MAGISTRATES' COURT INDEX

MAGISTRATES' COURT INDEX

THIRTEENTH EDITION

His Honour Ian McLean
Formerly a Metropolitan Stipendiary Magistrate

Peter Morrish
Barrister, sometime Deputy Chief Clerk
Inner London Magistrates' Courts

and

John Greenhill
Barrister, formerly Chief Clerk
Inner London Magistrates' Courts

ADVISORY EDITOR
Andrew Mimmack LLB MSc
Barrister, Clerk to the Central Devon and North Devon Justices

OXFORD
UNIVERSITY PRESS

OXFORD
UNIVERSITY PRESS

Great Clarendon Street, Oxford OX2 6DP

Oxford University Press is a department of the University of Oxford.
It furthers the University's objective of excellence in research, scholarship,
and education by publishing worldwide in

Oxford New York

Auckland Bangkok Buenos Aires Cape Town Chennai
Dar es Salaam Delhi Hong Kong Istanbul Karachi Kolkata
Kuala Lumpur Madrid Melbourne Mexico City Mumbai Nairobi
São Paulo Shanghai Taipei Tokyo Toronto

Oxford is a registered trade mark of Oxford University Press
in the UK and in certain other countries

Published in the United States
by Oxford University Press Inc., New York

First published 2003

British Library Cataloguing in Publication Data
Data available

Library of Congress Cataloging in Publication Data
Data available

ISBN 0–19–926575–5

1 3 5 7 9 10 8 6 4 2

Typeset by Hope Services (Abingdon) Ltd
Printed in Great Britain
on acid-free paper by
Biddles Ltd,
Guildford and King's Lynn

PREFACE

THIS EDITION seeks to provide, once again, a condensed guide to procedure and sentencing for those who work and practice in the magistrates' courts. It is in no way a textbook, but is presented as an *aide memoire*, in the first instance for District Judges, Justices' Clerks, legal advisers and practitioners, though the authors think that there is much of value in it for lay magistrates and others needing a practical oversight of the functions of these courts.

Statements of law are based on the text of the relevant statute, interpreted and augmented by case law and, where appropriate, drawing on the varied experience of the several authors. In order to achieve this aim, while repetition has been kept to a minimum, the authors have sought to create, where possible, self-contained sections, so that some repetition from the general to the particular has been necessary, if only to maintain the flow and make for easy reference. The book is written for today. Where a topic, e.g. suspended sentences, has less relevance than it used to have, less space has been devoted to it; where Parliament has already indicated an intention to abolish a power, e.g. detention in a young offender institution, it is dealt with, but less prominence is given to it. The difficulty of maintaining the currency of any work on the administration of criminal justice is that not only have successive governments constantly tinkered with the system, but much of this tinkering has been effected by prospective legislation to be brought into effect by notice. Some of these provisions are not yet in force, though the statute may have been in operation for several years. Constant amendment has resulted in difficulties in their usual format. The authors have decided, in this edition, to limit references in side notes to the principal statutory provision upon which the text is based, e.g. to MCA 1980, leaving the words 'as amended by subsequent legislation' to be understood. There will be exceptions, of course.

References to 'justices' and 'justices of the peace' which appeared in earlier editions have been abandoned in favour of the generic 'magistrate' or 'magistrates'; the new title of District Judge (Magistrates' Courts) sits uneasily with those historic references. Where possible the term 'court' has been used rather than 'bench'. The term 'Clerk' indicates not only the Justices' Clerk himself, but, unless the context prevents it, also legal advisers and other persons authorised by the Justices' Clerk under the Justices' Clerks Rules 1991. For the sake of convenience that term has also been used to include the 'Justices' Chief Executive'. 'Accused' and 'offender', terms which are universally understood, have been used, where the text allows, instead of 'defendant', which, in its criminal connotations, is peculiar to England and Wales. The pronouns 'he' and 'his' have been used throughout to indicate gender, though 'she' and 'her' are to be understood in the proper context.

Abbreviations are used, as in earlier editions, for references to statutes, statutory instruments and occasionally to practice notes or directions; a list of these appears at the beginning of the work. Wherever possible, authorities are cited from the All England reports and the Criminal Law Review, those being the most readily available in most magistrates' courts. Where reports are not available in them, the Weekly Law Reports and the Justice of the Peace Reports, are preferred, and only in the last resort is reference made to other reports not readily available to magistrates.

In regard to Wales, only one or two special provisions are set out in the text. It must be noted, however, that under the Welsh Language Act 1993, s 1, the Welsh language may be spoken in any legal proceedings in a magistrates' court in Wales, by any party, witness or other person who desires to use it, without prior notice. Two sets of rules have been made under former legislation, The Magistrates' Courts (Welsh Forms) Rules 1986 (SI 1986/1079) and The Magistrates' Courts (Children and Young Persons)(Welsh Forms) Rules 1973 (SI 1973/1119). Further directions are to be found in *Practice Direction (criminal law:consolidated)* [2002] 3 All ER 904, at para 23.

The Criminal Justice Bill 2003 was not law at the time of going to print, and its provisions are, therefore, not included in this edition.

The authors apologise in advance for the absence of their traditional stepped thumb-index; the rising cost of such an aid has resulted in its abandonment.

We have sought to state the law as at 30 April 2003.

TABLE OF ABBREVIATIONS

STATUTES

ABOOA 1956	Appeals (Binding Over Orders) Act 1956
AEA 1971	Attachment of Earnings Act 1971
AJA 1999	Access to Justice Act 1999
BA 1976	Bail Act 1976
BAA 1993	Bail (Amendment Act) 1993
BBEA 1879	Bankers' Books Evidence Act 1879
CA 1960	Children Act 1960
CAA 1995	Criminal Appeals Act 1995
CCA 1981	Contempt of Court Act 1981
CDA 1971	Criminal Damage Act 1971
CDA 1998	Crime & Disorder Act 1987
CDDA 1986	Company Directors' Disqualification Act 1986
C&EMA 1979	Customs and Excise Management Act 1979
CJA 1967	Criminal Justice Act 1967
CJA 1982	Criminal Justice Act 1982
CJA 1987	Criminal Justice Act 1987
CJA 1988	Criminal Justice Act 1988
CJA 1991	Criminal Justice Act 1991
CJA 1993	Criminal Justice Act 1993
CJCSA 2000	Criminal Justice and Court Services Act 2000
CJ(IC)A 1990	Criminal Justice (International Cooperation) Act 1990
CJPA 2001	Criminal Justice and Police Act 2001
CJPOA 1994	Criminal Justice and Public Order Act 1994
CLA 1977	The Criminal Law Act 1977
CLSA 1990	Courts and Legal Services Act 1990
CPIA 1996	Criminal Procedure and Investigation Act 1996
CYPA 1933	Children and Young Persons Act 1933
CYPA 1963	Children and Young Persons Act 1963
CYPA 1969	Children and Young Persons Act 1969
DTA 1986	Drugs Trafficking Offences Act 1986
DTA 1994	Drug Trafficking Act 1994
DTCFR	Magistrates' Courts (Detention and Forfeiture of Drug Trafficking Cash) Rules 1991
FA 1968	Firearms Act 1968
FAA 1976	Fatal Accidents Act 1976
FDA 2000	Football Disorder Act 2000
FSA 1989	Football Spectators Act 1989
FOD 1999	Football (Offences and Disorder) Act 1999
GA 1831	Game Act 1831
GIWA 1999	Government in Wales Act 1999
GWA 1998	Government of Wales Act 1998
HRA 1998	Human Rights Act 1998

IA 1971	Immigration Act 1971
ICA 1985	Interception of Communications Act 1985
IWCA 1960	Indecency with Children Act 1960
JPA 1361	Justices of the Peace Act 1361
JPA 1949	Justices of the Peace 1949
JPA 1968	Justices of the Peace Act 1968
JPA 1979	Justices of the Peace Act 1979
LAA 1988	Legal Aid Act 1988
LP(E)A 1980	Licensed Premises (Exclusion of Certain Persons) Act 1980
MCA 1980	Magistrates' Courts Act 1980
MDA 1971	Misuse of Drugs Act 1981
MHA 1959	Mental Health Act 1959
MHA 1983	Mental Health Act 1983
MH(A)A 1982	Mental Health (Amendment) Act 1982
OAPA 1861	Offences Against the Person Act 1861
OSA 1911	Official Secrets Act 1911
OSA 1920	Official Secrets Act 1920
PACE 1984	Police and Criminal Evidence Act 1984
PCA 1995	Proceeds of Crime Act 1995
PCA 2002	Proceeds of Crime Act 2002
PCC(S)A 2000	Powers of Criminal Courts Act 2000
PHA 1997	Protection from Harrassment Act 1997
POA 1985	Prosecution of Offences Act 1985
POCA 1978	Protection of Children Act 1978
POrA 1986	Public Order Act 1986
P(P)A 1897	Police (Property) Act 1897
ROA 1974	Rehabilitation of Offenders Act 1974
RTA 1988	Road Traffic Act 1988
RTOA 1988	Road Traffic Offenders Act 1988
RTRA	Road Traffic Regulation Act 1984
SCA 1981	Supreme Court Act 1981
SOA 1956	Sexual Offences Act 1956
SOA 1967	Sexual Offences Act 1997
SO(A)A 1976	Sexual Offences (Amendment) Act 1976
SO(A)A 2000	Sexual Offences (Amendment) Act 2000
TA 1968	Theft Act 1968
TA 2000	Terrorism Act 2000
TTPA 1989	Prevention of Terrorism (Temporary Provisions) Act 1989
VATA 1994	Value Added Tax Act 1994
YJCEA 1999	Youth Justice and Criminal Evidence Act 1999

RULES, REGULATIONS ETC

AER 1971	Attachment of Earnings Rules 1971
AIR 1985	Magistrates' Courts (Advance Information) Rules 1985
CCR 1982	Crown Court Rules 1982
CC(G)R 1986	Costs in Criminal Cases (General) Regulations 1986
CPR 1998	Civil Procedure Rules 1998
CTLR 1987	Prosecution of Offences (Custody Time Limits) Regulations 1987

CYPR 1992	Magistrates' Courts (Children & Young Persons) Rules 1999
DISR 1992	Fines (Deductions from Income Support) Regulations 1992
GR 2001	Costs in Criminal Cases (General) Regulations 2001
JCR 1999	Justices' Clerks Rules 1999
MCR 1981	Magistrates' Courts Rules 1981
MC(CJIC)R	Magistrates' Courts (Criminal Justice International Co-operation) Rules 1991
MC(F)R 1981	Magistrates' Courts (Forms) Rules 1981
NTR 1988	Magistrates' Courts (Notice of Transfer) Rules 1988
NTR 1992	Magistrates' Courts (Notice of Transfer) Rules 1992
NTRC 1992	Magistrates' Court (Notice of Transfer) Regulations 1992
PHR 1988	Criminal Justice Act (Preliminary Hearings) Rules 1988
POR 1987–91	Prosecution of Offences (Custody Time Limits) Regulations 1987–91
RDCR 2001	Criminal Defence Service (Recovery of Defence Costs Orders) Regulations 2001
ROAR 2001	Representation Orders (Appeal) Regulations 2001
RSC 1965	Rules of the Supreme Court 1965
SCR 1981	Supreme Court Rules 1981
SMDR 2002	Magistrates' Courts (Special Measures Directions) Rules 2002
SPER 1998	Crime and Disorder Act 1998 (Service of Prosecution Evidence) Regulations 1998
VHCCR 2001	Criminal Defence Service (Very High Costs) Regulations 2001
YCTLR 1999	Prosecution of Offences (Youth Court Time Limit) Regulations 1999

HO is an abbreviation for the Home Office publication 'Sentence of the Court' which last appeared in 1990. DPP speaks for itself. YOT stands for Youth Offending Team. MC and YC in case references refer to Magistrates' Court and Youth Court respectively. ECHR is the European Convention on Human Rights.

CONTENTS—SUMMARY

Mode of Trial Procedure
(MCA 1980, ss 19–21)

[Either-Way Offence]

(advance information)
(charge read to the accused)
Plea before venue: not guilty plea indicated or no plea indicated

Representations by prosecution as to suitability for summary trial or trial in the Crown Court

Representations by defence as to suitability for summary trial or trial in the Crown Court

Magistrate(s) to Decide

- Do the circumstances make the offence one of a serious character?
- If the accused were to be convicted, would the magistrates' courts powers of punishment be adequate?
- Are there any other circumstances which make the case more suitable to be tried in the magistrates' court or in the Crown Court?

Magistrates Announce Decision

(1) Either summary trial or trial by jury in the Crown Court appears more suitable.
(2) If summary trial appears more suitable accused may consent to summary trial in the Crown Court

(Note: Mode of trial proceedings are concerned with the nature of the offence and not the character of the accused. Therefore any previous convictions of the accused must not be disclosed or considered.)

Committal for Trial: MCA 1980, s 6(2)
(Without Consideration of the Evidence: MCR 1981, r 6)

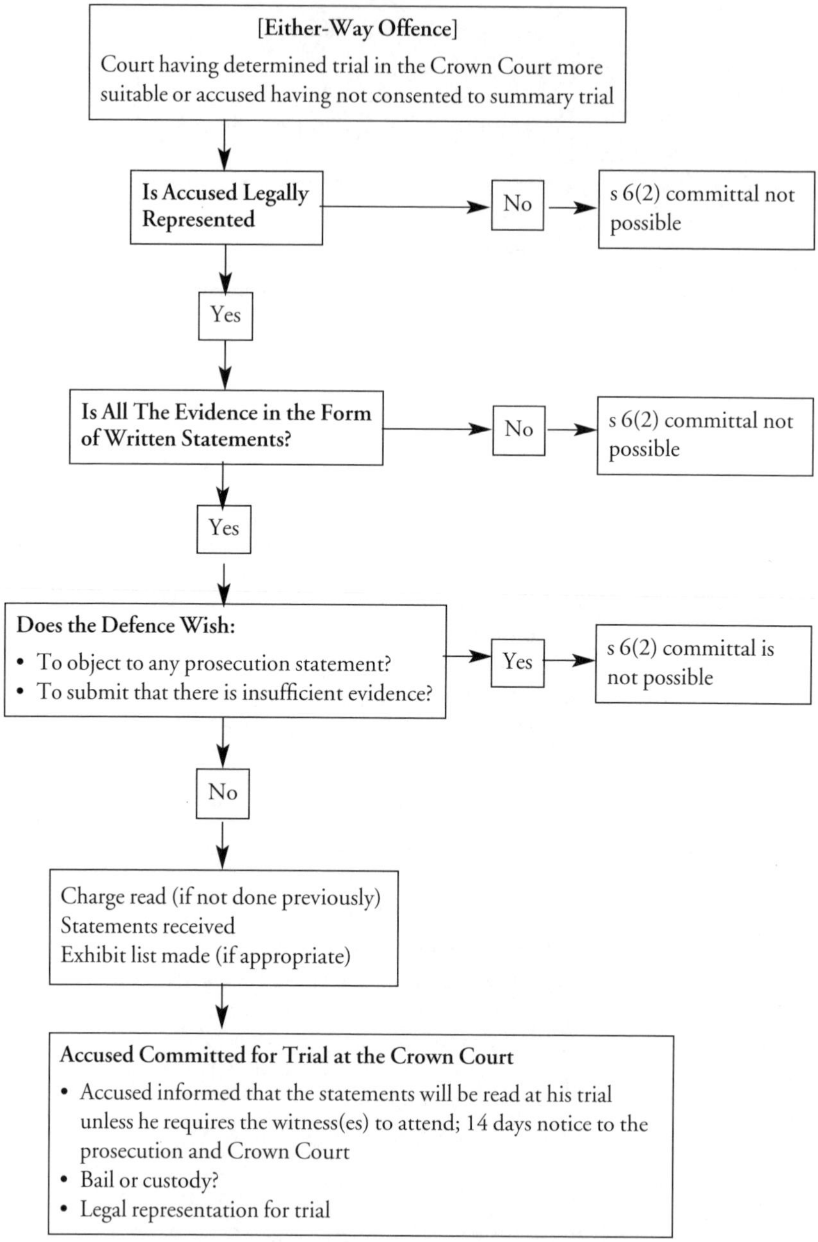

(The court may also deal with applications to lift reporting restrictions).
For documents to be sent to the Crown Court, see MCR 1981, r 11.

Committal for Trial: MCA 1980, s 6(1)
(Consideration of the Evidence: MCR 1981, r 7)

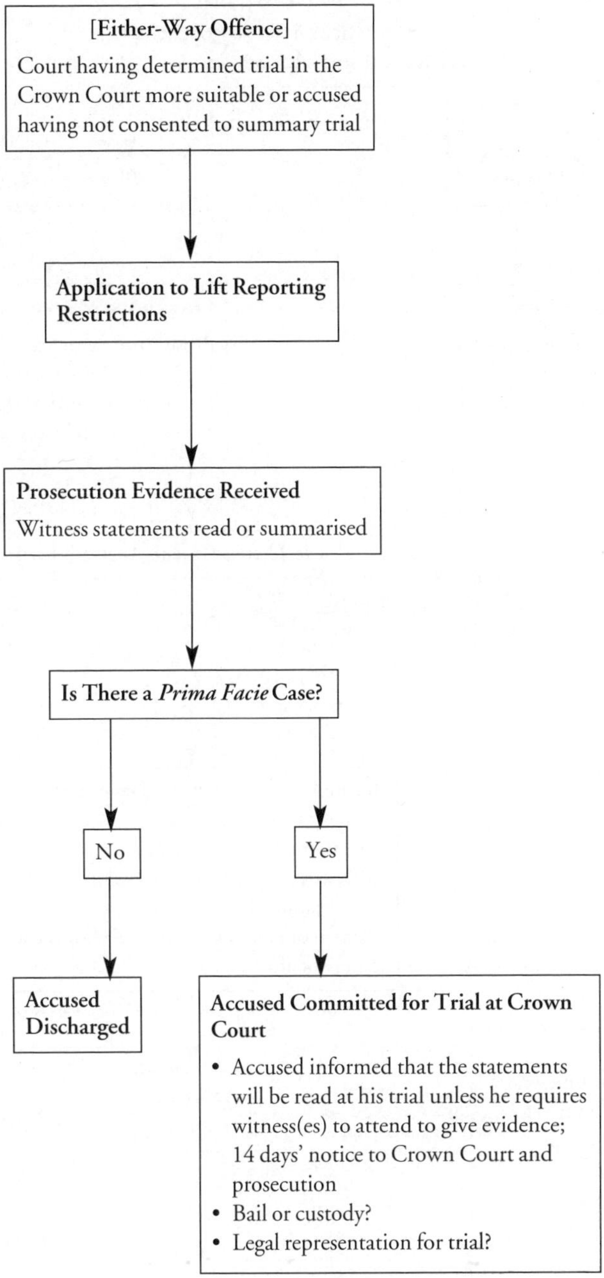

Procedure on Summary Trial

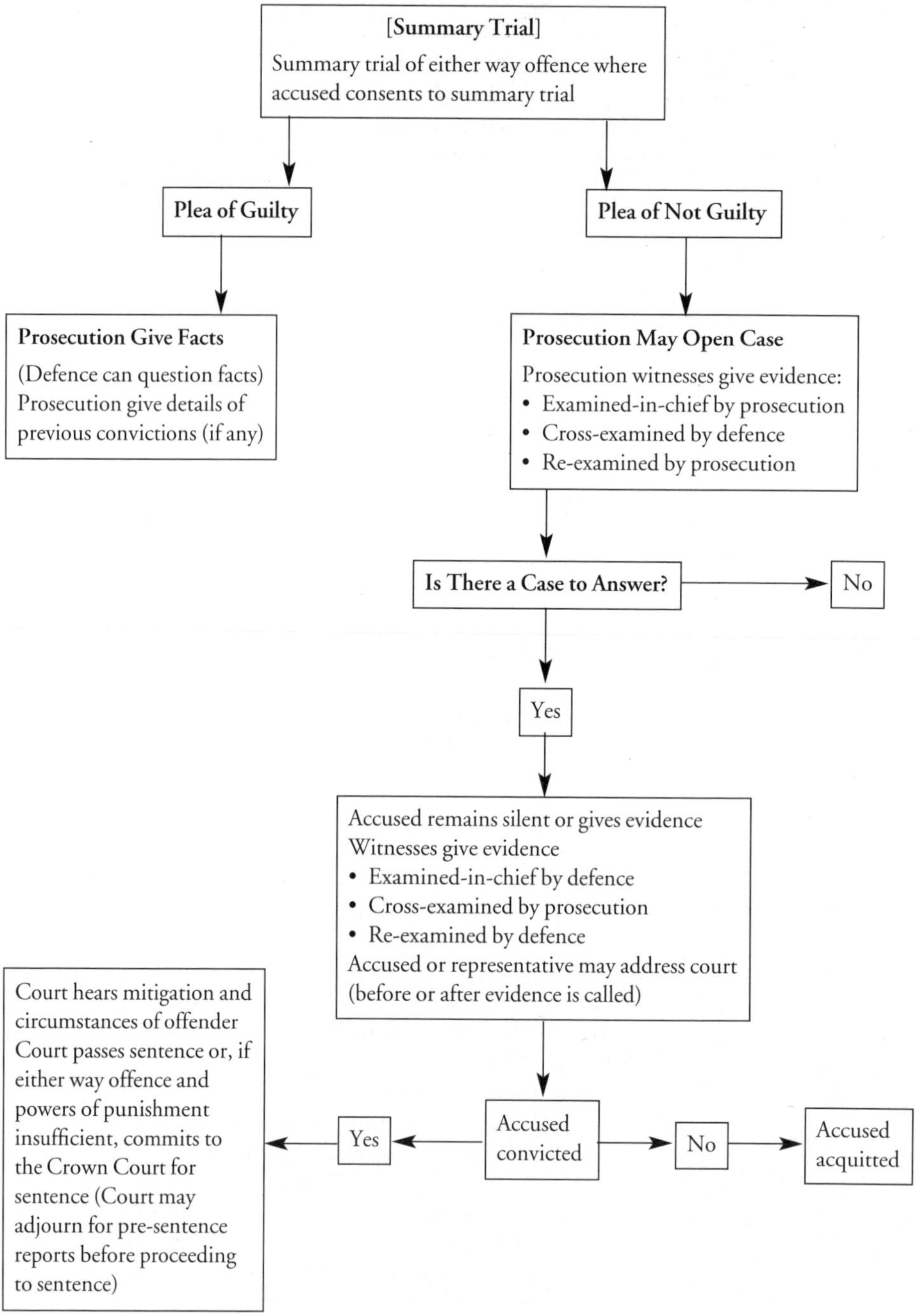

TABLE OF CASES

TABLE OF STATUTORY INSTRUMENTS

TABLE OF LEGISLATION

EUROPEAN LEGISLATION

HOME OFFICE PUBLICATIONS

ABSOLUTE AND CONDITIONAL DISCHARGE

A discharge is appropriate in both the adult and the youth court: PCC(S)A 2000, s 12(1)

(1) for any age of offender,

(2) where:

  (a) the nature of the offence, and

  (b) the character of the offender

  make punishment inexpedient

(unless he falls within the provisions of CDA 1998, s 65 (*below*)).

A discharge is not a 'community order' in terms of PCC(S)A 2000, s 33.

Absolute discharge

An absolute discharge may be imposed where the court considers no action is required beyond the mere finding of guilt, reflecting the triviality of the offence (*R v King* [1977] Crim LR 626), the circumstances in which it came to be prosecuted (*Smedleys Ltd v Breed* [1973] 3 All ER 339), or factors affecting the offender (*R v O'Toole* (1971) 55 Cr App Rep 206).

Conditional discharge

A conditional discharge has the effect of discharging an offender subject to a single condition that he commit no offence during the operational period of the order, which period must not exceed three years. He must be told in ordinary language that if he commits a further offence during the period, he is liable to be sentenced for the offence for which the order is being made.

A conditional discharge differs from other 'conditional' orders, eg from:

(1) a bind over, because recognisances may be estreated for conduct which does not amount to an offence;

(2) a community rehabilitation order, because there is no age restriction (see AGE OF OFFENDER), no supervision is involved and only the single condition may be imposed, and

(3) a suspended sentence of imprisonment because there are no statutory restrictions on the type of offence for which it may be imposed, no determinate sentence to be put into effect, and only a discretionary obligation to deal with the offender on a breach.

CDA 1998: constable's warning

Where a person has already been the subject of a warning from a constable under CDA 1998, s 65, and is convicted of an offence within two years of CDA 1998, ss 55(4), 65 that warning, the court may not impose a conditional discharge unless there are exceptional circumstances which must be stated in open court.

Ancillary orders: (1) General

In an appropriate case, the court

(1) must, where personal injury, loss or damage is involved and it makes no compensation order, state its reasons for *not* making such an order (see COMPENSATION);

(2) must discharge any duty under RTOA 1988, s 46(1) to disqualify or endorse the licence of a road traffic offender (see DISQUALIFICATION AND ENDORSEMENT);

PCC(S)A 2000, s 12(6)

(3) may, if it thinks it expedient for the purpose of the offender's reformation, allow any person who consents to do so to enter into a recognisance for his good behaviour (see BIND OVER).

Ancillary orders (2) improper combinations

Since the underlying basis of a discharge is that 'punishment is inexpedient', it follows that the court:

PCC(S)A 2000, s 12(7)

(1) *may not,* unless specifically authorised by statute, combine with a discharge, *on the same charge,* any additional order with a punitive element, such as a fine (*R v McClelland* (1951) 35 Cr App Rep 22, *R v Saniu* (1990) 12 Cr App R (S) 262), a deprivation order (*R v Hunt* [1978] Crim LR 697) or a company officer's disqualification order (*R v Young* [1990] Crim LR 818); but

(2) *may, for another offence,* even on the same occasion, combine with a discharge, a fine, a community punishment order, or even a suspended sentence of imprisonment (*R v Bainbridge* (1979) 1 Cr App R 36); and

(3) *may* make an order for costs against him, impose any appropriate disqualification on him, or make a compensation order in respect of him, (see *below*), or a restitution order (see FORFEITURE), or a recommendation for deportation (*R v Akan* [1972] 3 All ER 285).

Legal effect of discharge

PCC(S)A 2000, s 14

A conviction of an offence for which a discharge, whether absolute or conditional, is imposed is deemed not to be a conviction for any purpose other than the purposes of the proceedings in which the order is made or of any subsequent proceedings taken against the offender under PCC(S)A 2000, s 13 for a breach, although this provision:

(1) does not apply where the offender was aged 18 or over at the time of his conviction and is subsequently sentenced under s 13 for the offence;

(2) does not affect the offender's right to rely on his conviction in bar of any subsequent proceedings for the same offence, nor does it affect the restoration of any property in consequence of the conviction;

(3) has effect subject to MCA 1980, s 108(1A) in relation to rights of appeal;

(4) does not affect the operation in relation to the offender of any enactment or instrument in force on 4 July 1974, which is expressed to extend to persons dealt with under POA 1907, s 1(1) as well as to convicted persons;

(5) is to be disregarded for the purposes of any enactment or instrument which imposes a disqualification or disability on 'convicted persons', or authorises or requires the imposition of such.

Termination of order

A conditional discharge ceases to have effect: PCC(S)A 2000, s 12(5)

(1) on the expiry of the period for which it was made; or

(2) if the offender is subsequently sentenced for the offence for which it was imposed, but

termination does not affect any compensation order which was made ancillary to it, which may be enforced despite any sentence imposed on the breach (*R v Evans* [1961] 1 All ER 313).

Conditional discharge: breach

If an offender is convicted in any part of Great Britain of an offence committed during the 'operational period', and is dealt with in respect of that further offence, he is liable to be dealt with for the offence for which the original conditional discharge was made. PCC(S)A 2000, s 13

Where the original discharge was made:

(1) by a magistrates' court, and the subsequent conviction is by another magistrates' court, the latter, *with the consent of the first court*, may deal with him in any manner in which he could have been dealt with for the original offence;

(2) by the Crown Court, that court must deal with its own orders, and the offender may be committed to the Crown Court on the breach

(see COMMITTAL FOR SENTENCE).

As to the power of the Justices' Clerk to give consent for another magistrates' court to deal with the breach of a conditional discharge, see (JUSTICES' CLERK/LEGAL ADVISERS).

A summons, or if appropriate a warrant, may be issued to bring the offender before the court which made the original order. PCC(S)A 2000, s 13(3)(4)

Procedure on the breach

Before imposing any sentence on the breach of a conditional discharge, the court must put to the offender and obtain from him admissions that:

(1) he was, on the date specified, convicted of the offence and made the subject of a conditional discharge;

(2) his subsequent conviction was within the 'operational period' of that order; and

(3) he realises that he is liable to be dealt with for the original offence.

Where the offender disputes any of these issues the court must decide the matter (*R v Devine* (1956) 120 JP 238, *R v Long* (1960) 124 JP 35).

Sentence on the breach

Although there is only a *power* and no statutory *obligation* to deal with an offender for the further offence, failure to deal with it makes a nonsense of the warning given to him at the time of making the order.

In sentencing an offender on the breach:

(1) it is not a matter of taking the breach into consideration;

(2) a separate sentence ought to be passed for the offence for which the original order was made; and

(3) that sentence should be more than nominal;

(4) if a term of imprisonment is imposed, it may be expressed to run consecutively to the new sentence (see *R v Webb* (1955) 117 JP 319, *R v Stuart* (1964) 129 JP 35).

There may be exceptional circumstances where, for instance, a further conditional discharge is warranted.

The relevant date for considering the appropriate sentencing options on the breach is the date of the subsequent sentence (*R v Keelan* (1975) 61 Cr App Rep 212).

Ancillary orders made on the original order continue in force despite the termination of the order (*R v Fry* (1986) 119 JP 75).

Offenders under 18

PCC(S)A 2000, s 12(9)

Where a conditional discharge was made in the case of an offender under 18, in respect of an offence triable only on indictment in the case of an adult, the court which deals with him after he has attained the age of 18, may:

(1) impose on him a fine not exceeding £5,000; or

(2) deal with him in any way that a magistrates' court could deal with him if it had just convicted him of an offence punishable with imprisonment for a term not exceeding six months.

Order made on appeal

An order made on appeal is deemed to have been made by the lower court, so that for the purposes of proceedings under s 13 for a breach, if the order was made by the Crown Court on appeal from a magistrates' court, there is no power to commit the offender to the Crown Court on a breach (*R v Waltham Forest MC ex p Brewer* [1992] Crim LR 73). PCC(S)A 2000, s 15(2)

ABUSE OF PROCESS

The court has the power to protect its process from abuse that might prejudice the fairness of its proceedings. In the case of a magistrates' court, this power is limited to the trial of an accused person before it (*R v Horseferry Road MC ex p Bennett* [1993] 3 All ER 138, *R v Staines MC ex p Westfallen* [1998] 3 All ER 210). Where abuse is made out the court may take the extreme step of dismissing an information, though this is a step which ought not to be taken lightly.

A vast amount of court time is taken up by unwarranted abuse applications. The trial process itself is equipped to deal with most of the complaints on which applications to stay are founded, and it is undesirable that that process be complicated, and distorted, by unnecessary allegations of abuse. There are, of course, cases in which an argument is warranted and the defence must be permitted to put it forward, but the court should be quick to take action where they are put forward 'as mere embroidery of a case which could be advanced equally satisfactorily without them' (*R v Childs* (2002) *The Times*, 30 November).

Approach to application

In considering an application to stay proceedings on the ground of abuse of process, the court needs to apply two well-known principles, namely that:

(1) the ultimate objective of the discretionary power to stay proceedings is to ensure that there should be a fair trial according to law, which involves fairness *both* to the accused and to the public as represented by the prosecutor; but

(2) if the conduct of the prosecution has been such that it would be unfair to try the accused at all, or that if tried he cannot receive a fair trial (*R v R* [1994] Crim LR 948) proceedings should be stayed on that ground.

A useful test is for the court to ask itself:

(a) firstly, whether there is an element of bad faith, or at the very least some serious fault on the part of the police, the prosecuting authority or other complainant (*R v Feltham MC ex p Ebrahim, Mouat v DPP* [2001] 1 All ER 831); proceedings should rarely be stayed in the absence of such fault (*Attorney-General's Reference* (*No 1 of 1990*) [1992] 3 All ER 169);

(b) the further and quite separate question, whether, if (a) is made out, there is *substantial* potential prejudice to the accused.

Proceedings ought to be stayed where their continuance would be to bring the administration of justice into disrepute (*Hunter v West Midlands Chief Constable* [1981] 1 All ER 727).

The power to stay is discretionary, and even where abuse is established, the court may still exercise its undoubted discretion to allow the proceedings to continue where there is no potential prejudice to the accused. Proceedings should not be halted where there are other means of achieving a fair trial (*DPP v Hussain* [1994] 158 JPN 570 DC).

Circumstances where abuse is to be found

Abuse may arise where:

(1) the prosecution has so manipulated or misused the process of the court as to deprive an accused of a protection afforded by the law, or to take advantage of a technicality (*R v Liverpool MC ex p Slade* [1998] 1 All ER 60); or

(2) the proceedings have been brought before the court by acts which offend the court's conscience as being contrary to the rule of law, or as otherwise bringing the administration of justice into disrepute (*Hunter v West Midlands Chief Constable* (*above*)) as where:
   (a) the accused has been brought within the jurisdiction in illegal disregard of extradition provisions and as a consequence of illegal acts (*R v Horseferry Road MC ex p Bennet* (*above*));
   (b) in exceptional circumstances, where an unequivocal promise has been made to an accused that he will not be prosecuted (see *R v Croydon JJ ex p Dean* (*below*)); or

(3) the accused has been, or will be, prejudiced in the preparation or conduct of his defence by delay on the part of the prosecution which is inordinate and unjustifiable (*R v Derby JJ ex p Brooks* (1984) 184 JP 609, *R v W London Stipendiary Magistrate ex p Anderson* (1984) 14 8 JP 683, *R v Sunderland MC ex p Z* [1989] Crim LR 61) and not due, for example to:
   (a) the complexity of the investigation and the preparation of the case;
   (b) the action(s) of the accused or co-accused (*R v W London Stipendiary Magistrate ex p Anderson* (*above*)); or
   (c) genuine difficulties of service (*R v Derby CC ex p Brooks* (*above*)).

Factors to be considered

The complexities of the case and the difficulties of the investigation are factors which need to be considered; there may be cases so complex that despite all the prosecutor's efforts the delay is such that a fair trial is impossible (*R v Telford JJ ex p Badham* [1991] 2 All ER 884, *Hayter v L* [1998] 1 WLR 854).

Failure, through inefficiency, to disclose advance information does not amount to abuse (*R v Willesden MC ex p Clemmings* (1988) 152 JP 286).

Mere petty spite or animosity in the bringing of the proceedings does not, of itself, amount to abuse (see *R v Telford JJ, ex p Badham* (*above*), *R v Rotherham JJ ex p Brough* [1991] Crim LR 522). As to abuse of process within the workings of the court itself, see *Gleaves v Insall* [1999] 2 Cr App R 466.

Undertaking not to prosecute

There are cases in which an unequivocal undertaking not to prosecute an accused may bar the prosecution from later attempting to bring a case before the court, but there must be exceptional circumstances (*R v Croydon JJ ex p Dean* [1994] 98 Cr App Rep 76, *R v Horseferry Road MC ex p Bennett* (*above*), *R v Slesinger* [1995] Crim LR 137, *R v Latif* [1996] 1 WLR 104, *R v Mullen* [1999] 2 Cr App R 143).

Note that:

(1) the breach of an undertaking not to prosecute, without more, does not *necessarily* give rise to abuse (*R v Townshend & Ors* [1997] 2 Cr App Rep 540, see also *R v Henworth* (2001) *The Times*, 30 January, *DPP v Edgar* (2000) 164 JP 471);

(2) where the prosecutor elects not to proceed against co-accused, although such proceedings were possible, abuse of process does not arise (*R v Forsyth* [1997] Crim LR 581);

(3) the fact that the prosecutor decides not to proceed with an either way offence, but relies on an alternative summary offence, thus depriving the accused of trial by jury, does not, without more, amount to abuse (*R v Liverpool Stipendiary Magistrate ex p Ellison* [1989] Crim LR 369).

Delay

Claims of unreasonable delay are a frequent basis for claims of abuse. This may be particularly significant in relation to summary offences in view of the six month general time limit for the institution of proceedings. There is a distinction to be made in this respect in the case of indictable offences (*R v Derby MC ex p Brooks* (*above*), *R v Willesden MC ex p Clemmings* (1988) 152 JP 286, *R v Grays JJ ex p Graham* [1982] 3 All ER 653).

Where delay is made the subject of an application, the court needs to consider both:

(1) the reasons for any delay (normally considered to run from the date of the charge or summons): *Attorney-General's Reference* (*No 2 of 2001*) [2002] Crim LR 207); and

(2) the potential unfairness, if any, to the accused, bearing in mind that any use of the power to stay proceedings on the ground of delay is exceptional (see generally *R v West London Stipendiary Magistrate, ex p Anderson* (1984) 148 JP 683). See, however, *R v Oxford City JJ ex p Smith* [1982] RTR 201 and *R v Newcastle JJ ex p Hindle* [1984] 1 All ER 770).

Relevant factors

In considering (2) *above*, 'a further and separate question', relevant factors will be:

(1) whether the delay can be said to be 'inordinate'; and

(2) any efforts made by the accused to assert his rights.

The longer the delay, the more likely that the prosecution is at fault, and that the delay will cause prejudice to the accused. The less the prosecution has to offer by way of explanation the more easily will prejudice be inferred. But the establishment of these facts is only a step on the way to consideration of whether, in all the circumstances, the situation created by the delay renders the proceedings unfair.

Delay by a young victim in reporting an alleged sexual assault due to reticence is not uncommon and is wholly understandable (*R v LPB* (1990) 91 Cr App Rep 359).

A finding that there has been unreasonable delay in relation to ECHR Article 6(1) does not, of itself, justify dismissing an information where no serious prejudice to the accused has been established (*Attorney-General's Reference* (*No 2 of 2001, above*).

Missing exhibits

The loss or absence of an exhibit, without more, is unlikely to amount to abuse of process (*R v Beckford* [1995] Crim LR 712); it is a matter which affects the strength of the evidence and can be dealt with during the trial. A distinction needs to be drawn between:

(1) loss (*R v McNamara* [1998] Crim LR 278, *R v Medway* [2000] Crim LR 415, *R v T* [2000] Crim LR 832, *R v Feltham MC ex p Ebrahim* [2001] Crim LR 741, *Mouatt v DPP* [2001] 1 All ER 831 DC); and

(2) the deliberate destruction of evidence (*R v Sunderland MC ex p Z* [1989] Crim LR 61, *R v Birmingham* [1992] Crim LR 117).

The court should approach such an issue as follows:

(a) What was the nature of the investigator/prosecutor's duty to obtain and/or retain the evidence? If there was none before the defence first sought its retention, there can be no question of a trial being unfair on that ground.

(b) If the evidence was not obtained and/or retained in breach of the obligations set out in the Code of Practice (CPIA 1996, ss 23, 25) or under the Attorney-General's Guidelines of 29 November 2000, then:
   (i) the ultimate objective is to ensure that there should be a fair trial according to law;
   (ii) this involves fairness both to the prosecutor and to the defence;
   (iii) the trial process is equipped to deal with the examination of complaints, and there will be few cases in which a court will be able to conclude that a trial will be unfair;
   (iv) it is commonplace in criminal trials for the defence to rely on gaps in the prosecutor's case, and if, in such a case, there is sufficient credible evidence which, if believed, would justify a safe conviction, then a trial can proceed, leaving the defence to seek to persuade the court not to convict owing to the unavailability, through no fault of their own, of the evidence in question.

(c) If the conduct of the prosecutor has been such that it would be unfair to put the accused on trial, the proceedings should be stayed. The most useful test is to ask whether there has been bad faith, or at least some serious fault on the part of the police or of the prosecutor (see *R v ARA* [2001] 4 All ER 559).

(*R v Feltham MC ex p Ebrahim* (*above*) and see *Practice Direction* (*Abuse of Process*) [2000] 3 All ER 34, and Code of Practice, CPIA 1966).

Publicity

As to staying the proceedings owing to the publicity surrounding a case, see *R v Stone* (2001) *The Times*, 22 February, and the Scots cases of *Montgomery v HMA* [2001] 2 WLR 779 and *Coulter v HMA* (2000) *The Times*, 6 December.

Spelling it out

Where the court dismisses an information on the grounds of abuse of process, it should gives its reasons (and the advocate has a duty to note them). A few sentences will ordinarily suffice, showing the court's appreciation of the principles, and a short summary of its reasons for granting or refusing the application (*R v Manchester CC ex p Brockenbrow* (1991) *The Times*, 31 October, DC, *R v Feltham MC, Mouat v DPP* (*above*)).

ADJOURNMENT AND REMAND

The court has wide powers of adjourning *summary* proceedings. Such an adjournment may be quite informal, granted even by a single magistrate, and while it may, there is no obligation to, fix the date of the next hearing. Before conviction an adjournment may be *sine die*. A case may be adjourned by the Clerk. MCA 1980, s 10(1)(2)(3); JCR 1999, Schedule

An adjournment is a matter within the court's discretion, but it ought not to be unreasonably refused (*R v Neath and Port Talbot JJ ex p DPP* [2000] Crim LR 624). The court may consider:

(1) any likely adverse consequences or prejudice to the respective parties if the application is granted or refused;

(2) the convenience of the court and likely delay to other cases; and

(3) the extent to which the applicant has been the author of his difficulty.

Before proceeding with the trial of an absent accused, it is important to ensure that any notice of adjournment has been received by him (*R v Seisdon JJ ex p Dougan* [1983] 1 All ER 6). MCR 1981, ss 12(2), 99

Adjournment and Remand

TV links

CDA 1998, s 57 provides for pre-trial hearings involving an accused in custody to be conducted over a live television link between the prison and the court; either party may make representations where the court has this facility. Where the court has power to give a direction for use of a live television link but decides not to do so it must give its reasons for that decision.

Need for remand

In relation to *indictable offences*, an accused, or offender, must be remanded to a fixed date, and a decision must be taken as to whether he be remanded on bail or in custody, where proceedings .

(1) *at any time* are adjourned for:
   (a) an intended plea (see p 300); MCA 1980, s 17C
   (b) to determine mode of trial; or MCA 1980, s 18(4)
   (c) to commit for trial; MCA 1980, s 5(1)

(2) *after conviction*:
   (a) for the purpose of enabling enquiries to be made; MCA 1980, s 10(1)
   (b) for determining the most suitable method of dealing with the offender; MCA 1980, s 10(3)
   (c) for a medical report. PCC(S)A 2000, s 11

MCA 1980, s 10(3) After conviction, if the remand is on bail the adjournment must not exceed four weeks at a time. If the remand is in custody the adjournment must not exceed three weeks at a time.

Where the court proposes to consider a particular aspect of the sentence, eg disqualification, it must adjourn the question of sentence as a whole, to be disposed of as one matter on the adjourned hearing (*R v Talgarth JJ ex p Bithell* [1973] 2 All ER 717).

Notice of reasons; absent accused

MCA 1980, ss 11(4), 12(2)(b), (6), 10(3)

Where an accused is absent, and an adjournment is occasioned by:

(1) the court's decision not to proceed in his absence, albeit he has pleaded guilty in writing; or

(2) an intention to impose a disqualification from driving, when the hearing is resumed,

the notice of adjournment must give reasons for that adjournment.

Constitution of court on adjourned hearing

In general:

MCA 1980, s 121(6)

(1) the magistrates comprising the court before which any proceedings take place must be present throughout the whole of those proceedings; if any one of them absents himself he must cease to act in the case, although the case may continue if the magistrrates remaining suffice to make up a quorum;

MCA 1980, s 121(7)

(2) where the trial of an information is adjourned after conviction and before sentence, the court which deals with sentence need not be composed of the same members as the court which convicted. If that is the position, the court must make such enquiry into the facts and circumstances of the case as will enable them to be fully acquainted with them;

MCA 1980, s 42

(3) a magistrate cannot take part in trying the issue of an accused's guilt in summary proceedings if, in the course of the same proceedings he has been informed, for the purposes of determining bail, that he has one or more previous convictions.

Obligation to remand

Where an accused, or offender, is remanded, a decision must be taken either to release him on bail subject to a duty to surrender (see BAIL), or to commit him to custody. Special rules (see *below*) apply to juveniles not released on bail.

The court:

(1) *may* remand the accused when adjourning the hearing of an information charging a summary offence;

(2) *may* remand an accused, charged with an offence punishable on summary conviction with imprisonment, when adjourning for a medical examination under PCC(S)A 2000, s 11; PCC(S)A 2000, s 11

(3) *may* remand an offender on adjourning after conviction, for enquiries to be made, or for determining the most suitable method of dealing with him; MCA 1980, s 10(3)

(4) *must* remand an accused:
   (a) on adjourning committal proceedings; and MCA 1980, s 5(1)
   (b) on adjourning the summary trial of an information, where the accused is 18 years of age or over and the offence is triable either way, if: MCA 1980, s 10(4)
      (i) on the first occasion on which he appeared or was brought before the court to answer the information he was in custody, or having been on bail, he surrendered to the custody of the court; or
      (ii) the accused has been remanded at any time in the course of the proceedings on the information.

Subject to MCA 1980, s 128(3) (*below*), the time fixed for resumption of the trial will be the time at which he is required to appear or be brought before a court in pursuance of the remand.

As to the limited powers of the Clerk to deal with remands, see JUSTICES' CLERK/LEGAL ADVISER.

Adjournment and Remand

No remand on deferment

There is no power to remand an offender on the occasion when the court defers sentence. PCC(S)A 2000, s 1(4)

Custody or bail

Where the court has power to remand any person, subject to BA 1976, s 4, it may: MCA 1980, s 128

(1) remand him in custody, to be brought before the court (subject to MCA 1980, s 128(3A)) at the end of the period of remand, or at such earlier time as required; or

(2) where it is enquiring into an offence alleged to have been committed by him, or has convicted him of an offence, remand him on bail in accordance with BA 1976; or

(3) except in a case falling within (2) remand him on bail, by taking from him a recognisance (with or without sureties) conditioned for his appearance on the adjourned date.

In this last case, as under BA 1976, the court may, instead of taking the recognisances forthwith, fix the amount(s) with a view to their being taken later, in which case the person must be remanded in custody in accordance with (1) *above.*

Period of remand

The limits placed on the maximum period of remand are variable and depend on the stage in the proceedings reached, whether the remand is on bail or in custody and, in some circumstances, whether the accused consents to the period suggested. The periods are as follows:

(1) on bail:

MCA 1980, s 128(6)

  (a) before conviction – the norm is eight clear days unless both parties agree to a longer period;

MCR 1981, r 23

  (b) after conviction – four weeks for enquiries or reports; though a person in custody for want of recognisances must be brought before the court at the expiry of the eight day period.

(2) in custody:

  (a) *before* conviction –
    (i) three clear days, if detention is at a police station;
    (ii) eight clear days to a prison establishment, or to the next occasion the court can be properly constituted, in the case of an either way offence being tried summarily, if the court cannot be properly constituted in the time;
    (iii) 28 clear days where an order under MCA 1980, s 128A (see *below*) applies;

MCA 1980, s 131

    (iv) 28 clear days if the accused is serving a custodial sentence and has at least that period to serve;
    (v) three weeks, for a medical examination in a case under PCC(S)A 2000, s 11;
    (vi) until appearance at the Crown Court where a person is committed, transferred or sent there for trial;

  (b) *after* conviction –
    (i) three weeks for enquiries or reports;
    (ii) until appearance at the Crown Court if committed for sentence.

There are further remand provisions under MHA 1983 (see MENTALLY DISORDERED OFFENDERS).

As to remand in absence, see pp 18–19 *below.*

Fixed date; continuous bail

MCA 1980, s 128(4)(5)

When remanding an accused on bail the court may direct him to appear:

(1) on a fixed date, that is to say before the end of the period of remand; or

(2) at every time and place to which the proceedings may from time to time be adjourned, that is to say 'continuous bail'; or

(3) where the accused is remanded on bail with a surety during committal proceedings, the surety's recognisance may be conditioned for the accused's appearance at every time and place to which the proceedings are adjourned, and before the Crown Court in the event of the accused being committed for trial.

Remands to police detention

Where the court has a power to remand a person in custody, it has power to commit him to detention at a police station for up to three clear days in the case of an adult, 24 hours in the case of a juvenile, but only where there is a need for it for the purposes of enquiring into other offences, which include offences relating to those with which the person has already been charged (*R v Bailey & Smith* [1993] 3 All 513). MCA 1980, 128(7)

A person so committed:

(1) must be brought back before the court which commits him (*R v Penrith JJ, ex p Morley* [1990] Crim LR 592) as soon as that need ceases;

(2) must be treated as a person in police detention to whom the duties under PACE 1984, s 39 relate; and

(3) must have his detention periodically reviewed in accordance with PACE 1984, s 40 (see POLICE DETENTION).

On an application of this sort the court needs only to be informed of those matters directly relevant to the need for the person's detention at a police station (*R v Bailey & Smith* (*above*)).

Remands to customs detention

Where a person aged 17 or over is brought before the court on a charge of an offence against MDA 1971, s 5(2) or a drug trafficking offence as defined in the 1986 Act, and: CJA 1988, s 152

(1) the court has power to remand him; and

(2) it considers it appropriate to do so,

it may remand him to customs detention, that is to commit him to the custody of a customs officer for a period not exceeding 92 hours.

Further remand: (1) s 128A

The court may remand an accused in custody for a period exceeding eight clear days, provided: MCA 1980, s 128A

(1) it has previously remanded him in custody for the same offence; and

(2) he is before the court,

but only if, after affording the parties an opportunity to make representations, it has set a date on which it expects that it will be possible for the next stage in the proceedings, other than a hearing relating to a further remand in custody or on bail, to take place and only:

(a) for a period ending not later than that date; or

(b) for a period of 28 clear days, whichever is the less.

BA 1976, Sched 1, para 9B

These provisions do not affect the right of the accused to apply for bail during the period of the remand.

When considering whether to exercise this power, the court must have regard to the total length of time which the accused will spend in custody if it is exercised.

As to the limited powers of the Clerk to deal with such remands, see JUSTICES' CLERK/LEGAL ADVISER.

Further remand: (2) enlargement of bail

MCA 1980, s 129(1)(2)

The court may further remand any person who:

(1) appears or is brought before the court at the end of the remand period; or

(2) is unable to appear or be brought before the court by reason of illness or accident, and,

in the latter case, the eight clear day rule does not apply to the further remand.

If the person was granted bail in criminal proceedings, the recognisance of any surety may be enlarged to the new date; if bail was granted in non-criminal proceedings, the recognisances of principal and surety may be likewise enlarged.

As to the limited powers of the Clerk to enlarge bail, see JUSTICES' CLERK/LEGAL ADVISER.

Further remand: (3) absence of accused

MCA 1980, s 128(1A)(1B)(3B)

In general, except as noted above, the accused must not be remanded further unless he is present before the court.

However, where the court:

(1) adjourns proceedings with a view to committal for trial, to determine mode of trial, or the summary trial of an information; and

(2) proposes to remand, or further remand, the accused in custody; and

(3) the accused:
   (a) is present in court; and
   (b) is legally represented in those proceedings (whether that representative is present in court or not),

the court has a specific duty to inform the accused that, if he consents, future remands will be determined in his absence.

If he consents, the court may remand him for up to three occasions in his absence, provided counsel or a solicitor continues to act. The accused will be brought before the court only for the hearing of at least every 4th application. The accused must be so informed.

Preconditions for remand in absence

Where the above situation arises, the court may further remand the accused if satisfied that:

MCA 1980, s 128(3A)(3B)(3D)(3E)

(1) he gave his consent to such an application being heard or determined in his absence;

(2) he has not withdrawn his consent; and

(3) he was 17 or over when he gave his consent; and

(4) he has not been further remanded in his absence in accordance with these provisions on more than two previous occasions immediately preceding the application it is hearing; but if
   (a) there is no solicitor acting for him, the court is not entitled to exercise its power;
   (b) if the court, on the further remand, is not satisfied that the preconditions are fulfilled, the proceedings must be adjourned for the shortest period possible for the accused to be brought before it; and
   (c) if it appears to the court, on a further remand (whether it is the court which originally remanded him or a court to which a hearing is transferred under s 130) that the accused ought not to have been remanded in his absence, it must, again, require him to be brought before it at the earliest opportunity.

Transfer of remand hearing

On adjourning the hearing of an information in committal proceedings, in determining mode of trial and remanding the accused in custody, the court may (if the accused has attained the age of 17) order that:

MCA 1980, s 130(1)–(3)

(1) he be brought up for any subsequent remands before; or

(2) any applications for subsequent remands (in a case under s 128(3A)) be made,

to an 'alternate' court, nearer to the prison in which he is to be confined on remand.

Such an order requires the accused to be brought up before, or for any application for a further remand to be made to, the alternate court at the end of the period of remand, or at such earlier time as that court requires.

Effect of transfer

MCA 1980, s 130(3)

Whilst the order is in force, the alternate court has all the powers in relation to further remand, and to the grant of any representation order (see DEFENCE PUBLIC FUNDING) which the original court would have had, to the exclusion of the original court.

MCA 1980, s 130(4)(4A)

On remanding the accused in custody, where the remand is not a remand for more than eight clear days (s 128(3A)) the alternate court may require any applications for subsequent remands to be made to the court which made the order, at the end of the period of the remand or at such earlier time as that court may require.

Where this is done, or where the accused is released on bail, the transfer order ceases to have effect.

Note that when making an order under these provisions:

MCA 1980, s 130(5)

(1) the court is not obliged then and there to fix the time and place at which the case is to be resumed, but must do so as soon as practicable after the order ceases to have effect;

MCA 1980, s 130(5)

(2) in the course of committal proceedings, such proceedings before the alternate court have the same nature for the purposes of restrictions on reporting;

(3) the court must notify the terms of the order to the alternate court.

MCA 1980, s 130(5)

If a person to whom such an order applies is bailed by the alternate court, he must be bailed to appear before the court which made the original order.

'Cross-remanding' to courts within the same commission area is a lawful and proper exercise of the power and a court is entitled to remand an accused to appear before a different magistrates' court sitting in a different petty sessions area of the same county *(R v Avon MC Committee, ex p Bath Law Society* [1988] 2 WLR 137).

Remand after conviction 'for reports'

When remanding after conviction for reports under s 10(3), a long line of cases, commencing with *R v Gillam* [1981] Crim LR 55, has emphasised the importance of not raising in the offender's mind an expectation that he is going to receive a non-custodial sentence on the date to which the case is adjourned. The proper course is to indicate that the court 'is keeping its options open', including, in the case of an either way offence, the power to commit the offender to the Crown Court for sentence.

Even if the report 'recommends' a certain course, there is no obligation on the court to follow it (*R v Horton & Alexander* (1985) 7 Cr App R(S) 299).

Juveniles who are refused bail

Where an accused is remanded, or committed or sent for trial, or his case is transferred to the Crown Court, and bail is refused, if he is:

(1) a child, he must be remanded into local authority accommodation, except that:

(2) if he is aged 12–16 he may be remanded into local authority secure accommodation or to Prison Service accommodation (ie a 'secure remand')

although CJPA 2001, s 130(3) places an express duty on the court *to consider all other options* for the remand of a child or young person before making a decision as to a secure remand. CYPA 1969, s 23(5AA)

'Young person' means a person who has attained the age of 14 years and is under the age of 17. The adult remand provisions apply in the case of a person aged 17.

Those other options are:

(a) unconditional bail;

(b) conditional bail;

(c) conditional bail with tagging (see p 58);

(d) bail supervision and support;

(e) bail supervision and support with tagging;

(f) bail ISSP (see *below*) where available;

(g) bail ISSP with voice verification (where available);

(h) bail ISSP with tagging (where available);

(i) remand to local authority accommodation;

(j) remand to local authority accommodation with conditions;

(k) remand to local authority accommodation with tagging.

Local authority accommodation

A court remanding such a person to local authority accommodation must designate the local authority which is to receive him, and that authority must be:

(1) in the case of a person who is being looked after by a local authority, that authority; and

(2) in any other case, the local authority in whose area it appears to the court that he resides or the area in which one of the offences was committed.

Where a person is remanded to local authority accommodation, it is lawful for any person acting on behalf of the designated authority to detain him.

Secure remand: criteria

CYPA 1969, s 23(4)(5)(5A)(5AA)(6)

The court remanding a person to local authority accommodation may, after consultation with the designated authority, require that authority to comply with a security requirement, that is to say, a requirement that the person in question be placed and kept in secure accommodation.

CYPA 1969, s 23(12)

'Secure accommodation' means accommodation which is provided in a community home, a voluntary home or a registered childrens' home for the purpose of restricting liberty and is approved for that purpose by the Secretary of State.

Such a requirement must *not* be imposed unless the child or young person:

(1) is charged with, or has been convicted of, a violent or sexual offence, or an offence punishable in the case of an adult with imprisonment for 14 years or more; or

(2) is charged with, or has been convicted of, one or more imprisonable offences which, together with any other imprisonable offences of which he has been convicted in any proceedings, amount to, or would, if he was convicted of the offences with which he is charged, a 'recent history of repeatedly committing imprisonable offences' while remanded on bail or to local authority accommodation (see *below*); and, in addition

(3) in either case, the court is of opinion:
   (a) *after considering all the options* for that child or young person's remand, that
   (b) only a secure remand would be adequate:
      (i) to protect the public from serious harm from him; or
      (ii) to prevent the commission by him of imprisonable offences.

Under (i) above it is harm from that (particular) offender (*R v Jacobs & Kinsella* [1989] Crim LR 597) that is relevant. As to 'violent' and 'sexual' offences, see *below*. 'Serious harm', in this context, means harm which can sensibly be called serious to the general public, and not merely the risk of a repetition of the offences involved (*R v Croydon YC, ex p G* (1995) *The Times*, 13 May). What is 'recent' and what amounts to 'repeatedly' are matters for the court.

'Sexual' and 'violent' offences

A 'sexual offence' means an offence under:

(1) the Sexual Offences Act 1956;

(2) the Indecency with Children Act 1960;

(3) the Sexual Offences Act 1967;

(4) the Criminal Law Act 1977, s 54;

(5) the Protection of Children Act 1978,

other than:

(a) an offence under SOA 1956, ss 12 and 13, which would not be an offence but for SOA 1967, s 2;
(b) an offence under SOA 1956, ss 30, 31, 33–36; and
(c) an offence under SOA 1967, ss 4 and 5.

'Violent offence' means an offence which leads or is intended or likely to lead, to a person's death, or to physical injury to a person, and includes an offence which is required to be charged as arson, whether or not it would otherwise fall within this definition.

Legal representation

The court may not impose a security requirement in respect of a child or young person, who is not legally represented, unless: CYPA1969, s 23(5A)

(1) having been informed of his right to apply for a representation order (see DEFENCE PUBLIC FUNDING) and having had the opportunity to do so, he refused or failed to apply; or
(2) he was granted a right to representation under the Criminal Defence Service but the right was withdrawn because of his conduct.

Spelling it out

Where the court imposes a security requirement, it must: CYPA 1969, s 23(6)

(1) state in open court that it is of the opinion set out above; and
(2) explain to the person remanded or committed in open court and in ordinary language why it is of that opinion, and the reason(s) must be entered in the register.

Remand of males aged 15 or 16

Where a male aged 15 or 16 is eligible for a secure remand, he will ordinarily be remanded to a remand centre or to prison. CYPA 1969, s 23(5A)

If, however, the court declares him to be 'vulnerable', that is to say that:

(1) by reason of his physical or emotional immaturity, or
(2) his propensity to harm himself,

it would be undesirable for him to be remanded to a remand centre or to prison, it must:

(a) state in ordinary language in open court the reason;
(b) and remand him to local authority secure accommodation.

The distinction between males and females in this context has been held (*R (on the application of SR) v Nottingham MC* [2001] 166 JP 132) to be justifiable.

Local authority accommodation with conditions

CYPA 1969, s 23(7)(8)

A court remanding a person to local authority accommodation without imposing a security requirement, may, after consultation with the designated authority require that person to comply with:

(1) any such bail conditions as might be imposed under BA 1976, s 3(6) (see BAIL) if he were then being granted bail, and where such conditions are being imposed, must explain in open court and in ordinary language why they are being imposed, and cause the reasons to be entered in the register; and

(2) any conditions imposed for the purpose of securing the electronic monitoring of his compliance with any other imposed.

CYPA 1969, s 23(9)(10)(12)

Where a person is remanded to such accommodation, a 'relevant court' may:

(a) on the application of the designated authority impose on that person any such conditions as might be imposed under BA 1976, s 3(6); and

(b) where it does, may impose on the authority any requirements for securing compliance with the conditions imposed; and

(c) on the application of the authority or the person remanded, vary or revoke any such conditions.

'Relevant court' for these purposes means the court by which such person was remanded or any magistrates' court having jurisdiction over the place where he is for the time being.

CYPA 1969, s 23

Where a juvenile is so remanded with conditions, and a constable has reasonable grounds for suspecting that he has broken any of those conditions, he may be arrested and taken before a magistrate in a manner similar to that applying in breach of bail (see p 61 *below*).

Local authority application for security requirement

CYPA 1969, s 23(9A)

Where the court has remanded a juvenile into local authority accommodation without imposing a security requirement, it may, on the application of the local authority:

(1) declare the juvenile to be a person to whom the provisions of s 23(5) apply; and

(2) require him to be placed and kept in secure accommodation.

ISSP – Intensive Supervision and Surveillance Programme

ISSP requirements may be attached to a grant of bail in the case of a juvenile. These requirements include provisions for the juvenile's education and training, including the provision of work to change his behaviour, the provision of support for his family and his surveillance in the community, which may include electronic tagging (see *below*).

Before an ISSP can be applied the juvenile must:

(1) have been warned, charged or convicted of offences committed *on four or more separate occasions,* within the previous 12 months;

(2) have received at least one custodial or community penalty; and/or

(3) he is at risk of custody because:
   (a) the current charge relates to an offence which is sufficiently serious that an adult could be sentenced for it to 14 years' imprisonment or more; or
   (b) he has a history of repeatedly offending on bail (see *above*) and is at risk of a secure remand under CJPA 2001, s 130.

Electronic monitoring condition

A court must not impose an electronic monitoring condition unless the person: CYPA 1969, ss 23AA, 23A

(1) has attained the age of 12; and

(2) is charged with or has been convicted of a violent or sexual offence, or an offence punishable in the case of an adult with imprisonment for 14 years or more; or

(3) is charged with or has been convicted of one or more imprisonable offences which, together with any other imprisonable offences of which he has been convicted in any proceedings, amount, or would, if he were convicted of the offences with which he is charged, amount to a recent history of repeatedly committing imprisonable offences while remanded on bail or to local authority accommodation; and

(4) arrangements for electronic monitoring are available in the area; and

(5) a youth offending team has informed the court that in its opinion the imposition of such a condition will be suitable in that person's case.

AGE OF OFFENDER

An offender 10 years or over but under 18 who is convicted by the adult court must be remitted to a youth court for sentence unless the adult court proposes to deal with him by means of a deferral order, a fine, absolute or conditional discharge or by binding his parent or guardian over to take proper care of, and exercise proper control over him, with or without any other ancillary order that the adult court has power to make when absolutely or conditionally discharging him. CYPA 1969, s 7(8)

The Table on p 29 shows the availability of primary sentencing options and, in the case of juveniles, indicates where an option is available only to a youth court. Reference should be made to the appropriate title for the criteria governing each particular option.

Proof of age

MCA 1980, s 150(4)

An offender's age at any material time is deemed to be or to have been that which the court, after considering any available evidence, believes to be or to have been his age at the time. If there is any doubt as to his age, the court should examine the available evidence and, if necessary, cause enquiries to be made.

The determining factor in relation to the availability of a particular sentence is normally the offender's age on the date he is convicted or found guilty, and it is improper to adjourn proceedings for the sole purpose of the offender attaining a greater age (*R v Danga* [1992] Crim LR 219; *Arthur v Stringer* (1986) 151 JP 97; *R v Starkey* [1994] Crim LR 380).

CYPA 1963, s 29

Where proceedings are begun when a defendant is under 18 and he attains that age before the conclusion of the proceedings the court may, after conviction, make any order which it could have made had the offender not attained the age of 18.

PCC(S)A 2000, s 9

Where a person who is before the youth court attains the age of 18, that court may, at any time after conviction and before sentence, remit him to the adult court.

Where a defendant crosses a relevant age threshold between the date of the commission of the offence and the date of conviction, the starting point for sentence is the sentence the defendant would have received if he had been sentenced at the date of the commission of the offence. Other factors may have to be considered but there have to be good reasons for departing from the starting point. It will be most unusual for a court to consider passing a sentence that is more severe than the maximum that would have applied to the defendant at the date of the offence. Where the date of conviction is only a few months after the date of the offence, it will rarely be appropriate to pass a longer sentence that would have been passed at the date of the offence (*R v Ghafoor* [2002] 116 JPR 601).

Sentence	10	11	12	13	14	15	16	17	18	19	20	21 + over
Absolute discharge	●	●	●	●	●	●	●	●	●	●	●	●
Conditional discharge	●	●	●	●	●	●	●	●	●	●	●	●
Action plan order	◍	◍	◍	◍	◍	◍	◍	◍				
Attendance centre*	◍	◍	◍	◍	◍	◍	◍	◍	●	●	●	●
Bind over	●	●	●	●	●	●	●	●	●	●	●	●
Bind over (parental)	●	●	●	●	●	●	●	●				
Committal for sentence PCC(S)A 2000, s 3*									●	●	●	●
Community rehabilitation order							◍	◍	●	●	●	●
Community punishment order*							◍	◍	●	●	●	●
Community punishment & rehabilitation order*							◍	◍	●	●	●	●
Compensation order	◍	◍	◍	◍	◍	◍	◍	◍	●	●	●	●
Curfew order	●	●	●	●	●	●	●	●	●	●	●	●
Detention & training order*			◍	◍	◍	◍	◍	◍				
Detention young offender institution*									●	●	●	
Drug abstinence order*									●	●	●	●
Drug treatment & testing order							●	●	●	●	●	●
Fine	●	●	●	●	●	●	●	●	●	●	●	●
Guardianship order (MHA)	◍	◍	◍	◍	◍	◍	◍	◍	●	●	●	●
Hospital order*	◍	◍	◍	◍	◍	◍	◍	◍	●	●	●	●
Imprisonment												●
Referral to youth offender panel	◍	◍	◍	◍	◍	◍	◍	◍				
Reparation order (other than money)	◍	◍	◍	◍	◍	◍	◍	◍				
Supervision & treatment order PCC(S)A 2000, Sched 6 para 6	●	●	●	●	●	●	●	●				
Supervision order	◍	◍	◍	◍	◍	◍	◍	◍				

Sentence available ● **Sentence available in youth court only** ◍ **Sentence not available** ☐

* Only where offence(s) punishable by imprisonment in the case of an offender aged 21 or over.

APPEALS

Appeals

1. APPEALS TO MAGISTRATES' COURTS

A number of statutes provide for an appeal to a magistrates' court from public or local government bodies.

The powers of the court in dealing with such an appeal will depend upon the particular statute governing the appeal. The appeal is initiated by the appellant making a complaint for an order, within the time prescribed by the statute, followed by the issue of a summons.

Procedure on appeal

The procedure follows that laid down for hearing a complaint, ie:

MCR 1981, r 34

(1) the complainant/appellant opens the appeal;
(2) witnesses are called in such order as the party calling them desires;
(3) evidence is given on oath or on affirmation;
(4) the rules as to adjournments apply; and
(5) speeches follow the usual order.

An appeal involves a rehearing of the whole matter: the parties are not restricted to adducing the evidence which was adduced, or to the arguments which were advanced at the lower hearing. The court must form its own opinion on the subject-matter of the appeal and is entitled to substitute that opinion for the opinion of the body or tribunal from which the appeal is brought (see *Fulham BC v Santilli* (1933) 97 JP 174; *Tower Hamlets BC v Whitehouse* (1971) 68 LGR 426; *Sagnata Investments v Norwich Corporation* [1971] 2 All ER 1441; *Northern Ireland Trailers Ltd v Preston Corporation* (1971) JP 149; *Thameside MBC v Grant* (2001) 165 JPN 875).

Powers on appeal

On determining an appeal, the court may either make the order for which complaint is made, or dismiss the complaint, thus dismissing the appeal. MCA 1980, s 63

Where the court makes an order, it may include in it provisions as to:

(1) the manner in which anything is to be done;
(2) the time within which anything is to be done or during which anything is not to be done; and
(3) any other provision for giving effect to the order, as the court thinks fit.

Costs of the appeal

MCA 1980, s 64

As part of the adjudication, the court may make such order as to costs as it thinks just and reasonable to be paid:

(1) on the making of an order, by the defendant to the complainant; and

(2) on dismissing a complaint, by the complainant to the defendant,

the amount of any sum ordered to be paid being specified in the order, or the order for dismissal, as the case may be.

Those costs may include the witnesses' expenses and professional representation.

The general principles as to the award of costs apply; in particular:

(a) the costs awarded should not exceed the proper costs incurred; and

(b) the order must not be a penalty under the guise of costs.

If an excessive award is made, or if the court is shown to have taken account of irrelevant factors, the court acts outside the discretion conferred upon it, and the award is liable to be quashed by the High Court *(R v Pwllheli JJ, ex p Soane* [1948] 2 All ER 815; *R v Highgate JJ, ex p Petrou* [1954] 1 All ER 406; *R v Tottenham JJ, ex p Joshi* (1982) 146 JP 268).

2. APPEALS FROM MAGISTRATES' COURTS

The acts, orders or decisions of a magistrates' court are subject to control and review by superior courts. They may be challenged:

(1) by appeal to the Crown Court against conviction and/or sentence, which takes the form of a rehearing of the case; or

(2) by appeal to the Queen's Bench Division of the High Court by way of case stated, which takes the form of a consultation with the High Court, to obtain an answer on a point of law on facts found by the magistrates' court; or

(3) the Criminal Cases Review Commission may, under CAA 1995, Pt II refer to the Crown Court the conviction or sentence of a person convicted summarily, which is then treated for all purposes as an appeal by that person under MCA 1980, s 108(1).

There is also provision for challenging certain bail decisions of the magistrates' court in the Crown Court (see BAIL). There is no appeal from a magistrates' court to the Criminal Division of the Court of Appeal.

Proceedings for judicial review of magistrates' decisions, while not strictly counting as appeals, are dealt with at pp 43–45 (*below*)).

In certain circumstances, where an accused serves on the magistrates' court a statutory declaration that he was unaware of the proceedings in his absence they may be treated as invalid and commenced afresh. MCA 1980, s 14

3. APPEAL TO THE CROWN COURT

In its appellate jurisdiction, the Crown Court exists primarily to deal with disputed questions of fact. An appeal against:

(1) conviction takes the form of a rehearing of the whole case, with the prosecutor having to prove his case afresh. Either party may call relevant and admissible evidence in support of his case, whether or not that evidence was called below;

(2) sentence is a rehearing of the case from the point of conviction onwards (*Dyson v Ellison* [1975] RTR 205); the Crown Court will consider what the right sentence should be, and will not confine itself to considering whether the sentence passed was within the jurisdiction of the court below (*R v Swindon CC, ex p Murray* (1997) 162 JP 36).

As to conducting a 'Newton Hearing' where there is a sharp divergence in the versions of the facts, see *R v Williams* (1983) 148 JP 375, *Bussey v DPP* [1999] Crim LR 908.

On hearing an appeal against conviction, the powers of the Crown Court are the same as those of the magistrates' court, and save as is expressly authorised (eg as by the provisions of RTA 1988, s 24, as amended by RTA 1991, s 24) it has no power:

(a) to amend an information (*Garfield v Maddocks* [1973] 2 All ER 303); or

(b) to substitute an alternative charge for the one before the court below (*R v Manchester Crown Court, ex p Hill* (1985) 149 JP 257; *Arthur v Stringer* (1987) 151 JP 97); or

(c) to convict on an information in different form from that before the lower court (*Fairgrieve v Newman* [1986] Crim LR 47; *R v Swansea CC, ex p Stacey* [1990] RTR 183; *R v Norwich CC, ex p Russell* [1993] Crim LR 518).

Right of appeal: (1) general

A person convicted before a magistrates' court has a general right of appeal to the Crown Court: MCA 1980, s 108

(1) if he pleaded guilty, against his sentence; or

(2) if he pleaded not guilty, against his conviction and/or sentence.

Where an appeal is brought against conviction, the question of sentence is also at large, enabling the court to adjust it by reducing it or increasing it.

The term 'sentence' is defined to include any order made on conviction, except:

(a) an order for payment of costs, which must be challenged by judicial review (*R v Tottenham JJ, ex p Joshi* (1982) 146 JP 268); or

(b) an order under the Protection of Animals Act 1911, s 2 which enables a court to order an animal's destruction.

PCC(S)A 2000, s 14, under which a conviction of an offence for which an order for absolute or conditional discharge is made is deemed not to be a conviction, does not prevent an appeal, whether against conviction or against sentence, and a person sentenced for an offence in respect of which a conditional charge has been previously made, may appeal to the Crown Court against the sentence.

Right of appeal: (2) 'order made on conviction'

The basis of an 'order made on conviction' is that it must have been made *in consequence of the conviction* for the particular offence of which the offender stands convicted (*R v London Sessions Appeal Committee, ex p Beaumont* (1951) 115 JP 108; *R v London Sessions Appeal Committee, ex p Rogers* [1951] 1 All ER 343; *R v Hayden* [1975] 2 All ER 558).

No appeal lies against an order:

(1) committing, sending or transferring an accused to the Crown Court for trial; or

(2) committing an offender to the Crown Court for sentence or to be dealt with under PCC(S)A 2000, s 3.

The decision of a 'designated authority' to give notice of transfer of a serious fraud case, or of the DPP to transfer a case involving a child to the Crown Court for trial, is not liable to be appealed.

By statute, however, appeal lies against:

IA 1971, s 6(5)(a) (a) a recommendation for deportation made under the Immigration Act 1971;

MHA 1983, s 70 (b) a guardianship order under the Mental Health Act 1983;

RTOA 1988, s 38 (c) an obligatory disqualification under the Road Traffic Acts.

Right of appeal: (3) other specific cases

In addition to the general right of appeal conferred by s 108(1) a right of appeal is given by statute to:

(1) an offender sentenced for an offence in respect of which a community rehabilitation order or an order of conditional discharge was previously made; MCA 1980, s 108(2)

(2) an offender sentenced for breach of the requirements of a community rehabilitation order, a community punishment order, a curfew order or a drug testing treatment and testing order; PCC(S)A) 2000 Sched 8, para 4(6)

(3) an offender sentenced for breach of an attendance centre order, or a breach of the centre's rules; PCC(S)A 2000, Sched 5, para 2(6)

(4) a person ordered, under JPA 1361 or otherwise, to enter into recognisances to keep the peace; ABOOA 1956, s 1

(5) a parent or guardian ordered to pay the fine, costs or compensation order in respect of a juvenile offender; PCC(S)A2000, s 137(6)

(6) a parent or guardian ordered to enter into recognisances to ensure that a juvenile offender pays sums in respect of fines, costs etc. incurred by him; MCA 1980, s 81(6)

(7) a parent or guardian ordered to enter into recognisances to take proper care and exercise proper control of a relevant juvenile; PCC(S)A 2000, s 150(8)

(8) against the extension or further extension of the overall custody time limit, or the giving of a direction under POA 1985, s 6A; POA 1985, s 22(8)

(9) a person aggrieved by a decision to make an order under FOD 1999, s 7; FSA 1989, s 22(7)

(10) a party to any proceedings in which forfeiture of cash is made by the court under CJ(IC)A 1990, s 26; CJ(IC)A 1990, s 24A

(11) against the making of an anti-social behaviour order, or a sex offender order; CDA 1998, s 4(1)(2)

(12) by a parent or guardian against the making of a parenting order; CDA 1998 s 10(1)

(13) by an offender against any order made on the breach of an action plan order or reparation order, except one that could have been have been made in his absence by virtue of para 6(9), and against the dismissal of an application to revoke an order; PCC(S)A 2000, ss 72, 75, Sched 8 para 7

(14) by a young offender dealt with for an offence on the revocation of a referral order made under PCC(S)A 2000, ss 16–32; PCC(S)A 2000, s 32

(15) against a person against whom a forfeiture order has been made under TA 2000, para 5(4); TA 2000, s 29

(16) a person dealt with by a magistrates' court for contempt, in relation to the sentence, but *quaere* whether the Crown Court has power to entertain an appeal against the finding (*R v Havant JJ, ex p Palmer* [1985] Crim 658). CCA 1981, s12(5)

Appeals

Right of appeal by unsuccessful prosecutor

An unsuccessful prosecutor has no right of appeal to the Crown Court against the dismissal of an information or an acquittal in the magistrates' court unless conferred by statute, eg under C&EMA 1979, s 147(2).

An appeal under (8) above lies at the instance of either prosecutor or accused. As to a prosecutor's right to appeal bail decisions, see BAIL.

Initiating the appeal

The initiation of an appeal is governed by the Crown Court Rules.

CCR 1982, r 7(1)(2)(3)

An appeal is initiated by the appellant giving notice in writing to:

(1) the clerk of the magistrates' court; and
(2) any other party to the appeal.

That notice must state whether appeal is against conviction or sentence or both, and must be given not later than 21 days after:

(a) the day on which the decision appealed against was given; or
(b) where the proceedings were adjourned after conviction, the day on which sentence was passed or the offender was otherwise dealt with; or
(c) where the court deferred sentence, in the case of an appeal against conviction, the day on which the court exercised that power.

CJ(IC)A 1990, s 26A

An appeal against an order for forfeiture of cash in accordance with CJ(IC)A 1990, s 26 must be brought within the period of 30 days beginning with the date on which it was made.

CCR 1982, r 7(1)(5)(6)

The time may be extended by the Crown Court, whether before or after it expires. Any application for extension will need to be in writing, specifying the grounds for the extension, together with the grounds of appeal, and must be sent to the appropriate officer of the Crown Court.

On appeal against conviction, an appellant on public funding is entitled to require from the clerk of the magistrates' court a copy of any notes of evidence; an appellant not so represented has no such right, but clearly requests from such a person ought to be sympathetically considered (*R v Clerk to Highbury Corner JJ, ex p Hussein* [1986] Crim LR 812).

Grounds of appeal

In certain specific cases (for which see the Crown Court Rules 1982, Sched 3, Pt III) detailed grounds of appeal are required, but normally a formula such as 'the conviction is against the weight of the evidence' or 'the sentence is excessive' is acceptable.

In the case of a Welsh devolution issue under GWA 1998, notice of appeal must specify whether the issue was considered in the magistrates' court. If it was not, the notice should specify: GWA 1998, s 20

(1) that the appeal raises such an issue, and the relevant provisions of GWA 1998; and
(2) the facts and circumstances and points of law on the basis of which it is alleged that the issue arises, in such detail as to enable the court to determine whether a devolution issue arises.

Representation of magistrates

It is the invariable practice for the prosecutor in the proceedings before the magistrates' court to take upon himself the duty of responding to the appeal (*R v Kent JJ, ex p MPC* [1935] All ER 817; *R v Preston Crown Court, ex p Pamplin* [1981] Crim LR 338). In any event, the magistrates whose decision is questioned have, in law, an absolute right to appear, to instruct counsel and to call evidence in support of the decision at which they arrived. Where they do, however, they appear as *amicus curiae,* and should not enter into any dispute since they cannot be cross-examined, do not make themselves parties to the appeal, and no costs can be awarded against them.

Case notes

Any case notes should be sent to the Crown Court when there is an appeal, thereby making them available to the judge if the judge requires them in order to decide before the hearing questions of listing or representation or the like. They will also be available to the court during the hearing if it becomes necessary or desirable for the court to see what happened in the magistrates' court (*Practice Direction* (*criminal: consolidated*) [2002] 3 All ER 904, para 52.1).

Equivocal plea; change of plea

An offender pleading guilty in the magistrates' court has no right of appeal to the Crown Court against his conviction unless he can persuade the Crown Court that the plea he entered below was 'equivocal', or, in exceptional circumstances, that his plea was entered under duress (*R v Huntingdon CC, ex p Jordan* [1981] 2 All ER 872).

For a plea to be 'equivocal' in this sense it must be shown that the accused added to his plea of guilty in the lower court some qualification which, if true, might show that he was not really admitting his guilt of the offence charged (*R v Durham* QS, *ex p Virgo* [1952] 1 All ER 466; *R v Huntingdon CC, ex p Jordan, above*).

Magistrates' courts are sometimes faced with a case sent back from the Crown Court with a direction to enter a plea of not guilty and start again.

The Crown Court is only entitled to take such a step:

(1) where the judge has properly determined the issue as a preliminary matter;

(2) after hearing evidence as to what happened before the lower court; and

(3) if necessary, calling for, and considering, affidavit evidence from the chairman and/or Clerk to the magistrates' court

(*R v Marylebone Magistrates, ex p Westminster City Council* (1971) 135 JP 239.)

The Crown Court has a limited power, on an appeal against conviction, to embark upon an enquiry as to whether the plea was entered under a mistake or misapprehension (*R v Durham QS, ex p Virgo* (*above*); also *R v W Kent QS, ex p Files* [1951] 2 All ER 728), but if the Crown Court finds, on the evidence that eg:

(a) the plea was entered under duress (*Huntingdon CC, ex p Jordan* (*above*)); or

(b) that a plea in bar of trial was open to the appellant in the magistrates' court (*Cooper v New Forest DC* [1992] Crim LR 877),

the case will be remitted to the magistrates' court (cf *R v Birmingham CC, ex p Sharma* [1988] Crim LR 741).

If the Crown Court finds, on the evidence, that the plea before the lower court was equivocal, it may treat the conviction as a nullity and remit the case to the magistrates' court to be reheard (*R v Rochdale JJ, ex p Allwork* (1982) 146 JP 33).

If the case is properly remitted, the magistrates' court must follow the Crown Court's direction and rehear the case (*R v Plymouth JJ, ex p Hart* [1986] 2 All ER 452); it may be compelled to do so by mandatory order.

A new trial commences when the evidence is called; the preliminaries may therefore be taken as read. In the case of an offence triable either way, the magistrates are not obliged to put the accused again to his election; if they do so, they are not obliged to permit him to change his original election. It is a matter of discretion and will depend on how they see 'the broad justice of the whole situation' (*R v Bradfield & Sonning JJ, ex p Jones* [1975] Crim LR 518; *R v Southampton JJ, ex p Briggs* [1972] 1 All ER 573).

Ancillary matters

A number of ancillary matters may be noted:

(1) apart from any special enactment (eg under the betting, gaming and licensing legislation), the giving of notice of appeal does not necessarily stay the execution of any order or sentence of the magistrates' court;

(2) a compensation order (see COMPENSATION) made by the magistrates' court, is suspended until the time for giving notice of appeal has expired, and if notice is given within time, until the determination of the appeal;

(3) bail pending appeal may be granted, subject to the provisions of CJPOA 1994, s 25, once notice of appeal has been given:
   (a) by the magistrates' court; or MCA 1980, s 113
   (b) by the Crown Court; or SCA 1981
   (c) by the High Court. BA 1976, s 4(1)(2)

There is, however, no general right to bail after conviction .

Abandonment of appeal

A person giving notice of appeal to the Crown Court may abandon the appeal by giving notice in writing to the Clerk of the magistrates' court not later than the third day before the day fixed for the hearing of the appeal. He must also send a copy to the appropriate officer of the Crown Court. CCR 1982, r 11

In computing the 'third day', Saturdays, Sundays and bank holidays are disregarded.

The advantage of giving notice of abandonment in this way instead of waiting until the day of the hearing, is that no costs may be ordered against the appellant.

4. APPEAL BY WAY OF CASE STATED

Any person who was a party to proceedings before a magistrates' court, or who is is aggrieved by the conviction, order, determination or other proceedings of a magistrates' court, may, unless: MCA 1980, s 111(1)

(1) there is a right of appeal directly to the High Court; or

(2) by virtue of any enactment, the decision of the magistrates' court is final,

question the same on the ground that it is *wrong in law or in excess of jurisdiction,* by applying to the magistrate(s) composing the court to state a case for the opinion of the High Court on the question of law or jurisdiction involved.

On making an application to state a case, any right of appeal to the Crown Court ceases, and this is so even though the application to state the case is out of time and therefore invalid (*P & M Supplies (Essex) Ltd v Hackney LBC* [1990] Crim LR 569), although a person appealing by way of case stated against his *conviction,* whose appeal is dismissed, is not debarred from MCA 1980, s 111 appealing to the Crown Court against his *sentence* (*Sivalingham v DPP* [1975] CLY 2037; *Universal Salvage Ltd etc v Boothby* [1984] RTR 289).

In all but the most exceptional case, challenge to a sentence ought to be by way of appeal to the Crown Court, and not by case stated to the High Court (*Tucker v DPP* [1992] 4 All ER 901, see also *Allen v W Yorks Probation Service* (2001) *The Times*, 20 February). The Crown Court is the proper forum for the resolution of disputed facts (*James v Kent Chief Constable* (1986) *The Times*, 7 June).

Nature of appeal

An appeal by way of case stated is not, like an appeal to the Crown Court, a rehearing. It is by way of argument, upon a case stated by the magistrates and any affidavits submitted or required. The High Court does not sit as a general court of appeal against the decisions of magistrates in the way the Crown Court does. It sits only to review the lower courts' decisions in point of law, being bound by the facts to which the magistrates have come, provided there was evidence on which they could come to the conclusions that they did. It will not entertain an appeal by way of case stated until the magistrates have reached a final decision (*Loade v DPP* (1990) 90 Cr App R 162).

There will be few cases in which this procedure is appropriate for appealing an interlocutory decision (see *R v Greater Manchester JJ ex p Aldi GmbH* (1994) 159 JP 717).

Initiating an appeal

MCA 1980, s 111(2)

An appeal is initiated by applying to the magistrates comprising the court whose decision is appealed against, within 21 days after the day on which the decision was made, to state a case for the opinion of the High Court on the question of law or jurisdiction involved. Note that:

MCR 1981, r 76(1)(2)

(1) the application must be made in writing and be signed by or on behalf of the appellant, and must identify the questions of law or jurisdiction on which the High Court's opinion is sought;

(2) where one of those questions is whether there was evidence on which the lower court could come to its decision, the particular finding of fact which it is claimed cannot be supported must be specified;

(3) where the court adjourned the trial of an information after conviction, the day on which its decision was 'given' is the day on which the offender was sentenced or otherwise dealt with.

Consideration of draft case

MCR 1981, r 77

Unless the magistrates refuse to state a case, the Clerk must, within 21 days of the receipt of the application, send to the applicant and to the respondent, or their solicitors, a draft case in which is stated:

(1) the facts found by the magistrates; and

(2) the questions of law or jurisdiction on which the opinion of the High Court is sought.

The case must not contain a statement of the evidence unless one of the questions on which an opinion is sought is whether there was evidence upon which the magistrates could come to their decision; nor is the High Court competent to receive notes of evidence (*Cotgreave and Cotgreave v Chester CC* (1992) 157 JP 85). In such a case, the particular finding which it is claimed cannot be supported must be specified in the case.

Where a properly formulated question to the High Court is submitted to the magistrates, it should not be fundamentally altered without giving the party submitting it an opportunity to comment on any alteration (*Waldie v DP* (1995) 159 JP 514).

If the Clerk is unable to send the draft case to the appellant within the 21 days, he must do so as soon as practicable thereafter, attaching to the draft case, and to the final case when it is sent to the appellant or his solicitor, a statement of the delay and the reasons for it. MCR 1981, r 79(1)

Representation by the parties

Each party to the proceedings has the right, within 21 days of the receipt of the draft case, to make representations on it. MCR 1981, r 77(2)

These representations must be:

(1) in writing;

(2) signed by or on behalf of the party; and

(3) sent to the Clerk of the magistrates' court.

If, within that time, the Clerk receives an application from either party, with reasons given, he may extend the time within which representations must be made. In such circumstances, he must give notice to the parties, and the final case sent to the appellant or his solicitor must bear a statement of the extension and the reasons for it. MCR 1981, r 79(2)

Preparation and submission of final case

Within 21 days of the day on which representations should have been made, the magistrate(s) may make such adjustments as they think fit to the draft case, considering any representations made, and then state the case. The case may be stated on behalf of the magistrates whose decision is questioned by any two or more of them, and, if they so direct, may be signed by the Clerk on their behalf. MCR 1981, r 78(1),(2)

If they are unable to state the case within the 21 days, they must do so as soon as practicable thereafter, attaching to the final case sent to the appellant a statement of the delay and the reasons for it. MCR 1981, r 79(3)

When the case has been stated and signed, it will be sent to the appellant or his solicitor forthwith.

Filing the case

CPR 1998, r 52

On receiving the case, the appellant must:

(1) within ten days after receipt, file notice with the High Court; and

(2) with the notice, lodge the stated case, a copy of the judgment, order or decision in respect of which the case has been stated; and

(3) within four days after they are filed with the High Court, serve on all other respondents his notice and the accompanying documents.

Procedure in the High Court is governed by CPR 1998.

Refusal to state a case

The magistrates have a legal duty to state a case when an application is made unless they consider the application to be frivolous (*P & M Supplies (Essex) Ltd v Walsall MBC* [1994] Crim LR 580), that is 'futile, misconceived, hopeless or academic', in which case they must, if briefly, indicate their reasons for so finding (*R v Mildenhall JJ, ex p Forest Heath DC* (1997) 161 JP 401).

MCA 1980, s 111(5)

If they are of the opinion that an application to state a case is frivolous, the magistrates may refuse the application, giving the applicant, if he so desires, a certificate stating that the application is refused, but an application cannot be refused on the ground that it is frivolous:

(1) where there is an arguable point of law (*R v Petersfield JJ, ex p Levy* [1981] RTR 204); or

MCA 1980, s 111(5)

(2) it is made by or on behalf of the Attorney-General.

Where an application is refused as frivolous, the applicant may apply for judicial review of that decision (*Sunworld Ltd v Hammersmith & Fulham LBC* [2000] 2 All ER 837).

MCR 1981, r 77(3)

If they are then required to do so by mandatory order (see *below*) the Clerk must send the draft case to the applicant, and a copy to the respondent, within 21 days after the date on which the mandatory order was made.

Refusal to state a case after being ordered to do so by mandatory order will render the magistrates liable to costs (*R v Huntingdon MC, ex p Percy* (1994) *The Times*, 4 March).

Bail

MCA 1980, s 113(1)(2)

Where a person who is in custody has applied to the magistrates to state a case, they may (subject to CJPOA 1994, s 25) grant him bail, and in such a case the time and place at which he is to appear, unless the magistrates' determination is reversed by the High Court, will be the magistrates' court, at such time within ten days after the judgment of the High Court has been given, as may be specified by the magistrates, any recognisance taken from him, or surety for him, being conditioned accordingly.

Recognisances

The magistrates are not bound to state the case until the applicant has entered into a recognisance, with or without sureties, to prosecute the appeal without delay and to submit to the judgment of the High Court, paying such costs as that court may award. MCA 1980, s 114

As in other cases where recognisances are being considered, the magistrates are bound to have regard to the appellant's means in deciding whether recognisances are appropriate, and if so, in fixing the amount (*R v Newcastle-upon-Tyne JJ, ex p Skinner* [1987] 1 All ER 349, *R v Croydon MC, ex p Morgan* (1998) 161 JP 169).

Abandonment

An appellant whose case stated is pending before the High Court may withdraw his appeal without leave of the court (*Collett v Bromsgrove DC* [1997] Crim LR 206).

5. JUDICIAL REVIEW

Judicial review is the appropriate remedy where it is sought to challenge the acts, orders or decisions of magistrates' courts in circumstances in which no right of appeal as such is conferred, or where existing rights of appeal do not apply to the specific matter which it is sought to challenge. These matters will often be interlocutory orders, such as irregularities in the issue of process, determinations as to mode of trial, decisions on representation, adjournments and so on.

This jurisdiction is exercised by the issue of:

(1) a mandatory order (CPR 1998, r 54.1), to compel the lower court to exercise its proper jurisdiction;

(2) a prohibiting order, to restrain the lower court from proceeding improperly; and

(3) a quashing order, to quash an order which has been made improperly.

Nature of judicial review

While judicial review provides a speedy and effective remedy in a proper case, it is a discretionary remedy (see *R v Peterborough MC, ex p Dowler* [1997] 2 WLR 843, *R v Hereford MC, ex p Rowlands* [1997] 2 WLR 854). Its ambit is restricted; in particular:

(1) the issue of these orders is reserved for simple and straightforward cases; the High Court will not attempt to resolve direct conflicts of evidence on material facts;

(2) their ambit is confined essentially to matters of jurisdiction, thus the proper exercise of a discretion to admit or reject evidence in committal proceedings is not subject to control;

(3) the High Court will not permit the machinery of judicial review to be used as a means of appeal; and

(4) the court will not interfere where the statutory framework for the hearing of appeals from the lower court has not been exhausted.

Where judicial review not appropriate

In a case where the facts are of material importance, the proper method is to proceed by way of case stated, rather than judicial review (*R v Felixstowe JJ, ex p Baldwin* [1981] Crim LR 282). The procedure:

(1) is not appropriate for attacking decisions on the grant of bail or conditions attached to bail, until the procedure under SCA 1981, s 81 and CJA 1967, s 22 has been exhausted (*R v Guildhall JJ, ex p Prushinowski* (1985) *The Times*, 14 December);

(2) will only rarely be appropriate for appealing an interlocutory decision (see *R v Greater Manchester JJ, ex p Aldi GmbH* (1994) 159 JP 717).

As to the court's approach to cases where the magistrates dismiss an information on grounds of abuse of process, see *R v Liverpool City JJ, ex p Price* (1998) 162 JP 766.

Sentence cases

Just as it is prepared to interfere with a sentence passed by the Crown Court in the exercise of that court's 'magistrates' powers', the High Court will intervene:

(1) where it is clear that there is an error of law in the sentencing process (*R v Liverpool CC, ex p Baird* (1985) 7 Cr App R(S) 437);

(2) where the sentence is harsh and oppressive, and so far outside the normal sentence for such offences as to amount to an error of law (*R v St Albans CC, ex p Cinnamond* [1981] All ER 802; *R v Croydon CC ex p Miller* (1987) 85 Cr App R 152);

(3) where the sentence is 'irrational and truly astonishing' (*R v Acton CC, ex p Bewley* (1988) 152 JP 327); *R v Chelmsford CC, ex p Birchall* (1989) 11 Cr App R(S) 510); *R v Northampton MC, ex p Customs & Excise Commissioners* [1994] Crim LR 598); and

(4) where the sentence imposed is 'outside the broad area of the lower court's jurisdiction' (*R v Southwark CC, ex p Smith* [2001] 2 Cr App R(S) 163).

Application for permission

Procedure for judicial review is under CPR 1998, r 54. The permission of the High Court must first be obtained before a claim for judicial review is made. CPC 1998, r 54

A claim is made by filing a claim form:

(1) promptly; and

(2) in any event not later than three months after the grounds to make the claim first arose (unless any other enactment specifies a shorter time limit), and

this time limit may not be extended by agreement between the parties.

Bail

Bail may be granted (subject to CJPOA 1994, s 25) by the High Court to a person convicted or sentenced in the magistrates' court and who applies for a quashing order under CPR 1998 or who has applied for leave to make such an application.

Costs against the magistrates

In general, magistrates should not appear before the High Court in appeals by way of case stated, or applications for judicial review unless their *bona fides* are called in question or there are other exceptional circumstances.

If they do:

(1) they are unlikely to recover costs if successful; and

(2) they risk a costs order being made against them if they lose.

Magistrates who merely file affidavits and do not appear before the court will not normally be visited with a costs order (even though in judicial review proceedings they are parties) unless they have done something which calls for strong disapproval (*R v Newcastle-under-Lyme JJ* [1995] 1 All ER 120).

6. TAINTED ACQUITTALS

CPIA 1996 provides a form of judicial review in a case where a person has been acquitted of an offence, and a person is convicted of perverting the course of justice, intimidation of witnesses, jurors etc under CJPOA 1994, s 51(1) or aiding, abetting, counselling, procuring, suborning or inciting another to commit an offence under s 1 of the Perjury Act 1911, involving interference or intimidation of a juror or a witness (or a potential witness), in any proceedings which led to the acquittal.

Appeals

Need for certificate

CPIA 1996, s 54(1)(2)(5)

Where it appears to the court before which the person was convicted that there was a real possibility that, but for the interference or intimidation, the acquitted person would not have been acquitted, and there is no question, because of lapse of time or any other reason, that it would be contrary to the interests of justice to take proceedings against the acquitted person for the offence of which he was acquitted, the court must certify that fact.

Application to High Court

CPIA 1996, s 54(3)(4)

Where a court so certifies, an application may be made to the High Court for an order quashing the acquittal, and if such an order is made proceedings may be taken against the acquitted person for the offence of which he was acquitted.

Conditions precedent to order

CPIA 1996, s 54(3), 55

The High Court may not make such an order unless four conditions are fulfilled. These are that it appears to the High Court likely, taking into account all the information before it, but ignoring the possibility of new factors coming to light, that:

(1) but for the interference or intimidation, the acquitted person would not have been acquitted;

(2) that because of lapse of time or for any other reason, it would not be contrary to the interest of justice to take proceedings against the acquitted person for the offence of which he was acquitted;

(3) that the acquitted person has been given a reasonable opportunity to make written representations to the court; and

(4) that the conviction for the administration of justice offence will stand. The High Court will not make an order if, for instance, the time of giving notice of appeal has not expired, or an appeal is pending.

Time limits

CPIA 1996, s 56

Where an order is made quashing an acquittal and it is proposed to take proceedings against the acquitted person, any time limits within which, by statute, a prosecution must be commenced, will run from the making of the order.

BAIL

Bail granted in criminal proceedings, that is bail grantable:

(1) in, or in connection with, proceedings for an offence, or an alleged offence, to a person who is accused or convicted of that offence; or BA 1976, ss 1(5), 11(1), 2

(2) in connection with an offence, to a person who is under arrest for the offence, or for whose arrest a warrant, backed for bail, is being issued,

is governed by BA 1976.

A person granted bail in criminal proceedings is under a duty to surrender to the custody of the court, at the time and place appointed, and if, at the time and place appointed: BA 1976, ss 2(2),3(1)(2), 6(1)

(a) he fails, without reasonable cause, to surrender to custody: or

(b) having reasonable cause for failure, fails to surrender as soon after the appointed time as is reasonably practicable,

he commits an offence.

No recognisance is taken from him, though recognisances may still be taken from a surety, and in certain quasi-criminal matters (particularly binding-over orders).

Special considerations apply to bail on the expiry of the custody time limits as to which see CUSTODY TIME LIMITS.

If bail is not granted to a person aged 17 or over he is remanded to prison; as to juveniles, see ADJOURNMENT AND REMAND.

Scheme of section

The scheme of this section is as follows:

(1) whether bail is appropriate (see pp 48–54 *below*);

(2) unconditional or subject to conditions (see pp 54–55 *below*);

(3) sureties/security (see pp 55–57 *below*);

(4) other requirements of bail (see pp 57–59 *below*);

(5) variation/reconsideration of bail (see pp 59–61 *below*);

(6) breach and absconding (see pp 61–64 *below*);

(7) forfeiture of recognisances security (see p 64–67 *below*);

(8) challenging a decision (see pp 68–69 *below*).

Bail

1. WHETHER BAIL IS APPROPRIATE

There is no right to withhold bail save on prescribed grounds. There are cases in which bail is restricted and cases in which the general right to bail may be displaced on one of the grounds set out in the Act.

Right to bail: (1) before conviction

MCA 1980, s 41; BA 1976, s 4(1)(2)(3)(7), Sched 1

Subject to CJPOA 1994, s 25 (*below*), *before conviction*, there is a general right to bail, unless one of the exceptions in Sched 1 is made out, where a person:

(1) appears, or is brought, before the court in the course of or in connection with, proceedings for an offence; or

(2) applies to the court for bail in connection with the proceedings.

Right to bail: (2) after conviction

There is no general presumption to bail after a person's conviction for an offence, though it may be granted, (subject to CJPOA 1994, s 25) where:

(1) the offender appears or is brought before the court to be dealt with for breach of the requirements of a community rehabilitation order or a community punishment order; or

(2) the offender's case is adjourned for the purpose of enabling enquiries and a report to be made, to assist the court in dealing with him for the offence (see p 51 *below*).

BA 1976, s 4(1) Sched 1, Pt I

Where an offender's case is adjourned for enquiries or reports, and the offence or one of the offences, of which he is convicted in the proceedings is punishable with imprisonment, he need not be granted bail if it appears that it would be impracticable to complete the enquiries or to make the report without keeping him in custody.

In other cases after conviction, as pending appeal or committal for sentence, grant of bail is a matter for the magistrates' discretion.

General considerations

BA 1976, s 4(1), Sched 1, Pt I

In considering whether or not to grant bail, balancing the right to bail, if it applies, against the statutory exceptions to it, the court must have regard to such of the following considerations as appear to be relevant (see also the ECHR approach set out in *Letellier v France* (1992) 14 EHRR 83):

(1) the nature and seriousness of the offence;

(2) the character and antecedents, associations and community ties of the accused;

(3) the accused's record as regards the fulfilment of his obligations under previous grants of bail; and

(4) except in 'reports' cases, the strength of the evidence; and
(5) any misuse of controlled drugs by the accused (BA 1976, s 4(9); CJCSA 2000, s 58).

Where a 28 day remand is being considered under MCA 1980, s 128A the court should also consider the total period of time which the accused will spend in custody if not granted bail.

There should be evidence to support objections to bail. Any evidence on which the prosecutor seeks to rely should be disclosed, though the strict rules of evidence do not seem to apply (*Lamy v Belgium* (1989) 11 EHRR 529).

Where the accused indicates that he does not intend to comply with any requirement imposed, this is not a ground for refusing bail; breach of any requirement may be dealt with subsequently under BA 1976, s 7 (see p 61 *below*) (see *R v Bournemouth MC, ex p Cross etc* [1989] Crim LR 207).

Other relevant considerations

A number of pertinent points may also be made (see the Scottish case of *Smith v M* [1982] SLT 421):

(1) where the presumption applies, an accused ought to be granted bail unless it can be shown that there are good grounds for not granting it;
(2) while the presumption of innocence is a factor, it does not exclude competing factors which may be more formidable in the circumstances of the case;
(3) previous convictions should not be regarded, by themselves, as an automatic reason for refusing bail, but if there is a significance in the record and the nature of the charges preferred, the consideration of protection of the public arises;
(4) vague or unspecified arguments that the police are still making enquiries are hardly a good ground for refusing bail: it is otherwise, of course, where the prosecution can show that it is in the interests of the public or the administration of justice that an accused be detained until enquiries are complete;
(5) an important factor is the allegation that, at the time of the commission of the alleged offence, the accused was under an obligation to be of good behaviour, as where, eg, he was subject to a community sentence or to a deferred sentence, or is on licence from prison.

Restrictions on bail; homicide and rape cases

A person charged with murder, attempted murder, manslaughter, rape or attempted rape, who: CJPOA 1994, s 25

(1) has been previously convicted in any part of the United Kingdom of such an offence, or

(2) in the case of a previous conviction for manslaughter or culpable homicide (in Scotland) was then a child or young person and was sentenced to long-term detention under any of the relevant enactments,

may be granted bail only if the court is satisfied that there are exceptional circumstances which justify it.

The court must announce in open court its reasons for that justification. As to the conditions appropriate in a murder case where bail is granted, see *below*.

Exceptions to bail: (1) other imprisonable offences

BA 1976, Sched 1, Pt I

Subject to the expiry of the custody time limits (see CUSTODY TIME LIMITS), if the offence, or one of the offences, of which the applicant is accused or convicted in the proceedings is punishable with imprisonment, he need not be granted bail:

(1) if the offence is an indictable offence or one triable either way, and it appears that he was on bail in criminal proceedings on the date of the offence; or

(2) if released on bail, whether subject to conditions or not, there are substantial grounds for the *belief* (see *R v Slough JJ, ex p Duncan* (1982) 75 Cr App R 384; *R v Mansfield JJ, ex p Sharkey* [1985] 1 All ER 193) that he would:
  (a) fail to surrender to custody; or
  (b) commit an offence while on bail; or
  (c) interfere with witnesses or otherwise obstruct the course of justice, whether in relation to himself or another person; or

(3) he should remain in custody for his own protection, or, if he is a juvenile, for his own welfare; or

(4) he is already in custody in pursuance of the sentence of a court, or of any authority acting under the Services Acts; or

(5) the court is satisfied that it has not been practicable to obtain sufficient information for the purpose of taking the decisions in (1)–(3) above for want of time since the institution of proceedings, or

(6) he has been arrested under BA 1976, s 7(1)(2) for failing to surrender to custody or for breach of a condition of bail.

Murder cases

Where a person is accused of murder (and CJPOA 1994, s 25 does not apply):

(1) the court should consider remanding him in custody, at any rate for a period long enough for medical reports to be made, so that any relevant matters concerning his state of mind at the time of the com-

mission of the alleged offence may be considered (*R v Vernege* [1982] 1 All ER 403n);

(2) if bail is granted, then unless satisfactory reports as to the accused's state of mind have been obtained, the court should impose, as a condition of his bail, a requirement that he: BA 1976, s 3(6A)
   (a) undergo examination by two medical practitioners for the purpose of such reports being prepared; and
   (b) attend for the purpose at such institution or place as they direct, and comply with any directions he may be given.

One of the medical practitioners must be approved for the purposes of MHA 1983, s 12. Failure to impose a requirement renders the grant of bail a nullity (*R v CCC, ex p Porter* [1992] Crim LR 121). The costs of any such report will be paid out of central funds by the Crown Court (MH(A)A 1982, s 34(5)). BA 1976, s 3(6B)

Medical reports: PCC(S)A 2000, s 11

Where the court, on the summary trial of an offence punishable with imprisonment, remands the accused for medical reports on being satisfied that he did the act or made the omission charged, but is of opinion that an enquiry ought to be made into his physical or mental condition before determining the method of dealing with him:

(1) the remand, if on bail, must not exceed four weeks at a time; and
(2) the conditions imposed under s 3(6)(d) must include a requirement that the accused:
   (a) undergo medical examination by a registered medical practitioner, or where the enquiry is into his mental condition and the court so directs, two such practitioners; and
   (b) for that purpose, attend such institution or place, or on any such practitioner, as the court directs and, where the enquiry is into his mental condition, comply with any of the directions given him for the purpose.

Non-imprisonable offences

Part II of BA 1976, Sched 1 makes different, less stringent, provisions where the accused faces, or is convicted of, a non-imprisonable offence, applicable only where it appears to the court that, having been previously granted bail in criminal proceedings:

(1) he has failed to surrender; and
(2) in view of that failure, it is probable that if released, whether subject to conditions or not, he will fail to surrender to custody.

There is nothing to prevent conditions being imposed in such a case (*R v Bournemouth MC, ex p Cross etc* [1989] Crim LR 207).

Application and decision; subsequent consideration

An application for bail is generally made quite informally. The prosecutor will outline any objections, and the accused or his representative may answer these and advance any arguments in favour of bail. While evidence may be called, if appropriate, the strict rules of evidence do not apply (*Re Mole* [1981] Crim LR 170). The decision on bail is an important, and often a difficult one, necessitating a weighing of conflicting interests. The fact that, eg, the prosecutor has no objections to bail, or to unconditional bail, is not an end of the matter, it is merely a factor in the case. The decision on bail is one for the court.

BA 1976, Sched I, Pt 1, para 11A

Where the court decides not to grant bail:

(1) it must consider at each subsequent hearing while the accused continues to have a right to bail under s 4, and remains in custody, whether he ought to be granted bail; and

(2) at the first hearing after that in which the court decided not to grant bail the accused may support his application with any argument as to fact or law which he desires (whether or not he has advanced that argument previously); but

(3) at subsequent hearings the court need not hear arguments as to facts or law which it has heard previously. (see *R v Barking JJ, ex p Shankshaft* (1983) 147 JP 399).

Note that 'previous hearings' for these purposes do not include:

(a) an earlier hearing at which the court found that it had not been practicable to obtain sufficient information to make a decision (*R v Calder JJ, ex p Kennedy* [1992] Crim LR 496);

(b) previous occasions where an accused has been remanded with his consent in his absence (*R v Dover & East Kent JJ, ex p Dean* (1991) 156 JP 357);

(c) committal proceedings, where they disclose the strength or otherwise of the prosecution case, may be a new circumstance, even though the fact of committal is not *(R v Slough JJ, ex p Duncan* & *Anor* (1983) 147 JP 1).

As to the position of juveniles refused bail, see ADJOURNMENT AND REMAND.

New circumstances which emerge during the course of remand hearings may, of course, militate against bail being granted, as where there are grounds for believing that the accused's mental state may result in further offences being committed on bail (*R v Tower Bridge MC, ex p Gilbert* (1988) 152 JP 307).

MCA 1980, s 42

A magistrate who has been informed, for the purposes of determining whether an accused should have bail, that he has one or more previous convictions, may not take part in trying the issue of his guilt on the summary trial of an information, if those facts were given in the course of the same proceedings.

Reasons and record

Where bail in criminal proceedings is granted or withheld, or conditions are imposed or varied in respect of a person to whom the general presumption in favour of bail before conviction applies, a record must be kept in the prescribed manner containing the prescribed information: BA 1976, s 5(1)(4), Sched 1, Pt I, para 9A

(1) the court must, with a view to enabling the accused to apply to another court:
   (a) give its reasons for *withholding bail,* or for imposing or varying conditions and include a note of them in the record of its decision;
   (b) give its reasons for *granting bail* in cases of murder, manslaughter, rape, attempted murder and attempted rape; and
   (c) give a copy of the note to the accused;

(2) the clerk must make a record in the prescribed manner, containing the prescribed particulars, and a copy must be given to the accused as soon as is reasonably practicable.

The record, properly authenticated, is admissible as evidence in any enforcement proceedings.

Where the court withholds bail from a person who is not represented, it must, if committing him for trial, or if it issues a certificate of full argument (see below), inform him that he may apply to the High Court or to the Crown Court to be granted bail. In any other case, he may apply to a judge of the High Court. BA 1976, s 5(6)

These are the appropriate courts to which application should be made; applications challenging bail decisions of magistrates should not be made by way of judicial review to the High Court (see *R v Blyth JC, ex p G* [1991] Crim LR 693). Applications for bail to the judge in chambers at the High Court are made under RSC 1965, r 79 (see p 69 *below*).

Certificate of full argument

Where the court remands a person in custody on: BA 1976, s 5(6A)–(6C)

(1) a remand for medical reports (PCC(S)A 2000, s 11); or
(2) the adjournment of an enquiry into an offence (MCA 1980, s 5); or
(3) the adjournment of a summary trial (MCA 1980, s 10); or
(4) the initial procedure on information against an adult for an offence triable either way (MCA 1980, s 18),

after hearing full argument on an application for bail where it has:

(a) not previously heard such argument on an application from him in those proceedings; or

(b) has previously heard full argument, but is satisfied that there has been a change in his circumstances or that new considerations have been placed before it,

it must issue a certificate in the prescribed form that it heard full argument before it refused the application, or as the case may be, state the nature of the change of circumstances or the new considerations which caused it to hear a further fully argued bail application.

2. UNCONDITIONAL OR SUBJECT TO CONDITIONS

BA 1976, ss 1(6), 3(4)–(6), Sched 1, Pt 1

Bail may be unconditional or conditional. No conditions are to be imposed unless it appears necessary for the purpose of preventing the occurrence of any of those events for which bail may be refused, or, in an appropriate case, that the accused or offender makes himself available for the purpose of enabling enquiries a report to be made to assist the court in dealing with him for the offence, and in this case only where it is necessary, or before the appointed time for his surrender, to attend an interview with an authorised advocate or an authorised litigator as defined in CLSA 1990, s 119(1).

The power to impose requirements applies whether the offence is punishable with imprisonment or not (*R v Bournemouth MC, ex p Cross etc, above*).

An accused may be required:

(1) before his release, to provide a surety or sureties (see pp 55–57 *below*) to secure his surrender;

(2) before his release, to give security (see p 57 *below*), which may be given by himself or on his behalf; and

(3) before release, or later, to comply with such requirements as appear to be necessary to secure the purposes of the Act, or to make himself available for the purposes of enquiries or a report being made;

BA 1976, s 3(6ZAA)

(4) if he is a child or young person, then subject to certain conditions, he may be required to comply with certain requirements imposed for the purpose of securing the electronic monitoring of his compliance with any other requirement imposed on him as a condition of bail (see p 58 *below*).

Note that:

(a) the requirements under (1) and (2) above do not apply where bail is granted on the expiry of custody time limits (see CUSTODY TIME LIMITS);

(b) the former requirement under (2) above, that the accused was unlikely to remain in the United Kingdom to stand trial has been removed;

(c) where one of the conditions imposed is residence in a bail or probation hostel, he may also be required to comply with the rules of the hostel. BA 1976, s 3(6ZA)

Otherwise, subject to PCC(S)A 2000, s 11 in relation to remands for medical reports (see DEALING WITH AN OFFENDER), no security may be taken from an accused, no surety may be required, and no other condition imposed, except as provided by BA 1976.

3. SURETIES/SECURITY

Sureties: (1) suitability

Where bail is granted in criminal proceedings on condition that the accused provide one or more sureties for securing his surrender to custody, the court is entitled to have regard, among other things, to the surety's: BA 1976, s 8(1)(2)

(1) financial resources;

(2) character and previous convictions, if any; and

(3) proximity, whether in point of kinship, place of residence or otherwise, to the person to whom he or she is to be surety.

There will be cases where only a token enquiry into the surety's resources is necessary; in other cases the court should insist on having proof of resources, examining bank accounts, building society books and other documents. 'Jewellery' will seldom be worth the value put upon it, nor is there likely to be an opportunity to sell a house or other immoveable property.

When considering financial resources:

(a) it is those of the surety, not the accused, which must be considered (*R v Southampton JJ, ex p Green* [1975] 2 All ER 1073); and

(b) in deciding whether to accept the accused's wife as a surety, it is her own resources which must be considered, disregarding any joint property or the matrimonial home;

(c) it is important to establish that a proposed recognisance is realistic, and that the surety will be able to meet his or her financial obligations in the event of the recognisance being declared to be forfeited (*R v Birmingham CC, ex p Rashid Ali* [1998] Crim LR 504).

Before the surety formally accepts his obligations, the nature of the obligation ought to be explained to him, and he ought to be warned of the consequences which may ensue, including the risk of imprisonment, should the accused abscond (*R v Kent CC, ex p Jodka* (1997) 161 JP 638). It is sensible to warn a surety of the possibility of the terms of bail being varied, in order to avoid the sort of problems which arose in *R v Wells St MC, ex p Albanese* [1981] 3 All ER 769 (see p 60 *below*).

Sureties: (2) postponement of taking recognisances

BA 1976, s 8(3)(4)(5)(7)

Where the court is unable to release an accused because no surety, or no suitable surety, is available, the proper procedure is for the court:

(1) to fix the amount in which any surety is to be bound; and

(2) to allow the recognisances to be entered into subsequently, before such of the prescribed persons as it may order,

and the same consequences follow as if the recognisances had been entered into before the court. Provisions exist, where the court is satisfied of the suitability of the surety, for the recognisance to be taken in Scotland before a constable having charge of any police office or station, in the like manner.

If the person responsible for taking the recognisances declines to take them because he is not satisfied of the surety's suitability, the surety may apply, either to:

(a) the court which fixed the amount in which the surety was to be bound; or

(b) a magistrates' court acting for the petty sessions area in which the surety resides,

for that court to take the recognisance(s). If satisfied of the surety's suitability, that court *must* take the recognisance(s).

Similar provisions apply in relation to recognisances taken otherwise than in criminal proceedings (MCA 1980, s 119; MCR 1981, r 86).

Sureties: (3) parent or guardian

BA 1976, s 3(7)

Where the parent or guardian of a juvenile consents to be a surety for him, that person may be required to secure that the juvenile complies with any requirement imposed on him under BA 1976, s 3(6) or (6A) as a condition of bail, except that:

(1) no such requirement is to be imposed where it appears that the juvenile will attain the age of 17 before the time appointed for his surrender; and

(2) that person cannot be required to secure compliance with any requirement to which he does not consent; and

(3) that person is not to be bound in respect of the requirements to which he or she does consent, in a sum greater than £50.

Sureties: (4) Withdrawal

A surety is entitled to make an application in writing at a police station stating that the accused is unlikely to surrender; this empowers an officer to arrest the accused without warrant (*R v Wood Green CC, ex p Howe* [1992] 3 All ER 366), but a surety has no other right, to 'withdraw', even if he believes his principal is about to abscond, unless his principal is before the court (and see p 67 *below*); and an application is made under BA 1976, s 3(8) (*R v Ipswich CC, ex p Reddington* [1981] Crim LR 618). BA 1976, s 3(8)

Security: s 3(5)

A person granted bail may be required, before his release, to give security, which may be deposited by himself or on his behalf. The former requirement that the accused was unlikely to remain in the United Kingdom to stand trial has been removed. It is permissible for a third party to make available to the accused an asset in order to enable him to give security (*R (Stevens) v Truro MC* [2002] 1 WLR 144). As to forfeiture of security see p 67 *below*.

4. OTHER REQUIREMENTS OF BAIL

(1) Common requirements

There can be no closed list of requirements or conditions which may be attached to the grant of bail, but common requirements are those as to:

(1) residence;
(2) sleeping every night at a specified address;
(3) reporting periodically at a named police station between specified hours on specified days;
(4) observing a curfew between specified hours;
(5) surrendering a passport; also
(6) restrictions on entering or leaving specific places or areas.

Note also:

(1) a requirement may be added that, before the time appointed for surrender to custody, the accused attend an interview with an advocate or authorised litigator as defined by CLSA 1990, s 119(1); BA 1976, s 3(6)(e)
(2) in cases where bail is granted pending reports, a condition may be attached that the offender 'attend on a member of a local probation board' or on a medical officer, as the case may be;
(3) a requirement 'not to drive' may be imposed, but before imposing it the court should consider whether it may have unjust results (*R v Kwame* (1975) 60 Cr App R 65); as to interim RT disqualifications, see DISQUALIFICATION AND ENDORSEMENT;

(4) where the court orders the surrender of a passport, it must notify the United Kingdom Passport Service of:
  (a) the details of the order to surrender it;
  (b) the date, where appropriate, the order was lifted;
  (c) the date of the final disposal of the proceedings, or of the committal, sending or transfer of the proceedings to the Crown Court.

If the Passport Service is not provided with these details it will be unable to initiate a 'stop file' preventing the person in respect of whom it is made from obtaining a duplicate or replacement.

(2) Electronic monitoring: children and young persons

BA 1973, s 3AA

Where arrangements are available, a child or young person who:

(1) has attained the age of 12 years; and;
(2) is charged with or has been convicted of:
  (a) a violent or sexual offence (see pp 22, 23);
  (b) an offence punishable in the case of an adult with imprisonment for 14 years or more; or
  (c) one or more imprisonable offences, which, together with any other imprisonable offences of which he has been convicted in any proceedings, amount, or would amount, if he were convicted of the offences with which he is charged, to a recent history of repeatedly committing imprisonable offences while remanded on bail or to local authority accommodation,

may be required to comply with the requirements imposed for the purpose of securing the electronic monitoring of his compliance with any other requirement imposed upon him as a condition of bail, provided that:

(i) the court has been notified that such arrangements are available, and the necessary provision can be made; and
(ii) a youth offending team has informed the court that in its opinion the imposition of such a requirement is suitable in the case of the accused.

The requirement must include a provision making a person responsible for the monitoring.

(3) 'Door stepping' condition

A 'door stepping' condition, that is a requirement that a person on bail to which a curfew requirement has been attached present himself to a constable who attends at his address during the specified hours of the curfew, is permissible provided that it appears to be necessary for the purpose of securing one or more of the purposes of the Act, namely that the accused:

(1) surrenders to custody;

(2) does not commit any offence; and

(3) does not interfere with the course of justice.

(*R v Chorley JJ* (2002) *The Times*, 22 October).

5. VARIATION/RECONSIDERATION OF BAIL

Variation

Where a magistrates' court has: BA 1976, s 3(8)(8A)(8B)

(1) granted bail in criminal proceedings; or

(2) released an accused on bail on transferring the case against him to the Crown Court for trial; or

(3) committed an offender to the Crown Court for sentence or to be dealt with;

(4) received notice of transfer under CJA 1987, s 4; or

(5) sent a person to the Crown Court for trial under CDA 1998, s 51,

then, subject to PCC(S)A 2000, s 11(3) as to bail on remand for medical examinations, either the magistrates' court *or* the Crown Court is empowered, on an application by the accused, or the prosecutor or a constable:

(a) to vary the conditions of bail; or

(b) to impose conditions where bail was originally unconditional.

Where the accused has been committed for trial, sent or transferred for trial or to be sentenced or otherwise dealt with, the magistrates' court and the Crown Court have a concurrent jurisdiction to vary conditions of bail during the period between committal to the Crown Court and surrender to the custody of the Crown Court.

Once an accused has surrendered to the Crown Court, however, and the Crown Court releases him on bail again, only the Crown Court can vary conditions of bail thereafter (*R v Lincoln MC, ex p Mawer* [1995] Crim LR 878).

Reconsideration

The prosecutor may apply to the court to reconsider its decision, in which case the court may decide to vary the conditions, impose conditions in respect of bail granted unconditionally, or withhold bail, but: BA 1976, s 5B

(1) only in respect of an indictable or either way offence; and

(2) only where the application is based on information not available to the court when the decision was taken; and

(3) if bail is withheld the accused must be remanded in custody or ordered to surrender as the case may be.

MCR 1981, r 93B The procedure is as for variation, for which see *above.*

A person ordered to surrender may be arrested on a warrant if he fails to do so without reasonable cause, and taken before a magistrate.

There is no general requirement that the court notify any surety of a variation in the terms of an accused's bail, though he ought to have been told when he was accepted that the court had power to vary. A variation may become relevant in deciding to what extent a surety is liable to forfeiture of his recognisance (*R v Wells St MC, ex p Albanese* [1981) 3 All ER 769).

Non-criminal matters

MCA 1980, s 118 Where, in proceedings other than criminal proceedings, the court has committed a person to custody in default of finding sureties, it may, on application by or on behalf of that person and after hearing fresh evidence, reduce the amount in which any proposed surety is to be bound, dispense with any of the sureties, and otherwise deal with the case as they think just.

Variation of police bail

MCA 1980, s 43B Where the custody officer at a police station:

(1) grants bail to a person under PACE 1984, Pt IV in criminal proceedings and imposes conditions; or

(2) varies conditions of bail under BA 1976, s 3(8),

the court may, on application by or on behalf of that person, grant bail or vary the conditions, even if it means imposing more onerous conditions, and the bail granted by the custody officer then lapses.

MCA 1980, s 43(1) Subject to a duty to surrender to a magistrates' court, the court may appoint a later time as the time at which the person is to appear, and may enlarge the recognisances of any surety to that time.

JCR 1999, Schedule The Clerk may appoint a time at which a person under a duty to appear at the magistrates' court, is to appear, and, provided there is no objection by the prosecutor, enlarge the recognisances of any sureties under MCA 1980, s 4(1); he may also appoint an earlier time for the appearance of such a person at the magistrates' court.

Application needs to be made in writing:

MCR 1981, r 84A

(a) to the clerk of the magistrates' court (if any) appointed by the custody officer or the court before which the applicant has a duty to appear; or

(b) if no such court is appointed, to a court acting for the petty sessions area in which the police station at which he was granted bail, or at which the conditions were varied, is situated.

The notice needs to specify the grounds on which it is made, the offence with which the applicant is charged, the reasons given by the custody officer for imposing or varying any conditions, and the name and address of any surety.

The Clerk will notify the other parties of the date, time and place of the hearing, which must not be more than 72 hours after the receipt of the notice, excluding Saturday and Sunday and the customary public holidays.

6. BREACH AND ABSCONDING

Breach of bail: (1) arrest

A person who has been released on bail in criminal proceedings, and who is therefore under a duty to surrender, may be arrested without warrant by a constable, if the latter has reasonable grounds for believing that he: BA 1976, s 7(2)

(1) is not likely to surrender; or

(2) is likely to breach any of the conditions of his bail; or

(3) has broken any such condition,

or, where that person was released on bail with one or more sureties, if a surety notifies a constable in writing that the principal is unlikely to surrender, and for that reason he wishes to be relieved of his obligations.

The court may also issue a warrant under MCA 1980, s 7(1).

Breach of bail: (2) disposal

BA 1976, s 7(4) provides a 'simple, expeditious and informal procedure' for dealing with a person arrested under the above provisions (even where bail was granted by the Crown Court):

(1) he must be brought, as soon as possible, and in any event within 24 hours after his arrest, before a magistrate for the petty sessions area in which he is arrested; except where BA 1976, s 7(4)

(2) he is arrested within 24 hours of the time appointed for his surrender, in which case he must be brought before that court; and

(3) the magistrate must give the arrested person an opportunity to respond to the constable's allegations, though there is no strict need for giving evidence on oath, nor need an opportunity be given for cross-examining the constable;

(4) the magistrate, if he finds any of the grounds put forward proved, may either:
   - (a) remand the accused in, or commit him to, custody, as the case may require; or
   - (b) grant him bail again on the same or different conditions;

(5) if the magistrate is not of the opinion that any of the appropriate grounds are made out, he must grant the arrested person bail again, subject to the same conditions;

(6) the magistrate has no power to adjourn the proceedings (but see *R (Hussein) v Derby MC* [2002] 1 WLR 347), or in the case of bail granted by the Crown Court, to send him to that court to be dealt with for the breach.

(*R v Liverpool City MC, ex p DPP* [1993] 3 All ER 249, *R v Havering MC, ex p DPP, R v Wirral Borough MC, ex p McKeown* (2000) *The Times*, 7 February.)

BA 1976, s 7(6) If that person is a juvenile and is not granted bail, CYPA 1969, s 23 relating to remand into the care of a local authority applies (see ADJOURNMENT AND REMAND).

These provisions must be strictly complied with (*R v Governor of Glen Parva YO Institution, ex p G* [1998] 3 WLR 13).

Nothing precludes the arrested person from making a fresh application for bail.

Absconding: (1) warrant

BA 1976, s 7(1)(2) Where a person under a duty to surrender to custody at court fails to do so at the time appointed, the court may issue a warrant, with or without bail, for his arrest.

A warrant may also be issued for the arrest of a person who absents himself from court at any time after he has surrendered and before the court is ready to begin or resume the hearing, unless he is absent in accordance with leave given to him by or on behalf of the court.

Absconding: (2) the offence

BA 1976, s 6(1)(7) It is an offence (see p 64 *below*) for a person who has been released on bail in criminal proceedings:

(1) to fail, without reasonable cause, to surrender to custody; or

(2) having had reasonable cause, and failing to surrender, to fail to surrender at the appointed place as soon after the appointed time as is reasonably practicable.

The offence is also punishable by the Crown Court, as if for a criminal contempt of court, but only where the offender is committed to that court for sentence. Otherwise the offence is triable only by the court in respect of which a failure to surrender has occurred (*Schiavo v Anderson* [1986] 3 All ER 10, *Practice Note* (*Bail: Failure to Surrender*) [1987] 1 All ER 128).

A person 'surrenders' to the custody of the court when he complies with the procedure of the court at which he is due to appear, directing him to report to a particular office or a particular official. It is not sufficient for him simply to attend at the courthouse; he must overtly submit himself to the direction of the court (*R v CCC, ex p Gurney* [1995] 2 All ER 577). Thereafter, though not physically restrained, he is in the custody of the court and should be instructed not to leave the building without consent *(DPP v Richards* [1988] 3 All ER 406).

Absconding: (3) the procedure

Practice Direction (*criminal; consolidated*) [2002] 3 All ER 904, para 56 makes it clear that, on arrest, the accused should be brought before the court at which the proceedings in respect of which bail was granted are to be heard.

In the case of bail granted by a magistrates' court:

(1) it is neither necessary nor desirable to lay an information in order to commence proceedings for absconding;
(2) the court should initiate the proceedings of its own motion, following an express invitation by the prosecutor;
(3) which will be made only if, in all the circumstances, the prosecutor considers that proceedings are appropriate (*France v Dewsbury MC* [1988] Crim LR 295); and
(4) the prosecutor will conduct the proceedings and, if the matter is contested, will call evidence.

In the case of bail granted from a police station there is not the same compelling justification for the court to act of its own motion; such a case must be initiated by charge or by laying an information (*Murphy v DPP* [1990] 2 All ER 390). Where an information is laid, the time limits of MCA 1980, s 127 (see pp 295, 296) will apply (*ibid*).

A trial for absconding should normally take place after and immediately following the disposal of the case in respect of which bail was granted (*Practice Direction* (*Bail: failure to surrender*) (*above*); *R v Boyle* [1993] Crim LR 40). The fact that the accused is acquitted of the substantive charge, however, does not preclude the court, in a proper case, from imposing an immediate custodial sentence for the absconding (*R v Kohli* (1984) 5 Cr App R(S) 177; *R v Clarke* [2000] 1 Cr App R(S) 224).

Absconding: (4) evidence

A document which purports to be a copy of, or part of the prescribed record relating to the time and place appointed for the accused to surrender is evidence of that time and place, provided it is duly certified to be a true copy. BA 1976, s 6(8)(9)

It is for the accused to prove that he had reasonable cause for his failure to surrender to custody. Failure to give him a copy of the record does not constitute such reasonable cause, nor does mistake on the part of the accused as to BA 1976, s 6(3)(4) the date, caused by confusion or forgetfulness (*Laidlaw v Atkinson* (1986) *The Times*, 2 August).

Note that:

(1) the 'prescribed record' is the record of the decision of the court, officer or constable, made in pursuance of BA 1976, s 5(1);

(2) the copy of such record is duly certified by the clerk of the court, the constable who took the decision, or a constable designated for the purpose at the police station from which the accused was released.

Absconding: (5) penalty

BA 1976, s 6(6)(7)

A person convicted of an offence of absconding from bail may be:

(1) sentenced to a term of imprisonment not exceeding three months or to a fine not exceeding level 5 on the standard scale, or both; or

(2) committed, in custody or on bail, to the Crown Court for sentence, where the magistrates' court thinks:
   (a) that the circumstances of the offence are such that greater punishment should be imposed than that court has power to inflict; or
   (b) where it commits the accused to the Crown Court for trial for another offence, that it would be appropriate for him to be dealt with for his failure to surrender by the court which tries him for that offence.

Where the magistrates' court commits to the Crown Court, it will need to commit the bail offence expressly under BA 1976, s 6(6) to overcome the rule that only the court before which the accused should have appeared can deal with the offence of absconding. A person committed to the Crown Court may be sentenced to a term of imprisonment not exceeding 12 months.

A magistrates' court dealing with an offence ought to make some specific, appropriate order, and not just leave the matter in limbo. If it imposes a custodial sentence, that sentence ought to be distinct from, and if necessary, consecutive to, any custodial sentence for the substantive offence. If the court tells the offender that it proposes to overlook the bail offence, it cannot be revived later (*France v Dewsbury MC* [1988] Crim LR 295).

7. FORFEITURE OF RECOGNISANCES/SECURITY

Forfeiture: (1) general

MCA 1980, s 120

Where a recognisance, whether conditioned for the appearance of a person before a magistrates' court, or taken under a bind over (see BINDING OVER), appears to be forfeit, the court has the power to order that:

(1) the whole of the amount be forfeited; or
(2) part of the amount be forfeited; or
(3) the whole or part of the amount be remitted.

Payment of any sum adjudged to be paid as a result may be enforced as a fine (see FINES AND ENFORCEMENT), and as if the adjudication were the summary conviction of an offence not punishable with imprisonment.

The recognisance of a surety for a person granted bail subject to a duty to return to a police station may be enforced as if it were conditional for his appearance before a magistrates' court for the petty sessions area in which the police station named in the recognisance is situate. MCA 1980, s 120(2)

There is no right of appeal to the Crown Court against forfeiture of a surety's recognisance, but, where appropriate, the order may be challenged by an application for judicial review (*R v Durham JJ, ex p Laurent* [1944] 2 All ER 530).

Forfeiture: (2) procedure

The failure of an accused person to surrender to bail when required triggers the power of the court to order forfeiture of a surety's recognisance. But before deciding what should be done in such a case the court must enquire into the question of fault (*R v Reading Crown Court, ex p Bello* (1991) 92 Cr App R 303).

It must consider, amongst other things, the surety's conduct and whether it is open to criticism, though it is clear from *R v Maidstone Crown Court, ex p Lever* [1995] 2 All ER 35, that the surety's degree of culpability is not the guiding principle; *the basis of forfeiture is non-attendance.*

The principles were re-stated in the above case and in the cases of *R v Uxbridge JJ, ex p Heward-Mills* [1983] 1 All ER 530, and *R v Leicestershire Stipendiary Magistrate, ex p Kaur* (1999) 164 JP 127, as follows:

(1) where an accused for whom a person has stood surety fails to surrender, the full recognisance should be forfeited, unless it appears fair and just that a lesser sum, be forfeited, or the whole remitted;
(2) the burden of satisfying the court that the full sum should not be forfeited is on the surety and is a heavy one; it is for the surety to lay before the court the evidence of lack of culpability, and/or want of means on which he relies;
(3) where a surety is unrepresented, the court should assist him by explaining the principles in ordinary language and giving him an opportunity to call evidence and/or advance any argument.

Forfeiture: (3) result of enquiry

As a result of any such enquiry, the court may consider that:

(1) the surety connived at, or aided and abetted, the disappearance of the principal, and ought to forfeit the whole amount of the recognisance; or

(2) the surety was lacking in diligence, and a portion of the recognisance ought to be forfeited, the amount depending on the degree of fault; or

(3) a lack of culpability on the surety's part, or even a commendable diligence, is not of itself a reason for reducing or setting aside the obligation into which he has freely entered,

but the court has a broad discretion as to whether and to what extent it will be fair to remit some or all of the recognisance (*R v Maidstone CC, ex p Lever* (*above*)).

The matter of forfeiture should not be considered until the day appointed for the appearance of the accused (*R v ILCC, ex p Springall* (1987) 85 Cr App R 214).

The fact that a surety was unaware of a material and subsequent variation of bail may be relevant to the question whether the court ought to forfeit the whole or only part of a recognisance (*R v Wells St MC, ex p Albanese* [1981] 3 All ER 769 (bail subsequently varied allowing passport to be returned and security to be refunded); *R v Inner London CC, ex p Springall* (*above*) (reporting conditions omitted from prescribed record)).

In the case of the principal's spouse, any sum forfeited should come out of the spouse's own separate property. In a case where it may be necessary to sell the matrimonial home, the court ought to take into account the impact on others of such a sale (*R v Leicestershire Stipendiary Magistrate, ex p Kaur* (2000) 164 JP 127).

Forfeiture: (4) surety's means

The means of a proposed surety are essentially a matter for investigation by the court at the time he is considered for suitability, on the basis that he is entering into a serious obligation and ought to pay the amount of his recognizance if the accused fails to appear on the date(s) specified.

In recent years, however, the superior courts have laid down that on considering the question of forfeiture, the magistrates must enquire, as part of their duty to ensure that an order is fair and just, into:

(1) the ability of the surety to pay any amount ordered to be forfeited; and

(2) the consequences for him in ordering payment of an amount which will inevitably lead to a period of imprisonment in default.

(*R v Leicestershire Stipendiary Magistrate, ex p Kaur* (*above*). There may be cases where culpability is so great that payment should be ordered of an amount which makes a prison sentence likely (*R v Wood Green CC, ex p Howe* [1991] Crim LR 694).

Forfeiture: (5): surety purporting to 'withdraw'

In many cases a surety comes before the court purporting to 'withdraw' from his recognisance. He has no right to do so unless the accused is before the court and an application is made under BA 1976, s 3(8) (*R v Ipswich CC, ex p Reddington* [1981] Crim LR 618).

Where a surety becomes aware of the likelihood of an accused absconding or otherwise acting in breach of bail, the proper course is for him to make a statement in writing at a police station, and a constable is then empowered to arrest the accused under s 7(3) (*R v Wood Green CC, ex p Howe* (*above*); *R v Ipswich CC, ex p Reddington* (*above*)).

Forfeiture: (6) security under s 3(5)

Where a person gave security under BA 1976, s 3(5) and the court is satisfied that he failed to surrender to custody, then unless it appears that he has reasonable cause for such failure the security may be forfeited. In doing so the court may declare forfeiture to extend to such amount less than the full security as it thinks fit. Unless revoked, the order takes effect at the end of 21 days beginning with the day on which it is made. BA 1976, s 5(7)(8)(9)

Where the security:

(1) consists of money, it is accounted for and paid in the same manner as a fine imposed by the court; BA 1976, s 3(8A)

(2) does not consist of money, it is enforced in the manner specified by the order.

If, on an application made by or on behalf of the person who gave security, the court which forfeited it is satisfied that he did, after all, have reasonable cause for his failure to attend, it may either revoke the forfeiture altogether, or order that it extend to such lesser amount than the full value, as it thinks fit. BA 1976, s 3(8B)

If an order is made remitting the whole, or part, of the value of the security before the forfeiture has taken effect, any money which would fall to be repaid must be paid over to the person concerned. BA 1976, s 3(9A)

An application to revoke may be made before or after forfeiture takes effect, but must not be entertained unless the court is satisfied that the prosecution were given reasonable notice of the applicant's intention to make it. BA 1976, s 3(8C)

8. CHALLENGING A DECISION

(1) By the accused

The magistrates' decision on bail may be challenged by either party. The accused may make an application to the Crown Court or to the High Court under RSC 1965, r 75.

The Crown Court may grant bail to a person who:

(1) has been committed in custody for appearance before it;

(2) is in custody pursuant to a sentence imposed by a magistrates' court and who has appealed to it against conviction and/or sentence;

(3) is in custody pending disposal of his case by the magistrates' court; and

(4) if, and only if, the magistrates' court has certified that it heard 'full argument' (see pp 53, 54 *above*) before refusing bail, and he has been remanded in custody by the magistrates under the following provisions:
- MCA 1980, s 5 (adjournment of committal proceedings);
- MCA 1980, s 10 (adjournment of summary trial);
- MCA 1980, s 18 (adjournment of proceedings re mode of trial); or
- PCC(S)A 2000, s 11 (remand for medical examination).

(2) By the prosecutor

BAA 1993, s 1

In addition to the accused's right to ask the magistrate(s) to reconsider a bail decision, (see pp 59, 60 *above*) a 'prescribed prosecutor' may appeal to the Crown Court, against the granting of bail where:

(1) the offence is punishable by a term of five years or more, or is one under TA 1968, s 12 or 12A;

(2) the prosecutor is the DPP or other person prescribed by the Secretary of State; and

(3) the prosecution objected to bail.

In such a case the prosecutor needs to give oral notice at the conclusion of the proceedings in which bail was granted and before the accused is released, and must serve written notice within two hours. If notice is not so given, the appeal will be treated as having been disposed of; if notice is given, the accused must be remanded in custody until the appeal is determined (see *R v Isleworth CC, ex p Clarke* [1998] 1 Cr App R 257). But see *R. (Jeffrey) v Warwick CC & HM Customs & Excise* [2003] *Archbold News* for the position where the prosecutor is prevented from giving notice in time by circumstances beyond his control.

JCR 1999, Schedule

The Clerk may where the prosecutor appeals, give a direction under MCR 1981, r 93A(7) or (8).

Application by accused to High Court: RSC 1965, O 79 r 9

Where a magistrates' court withholds bail in criminal proceedings or imposes conditions in granting bail in such proceedings, the High Court may, subject to CJPOA 1994 (see pp 49, 50 *above*) grant bail or vary the conditions (which the Crown Court cannot do). CJA 1967, s 22(1)

Procedure is under RSC 1965, O 79 r 9 (not by way of judicial review: *R v Croydon CC, ex p Cox* [1997] Crim LR 52), whereby:

(1) an application must be served by way of claim form served on the prosecutor at least 24 hours before the return date, calling on the respondents to show cause why bail should not be granted, or as the case may, the conditions of bail should not be varied;

(2) the application must be supported by witness statement or affidavit;

(3) defence public funding is not available; but

(4) where the accused is in custody and unable to instruct solicitors he may make a written request to the judge of the High Court for the Official Solicitor to be assigned to act for him, and if the judge accedes to this request, service of the claim form and witness statement may be waived.

The application will be heard by a single judge sitting in chambers. If the application is refused, the applicant is not entitled to go to another judge of the High Court, but nothing prevents him from applying to the Crown Court (*R v Reading CC, ex p Malik* [1981] 1 All ER 249).

Where bail is granted subject to sureties, the sureties may enter into recognisances before the magistrates' court or other appropriate person (see p 56 *above*).

BINDING OVER

A magistrates' court has jurisdiction either in the course of criminal proceedings, or on complaint under MCA 1980, s 115 (*R v Morpeth JJ, ex p Ward* [1992] Crim LR 497) to require any person who, or whose case, is before the court to enter into recognisances, with or without sureties:

(1) in a specific sum;

(2) to keep the peace;

(3) for a specified period, usually, but not necessarily 12 months;

(4) or be committed to prison.

It is no longer appropriate to bind a person over to be of good behaviour (*Hashman & Harrap v UK* [2000] Crim LR 185; *Steel v UK* [1998] Crim LR 893).

The subject of the order must consent to its making, though that consent is not vitiated by the fact that a custodial sentence is the realistic alternative (*R v Williams* [1982] 1 WLR 1398). He cannot be compelled to consent, nor may the court treat him as bound when he declines to be.

In the case of:

(a) a person aged 18 or over who declines to be bound, may be committed to prison for up to six months, or until he sooner complies with the order (*Veater v Glennon* [1981] 2 All ER 304);

(b) a person under 18 there is no practicable remedy (*Veater v Glennon* (*above*); *Howley v Oxford* [1985] Crim LR 724, *Surrey Chief Constable v Ridley* [1985] Crim LR 725) unless he complies (*Conlan v Oxford* (1984) 148 JP 97), but see the power to bind over parents and guardians (*below*).

Typical situations – JPA 1968, s 1(7)

Essentially, the power is a valuable instrument to prevent breaches or potential breaches of the peace, and to deal with complaints about conduct which does not strictly constitute an offence but is likely to lead to the commission of one, by the subject of the complaint or by others.

There must be material before the court, though it need not consist of sworn evidence, justifying the conclusion that, unless such a step is taken, there is a risk of a breach of the peace (and see *Nicol & Selvanayagam v DPP* [1996] Crim LR 318).

'Person before the court'

The general power under JPA 1968, s 1(7) is exercisable not only in respect of accused persons, but of any person before the court. The exercise of the power is not dependent upon conviction, and even an acquitted accused may be bound over in appropriate circumstances (*R v ILCC, ex p Benjamin* (1987) 85 Cr App R 267).

'Persons before the court':

(1) includes witnesses who give evidence, whether for the prosecution or for the defence (*Sheldon v Bromfield* [1964] 2 All ER 131);

(2) does *not* include persons who are neither parties nor are called to give evidence (*R v Swindon CC, ex p Singh* [1984) 1 All ER 941, *R v Kingston CC, ex p Guarino* [1986] Crim LR 325, *R v Lincoln CC, ex p Jones* (1989) *The Times*, 16 June).

The standard of proof is the criminal standard (*Percy v DPP* [1995] Crim LR 714).

Procedure

Where the court is minded to bind over a person under the Act, the authorities show that:

(1) a witness or complainant who is to be bound over should be given the opportunity of being heard; this is not strictly necessary in the case of an accused in a criminal case;

(2) a person causing a disturbance in court need not receive a warning, nor need he be given an opportunity to make representations;

(3) an acquitted accused ought, as a matter of courtesy, to be warned of the court's intentions, and it is of particular importance in such a case that the court is *sure* that the accused is a potential threat to others and is a man of violence, not merely that the court believes that he *may* pose a threat (*R v Middlesex CC, ex p Khan* (1996) 161 JP 240, *R v Lincoln CC, Ex p Jude* [1997] 3 All ER 737).

Parents and guardians

PCC(S)A 2000, s 150(1)(2)

In the case of persons under 18, where such a person is convicted of an offence, the court:

(1) *may*; and

(2) *must* where the offender is under 16 when convicted,

if satisfied, having regard to the circumstances of the case, that it would be desirable in the interest of preventing the commission by him of further offences:

(a) with the consent of his parent or guardian,

(b) order the parent or guardian to take proper care of him and exercise proper control over him,

and if the latter refuses his consent, and the court considers that refusal unreasonable, it may order him to pay a fine not exceeding £1,000 and where a community sentence has been made in respect of the offender the court may include in the recognisance a requirement that the parent or guardian ensure that the offender complies with the requirements of that sentence.

If the court does not exercise its duty under (2) above, it must state in open court that it is not satisfied as mentioned in that paragraph, and why.

In fixing the amount of the recognisance, the court must take into account the means of the parent or guardian as they are known to it, and an order may not require him to enter into a recognisance for an amount exceeding £1,000 or for a period exceeding three years or, where the offender will attain 18 in a shorter period, that shorter period.

Appeal

A parent or guardian may appeal to the Crown Court against the making of an order. The court may vary or revoke an order if it appears, on an application by that person, to be in the interest of justice to do so.

Means

Unless the amount of the recognisance is trifling, the court must enquire into the means of the person to be bound over, and must give him or his advocate an opportunity to make representations on the matter (*R v CCC, ex p Boulding* [1984] 1 All ER 766; *R v Atkinson* [1989] Crim LR 457; *R v Nottingham CC, ex p Brace* (1990) 154 JPN 63; *R v S Molton JJ, ex p Ankerson* (1990) 90 Cr App R 158; *R v ILCC, ex p J* [1993] Crim LR 41; *R v Lincoln CC, ex p Jude* (*above*)).

Postponement of taking recognisances

Instead of taking the recognisances there and then, the court may: MCA 1980, 119(1); MCR 1981, r 86

(1) fix the sum on which the principal and any surety is to be bound; and

(2) permit the recognisances to be taken later by one of those persons prescribed in the Rules; and

the same consequences follow as if the recognisance had been entered into before the court.

Varying or dispensing with surety requirement

Where the court commits a person to prison in default of finding a surety it may, on an application by or on behalf of that person, *and* after hearing fresh evidence: MCA 1980, s 118

(1) reduce the amount in which it is proposed that any surety should be bound; or

(2) dispense with any surety,

or otherwise deal with the matter as it thinks fit.

Estreatment

Breach of recognisances is enforced by estreatment (see BAIL), and the court, before taking steps to estreat a recognisance must make such enquiries as are required before estreating the recognisances of sureties for bail, as to which see BAIL (*R v Marlowe JJ, ex p O'Sullivan* [1983] 3 All ER 578).

Appeal

ABOOA 1956, s 1 An appeal lies to the Crown Court against the making of a binding over order.

Such an appeal is by way of a rehearing, and unless the appellant is prepared to admit the evidence which was called before the magistrates' court, the facts justifying the order must be proved again by sworn evidence which may be the subject of cross-examination (*Shaw v Hamilton* [1982] 2 All ER 718].

While it is the invariable practice for the prosecutor in proceedings before a magistrates' court to take upon himself the duty of responding to an appeal, this is a class of case where the system frequently breaks down, particularly in a bind over made otherwise than on complaint. The magistrates' court needs to bear in mind that:

(1) though the magistrates have an absolute right to appear on the appeal, to instruct counsel and call evidence in support of the decision they arrived at;

(2) a better course is for them to maintain contact with the Crown Prosecutor in the matter;

(3) if they do appear, they appear as *amicus curiae* and should not enter into any dispute;

(4) they cannot be cross-examined, and do not make themselves parties to the appeal, and

(5) no costs may be awarded against them.

COMMITTAL PROCEEDINGS

Committal proceedings precede a committal to the Crown Court for trial:

(1) of an accused aged 18 or over, or a corporation, charged with an offence triable either way which the magistrates' court considers more suitable for trial on indictment, or

(2) the accused or corporation has either indicated a plea of not guilty or has not indicated a plea and elects trial on indictment in the Crown Court.

They have no application to an indictable only offence to which the procedure CDA 1998, s 51 applies (see SENDING FOR TRIAL s 51).

Though legislation has reduced the proceedings to little more than a formality, the avowed purpose of such proceedings is for the examining magistrates (the functions may be performed by a single magistrate) to ensure that no person is put upon his trial at the Crown Court unless a *prima facie* case has been made out against him (*R v Epping & Harlow JJ, ex p Massaro* (1973) 137 JP 373).

Where:

(a) the accused is represented, and his representative consents, committal will be without consideration of the evidence;

(b) where his representative so requires or the accused is unrepresented, committal must be on a consideration of the documentary evidence and exhibits submitted by the prosecutor and any submissions made.

The prosecutor's function is to adduce sufficient evidence to satisfy the court that there is a *prima facie* case (*R v Epping & Harlow JJ,* (*above*). He is entitled to choose what witness statements he proposes to rely on (*Wilkinson v DPP* [1998] Crim LR 743) and failure to call a particular witness does not invalidate the committal (*R v Grays JJ, ex p Tetley* (1979) 70 Cr App R 11). No evidence is given for the defence.

The order of procedure will depend upon whether the court is required to consider the evidence or not.

General

Where a person:

(1) aged 18 or over appears or is brought before the court on an information charging him with an offence triable either way, and

(2) the accused (under MCA 1980, s 17A) or his representative (under *ibid*, s 17B) has indicated that he will plead not guilty, or has not indicated a plea, and

(3) the court considers the offence more suitable for trial on indictment, or the accused does not consent to have it tried summarily,

MCA 1980, s 4

such offence(s) must be the subject of committal proceedings, which may take place, if necessary, before a single magistrate.

Note that:

(a) the date on which the age of an accused is to be determined is the date of his appearance before the court on which the decision as to mode of trial is made (*R v Islington North JC, ex p Daley* [1982] 2 All ER 321);

(b) joint committal proceedings may be held in respect of two or more accused in respect of different charges which may be joined in the same indictment, notwithstanding objections by the accused to such a course (*R v Camberwell Green Stipendiary Magistrate, ex p Christie* [1978] 2 All ER 794).

Powers of DPP etc

The DPP and the 'designated authority' under CJA 1987 have powers in relation to committal proceedings as follows:

POA 1985, s 23

(1) the DPP, if he has conduct of the proceedings, may, in the case of an either-way offence, at any time before the accused is committed for trial, give notice to the clerk of the court that he does not want the proceedings to continue, and they will be discontinued (though this does not prevent the bringing of fresh proceedings);

CJA 1987, s 4(1)(2)

(2) the 'designated authority' under CJA 1987, 'serious fraud cases' may give notice of transfer, before the court has begun to enquire into the case as examining justices, and the functions of the magistrates' court cease save in relation to bail, the grant of legal representation and witness orders.

1. COMMITTAL ON CONSIDERATION OF THE EVIDENCE

MCA 1980, s 6(1)

Where the pre-conditions stated above for committal without consideration of the evidence are *not* fulfilled the court must examine the evidence and hear any submissions that there is insufficient evidence before deciding whether to:

(1) commit the accused for trial if of opinion that there is sufficient evidence to put him on trial for an either way offence; or

(2) discharge him if there is insufficient evidence.

In such circumstances, once the court has ascertained that the accused is not legally represented, or that his legal representative has requested the court to consider a submission that there is insufficient evidence to put the accused upon his trial: MCR 1980, r 7

(a) the prosecutor may make an opening address if he wishes to do so, before any evidence is tendered;

(b) the evidence will then be tendered by being read aloud, unless the court otherwise directs or allows parts of it to be summarised;

(c) the court may view any exhibits produced and take possession of them; and

(d) the court will then hear any submissions on behalf of the accused, allowing the prosecutor to reply, and to make any submission where the court is not minded to commit, before deciding whether or not there is sufficient evidence to put the accused upon his trial.

Section 6(1) proceedings apply equally to accused persons under 18 as they do to those over that age. MCA 1980, s 5B(4),5C(4), 5D(4),5E(3)

Abuse of process

The court may discharge the accused without hearing evidence if there has been such a delay in bringing the proceedings as to render them vexatious and an abuse of the process of the court, but not normally without some proof of bad faith on the part of the prosecution, or real prejudice to the accused (*R v Grays JJ, ex p Graham* [1982] 3 All ER 683, *R v Bow St Stipendiary Magistrate, ex p DPP* [1990] Crim LR 318, and see generally ABUSE OF PROCESS).

Where an application is made, the court should hear evidence from both prosecution and defence (*R v Clerkenwell Stipendiary Magistrate, ex p Bell* [1991] Crim LR 468; *R v Crawley JJ, ex p DPP* (1991) 155 JP 841) as to the reasons for the delay and the likelihood of prejudice to the accused before embarking on the committal proceedings. The fact that the court has adjudicated on an abuse of process application does not signify that it has commenced committal proceedings for the purposes of MCA 1980, s 6(1) (*R v Worcester MC, ex p Bell* [1994] Crim LR 133).

Evidence in committal proceedings

When the court is enquiring into an offence as examining justices the *only* evidence which is admissible in the committal proceedings is that: MCA 1980, s 5A, 5B

(1) which is tendered by or on behalf of the prosecution; and

(2) which is:

 (a) a written statement complying with s 5B (with any documents or exhibits referred to in it);

 (b) a deposition complying with s 5C (with any documents or exhibits referred to in it);

(c) a statement which complies with s 5C, ie with the following conditions:
   (i) that the prosecutor notifies the court and each of the other parties to the proceedings that the statement might, by virtue of CJA 1988, s 23 or s 24 (first-hand hearsay and business, etc documents), be admissible as evidence if the case came to trial;
   (ii) that the statement would not be admissible as evidence otherwise than by virtue of those provisions if the case came to trial;
   (iii) that the prosecutor's belief is based on information available to him at the time he makes the notification;
   (iv) that he has reasonable grounds for his belief;
   (v) that he gives reasons for his belief when he makes the notification; and
   (vi) when the court or party is notified a copy of the statement is given to the court or party concerned;

(d) a document falling within s 5E which by virtue of any enactment:
   (i) is evidence in committal proceedings;
   (ii) is admissible, or may be used, or is to be admitted or received, in or as evidence in committal proceedings;
   (iii) may be considered in committal proceedings;
   (iv) constitutes proof in committal proceedings by its production;
   (v) is evidence by its production in committal proceedings.

MCA 1980, s 5B(6),5E(4)

A 'document' means anything in which information of any description is recorded. Where any evidence in (a)–(d) *above* is admissible, it may be proved by the production of:

(a) the statement, deposition or document; or

(b) a copy of it or the material part of it, whether or not the original is still in existence.

MCA 1980, s 5F(4)

'Copy' means anything onto which information recorded in the original has been copied, by whatever means and whether directly or indirectly.

It is immaterial how many removes there are between a copy and the original.

Written statements

MCA 1980, s 5B(2)(3)

For a written statement by a person to be admissible in committal proceedings it must:

(1) purport to be signed by the person who made it;

(2) contain a declaration by the maker to the effect that it is true to the best of his knowledge and belief and that he made the statement

knowing that if it is tendered in evidence he would be liable to prosecution if he wilfully stated in it anything which he knew to be false or did not believe to be true;

(3) if it is made by a person under 18, it gives his age;

(4) if it is made by a person who cannot read it, it is read to him before he signs it and is accompanied by a declaration by the person who so read it to the effect that it was read; and

(5) before it is tendered in evidence a copy of it is given, by or on behalf of the prosecutor, to each of the other parties to the proceedings; and

(6) if it refers to any document as an exhibit, a copy of the exhibit accompanies the copy statement or information is given to the other parties to enable them to inspect the exhibit or a copy of it.

Editing statements; composite statements

Where the prosecution proposes to tender written statements in evidence either under ss 5A and 5B or under CJA 1967, s 9 it will frequently be not only proper, but also necessary for the orderly presentation of the evidence, for certain statements to be edited. This will occur either because a witness has made more than one statement whose contents should conveniently be reduced into a single, comprehensive statement or where a statement contains inadmissible, prejudicial or irrelevant material. Editing of statements should in all circumstances be done by a Crown Prosecutor (or by a legal representative, if any, of the prosecutor if the case is not being conducted by the Crown Prosecution Service) and not by a police officer.

A composite statement giving the combined effect of two or more earlier statements or settled by a person referred above must be prepared in compliance with the requirements of ss 5A and 5B of the 1980 Act or CJA 1967, s 9 as appropriate and must then be signed by the witness (*Practice Direction* (*criminal: consolidated*) [2002] 3 All ER 904, paras 23, 24).

Procedure for editing

There are two acceptable methods of editing single statements:

(1) By marking *copies* of the statement in a way which indicates the passages on which the prosecution will not rely. In this case:
   (a) this merely indicates that the prosecution will not seek to adduce the evidence so marked, the *original signed statement* to be tendered to the court is not marked in any way. The marking on the copy statement is done by lightly striking out the passages to be edited so that what appears beneath can still be read, or by bracketing, or by a combination of both;
   (b) it is not permissible to produce a photocopy with the deleted material obliterated, since this would be contrary to the

Committal Proceedings

requirement that the defence and the court should be served with copies of the signed original statement;

(c) whenever the striking out/bracketing method is used, it will assist if the following words appear at the foot of the frontispiece or index to any bundle of copy statements to be tendered: 'The prosecution does not propose to adduce evidence of those passages of the attached copy statements which have been struck out and/or bracketed (nor will it seek to do so at the trial unless a notice of further evidence is served).'

(2) By obtaining a fresh statement, signed by the witness, which omits the offending material, applying the procedure of a composite statement.

(*Practice Direction* (*criminal: consolidated*) [2002] 3 All ER 904, para 24).

In most cases where a single statement is to be edited, the striking out/bracketing method will be the more appropriate, but the taking of a fresh statement is preferable in the following circumstances:

(a) when a police (or other investigating) officer's statement contains details of interviews with more suspects than are eventually charged, a fresh statement should be prepared and signed omitting all details of interview with those not charged except, in so far as it is relevant, for the bald fact that a certain named person was interviewed at a particular time, date and place;

(b) when a suspect is interviewed about more offences than are eventually made the subject of committal charges, a fresh statement should be prepared and signed omitting all questions and answers about the uncharged offences unless either they might appropriately be taken into consideration or evidence about those offences is admissible on the charges preferred, such as evidence of system. It may, however, be desirable to replace the omitted questions and answers with a phrase such as: 'After referring to some other matters, I then said . . .', so as to make it clear that part of the interview has been omitted;

(c) a fresh statement should normally be prepared and signed if the only part of the original on which the prosecution is relying is only a small proportion of the whole, although it remains desirable to use the alternative method if there is reason to believe that the defence might itself wish to rely, in mitigation or for any other purpose, on at least some of those parts which the prosecution does not propose to adduce; and

(d) when the passages contain material which the prosecution is entitled to withhold from disclosure to the defence.

Prosecutors should also be aware that, where statements are to be tendered under CJA 1967, s 9 in the course of *summary* proceedings, there will be a need to prepare fresh statements excluding inadmissible or prejudicial material rather than using the striking out or bracketing method.

None of the above principles applies, in respect of committal proceedings, to:

(i) documents which are exhibited (including statements under caution and signed contemporaneous notes); or

(ii) to oral statements of a defendant which are recorded in the witness statements of interviewing police officers, except in the circumstances referred to in para 24.4(b).

All this material should remain in its original state in the committal bundles, any editing being left to prosecuting counsel at the Crown Court (after discussion with defence counsel and, if appropriate, the trial judge).

Whenever a fresh statement is taken from a witness, a copy of the earlier, unedited statement(s) of that witness will be given to the defence in accordance with the Attorney-General's guidelines on the disclosure of unused material (*Practice Note* (*criminal evidence: unused material*) [1982] 1 All ER 734) unless there are grounds under para 6 of the guidelines for withholding such disclosure (*Practice Direction* (*criminal: consolidated*) [2002] 3 All ER 904, paras 24.3–24.7).

Depositions

For a deposition to be admissible:

(1) a copy of it must be given, by or on behalf of the prosecution to each of the other parties to the proceedings *before* the court begins to enquire into the offence concerned as examining justices; and MCA 1980, s 5C

(2) if it refers to any document as an exhibit, a copy of that exhibit accompanies that copy deposition or information is given to the other parties to enable them to inspect the exhibit or a copy of it.

Any document or other object referred to as an exhibit and identified in a deposition which is admitted in evidence is to be treated as if it had been produced as an exhibit and identified in court by the person who made the deposition.

In addition, if a deposition is taken in the circumstances outlined *below* a copy of it must be sent to the prosecutor. MCA 1980, s 97A

Person not voluntarily making statement or producing exhibit

Where any person in England or Wales for the purposes of committal proceedings before a magistrates' court: MCA 1980, s 97A

(1) is likely to be able to make *on behalf of the prosecutor* a written statement containing material evidence or produce a document or other exhibit likely to be material evidence; and

(2) will not voluntarily do so,

a magistrate acting for the commission area in which the magistrates' court is situated *must* issue a summons directed to that person requiring him to attend before that magistrate at a time and place specified in the summons to have his evidence taken as a deposition or to produce the document or other exhibit.

If the magistrate is satisfied by evidence on oath of the matters at (1) and (2) above and that it is probable that a summons would not produce the required result, he may, instead of issuing a summons, issue a warrant to arrest the person and bring him before a magistrate at a time and place specified in the warrant.

Only a summons may be issued if the magistrate is satisfied that the person is outside the British Isles.

A summons or warrant may not be issued after the court has begun to enquire into the offence as examining magistrates.

Failure to answer summons

MCA 1980, s 97A(5)

If a person fails to answer a summons under the above provision, then, provided:

(1) the magistrate is satisfied by evidence on oath that he is likely to be able to make the statement or produce the document or other exhibit; and

(2) it is proved on oath or other prescribed manner that the summons was served and a reasonable sum was paid or tendered to him for costs and expenses; and

(3) it appears to the magistrate that there is no just excuse for the failure,

he may issue a warrant to arrest him and bring him before a magistrate at a time and place specified in the warrant.

MCA 1980, s 97A(6)

Where a summons or warrant issued with a view to securing, that a person has his evidence taken as a deposition, the time specified to enable the evidence to be taken as a deposition must be a time before the court begins to enquire into the offence as examining justices.

MCA 1980, s 97A(7)

Where a person attending or is brought before a magistrate in pursuance of the above provision refuses without just excuse to have his evidence taken as a deposition or to produce a document or other exhibit, the magistrate may do one or both of the following:

(a) commit him to custody for up to one month, the period being specified in the warrant of commitment, or until he sooner has his evidence taken as a deposition or produces the document or exhibit;

(b) impose a fine not exceeding £2,500.

Duty of Clerk

MCA 1980, s 97A(9)–(11)

The Clerk is required, as soon as is reasonably practicable, to send a copy of the deposition and a copy of any document produced as an exhibit to the prosecutor. If a non-documentary exhibit is produced the Clerk must notify the prosecutor of that fact.

Evidence of children in committal proceedings

When the court is enquiring into any of the following offences as examining justices: MCA 1980, s 103

- an offence which involves an assault, or injury or a threat of injury to, a person;
- an offence under CYPA 1933, s 1 (cruelty to persons under 16);
- an offence under the SOA 1956, the IWCA 1960, SOA 1967, CLA 1977, s 54 or POCA 1978; or
- an offence which consists of attempting or conspiring to commit, or of aiding, abetting, counselling, procuring or inciting the commission of, any of the above offences,

a statement made in writing by or from a child is admissible in evidence of any matter.

Objecting to evidence

While objections may be taken to the tendering of inadmissible evidence at the committal proceedings stage, and MCR 1981, r 70 provides for the marking of portions of statements as 'treated as inadmissible', it will be only in the most crass instances that it will be proper to rule on it. Where the decision involves a discretion in the court, the matter should be left to be decided by the judge at the trial (*R v Highbury Corner MC, ex p Boyce* [1984] Crim LR 294), who will, in any event have the last word on the matter. There is no power to refer it to another bench to decide the issue of admissibility (*R v Ormskirk JJ, ex p Davies* [1994] Crim LR 850).

Open court: adjournment

Committal proceedings will ordinarily be held in open court, unless some enactment contains an express provision to the contrary, or the court considers that, as respects the whole or part of the proceedings, the ends of justice would not be served by sitting in open court. The proceedings must be held in the presence of the accused, though if he is represented by a legal practitioner he is deemed not to be absent (MCA 1980, s 122). See also *R v Liverpool City MC, ex p Quantrell* [1999] Crim LR 734. Evidence may be given in the absence of the accused where either, by reason of his conduct it is not practicable for it to be given in his presence, or he cannot be present for health reasons. MCA 1980, s 4(2)

There is a general power to adjourn (see ADJOURNMENT AND REMAND) before beginning to enquire into an offence or at any time during the enquiry; if the hearing is adjourned, the accused *must* be remanded. MCA 1980, s 5(1)

Reporting restrictions

MCA 1980, s 8(1)(2)(4)(8)

Committal proceedings may not be reported, save for certain specified formal details (see *below*), either in the press or by broadcasting, unless:

(1) the 'reporting restrictions' are lifted at the request of one of the accused; or

(2) the court decides not to commit the accused, or any of them, for trial; or

(3) at the Crown Court, the trial is concluded.

MCR 1981, r 5(1)

The accused must be told of the position and of his right to apply for the restrictions to be lifted, *before* any written statement or deposition is admitted and if any accused makes such an application:

(a) the court must lift the restrictions, except that

(b) in the case of two or more accused, if one objects to the restrictions being lifted, the court should only lift them if, after hearing representations, it is satisfied that it is in the interests of justice to do so. Where a case is made out for doing so, the court should lift the restrictions (*R v Leeds JJ, ex p Sykes* [1983] 1 All ER 460).

In the case of a number of accused, each must have the opportunity to make representations, and a balance of competing interests must be struck (*R v Wirral District MC, ex p Meikle* [1990] Crim LR 801).

If the restrictions are lifted the order must be entered in the court register, and must be repeated at the start of any adjournment.

An application may be made as soon as the accused is before the court, and need not await the admission of statements or depositions (*R v Bow Street Magistrates, ex p Kray* [1968] 3 All ER 872). An order applies to the whole proceedings; there is no room for limiting reporting to a particular accused (*R v Russell, ex p Beaverbrook Newspapers* [1969] 1 QB 342). Once lifted, the restrictions cannot be re-imposed and apply to any accused who are joined in the proceedings at a later stage (*R v Blackpool JJ, ex p Beaverbrook Newspapers* [1972] 1 All ER 388).

Where a transfer of remand order is made under MCA 1980, s 130 (see ADJOURNMENT AND REMAND), committal proceedings continue to be 'committal proceedings' when before the alternate court (*R v Newcastle upon Tyne JJ, ex p Vicker* (1981) *The Times*, 18 April).

Permitted formal details

Where the reporting restrictions are not lifted, the media are permitted to report or broadcast only:

(1) the identity of the court and the names of the examining justices;

(2) the names, addresses and occupations of the parties and witnesses, and the ages of the accused and the witnesses;

(3) the offence(s) or a summary of them, with which the accused is charged;

(4) the names of the legal representatives;

(5) any decision of the court to commit the accused for trial or any decision or disposal where the accused is not committed for trial;

(6) the charge(s) on which the accused has been committed for trial, and the location of the Crown Court to which he has been committed;

(7) if the proceedings are adjourned, the date(s) and places to which they have been adjourned;

(8) details of bail or custody; and

(9) the grant of any legal representation.

Presence of accused

In general, the written evidence must be submitted at committal proceedings in the presence of the accused, but:

(1) the court may allow the evidence to be submitted in the absence of the accused where:

 (a) the court considers that by reason of his disorderly conduct before it, it is not practicable for the evidence to be given in his presence; or

MCA 1980, s 4(3),(4)

 (b) the accused cannot be present for health reasons, but is represented by counsel or a solicitor and has consented to the evidence being given in his absence; and

(2) the court may enquire into an offence and commit an accused for trial in accordance with MCA 1980, s 6, where it is satisfied that:

MHA 1983, s 52(7)

 (a) on the written or oral evidence of the responsible medical officer that the accused is unfit to take part in the proceedings; and

 (b) the accused is represented by counsel or a solicitor.

Decision to commit

The court must commit if it is of opinion that there is sufficient evidence to put the accused on trial for any indictable offence, whether the offence for which the prosecution seeks committal or some other indictable offence, and if it is not of that opinion it must discharge the accused.

MCA 1980, s 6(1)

Note that:

(1) the defence is entitled to submit that there is no case to answer, and the prosecutor is entitled to reply;

(2) where there are several charges, the court may commit on one or more but not on others; but

MCR 1981, s 7(6)(12)

(3) if the court commits for an indictable offence not charged by the prosecutor, the charge must be written down and the defence must have the opportunity of addressing the court on it (*R v Gloucester MC, ex p Chung* (1988) 153 JP 75).

2. COMMITTAL WITHOUT CONSIDERATION OF THE EVIDENCE

MCA 1980, s 6(2)

The court may commit an accused for trial without considering the evidence provided that:

(1) all the prosecution evidence is in admissible form, ie falls within the requirements of s 5A(3);

(2) the accused, or each of them, has a legal representative acting for him in the case; and

(3) none of the legal representatives acting for the accused has requested the court to consider a submission that there is insufficient evidence to put the accused on trial at the Crown Court for the offence.

Section 6(2) proceedings apply equally to accused persons under 18 as they do to those over that age.

MCR 1981, r 6

In such circumstances:

(a) the accused is identified, and the court establishes that he is represented;

(b) the prosecutor informs the magistrate(s) that all his evidence falls within s 5A(3) and that a copy has been given to the accused;

(c) the charge is written down if this has not already been done, and is read to the accused; and

(d) the magistrate(s) ascertain whether the accused is making any submission on the sufficiency of the evidence.

If satisfied that the accused does not wish to make any such submission, after receiving any written evidence under (b) *above*, the court determines whether or not to commit for trial.

Where the court decides to commit, the procedure is as for a case where the evidence is considered (*above*). Where they decide not to commit they must discharge the accused.

JCR 1999, Schedule

The Clerk may commit an accused on bail for trial in accordance with MCA 1980, s 6(2) and (3)(b) where, having been remanded on bail on the previous adjournment, he is released on bail on the like terms and conditions.

3. PROVISIONS COMMON TO BOTH

Committal in absence

Where the required conditions are fulfilled (see p 85 *above*) the accused may be committed in his absence, whether committal is under s 6(1) or s 6(2), (*R v Liverpool City MC, ex p Quantrell* [1999] Crim LR 734).

Committal for summary offences – s 41

A court committing an accused to the Crown Court for trial on indictment for an offence triable either way, or a number of such offences, is also empowered to commit him for any summary offence with which he is charged, provided that: CJA 1988, s 41 (l)(3)

(1) it is punishable with imprisonment, or involves obligatory or discretionary disqualification from driving; and
(2) arises out of circumstances that appear to be the same as, or connected with, those giving rise to the offence(s) triable either way,

whether or not evidence relating to the summary offence(s) appears in the written statements or depositions. The trial of the information charging the summary offence will then be treated as if it had been adjourned under MCA 1980, s 10, *sine die.*

The court's decision to exercise this power is not subject to appeal or liable to be questioned in any court.

Notice under s 41

Where the court exercises this power, it will give to the Crown Court and to the accused a notice stating which of the offences triable either way appears to the court to arise out of circumstances which are the same as or connected with those giving rise to the summary offence(s). CJA 1988, s 41(2)

Procedure at the Crown Court

If the accused is convicted on the indictment at the Crown Court: CJA 1988, s 41(5)(6)(7)(8)(9)

(1) that court will consider whether the pre-conditions for committal of the summary offence(s) are made out; and
(2) if the court considers that they *are* satisfied, it will state to the accused the substance of the summary offence(s) and ask him if he pleads guilty or not guilty;
(3) if the accused pleads guilty to the summary offence(s) he may be dealt with for them in any manner in which the magistrates' court could have dealt with him;
(4) if he does not plead guilty, the powers of the Crown Court in respect of the summary offence(s) cease; and

(5) if the prosecution inform the Crown Court that they would not desire to submit evidence on the charge relating to the summary offence, the Crown Court will dismiss it.

CJA 1988, s 41(10) In any event, the Crown Court will inform the Clerk of the magistrates' court of the outcome of the proceedings.

Committals for trial: (1) general

MCA 1980, s 7(2) On committing the accused for trial the magistrate(s) must:

(1) specify the place of trial having regard to:
   (a) the convenience of the defence, the prosecution and the witnesses, and
   (b) the expediting of the trial, and
   (c) any directions of the Lord Chief Justice (see *below*);

MCR 1981, r 8 (2) remind the accused of his right to object by written notification to the prosecutor and the Crown Court within 14 days of being committed (unless the court permits the objection to be made outside that period) to any statement or deposition being read in evidence at the trial without oral evidence being given by the person who made it, and without the opportunity to cross-examine that person; and

Practice Direction [1995] 4 All ER 379 (3) specify the date on which the accused must appear at the Crown Court for an initial plea and directions hearing.

Committals for trial: (2) bail

An accused may be committed in custody or on bail to the Crown Court.

MCA 1980, s 6(3) Where his release on bail is conditional on his providing one or more sureties, and the court fixes the amount in which the surety is to be bound with a view to his entering into a recognisance subsequently, the court must, in the meantime, commit him in custody (as to juveniles, see ADJOURNMENT AND REMAND).

MCA 1980, s 6(4) Where the accused is committed in custody and if he is in custody for no other cause, the magistrates' court may at any time before his first appearance at the Crown Court, grant him bail subject to a duty to appear at the Crown Court on a specified date.

Where an application for bail is made to the Crown Court, CCR 1982, rr 19, 20 apply to the application, but before the Crown Court can deal with an application:

(1) it must be satisfied that the magistrates' court has issued a certificate under BA 1976, s 5(6A) that it heard full argument on the application for bail before it refused the application;

(2) a copy of the certificate should be issued to the applicant and not sent directly to the Crown Court;

(3) it will therefore be necessary for the applicant's solicitors to attach a copy of the certificate to the bail application form.

If the certificate is not enclosed with the application form it will be difficult to avoid some delay in listing (*Practice Direction* (*criminal: consolidated*) [2002] 3 All ER 904, paras 53.1, 53.2).

Applications should be made to the court to which the accused will be or would have been committed for trial. In the event of an application in a purely summary case, it should be made to the Crown Court centre which normally receives class 4 work (see p 90 *below*). The hearing will be listed as a chambers matter unless a judge has directed otherwise (*Practice Direction* (*criminal: consolidated*) [2002] 3 All ER 904, para 53.3).

Representation

The court, or the Clerk (JCR 1999, Schedule) may, where an accused is to be tried on indictment, grant a representation order for the purpose of the proceedings in the Crown Court. The order includes representation by counsel.

Venue: (1) classification of offences

For the purposes of trial in the Crown Court offences are classified as follows:

(1) Class 1:
  (a) misprision of treason and treason felony;
  (b) murder;
  (c) genocide;
  (d) torture, hostage-taking and offences under the War Crimes Act 1991;
  (e) an offence under the Official Secrets Actd (OSAs);
  (f) soliciting, incitement, attempt, or conspiracy to commit any of the above offences.

(2) Class 2:
  (a) manslaughter;
  (b) infanticide;
  (c) child destruction;
  (d) abortion (OAPA 1861, s 58);
  (e) rape;
  (f) sexual intercourse with a girl under 13;
  (g) incest with girl under 13;
  (h) sedition;
  (i) an offence under s 1 of the Geneva Conventions Act 1957;
  (j) mutiny;
  (k) piracy;
  (l) soliciting, incitement, attempt or conspiracy to commit any of the above offences.

(3) Class 3:
  (a) all offences triable only on indictment other than those in classes 1, 2 and 4;
  (b) soliciting, incitement, attempt or conspiracy to commit any of the above offences.

(4) Class 4:
  (a) wounding or causing grievous bodily harm with intent (OAPA 1861, s 18);
  (b) robbery or assault with intent to rob (TA 1968, s 8);
  (c) soliciting, incitement or attempt to commit any of the above offences;
  (d) conspiracy at common law, or conspiracy to commit any offence other than those included in classes 1, 2 and 3;
  (e) all offences which are triable either way.

(*Practice Direction* (*criminal: consolidated*) [2002] 3 All ER 904, para 21.1).

Venue: (2) location of Crown Court

Save as expressly provided for certain offences in class 2 and offences in class 3, on committing a person for trial under MCA 1980, s 6 (transferring a person under either CJA 1987, s 4, or CJA 1991, s 53, or sending a person under CDA 1998, s 51):

(1) a magistrates' court must, if the offence, or any of the offences, is included in classes 1 or 2, specify the most convenient location of the Crown Court where a High Court judge sits, or where the case is included in class 1, where a circuit judge duly appointed for the purpose by the Lord Chief Justice regularly sits. These courts will be identified by the presiding judges on each circuit. Where an offence is in class 4 the magistrates' court must specify the most convenient location of the Crown Court;

(2) the proviso is that where a presiding judge has directed that cases of rape, sexual intercourse with a girl under 13, incest with a girl under 13 or soliciting, incitement, attempt or conspiracy to commit any of these offences (all of which are within class 2) or class 3 offences, may be committed (transferred or sent) from a specified magistrates' court or courts to a specified location of the Crown Court at which a High Court judge does not regularly sit, the magistrates' court shall specify that location;

(3) in selecting the most convenient location of the Crown Court, the magistrates' court must have regard to the considerations referred to in MCA 1980, s 7 (and CDA 1998, s 51(1)) and to the location or locations of the Crown Court designated by a presiding judge as the location to which cases should normally be committed, from their petty sessions area;

(4) where on one occasion a person is committed in respect of a number of offences, all the committals must be to the same location of the Crown Court and that location must be the one where a High Court judge regularly sits if such a location is appropriate for any of the offences.

(*Practice Direction* (*criminal: consolidated*) [2002] 3 All ER 904, para 21.)

Notification of committal

Where an accused is committed for trial, or discharged, a notice will be displayed in public, giving his name, address and age, if known, the charge(s) on which he is committed, or the offence(s) charged and the determination to discharge him. MCA 1980, s 6(5)(6)

This information is subject, of course, to any restrictions as to identity imposed by SO(A)A 1976, s 4 (anonymity of *complainant* in rape cases), or restrictions on giving the name or address of juveniles.

Challenging the committal

The prosecutor's remedy where the magistrates refuse to commit is to apply to the Crown Court for leave to prefer a voluntary bill.

An accused may challenge the decision of the magistrates' court by applying for judicial review (see APPEALS) of eg a committal based on no, or on inadmissible evidence.

COMMITTAL FOR SENTENCE

Offenders aged 18 or over may be committed to the Crown Court for sentence, or to be dealt with as follows:

(1) on summary conviction of an offence triable either way;

(2) on indication of a plea guilty to an offence triable either way;

(3) on committal in respect of another offence;

(4) on conviction during the licence period of a previous sentence of imprisonment.

A committal for sentence may not be the subject of an appeal to the Crown Court, but may be challenged by judicial review (see APPEALS).

1. AFTER CONVICTION OF EITHER-WAY OFFENCE – S 3

Where, on the summary trial of an offence triable either way (other than an offence of criminal damage listed in MCA 1980, Sched 1, for which see Mode of Trial), a person aged 18 or over is convicted of that offence, and the court is of opinion: PCC(S)A 2000, s 3

(1) that the offence, or the combination of the offence and one or more offences associated with it (see pp 170, 171) was so serious that greater punishment should be inflicted for the offence than the court has power to impose, or

(2) in the case of a violent or sexual offence (see p 171), that a custodial sentence for a term longer than it has power to impose is necessary to protect the public from serious harm from him,

it may commit the offender in custody or on bail to the Crown Court for sentence, and also commit him in respect of certain other offences (under s 6, below).

A convicted corporation is treated as an individual aged 18 or over, but the custody and bail provisions do not apply. PCC(S)A 2000, s 3(5)

In *R v NE Essex JJ, ex p Lloyd* [2001] Crim LR 145, it was held under the previous legislation (MCA 1980, s 38) that the power under (1) *above* is not restricted to cases where the magistrates consider their powers of imposing a custodial sentence are inadequate. They may commit, for instance, if they consider a fine appropriate but the proper amount to be beyond their powers; note that (2) above refers only to a 'custodial term'.

Where the court determines a fact relevant to sentence (see DEALING WITH AN OFFENDER – 'Newton Hearing') it ought to communicate that approach to the Crown Court (*Munroe v DPP* [1988] Crim LR 823).

Time for forming opinion

That opinion may be formed after the court has assumed jurisdiction (see *R v Sheffield CC, ex p DPP* [1994] Crim LR 470; *R v Dover MC, ex p Pamment* [1994] Crim LR 470; *R v N Sefton MC, ex p Marsh* [1994] Crim LR 865; *R v Southampton MC, ex p Sansome* [1998] Crim LR 595) and unlike the position under the previous legislation, it need not be based on information emerging after that decision is made, although it has a duty to go into the issue in mode of trial proceedings, and on an indicated plea of not guilty, or where no plea is indicated, before assuming jurisdiction (*R v Warley MC, ex p DPP* [1998] Crim LR 684). Compare this with the other view that once jurisdiction has been accepted, the offender is entitled to assume that he will be dealt with in the magistrates' court (see *R v Doncaster JJ, ex p Goulding* [1992] 13 Cr App R(S) 428; *R v Manchester MC, ex p Kaymanesh* [1994] Crim LR 401; *R v Feltham JJ, ex p Rees* [2001] Crim LR 47).

Where the offender has been led to believe that he will be sentenced by the magistrates, it is quite wrong that he should subsequently be committed under s 3 (*R v Nottinghamshire MC, ex p Davidson* [2000] Crim LR 118; *R v Norwich MC, ex p Elliott* [2001] 1 Cr App R(S) 152; *R v Wirral MC, ex p Jermyn* [2001] Crim LR 45).

2. ON INDICATION OF PLEA OF GUILTY – S 4

PCC(S)A 2000, s 4(1)–(4)

Where a person aged 18 or over is brought before a magistrates' court on an information charging him with an offence triable either way and:

(1) he or his representative indicates that he would plead guilty if the offence were to proceed to trial; and

(2) proceeding as if MCA 1980, s 9(1) were complied with and he pleaded guilty under it, the court convicts him of the offence, then:
   (a) if the court has committed him to the Crown Court for *trial* for one or more offences which, in its opinion are related to the offence, it may commit him in custody or on bail to the Crown Court, to be dealt with in respect of the offence in accordance with s 5(1); or
   (b) if that power is not then available, but the court still has to enquire as examining magistrates into one or more offences, it must adjourn the proceedings relating to the offence until after the conclusion of its enquiries, and if it then commits him for trial for one or or more related offences, may exercise its power under (a),

provided that if it commits under s 4 it must also state that in its opinion it also has power under ss 3, 5(1) below, or the powers of the Crown Court on ss 4 and 5 will not apply.

The court normally observes any bail conditions as they were when the accused appeared before it, and if the accused was on bail at that stage, bail is continued unless there are good reasons for refusing it; if he was in custody at that stage, the accused should be remanded in custody (see *R v Rafferty* [1998] Crim LR 433).

If, at the Crown Court, it is shown that the committal was based on a wrong understanding of the facts, and the accused is permitted to change his plea, the matter may be remitted to the magistrates' court to reconsider (*R v Isleworth CC, ex p Buda* [2000] Crim LR 111).

3. CONDITIONAL SENTENCES – S 6

Where a magistrates' court commits an offender to the Crown Court under: PCC(S)A 2000, s 6

(1) The Vagrancy Act 1824;

(2) PCC(S)A 2000, ss 3 and 4 above;

(3) PCC(S)A 2000, s 13(5) (conditionally discharged offender convicted of further offence);

(4) PCC(S)A 2000, s 116(3)(b) (prisoner on licence); or

(5) PCC(S)A 2000, s 120(2) (offender convicted of further offence during the operational period of a suspended sentence),

to be sentenced or otherwise dealt with in respect of an offence and the relevant offence is:

(a) an *either-way offence*, it may also commit him in respect of any other offence in respect of which it has power to deal with him (being an offence of which he has been convicted by it or any other court); and

(b) a *summary offence*, it may commit him in respect of any other offence of which it has convicted him, being either one punishable with imprisonment, or one in respect of which it has a power or a duty to disqualify him under RTOA 1988, ss 34, 35, or 36, or any suspended sentence in respect of which it has power to deal with him under PCC(S)A 2000, s 120(1).

4. VENUE

Where the Crown Court has made a community rehabilitation order, an order for conditional discharge or a community punishment order, or a community punishment and rehabilitation order has been made, or a suspended sentence of imprisonment passed, and the offender is committed to be dealt with for the original offence or in respect of the suspended sentence, he must be committed in accordance with the following:

(1) If the order was made or the sentence was passed by the Crown Court, he must be committed to the location of the Crown Court where the order was made or the suspended sentence was passed, unless it is inconvenient or impracticable to do so.

(2) If he is not so committed and the order was made by a High Court judge he must be committed to the most convenient location of the Crown Court where a High Court judge regularly sits.

(3) In all other cases where a person is committed for sentence or to be dealt with he must be committed to the most convenient location of the Crown Court.

In selecting the most convenient location of the Crown Court, the magistrates' court must have regard to the location or locations of the Crown Court designated by a presiding judge as the locations to which cases should normally be committed from their petty sessions area.

(*Practice Direction* (*criminal: consolidated*) [2002] 3 All ER 904, paras 21.6–10).

5. POWERS OF CROWN COURT

PCC(S)A 2000, s 5 The powers of the Crown Court vary, according to whether the offender is committed under ss 3 and 4 or under s 6. On a committal under:

(1) ss 3 and 4, the Crown Court may deal with the offender in any way in which he could have been dealt if he had just been convicted there, but it may not remit him to the magistrates' court (*R v Isleworth CC, ex p Buda* [2000] Crim LR 111);

PCC(S)A 2000, s 7 (2) s 6, the Crown Court may deal with him in any way in which the magistrates' court could have dealt with him if it had just convicted him of the offence, save that:
   (a) if the offender is committed in respect of a suspended sentence, the powers in s 119 are exercisable; and
   (b) where the offender is committed in respect of an offence triable only on indictment in the case of an adult, but which was tried summarily because the offender was under 18 the judge's powers enable him to:
      (i) impose a fine not exceeding £5,000; or
      (ii) to deal with the offender in respect of the offence in any way in which the magistrates' court could have dealt with him if

it had just convicted him of an offence punishable with a term of imprisonment not exceeding six months.

Any duty or power which would, apart from these provisions fall to be discharged or exercised by the magistrates shall not be so exercised, but instead, will be discharged or exercised by the judge of the Crown Court. PCC(S)A 2000, s 7(3)

Where a person is committed to the Crown Court under PCC(S)A 2000, s 116, in respect of an offence committed during the currency of his original sentence ie a prisoner on licence, the Crown Court may order him to be returned to prison for the whole or any part of the period which: PCC(S)A 2000, s 116(4)

(1) begins with the date of the order; and
(2) is equal in length to the period between the date on which the new offence was committed and the date mentioned in s 40(1) (see PRISONER ON LICENCE).

Ancillary orders; interim RT disqualification

Since committal to the Crown Court is an alternative to the magistrates' court dealing with the offender, that court may not, on committal, make any ancillary orders, save that where it:

(1) commits an offender under s 6 or any enactment to which that section applies; and
(2) does not exercise its power or duty to disqualify for holding or obtaining a driving licence under RTOA 1988, ss 34, 35 or 36,

it may order him to be disqualified in the interim until the Crown Court has dealt with him in respect of the offence.

If the offender is not sentenced within six months of the date of committal, that interim disqualification lapses (see DISQUALIFICATION AND ENDORSEMENT). If the Crown Court, on dealing with the offender imposes a disqualification, it will be reduced by the length of the interim disqualification.

Case notes and reasons

Any case notes should be sent to the Crown Court when there is a committal for sentence, thereby making them available to the judge if the judge requires them in order to decide before the hearing questions of listing or representation or the like. They will also be available to the court during the hearing if it becomes necessary or desirable for the court to see what happened in the magistrates' court. Any reasons given by the magistrates for their decision should be included with the notes sent to the Crown Court (*Practice Direction* (*criminal: consolidated*) [2002] 3 All ER 904, para 52.1).

6. OTHER CASES

Apart from the general powers to commit for sentence, the Table below gives a list of those other circumstances in which magistrates have power to commit for sentence or to be dealt with.

1.	PCC(S)A, 2000, s 3	(a) offender not less than 18 convicted of either-way offence committed because offence(s) require greater punishment than magistrates have power to inflict; (b) offender convicted of violent or sexual offence requiring longer custodial term than magistrates have power to impose to protect public from serious harm. A corporation may be committed for sentence under these provisions and is treated as an individual of not less than 18. Bail/custody does not then apply (MCA 1980, s 38(4); CJA 1991, s 25(1)(2)).	Powers on indictment (PCC(S)A, 2000, s 5(1))
2.	PCC(S)A 2000, s 4	Accused not less than 18 charged with offence triable either-way indicating plea of 'guilty' if committed for trial and accordingly convicted by the magistrates and committed for sentence.	PCC(S)A, 2000, ss 4(5),5 Powers on indictment only if magistrates certify power to commit under s 3.
3.	PCC(S)A 2000, s 116 (3)	Prisoner on licence convicted in magistrates' court of new offence punishable with more than six months imprisonment and committed for greater punishment than the magistrates' maximum.	Return to prison (PCC(S)A 2000, s 116(4))
4.	PCC(S)A 2000, s 120 (3)	Offender convicted in the magistrates' court of offence committed during the operational period of a suspended sentence imposed by the Crown Court.	PCC(S)A 2000, s 119(1)
5.	PCC(S)A 2000, Sched 3, para 4(4)	Offender found by magistrates to be in breach of relevant community order made by the Crown Court.	PCC(S)A 2000, Sched 3, para 5(1)
6.	PCC(S)A 2000, Sched 3 para 13(3)	Offender in respect of whom a relevant community order made in the Crown Court is in force, committed by the magistrates with a view to revocation.	PCC(S)A 2000, Sched 3, para 14
7.	PCC(S)A 2000, Sched 3 para 11(1)(2)	Offender committed for sentence during the currency of a relevant community order.	PCC(S)A 2000, Sched 3, para 11(2)
8.	PCC(S)A 2000, s 6	Offender committed in respect of 1–5 above and also in respect of other offences joined.	PCC(S)A 2000, s 7
9.	MHA 1983, s 43(1)	Offender aged 14 or over committed with a view to a restriction order under MHA 1983, s 41, being made.	MHA 1983, s 43(2)

10.	PCC(S)A 2000, s 61 Sched 5, para 2(c)	Offender committed for failure to attend at, or in breach of the rules of an attendance centre.	PCC(S)A 2000, s 61, Sched 5, para 3
11.	PCC(S)A s 65, Sched 7, para 2(c)	Juvenile offender committed in respect of the breach of a supervision order.	PCC(S)A 2000, s 65, Sched 7, para 2(4)
12.	PCC(A) 2000, s 13(6)	Offender found by magistrates' court to be in breach of conditional discharge order made by Crown Court.	PCC(S)A 2000, s 13(6)
13.	PCA 2002, s 70	Offender convicted of offence and committed with a view to a confiscation order being considered.	PCA 2002, s 6

COMMUNITY SENTENCES

A sharp distinction is made between custodial sentences and Community sentences; they cannot be combined. A 'community sentence is one which includes one or more community orders. 'Community orders' are 10 in number: PCC(S)A 2000, s 33

(1) a curfew order (pp 105–106 *below*);

(2) a community rehabilitation order (formerly a probation order) (pp 108–115 *below*);

(3) a community punishment order (formerly a community service order) (p 115 *below*);

(4) a community punishment and rehabilitation order (formerly a combination order) (p 119 *below*);

(5) a drug treatment and testing order (pp 120–123 *below*);

(6) an attendance centre order (124–126 *below*);

(7) an exclusion order (pp 106–107 *below*);

(8) a drug abstinence order (p 123 *below*);

(9) a supervision order (pp 126–128 *below*);

(10) an action plan order (p 129 *below*).

Each of these orders is a separate order in its own right, though the objects of some may overlap with those of others.

Additional requirements

Additional requirements, intended to achieve a particular aim, may be inserted; Some of these are common to several orders. Thus additional requirements may be attached to secure:

(1) a curfew;

(2) residence;

(3) participation in activities;

(4) attendance at probation hostels;

(5) mental treatment;

(6) treatment for drug dependency;

(7) abstinence from Class A drugs; or

(8) exclusion from particular places or areas.

General restrictions on imposing community sentences

PCC(S)A 2000, s 35

A court must not pass a community sentence on an offender unless it is of the opinion that the offence, or the combination of the offence and one or more offences associated with it, was serious enough to warrant such a sentence and where it does pass such a sentence:

(1) the particular order or orders comprising or forming part of the sentence must be such, as in the court's opinion is, or taken together are, the most suitable for the offender, and

(2) the restrictions on liberty imposed by the order or orders must be such as in its opinion are commensurate with the seriousness of the offence or the combination of the offence and the one or more offences associated with it.

Improper combinations

PCC(S)A 2000, s 51

A community sentence must not consist of both a community punishment order and a community rehabilitation order, whether for a single offence or for two or more offences (*Golding v DPP* (1998) *The Times*, 20 May).

A community punishment and rehabilitation order may be made (see p 119 *below*) which combines features of both.

Special provisions apply under PCCC(S)A 2000, s 59 to curfew orders and community punishment orders for persistent petty offenders (see pp 105, 115, *below*).

Meaning of associated offence

PCC(S)A 2000, s 161(1)

An offence is associated with another offence:

(1) if the offender is convicted of it in the proceedings in which he is convicted of the other offence, or (although convicted of it in earlier proceedings) is sentenced for it at the same time as he is sentenced for that offence; or

(2) the offender admits the commission of it in the proceedings in which he is sentenced for the other offence, and requests the court to take it into consideration in sentencing him for that offence (see TICs).

Basis for court's opinion

The court, in forming its opinion as to:

PCC(S)A 2000, s 39(1)

(1) whether the offence is serious enough to warrant a cornmunity sentence, or as to whether the restriction on liberty is commensurate with the seriousness of the offence, must take into account all such information as is available to it about the circumstances of the offence, or as the case may be, the offence or offences associated with it, including any aggravating or mitigating factors; and

(2) whether the particular orders are the most suitable;

may take into account any information about the offender which is before it. PCC(S)A 2000, s 36(2)

Aggravating factors: (1) previous convictions

In considering the seriousness of any offence, the court: CJA 1991, s 29(1)

(1) may take into account any previous convictions of the offender, or any failure of his to respond to previous sentences; and

(2) must, in considering the seriousness of an offence committed while the offender was on bail, treat the fact that it was committed in such circumstances as an aggravating factor.

A probation order or conditional discharge made before 1 October 1992 (which by virtue of, PCCA 1973, ss.2, 13 and 17 would otherwise not have ranked as a conviction or sentence as the case may be) is treated as a conviction or sentence for these purposes. CJA 1991, s 29(3)(4)

Aggravating factors: (2) prevalence

The prevalence of offences of a particular class, and public concern about them, is relevant to the seriousness of an offence before the court (*R v Cunningham* [1993] Crim LR 149; *R v Cox* [1993] Crim LR 152).

Aggravating factors: (3) racially aggravated offences

Where the offence is racially aggravated (see RACIALLY ETC AGGRAVATED OFFENCES within the meaning of CDA 1998, s 28), the court must treat that as a factor increasing the seriousness of the offence and must state in open court that it was so racially aggravated.

Need for pre-sentence report

In relation to: PCC(S)A 2000, s 36(3)(4)(5)

(1) a community rehabilitation order which includes additional requirements authorised by PCC(S)A 2000, Sched 2;

(2) a community punishment order;

(3) a community punishment and rehabilitation order;

(4) a drug treatment and testing order;

(5) a supervision order which includes requirements authorised by Sched 6,

the court must obtain and consider a pre-sentence report before forming an opinion as to the offender's suitability for one or more of those orders, unless, in the circumstances of the case, it is of opinion that it is 'unnecessary' to do so.

Where:

(a) the offender is aged under 18; and PCC(S)A,2000, s 36(6)

Community Sentences

(b) the offence is not triable only on indictment; and

(c) there is no other offence associated with it that is triable only on indictment,

the court may not consider a report 'unnecessary' unless there is a previous report obtained in respect of him, and the court has had regard to the information in it, or, if there is more than one report, the most recent.

PCC(S)A 2000, s 36(7)(8)(9)

A community order is not invalidated by the court's failure to obtain and consider a report.

Specific sentence reports (SSRs)

The court has a discretion to sentence without a pre-sentence report where it considers such a report is unnecessary. Where the court considers an offence serious enough for a community sentence but the circumstances are such that a full pre-sentence report is not required but the Probation Service's advice is needed in respect of the community sentence the court has in mind, it may request a specific sentence report (SSR). An SSR is primarily directed towards community punishment and community rehabilitation orders. An SSR will most often be prepared on the day of the request after the offender has pleaded guilty or has been found guilty. The SSR reduces delay and makes better use of the Probation Service resources. If the SSR writer considers that an SSR does not adequately cover a risk assessment or that there are other matters that need further consideration (such as conditions that might be included in a community rehabilitation order) he will advise the court that a full pre-sentence report should be requested.

Pre-sentence drug testing

PCC(S)A 2000, s 36A

Where, in the case of an offender aged 18 or over convicted of an offence, the court is considering a community sentence, it may (provided it has been notified that it has that power), for the purpose of ascertaining whether the offender has any specified Class A drug in his body, (only heroin and crack/cocaine have so far been specified) make an order for him to provide specified samples. Failure, without reasonable excuse, to comply is punishable with a fine of an amount not exceeding level 4 on the standard scale (see FINES AND ENFORCEMENT).

Electronic monitoring

PCC(S)A 2000, s 36B

Where monitoring arrangements are available, and provision can be made under those arrangements, a community order may include a requirement securing the electronic monitoring of the offender's compliance with the order. However:

(1) where there is a person other than the offender without whose co-operation the order will not be practicable, the order must not be made without that person's consent; and

(2) a requirement shall not be included where one is already included; and

(3) the order must make an appropriate person responsible for monitoring the requirement.

COMMUNITY ORDERS AVAILABLE FOR OFFENDERS OF ANY AGE

1. Curfew orders

Where notified that such arrangements are available, both the adult court and the youth court may, subject to the general restrictions on the making of community orders (see pp 102, 103 *above*), make a curfew order, that is to say an order requiring the offender to remain for specified periods, at a specified place, in respect of an offender:

(1) of any age convicted before it of an offence; or PCC(S)A 2000, ss 37(1)(2), 59(3)

(2) aged 16 or over, who is a persistent petty offender (at present available in pilot areas only).

Restrictions on making an order under

In a case under (2) *above*, an order must not be made unless:

(1) the court is satisfied that: PCC(S)A) 2000, s 59(1)(2)

(a) one or more fines imposed on the offender in respect of one or more previous convictions have not been paid; and

(b) if a fine were imposed in an amount which was commensurate with the seriousness of the offence, the offender would not have sufficient means to pay it; and

(2) if it were not so satisfied it would be minded to impose a fine in respect of the offence.

Preconditions for curfew order

Before making such an order, the court must: PCC(S)A 2000, s 37(8)(9)(10)

(1) obtain and consider information about the place proposed to be specified in the order, including information as to the attitude of persons likely to be affected by the enforced presence of the offender there;

(2) in the case of an offender under 16 at the time of conviction, obtain and consider a report about his family circumstances and the likely effect of such an order on those circumstances; and

(3) explain to the offender in ordinary language:

(a) the effect of the order, including any additional requirements relating to electronic monitoring (see *above*):

(b) the consequences which may follow should he fail to comply with any of the requirements; and
(c) that the court has power to review the order on the application of either the offender or the person responsible for monitoring the offender's whereabouts during the specified curfew periods.

PCC(S)A 2000, s 37(11)

A copy of the order will be given to the offender and to the responsible officer.

Requirements of the order

PCC(S)A 2000, s 37(3)(4)

An order may specify different places or different periods for different days, but may not specify:

(1) periods which fall outside the period of six months beginning with the day on which it is made (three months in the case of an offender under 16 in respect of an offence committed after 1 January 1998); or
(2) periods of less than two hours or more than 12 hours in any one day.

PCC(S)A 2000, s 37(5)

As far as practicable the requirements of the curfew shall be such as to avoid:

(a) any conflict with the offender's religious beliefs or with the requirements of any other community orders to which he may be subject; and
(b) interference with the times, if any, at which he normally works or attends school or other educational establishment.

Amendment, revocation, and breach

PCC(S)A 2000, s 39

PCC(S)A 2000, Sched 3 has effect in relation to the amendment and revocation of orders, and also for dealing with failure to comply with its requirements (see pp 131–135 *below*).

2. EXCLUSION ORDERS
(at present available in pilot areas only)

PCC(S)A 2000, s 40A(1)(2)(3)(4)(5)(6)(12)

When notified that arrangements for monitoring the offender's whereabouts are available, the court may, subject to the general restrictions on the making of community orders (see CJCSA 2000, pp 102, 103 *above*), make, in respect of a person convicted of an offence, a s 46 exclusion order, that is to say an order prohibiting him from entering a specified place or area for a specified period, in the case of an offender:

(1) aged 16 or over, of up to two years; or
(2) under 16, of up to three months.

The order may:

(a) specify different places or areas for different periods or days; and

(b) provide for the prohibition to operate only during the periods specified in the order.

The order must include provision for making a person responsible for monitoring the offender's whereabouts during the periods when the prohibition operates.

Preconditions to making an order

Before making such an order, the court must:

(1) where the offender is under 16 on conviction, obtain and consider information about his family circumstances and the likely effect of such an order upon those circumstances; and PCC(S)A 2000, s 40A(9)(10)

(2) explain to the offender in ordinary language:
   (a) the effect of the order (including any additional requirements proposed to be included in it in accordance with PCC(S)A 2000, s 36B (electronic monitoring);
   (b) the consequences which may follow under Sched 3, Pt II if he fails to comply with any of the requirements of the order; and
   (c) that the court has power to review the order on the application of the offender, the responsible officer, or any affected person.

An 'affected person' is a person where a requirement of electric monitoring is included in the order by virtue of his consent, or a prohibition is included in the order for the purpose (or partly for the purpose) of protecting him from being approached by the offender.

As far as practicable, the requirements of an order should avoid any conflict with the offender's religious beliefs and with the requirements of any other community order to which he is subject, and any interference with the times, if any, at which he normally works or attends school or any other educational establishment. PCC(S)A 2000, s 40A(5)

A copy of the order will be given to the offender and to the responsible officer, and any information about the order which the court considers it appropriate for him to have will be given to any affected person. PCC(S)A 2000, s 40A(11)

Amendment, revocation, and breach

Schedule 3 (see pp 131–135 *below*) to the Act has effect in relation to the amendment and revocation of such orders, and is also for dealing with failure to comply with an order. PCC(S)A 2000, s 46

COMMUNITY ORDERS AVAILABLE ONLY WHERE THE OFFENDER IS AGED 16 OR OVER

1. Community Rehabilitation Orders

PCC(S)A 2000, s 41(1)(2)

Where a person aged 16 or over is convicted of an offence, and the court is of the opinion that his supervision is desirable in the interests of:

(1) securing his rehabilitation; and

(2) protecting the public from harm from him; or

(3) preventing the commission by him of further offences,

the adult court in the case of an offender aged 18 or over, and the youth court in the case of an offender aged 16 or 17, may, subject to the general restrictions on making community orders, make an order requiring him to be under supervision for a specified period of not less than six months nor more than three years.

PCC(S)A 2000, s 41(3)

The order will specify the petty sessions area in which the offender resides or will reside.

Offenders residing in Scotland or Northern Ireland

If the offender resides, or will be residing, in Scotland or Northern Ireland, at the time of the proposed making of the order, the order must not be made unless:

PCC(S)A 2000, Sched 4, para 1

(1) in the case of Scotland, the court is satisfied that suitable arrangements for the offender's supervision can be made by the council in whose area he resides or will be residing;

PCC(S)A 2000, Sched 4, para 2

(2) in the case of Northern Ireland, the court is satisfied that suitable arrangements can be made by the Probation Board for Northern Ireland.

Requirements of order

An order requires an offender:

PCC(S)A 2000, s 41(4)

(1) aged 18 or over at the time of his conviction to be under the supervision (subject to any change of address under Sched 3, para 18) of an officer of a local probation board appointed for or assigned to the petty sessions area specified in the order;

PCC(S)A 2000, s 41(5)(6)

(2) aged under 18 at that time, to be under the supervision either:
   (a) of such an officer as is mentioned in (1) above, or
   (b) of a member of a youth offending team, in the area in which he resides or will reside.

Preconditions to making the order

Before making the order, the court must:

(1) observe the restrictions on making a community order (see pp 102, 103 *above*);

(2) be satisfied that the offender has attained the age of 16; and

(3) be of opinion that his supervision is desirable in:
   (a) securing his rehabilitation, and
   (b) protecting the public from harm from him,
   (c) or preventing the commission by him of further offences;

   and

(4) explain to the offender in ordinary language: PCC(S)A 2000, s 41(7)
   (a) the effect of the order (including any additional requirements proposed to be included in the order;
   (b) the consequences which may follow under the Schedule if he fails to comply with the order; and
   (c) that the court has power to review the order on the application of the offender or the officer or member of the team responsible for his supervision.

While the PCC(S)A 2000 does not require the offender's consent to the making of an order, it is arguable that under the HRA 1998 he should indicate whether or not he is prepared to comply with the order. A condition requiring the offender to submit to treatment for his mental condition or his dependency on or propensity to misuse drugs or alcohol does, however, need the offender's consent.

The fact that a custodial sentence is the only realistic alternative will not vitiate that consent (*R v Marquis* [1974] 2 All ER 1216), but a suggestion by the court that custody is the only alternative when that is not the case will invalidate an order (*R v Barnett* (1986) 83 Cr App R 365).

Cannot be combined with custodial sentence

It is wrong in principle to make an order, or to extend an existing order, when the offender is sentenced to a custodial sentence (*R v Evans* [1958] 3 All ER 673; *R v Socratous* [1984] Crim LR 301; *R v Mullervy* (1986) 8 Cr App R (S) 42; *R v Carr-Thompson* [2000] Crim LR 401). There may, however, be cases where an offender is coming to the end of a current custodial sentence, where such a combination is permissible, even desirable (*DPP v Fontenau* [2000] Crim LR 611).

Security for good behaviour

On making an order, the court may, if it thinks it expedient for the purpose of his reformation, allow any person who consents to do so to give security for the offender's good behaviour. PCC(S)A 2000, s 41(8)

RT orders

RTOA 1988, s 46

An order of disqualification or endorsement under RTOA 1988 may be made ancillary to a community rehabilitation order.

Administrative provisions

PCC(S)A 2000, s 41(9)(10)

On the making of an order, the Clerk will:

(1) forthwith give copies of the order to:
   (a) if the offender is aged 18 or over, an officer of a local probation board assigned to the court, or
   (b) if the offender is aged under 18, to such an officer or member of a youth offending team so assigned;

(2) give copies to the offender, the responsible officer, and to the person responsible for the offender's supervision and to the person in charge of any institution in which he is required to reside; and

(3) send to the Clerk to the justices for the petty sessions area specified in the order, a copy of the order and any documents and information relating to the case likely to be of assistance to that court in the exercise of its functions in relation to the order.

General requirements

PCC(S)A 2000, s 41(11)

An order requires the offender to be under the supervision of an officer of a local probation board or a member of a youth offending team, and the offender must keep in touch with that person in accordance with any instructions given to him, and must notify him of any change of address.

PCC(S)A 2000, s 42(1)(3)

In addition, an order may require the offender to comply, during the whole or any part of the rehabilitation period with such requirements as the court, having regard to the circumstances of the case, considers desirable in the interests of:

(1) securing the rehabilitation of the offender;

(2) protecting the public from harm from him; or

(3) preventing the commission of further offences,

but may not, apart from making a compensation order under PCC(S)A 2000, s 130 (see COMPENSATION) order payment of sums by way of damages for injury or compensation for loss.

Additional requirements: (1) residence, hostels

PCC(S)A 2000, Sched 2, para 1

An order may include requirements as to the residence of the offender but:

(1) before making an order containing such a requirement the court must consider the offender's home surroundings; and

(2) where an order requires the offender to reside in an approved hostel or any other institution, the period for which he is to reside there must be specified,

and such a requirement should not be made where its making will render ineffective the other requirements of the order (eg 'to reside in Ireland') (*R v McCartan* (1958) 122 JP 465).

Additional requirements: (2) activities

An order may require the offender: PCC(S)A 2000, Sched 2, para 2(1)(2)(3)

(1) to present himself to a person or persons specified at a place or places specified;

(2) to participate, or refrain from participating, in specified activities ,

either on a specified day or days or during the period, or a specified portion of the period, of the order.

Such a requirement must not be included in the order unless:

(a) the court has consulted an officer of a local probation board as to the offender's circumstances, and the feasibility of securing compliance with the requirements; and

(b) is satisfied, having regard to that report, that it is feasible to secure compliance with them; and

(c) where participation in activities would involve the co-operation of a person other than the offender and his supervising officer, that such other person consents to the inclusion.

Such requirement obliges the offender: PCC(S)A 2000, Sched 2, para 2(6)

(i) as to (1) above, to present himself at a place or places approved by the local probation board, in accordance with any instructions given by his supervisor, for not more than 60 days in aggregate, and while there, to comply with any instructions given;

(ii) as to (2) above, to participate in activities, in accordance with any instructions given by his supervisor, for not more than 60 days in the aggregate (or in the case of a 'sexual offence', such greater number of days as may be specified) and while doing so, to comply with any instructions given.

Any such instructions given should as far as practicable be such as to avoid interference with the times, if any, at which the offender normally works or attends school or any other educational establishment. PCC(S)A 2000, Sched 2

Additional requirements: (3) probation centres

An order may require the offender, during the probation period, to attend at an approved centre or premises at which non-residential facilities are provided. PCC(S)A 2000, Sched 2, paras 3, 4

Attendance at such a centre includes attendance elsewhere for the purpose of participating in activities.

Such a requirement must not be included in an order unless the court:

(1) has consulted an officer of a local probation board; and

(2) is satisfied that arrangements can be made for the offender's attendance and the person in charge consents to the inclusion of the requirement.

Such a requirement obliges the offender to attend on not more than 60 days in accordance his supervisor's instructions and, while there, to comply with any instructions given to him.

Again, attendance should, as far as practicable, avoid any interference with working or school hours, religious beliefs and the demands of any other community order to which he is subject.

Additional requirements: (4) mental treatment, etc

PCC(S)A 2000, Sched 2, para 5

An order may include a requirement that the offender submit during the whole or any specified part(s) of the rehabilitation to treatment by, or under the direction of, a duly qualified medical practitioner, or a registered psychologist with a view to improving his mental condition.

This may meet the needs of an offender who does not need to be detained in a hospital under a hospital order, and it is generally much more effective than a guardianship order under MHA 1983 (see MENTALLY DISORDERED OFFENDERS).

The treatment specified may be:

(1) as a resident patient in a hospital or mental nursing home (not being a special hospital);

(2) as a non-resident patient at a specified place or institution; or

(3) by or under the direction of, a duly qualified medical practitioner or registered psychologist,

but the further nature of the treatment is not to be specified in the order.

Preconditions for mental treatment

PCC(S)A 2000, Sched 2, para 5(1)

Before including a requirement, the court must be satisfied, on the evidence of a medical practitioner approved for the purposes of MHA 1983, s 12, that the condition of the offender:

(1) is such as requires, and may be susceptible to, treatment; but

(2) is not such as to warrant his detention in pursuance of MHA 1983, Pt III,

PCC(S)A 2000, Sched 2, para 5(4)

and must be satisfied that arrangements have been made for such treatment (including arrangements for his reception in the case of his treatment as a resident patient) and that he has expressed his willingness to comply with such a requirement.

MHA 1983, s 54 (2)(3) (see MENTALLY DISORDERED OFFENDERS) as to proof applies here as it applies to proof of an offender's mental condition under MHA 1983, s 37(2). PCC(S)A 2000, Sched 2, para 5(9)

Arrangements under the order

While the offender is under such treatment as a resident patient, his supervisor's duties are only those necessary for the revocation or amendment of the order.

The responsible medical practitioner may be of the opinion that part of the treatment can be better or more conveniently given in, or at, an institution or place not specified in the order, which is one in or at which treatment will be given by him or under his direction. In that case he may, with the offender's consent, arrange for him to receive part of his treatment there, notwithstanding that the place or institution is not one which could have been specified in the order.

The medical practitioner will give notice to the supervisor, and such treatment is deemed to be treatment to which he is required to submit under the order.

Additional requirements: (5) drug/alcohol dependence

Where the court proposing to make such an order is satisfied on the evidence of a duly qualified medical practitioner that: PCC(S)A 2000, Sched 2 para 6

(1) the offender is dependent on drugs or alcohol;

(2) his dependency caused, or contributed to, the offence in respect of which the order is to be made; and

(3) his dependency requires, and may be susceptible to treatment,

the order may include a requirement that he submit, during the whole or any specified part of the rehabilitation period, to treatment by or under the direction of a medical practitioner, with a view to reducing or eliminating his dependency.

Such a requirement may not be included in the order unless the court has been notified that arrangements for implementing such orders are available in the area proposed to be specified.

Being 'dependent' on drugs or alcohol includes 'having a propensity towards the misuse of drugs or alcohol'. PCC(S)A 2000, Sched 2 para 6(8)

Similar provisions apply to this type of order as apply in the case of mental treatment. PCC(S)A 2000, Sched 2 para 6(4)–(8)

Additional requirements: (6) drug abstinence

PCC(S)A 2000, s 42(2A)–(F)

Where the offender was aged 18 or over on the date of his conviction and, in the court's opinion he is dependent on, or has a propensity to, misuse specified Class A drugs, then:

(1) where the offence is a 'trigger offence' (CJCSA 2000, Sched 6) the order *must,* and

(2) the offender's misuse of any specified Class A drug caused, or contributed to, the offence, the order *may,*

include a requirement that the offender:

(a) abstain from misusing specified Class A drugs; and

(b) provide, when instructed to do so, a sample for the purpose of ascertaining whether he has any specified Class A drug in his body.

Such a requirement must not be included unless the court is notified that arrangements exist for it to be carried out, nor must it be included if the order includes other requirements in respect of drugs under Schedule 6 or the sentence otherwise includes a drug testing and treatment order or a drug abstinence order.

'Trigger offences'

CJCSA 2000, Sched 6

For a magistrates' court, the trigger offences mentioned above are those under TA 1968, ss 1 (theft), 9 (burglary), 12 (taking a motor vehicle), 12A (aggravated vehicle taking), 15 (obtaining property by deception, s 25 (going equipped for theft, etc); under MDA 1971, if committed in relation to a class A drug offence under ss 4 (production and supply), 5(2) (possession), 5(3) (possession with intent to supply).

Additional requirements: (7) curfew

PCC(S)A 2000, Sched 2, para 7

A community rehabilitation order may:

(1) where the court is informed that monitoring facilities are in place; and provided that

(2) it has obtained and considered information about the place to be specified, and the attitude of persons likely to be affected by the offender's enforced presence,

include a requirement that he remain, for specified periods at a specified place, and may specify different places or different periods for different days, provided that it does not specify:

(a) periods falling outside the period of six months beginning with the day on which the order is made; or

(b) periods of less than two hours or more than 12 in any one day,

and provided that monitoring facilities are in place.

Like any other requirement, it should seek to avoid conflict with an offender's religious beliefs or the requirement of any other order, and to avoid interference with his education.

Additional requirements: (8) exclusion

Provided arrangements for monitoring such a requirement are in place, an order may include a requirement prohibiting the offender from entering any specified place or area for a specified period not exceeding two years, and may:

(1) provide for the prohibition to operate only during specified periods;

(2) specify different places or areas for different periods or days.

The order must provide for a person to monitor the offender's whereabouts.

An order must not be made where the overall sentence already includes an exclusion order.

Like any other requirement, it should seek to avoid conflict with an offender's religious beliefs or the requirement of any other order, and to avoid interference with his education.

Order made on appeal

An order made on appeal from a magistrates' court is deemed to have been made by that magistrates' court.

PCC(S)A 2000, Sched 3, para 2

Amendment, revocation and breach

As to amendment, revocation and breach of an order, see *below*, pp 131–135.

2. COMMUNITY PUNISHMENT ORDERS

An order is appropriate for an offender aged 16 or over who is convicted:

PCC(S)A 2000, ss 46, 59(6)

(1) of an offence punishable with imprisonment; or

(2) (when the power becomes generally available) of any offence, and is a persistent offender.

In either case the adult court in the case of an offender aged 18 or over, and the youth court in the case of an offender aged 16 or 17, may, subject to the general restrictions governing the making of community orders (see pp 102, 103 *above*), make a community punishment order, requiring him to perform unpaid work, but in the case of (2) above, the court must not make an order unless:

(a) it is satisfied that:

 (i) one or more fines imposed on the offender in respect of one or more previous convictions have not been paid; and

(ii) if a fine were imposed in an amount which was commensurate with the seriousness of the offence, the offender would not have sufficient means to pay it; and

(b) if it were not so satisfied it would be minded to impose a fine in respect of the offence.

Restrictions on making an order

PCC(S)A 2000, s 46(4)(6)

An order shall not be made unless the court is satisfied:

(1) after hearing, if it thinks it necessary, from an officer of a local probation board, or a local authority social worker, or in the case of an offender under 18, a member of a youth offending team, that the offender is a suitable person to do work under such an order; and

(2) that work is available under arrangements in force in the petty sessions area in which he resides or will reside.

'Punishable with imprisonment'

The requirement that an offence in respect of which an order is made is 'punishable with imprisonment' does not mean that it must be a direct alternative to a custodial sentence (*R v Lawrence* [1982] Crim LR 377; *R v Davies* (1984) 6 Cr App R (S) 224; *R v Barley* [1989] Crim LR 594; *R v Zaman* [1991] Crim LR 565).

Improper combinations

A community sentence may not consist of, or include, both a community rehabiliation order *and* a community punishment order, whether for a single offence, or for two or more offences. If the court desires to combine the two forms of sentence, it must make a community punishment and rehabilitation order (see p 119 *below*): *Golding v DPP* (1998) *The Times*, 20 May.

In relation to suspended sentences of imprisonment, it has been said that it is bad sentencing practice:

(1) to impose a community punishment order in respect of one offence and a suspended sentence on another (*R v Campbell* (1993) 14 Cr App R(S) 401); or

(2) to impose a community punishment order on the same occasion as activating a suspended sentence (*R v McElhorne* [1983] Crim LR 487).

Offenders residing in Scotland or Northern Ireland

If the offender resides or will be residing in Scotland or Northern Ireland, when the order comes into force, an order must not be made unless:

PCC(S)A 2000, Sched 4, para 3

(1) in the case of Scotland:

(a) the court has been notified by the Home Secretary that arrangements exist for persons residing in the locality, to perform such work; and

(b) provision can be made for the offender to work under those arrangements;

(2) in the case of Northern Ireland: PCC(S)A 2000, Sched 4, para 4

(a) the court has been notified that arrangements exist; and

(b) provision can be made for him to undertake work under those arrangements.

The number of hours

The number of hours to be worked must be specified in the order. They must, in the aggregate, whatever the age of the offender, be:

(1) not less than 40; and

(2) not more than 240.

Some credit ought to be given for time spent in custody awaiting trial (*R v Lawrence, above*).

Consecutive orders

Where convictions for two or more offences are concerned, the court may direct the hours specified in one to be concurrent with, or consecutive or additional to, the hours specified in another order, although:

(1) the hours specified in a single order must not exceed 240; and

(2) the total hours imposed on the same occasion should not exceed 240 (*R v Evans* [1977] 1All ER 228); though

(3) there is nothing to prevent different courts on different occasions from imposing orders which will in effect exceed 240 hours (*R v Siha* [1992] Crim LR 383, cf *R v Anderson* [1989] Crim LR 120), though it is undesirable; and

(4) it is wrong in principle to impose a consecutive order on an offender already subject to an order, if the effect is to create a combination exceeding 240 hours (*R v Anderson, above*) unless there are less than 240 hours still to be worked under the original order (*R v Siha, above*).

Other obligations of offender

In addition to performing work for the number of hours specified, at such times as he may be instructed, the offender must also keep in touch with his supervisor in accordance with any instructions given to him, and notify his supervisor of any change of address. PCC(S)A 2000, s 47(1)

In general (there are exceptions) the work must be performed within 12 months of the date of the order, but, unless revoked, it remains in force until the offender has worked the specified number of hours. PCC(S)A 2000, s 47(3)

Drug abstinence (at present in pilot areas only)

PCC(S)A 2000, s 47(3A)–(3C)

If the offender was 18 or over on the date of his conviction for the offence, and, in the court's opinion he is dependent on, or has a propensity to misuse Class A drugs, then:

(1) if the offence is a 'trigger offence' (see p 114 *above*), the order *must*; and

(2) if, in the court's opinion, the misuse by the offender of any specified Class A drug caused or contributed to the offence, the order *may*,

include a drug abstinence requirement (see p 114 *above*), but no such order should be made if the sentence, as a whole, contains a drug treatment and testing order or a drug abstinence order.

Explaining the effect of the order

PCC(S)A 2000, s 46(1)

Before making an order, the court must explain in ordinary language to the offender:

(1) the purpose and effect of the order, and in particular the requirements set out in s 47(1);

(2) the consequences which may follow under the Schedule if he fails to comply with any of those requirements; and

(3) that the court has power to review the order on the application either of the offender or the responsible officer.

Commencement of order; administrative provisions

PCC(S)A 2000, s 47(9)(12)

An order is effective from the moment it is pronounced (*Walsh v Barlow* [1985] Crim LR 46, *Thorpe v Griggs* (1985) 6 Cr App R (S) 286). It will specify the petty sessions area in which the offender resides or will reside, and, where he is under 18, may also specify a local authority where functions are to be exercised by a youth offending team.

Copies of the order will be given to the liaison officer of the local probation board, to the offender and to the relevant community service organiser, and sent to the Clerk of the relevant magistrates' court.

Failure to comply with order

If an offender fails to comply with the order as by:

(1) not notifying a change of address;

(2) not going to the place where he is told to do the work; or

(3) not working satisfactorily,

the organiser may apply for a summons or warrant to bring him before the relevant magistrates' court, where any further procedure will be governed by the provisions of Schedule 3 (see pp 131–135).

3. COMMUNITY PUNISHMENT AND REHABILITATION ORDERS

A community punishment and rehabilitation order combines the features of a community punishment order with those of a community rehabilitation order. Where: PCC(S)A 2000, s 51(1)(2)(3)

(1) a person over the age of 16;

(2) is convicted of an offence punishable with imprisonment (see p 116 *above*),

the adult court in the case of an offender aged 18 or over, and the youth court in the case of an offender aged 16 or 17, may, subject to the general restrictions on making community orders, if it is of the opinion that the order is desirable in the interests of:

(a) securing the rehabilitation of the offender;

(b) protecting the public from harm from him; or

(c) preventing the commission by him of further offences,

make such an order.

The order requires the offender both:

(i) to be under supervision for a specified period of not less than 12 months nor more than three years; and

(ii) to perform unpaid work for a specified number of hours, being in the aggregate not less than 40 nor more than 100.

Where such an order is made, subject to ss 41, 42, 46, 47, and Schedule 2, PCC(S)A 2000 applies to such an order, so far as (i) above is concerned, as if it were a community rehabilitation order, and as far as (ii) is concerned as if it were a community punishment order. PCC(S)A 2000, s 51(4)

Transfer to Scotland

Where such an order is transferred to Scotland, in so far as it imposes supervision it is to be treated as if it were a probation order and in so far as it imposes community service, as a community service order.

Consent to mental treatment

The offender's consent is required for the attachment of additional requirements stipulating mental treatment, or treatment for a drug or alcohol dependency.

Amendment, revocation, and breach

Amendment, revocation and breach of the order is dealt with under Schedule 3 (see pp 131–135 *below*).

4. DRUG TREATMENT AND TESTING ORDERS

PCC(S)A 2000, s 51(1)(2)(3)(5)(7)

Where an offender aged 16 or over is convicted of an offence committed after 30 September 1998, and the court has been notified that arrangements for implementing such orders are available in the area to be specified in the order, and is satisfied:

(1) that the offender is dependent on, or has a propensity to misuse, drugs and that his dependency or propensity is such as requires and may be susceptible to treatment; and

PCC(S)A 2000, s 53(3)

(2) that arrangements have been made or can be made for the treatment specified in the order (including arrangements for his reception where he is to be required to submit to treatment as a resident patient); and

(3) the offender expresses his willingness to comply with the requirements,

the court may make a drug treatment and testing order, specifying, for a period:

(a) treatment as a resident in a specified institution or place; or

(b) treatment as a non-resident in or at such an institution or place, at specified intervals.

Such an order:

(i) has effect for the period specified in the order, not being of less than six months or more than three years; and

(ii) includes certain specified requirements and provisions.

Provision of sample

PCC(S)A 2000, s 52(4)

For the purpose of ascertaining whether the offender has any drug in his body, the court may order him to provide such samples as it may specify, but it may not make such an order unless the offender expresses his willingness to comply.

Explanation in ordinary language

PCC(S)A 2000, s 52(6)

Before making an order, the court must explain to the offender in ordinary language:

(1) the effect of the order and of the requirements proposed to be included in it;

(2) that the order will be periodically reviewed at intervals as provided in the order; and

(3) that the order may be reviewed on the application whether of the offender or of the responsible officer.

Testing and treatment requirements

An order must include in its terms: PCC(S)A 2000, s 53(1)(2)(4)(5)

(1) 'the treatment requirement', that is a requirement that the offender submit, during the whole of the treatment and testing period, to treatment by or under the direction of a specified person having the necessary qualifications or experience ('the treatment provider') with a view to the reduction or elimination of his dependency on, or propensity to use, drugs;

(2) 'the testing requirement', that for the purpose of ascertaining whether he has any drug in his body during the treatment and testing period, he provide, at the times and in the circumstances determined by the treatment provider, specified samples. The requirement will specify for each month the minimum number of occasions on which samples are to be provided;

(3) a provision specifying the petty sessions area in which it appears that the offender resides or will reside; PCC(S)A 2000, s 54(1)(2)(3)

(4) a provision, that for the period, the offender will be under the supervision of an officer of a local probation board appointed for, or attached to, the petty sessions area specified in the order ('the responsible officer'):
   (a) with whom the offender will be required to keep in touch and to whom he must notify any change of address; and PCC(S)A 2000, s 54(4)
   (b) to whom will be communicated the results of any tests carried out on the samples he provides under the order, though his supervision will be carried on otherwise only so far as it is necessary to enable him to report on the offender's compliance or failure to comply with the order, and to determine whether the circumstances are such that an application should be made for the amendment or revocation of the order; and

(5) a provision for the order to be reviewed periodically at intervals of not less than one month. PCC(S)A 2000, s 53(5)

Administrative provisions

The court which makes or amends an order will give copies of the relevant orders to the offender, the treatment provider and the responsible officer. PCC(S)A 2000, s 57

Review hearings

In providing for the periodic review of the order at intervals of not less than than one month (see *above*), the order will also provide for: PCC(S)A 2000, s 54(6)

(1) (subject to s 55(6)) a 'review hearing' held for the purpose by the court which made the order, and will require the offender to attend;

(2) the supervisor to make, before each hearing, a report in writing on the offender's progress under the order, each report including the test results communicated to him, and the views of the treatment provider as to the offender's testing and treatment.

PCC(S)A 2000, s 55

At such a review, the court may amend any requirement or provision of the order though:

(a) the treatment and testing requirement may not be amended unless the offender expresses his willingness to comply with the requirement as amended;

(b) no provision may be amended so as to reduce the treatment and testing period below the minimum specified in s 52(1) or to increase it above the maximum there specified; and

(c) except with the consent of the offender, no provision or requirement shall be amended where an appeal against the order is pending.

PCC(S)A 2000, s 57(1)

Copies of any amending order must be given forthwith by the court to the responsible officer.

Informal review

PCC(S)A 2000, s 55(6)(7)(8)(9)

If, at a review hearing, the court, after considering the supervisor's report, is of opinion that the offender's progress under the order is satisfactory, it may so amend the order as to provide for each subsequent review to be made without a hearing.

Conversely, if at such an informal review, the court, after considering the supervisor's report, is of opinion that the offender's progress under the order is no longer satisfactory, it may require him to attend a hearing, specifying a time and place, and at that hearing, after considering the report, the court may:

(1) exercise any of the powers conferred by s 55; and

(2) amend the order to provide that each subsequent review be a review hearing.

Offender unwilling to comply with amendment of order

PCC(S)A 2000, s 55(3)

If the offender fails to express his willingness to comply with the treatment and testing requirement as proposed to be amended, the court may:

(1) revoke the order; and

(2) deal with him for the offence in respect of which the order was made, in any manner in which it could have dealt with him if he had just been convicted before it, taking into account the extent to which he has complied with the order.

A custodial sentence may be imposed, if appropriate, notwithstanding the provisions of PCC(5)A 2000, s 79(2) (see p 169 *below*).

Order made on appeal

An order made on appeal from a magistrates' court, it is deemed to have been made by that magistrates' court. PCC(S)A 2000, Sched 3, para 2(2)

Enforcement

A drug treatment and testing order, being a 'relevant' community order, is enforced under the provisions of Schedule 3 (see pp 131–135 *below*).

5. DRUG ABSTINENCE ORDERS

Where the adult court is notified that arrangements for implementing such orders are available, it may, subject to the general restrictions on the making of community orders, make: PCC(S)A 2000, s 58A(1)(2)(3)

(1) in respect of an offender aged 18 or over, convicted of an offence, where in its opinion the offender is dependent on, or has a propensity to misuse specified Class A drugs, or

(2) the offence in question is a 'trigger offence' as defined in CJCSA 2000, Schedule 6 (see p 114 *above*), or

(3) in its opinion the misuse by the offender of a specified Class A drug caused or contributed to the offence,

a drug abstinence order, that is to say, an order that the offender be under supervision for a period of not less than six months nor more than three years and requiring him:

(a) to abstain from misusing specified Class A drugs; and

(b) to provide, when instructed to do so by the responsible officer, any sample mentioned in the instruction for the purpose of ascertaining whether he has any specified Class A drug in his body.

Before making an order, the court must explain to the offender in ordinary language: PCC(S)A 2000, s 58B(1)

(i) the effect of the order and the requirements proposed to be included in it;

(ii) the consequences which may follow if he fails to comply with any of the requirements of the order; and

(iii) that the court has power to review the order on the application of the offender or the supervisor.

Amendment, revocation and breach

Schedule 3 to the Act (see pp 131–135 *below*) has effect in relation to the amendment and revocation of such an order, also for dealing with failure to comply with an order. PCC(S)A 2000, s 58B(3)

6. ATTENDANCE CENTRE ORDERS; OFFENDERS UNDER 21

PCC(S)A 2000, s 50(1)

An attendance centre order may be made, in three circumstances, namely:

(1) subject to the general restrictions on the making of community orders (see pp 102, 103 *above*), where a person aged under 21 is convicted of an offence punishable with imprisonment; or

(2) the court has power, but for s 89 (restrictions on the imprisonment of young offenders and defaulters) to commit a person aged under 21 to prison in default of payment of any sum of money or for failing to do or abstain from doing anything required to be done or left undone; or

(3) the court has power to commit a person aged at least 21 but under 25 to prison in default of the payment of any sum of money.

Only the youth court may make an order in respect of an offender under 18.

Pre-requisites of order

PCC(S)A 2000, s 60(1)(6)

Before an order can be made, the court has to be satisfied that:

(1) a centre is available for the reception of persons of his description, and

(2) the centre to be specified is readily accessible to him, having regard to his age, means of access and other circumstances.

Number of hours

PCC(S)A 2000, s 60(3)(7)(10)

In regard to the aggregate number of hours for which the offender may be required to attend the centre:

(1) the minimum is 12, except where he is under 14, and the court considers that to be excessive having regard to his age and other circumstances;

(2) the maximum is 12 except where the court is of opinion, having regard to all the circumstances, that 12 hours would be inadequate, in which case, the aggregate:
   (a) must not exceed 24 if he is under 16, and
   (b) must not exceed 36 where he is aged 16, but under 21, or in the case of (3) above, under 25,

and it should, as far as possible, avoid conflict with his religious beliefs, the requirements of any other community order to which he is subject, and any interference with the hours he normally works, or attends school, etc.

The offender cannot be required to attend on more than one occasion on any day or for more than three hours on any occasion.

Two or more orders

There is nothing to prevent the court making a further order while a previous one is still running, and the hours specified in the subsequent order may be determined without regard to the number specified in the previous order, or to the fact that that order is still in effect. PCC(S)A 2000, s 69(5)

Administrative provisions

A copy of the order will be delivered or sent to the offender and to the officer in charge of the centre, and the time of first attendance will be specified in the order. Subsequent times will be fixed by the officer in charge, avoiding interference, where practicable, with the offender's school or working hours. PCC(S)A 2000, s 60(8)(9)(11)

Order made on appeal

An order made on appeal from a magistrates' court is deemed to have been made by that court. PCC(S)A 2000, Sched 5, para 6

Defaulters

As to the making of an attendance centre order to enforce payment of unpaid fines (PCC(S)A 2000, s 60(12)), see FINES AND ENFORCEMENT).

Variation and discharge: Schedule 5

Special provisions are made for the variation and discharge of attendance centre orders, thus: PCC(S)A 2000, Sched 5, para 5

(1) applications to vary an order are made to a magistrates' court acting for the petty sessions area in which the centre is situate.

(2) an order may be discharged by application either to the court which made it, or to a magistrates' court acting for the petty sessions area in which the centre is situated, on behalf of the offender or of the officer in charge of the centre, unless the original order was made by the Crown Court which reserved to itself the power of discharge.

The power to discharge an order includes the power to deal with the offender for the offence for which the order was made, in any manner in which he could have been dealt with for that offence by the court which made the order, if the order had not been made.

A copy of the order will be sent or delivered to the offender and to the officer in charge of the centre.

Breach of the order: Schedule 5

If it is proved to the satisfaction of the court that an offender has:

(1) failed to attend under the order; or

(2) committed a breach of the rules of the centre which cannot be adequately dealt with under those rules,

he may be dealt with in any manner in which the court could have dealt with him if it had not made the order.

In the case of an offender who has willfully and persistently failed to comply with the requirements, the court may impose a custodial sentence, notwithstanding anything in PCC(S)A 2000, s 79(2) (as to which see p 169 *below*). Where a court deals with an offender under the above provision it must revoke the attendance centre order.

COMMUNITY ORDERS AVAILABLE ONLY WHERE OFFENDER AGED UNDER 18

1. SUPERVISION ORDERS

A supervision order is, in some ways like a community rehabilitation order for juveniles. It may include particular requirements and it may be varied. It may only be made by the youth court.

Making an order

PCC(S)A 2000, s 63(1)(2)(5)

A supervision order may be made where;

(1) a child or young person (that is to say any person aged under 18) is found guilty of an offence;

(2) the general restrictions on making community orders are fulfilled; and

(3) the court is satisfied that the offender will reside in a local authority area, (he may be required to reside there within the terms of Schedule 6 paragraph 1),

placing the offender under the supervision of a local authority designated by the order, an officer of a local probation board or a member of a youth offending team for a period specified in the order.

PCC(S)A 2000, s 63(7)

The order, unless it has been previously revoked, ceases to have effect at the end of the period of three years, or such shorter period as may be specified in it, beginning with the date on which it was made.

In making a supervision order, the court has power to discharge any other such order made by a magistrates' court.

Requirements

The requirements which may be included in such an order are set out in PCC(S)A 2000, Schedule 6, and include requirements as to:

(1) residence with a named individual (para 1);

(2) complying with the directions of the supervisor (para 2);

(3) activities, reparation and night restrictions (paras 3, 4);

(4) living in local authority accommodation (para 5);

(5) treatment for mental condition (para 6);

(6) education (para 7).

Provided that as to (3) *above*, the court;

(a) has first consulted the supervisor as to the offender's circumstances and the feasibility of securing compliance with the requirements;

(b) considers the requirements necessary for securing the good conduct of the supervised person or for preventing repetition by him of the same offence or the commission of other offences; and

(c) if the offender is aged under 16, he has obtained and considered information about his family circumstances and the likely effect of the requirements on such circumstances.

An order may also empower the supervisor to give directions requiring the supervised person to submit to certain requirements. PCC(S)A 2000, s 63, Sched 6, para 2

Directions by supervisor

An order may empower the supervisor to give directions requiring the offender:

(1) to live at a specified place or places for a specified period or to reside with a named individual who agrees to this requirement;

(2) to present himself to specified persons on dates and at places also specified; and

(3) to participate in specified activities.

A supervisor has a discretion as to how to apply the directions contained in the order. The total number of days to be spent by the supervised person in complying with directions under the order is not to exceed 90 days or such lesser number as specified in the order.

Night restriction order; activities

The order may require a supervised person: PCC(S)A 2000, s 63, Sched 6, paras 3, 4

(1) to remain for specified periods between 6 pm and 6 am at a place or places specified in the order. A 'night restriction order' of this nature may not, however, be for longer than 10 hours, last for longer than 30 days, nor relate to any day more than three months from the date of the order; it should normally specify the supervised person's place of residence and does not prevent his leaving if accompanied by his parent, guardian, supervisor or person specified by the court;

(2) to refrain from participating in specified activities.

Local authority accommodation

PCC(S)A 2000, s 63, Sched 6, para 5

Where a supervision order has previously been made in respect of the child or young person which included a night restriction order, a prohibited activities order or a residence order, and:

(1) he is found guilty of an offence committed while that order was in force, punishable in the case of an adult with imprisonment; and
(2) which, in the court's opinion, is serious; and,
(3) the court is satisfied that the behaviour which constituted the offence was due, to a significant extent, to the circumstances in which he was living (unless the original supervision order contained a residence requirement),

then, subject to a prior consultation with the local authority, the order may impose a requirement that the child or young person shall live for a specified period, not exceeding three months, in local authority accommodation.

Requirement as to mental treatment

PCC(S)A 2000, s 63, Sched 6, para 6

A requirement as to mental treatment may be included in a supervision order if the court is satisfied on the evidence of a medical practitioner approved for the purposes of MHA 1983, s 12, that the mental condition of the supervised person requires and may be susceptible to treatment but does not warrant a hospital order.

Similar provisions apply as those applicable to such a requirement in a community rehabilitation order.

Requirement as to education

PCC(S)A 2000, s 63, Sched 6, para 7

Such a requirement may, subject to consultation with the supervisor and the local authority, be included in an order if the court considers it necessary for securing the good conduct of the supervised person or to prevent him from re-offending.

Breaches, variation, and discharge

PCC(S)A 2000, s 65, Sched 7, para 2

Powers to deal with breaches of the requirements of, to vary, and to discharge, supervision orders are exercised normally by youth courts and other magistrates' courts. These powers extend to re-sentencing, but not to detention in a young offenders' institution.

Order made on appeal

PCC(S)A 2000, Sched 7, para 2(8)

Where an order is made on appeal, it is deemed, if it was made on an appeal brought from a magistrates' court to have been made by that court.

2. ACTION PLAN ORDERS

Where a person aged under 18 is convicted of an offence the youth court, if it is of the opinion that it is desirable to do so in the interests of securing the offender's rehabilitation, or of preventing the commission by him of further offences, and provided:

PCC(S)A 2000, s 69(1)(2)(3)(5)

(1) the court has been informed that arrangements for implementing such orders are available in the area;

(2) the offender is not already the subject of such an order; and

(3) the court does not propose to pass a custodial sentence on him, or to make a community rehabilitation order, a community punishment order, or a combination of both, a supervision order or an attendance centre order in respect of him,

may make an action plan order:

(a) requiring the offender, for a period of three months beginning with the date of the order, to comply with a series of requirements with respect to his actions and whereabouts;

(b) naming the petty session area in which it appears that the offender resides or will reside;

(c) placing him under the supervision for that period of an officer of a local probation board, a local authority social worker or a member of a youth offending team; and

(d) requiring him to comply with any directions given by that officer with a view to the implementation of the plan.

The general restrictions governing the making of community orders apply (see pp 102, 103 *above*).

Before making an order

Before making an order, the court must obtain and consider a written report from an officer of a local probation board, local authority social worker or member of of a youth offending team indicating:

PCC(S)A 2000, s 69(6)

(1) the requirements proposed to be included in the order;

(2) the benefits to the offender that the proposed requirements are designed to achieve;

(3) the attitude of the offender's parent or guardian to the proposed requirements; and

(4) in the case of an offender under the age of 16 information about his family circumstances and the likely effect of the order on those circumstances.

PCC(S)A 2000, s 69(11)

The court must, before making an order, explain to the offender in ordinary language:

(a) the effect of the order, and of the requirements proposed;

(b) the consequences which may follow if he fails to comply with any of them; and

(c) the power of the court, under the Schedule, to review the order on the application either of the responsible officer or the offender.

Requirements of the order

PCC(S)A 2000, s 70

The requirements included in an order (or the directions given by the responsible officer) may require the offender to do all or any of the following:

(1) participate in specified activities;

(2) present himself to specified persons at specified times and places;

(3) in a case where the offence committed by the offender is punishable with imprisonment in the case of an adult, attend for specified hours at an attendance centre;

(4) stay away from specified places;

(5) comply with specified arrangements for his education;

(6) make reparation to specified persons identified by the court as victims of the offence or as affected by it (provided that person consents to reparation being made) or to the community at large; and

(7) attend at subsequent hearings fixed by the court under s 71, *below*.

The directions will, as far as is practicable, avoid conflict with the offender's religious beliefs or the requirements of any other community order to which he is subject, and interference with the times, if any, at which he normally works or attends school or any other educational establishment.

Subsequent hearings

PCC(S)A 2000, s 71

Immediately after making an order, the court may:

(1) fix a further hearing, for a date not more than 21 days after the making of the order; and

(2) direct the responsible officer to make, at that hearing, a report as to the effectiveness of the order and the extent to which it has been implemented.

At that hearing the court will consider the report, and may, on the application either of the responsible officer or the offender, vary the order by cancelling any provision of it, or by inserting into it (either in addition to or in substitution for any of its provisions) any provision that could have been inserted in it originally.

Failure to comply

PCC(S)A 2000, Schedule 8 has effect for dealing with failure to comply with any requirement, and for varying or revoking any order. Breach proceedings may only be brought during the lifetime of the order. PCC(S)A 2000, s 72

BREACH OF 'RELEVANT' COMMUNITY ORDERS

The breach, amendment and revocation of:

- curfew orders;
- community rehabilitation orders;
- community punishment orders;
- community punishment and rehabilitation orders;
- drug treatment orders;
- exclusion orders;
- drug abstinence orders; and
- any other orders specified by the Home Secretary,

is dealt with under a common code, set out in PCC(S)A 2000, Schedule 3.

Where an order of the type set out in (1)–(4) was made on appeal from a magistrates' court it is deemed to have been made by that court. PCC(S)A 2000, Sched 3, para 2

In any type of breach proceedings, the court must:

(a) put the alleged breach to the offender; and

(b) obtain his admission as to it.

If he denies the breach it must be proved to the satisfaction of the court.

Any question whether an offender has failed to comply with the requirements of the order falls to be determined by the ordinary rules as to the presentation of the prosecution case (*R v Gainsborough JJ, ex p Green* (1983) 78 Cr App R 9).

Where the breach may result in re-sentencing, the prosecutor will need to put the facts of the original offence before the court. Where the case is presented by an officer of a local probation board, that officer well need to obtain any relevant facts from the Crown Prosecution Service (*R v Clarke* [1979] 2 Cr App R(S) 163).

Breach: (1) Issue of summons or warrant

If, at any time when a relevant order is in force, it appears on information being laid before a magistrate of the relevant magistrates' court that the offender has failed to comply with the requirements of the order, the magistrate may: PCC(S)A 2000, Sched 3, Pt II, para 3

(1) issue a summons requiring the offender to appear at the time and place specified in it; or

(2) if the information is in writing and on oath, issue a warrant for his arrest.

Breach: (2) Venue

The summons or warrant must direct that the offender appear or be brought:

(1) in the case of a drug treatment and testing order, or a drug abstinence order, before the court responsible for the order;

(2) in the case of any order made by the Crown Court which included a direction that any failure to comply with a requirement of the order be dealt with by the Crown Court, before that court;

(3) in the case of any order other than one set out in (1) above, before the relevant magistrates' court.

Breach: (3) Failure to comply with requirement

PCC(S)A 2000, Sched 3, Pt II, para 4(1)

If it is proved to the satisfaction of the court that the offender has failed *without reasonable cause* to comply with a requirement of an order, the court may deal with that failure in one of the following ways:

(1) impose on him a fine not exceeding £1,000;

(2) where the offender is aged 16 or over, make a community punishment order not exceeding 60 hours, in respect of him, (see further PCC(S)A 2000, para 7);

(3) where the order is:
   (a) a curfew order and the offender is under 16; or
   (b) a community rehabilitation or a community punishment and rehabilitation order, and the offender is under 21,

   make an attendance centre order;

(4) where the order was made by a magistrates' court, deal with him for the offence for which the order was made, in any way in which it could have dealt with him if he had just been convicted of the offence.

An offender required:

(a) by a community rehabilitation order to submit to treatment for his mental condition, or his dependency on, or propensity to misuse drugs or alcohol; or

(b) by a drug treatment and testing order, to submit to treatment for his dependency or propensity to misuse drugs,

is not to be treated for the purpose of these provisions as having failed to comply with a requirement on the ground only that he has refused to undergo surgical, electrical or other treatment if, in the court's opinion, his refusal was reasonable having regard to all the circumstances.

Where dealing with the offender under (4) above, the court: PCC(S)A 2000, Sched 3, Pt II, para 4(2)

(a) must take into account the extent to which he has complied with the requirements of the order;

(b) may, where he has persistently failed to comply with the requirements, impose on him a custodial sentence provided that the offence for which the order was made is punishable with imprisonment; and

(c) revoke the order if it is still in force.

There is no power, when dealing with an offender in respect of an offence triable either way, to commit him to the Crown Court for sentence under PCC(S)A 2000, s 3 (*R v Jordan* [1998] Crim LR 353).

Revocation; new circumstances

Where an order was made by a magistrates' court, and on application by the offender or the responsible officer it appears to that having regard to circumstances which have arisen since the order was made, it would be in the interests of justice: PCC(S)A 2000, Sched 3, Pt II, paras 10(1)(3)

(1) for the order to be revoked; or

(2) for the offender to be dealt with in some other way for the offence in respect of which the order was made,

the appropriate magistrates' court may:

(a) revoke the order; or

(b) revoke the order *and* deal with the offender in any way it could deal with him had he just been convicted by the court of the offence for which the order was made.

The circumstances in which: PCC(S)A 2000, Sched 3, Pt II, paras 10(4)(5)

(i) a community rehabilitation order;

(ii) a community punishment and rehabilitation order; and

(iii) a drug treatment and testing order,

may be revoked in this manner, without re-sentencing, include the offender's making good progress, or his responding satisfactorily to supervision or treatment.

Where revocation is on the ground that the offender is unable to comply by reason of illness or disability, a custodial sentence should, in general not be imposed (*R v Fielding* [1993] Crim LR 229), particularly where the offender made it clear from the outset that there might be difficulties (*R v Johnson* [2000] Crim LR 125), but may well be appropriate where the offender failed to disclose any difficulties at the time the order was proposed (*R v Hammon* [1998] Crim LR 293).

Where an offender is to be sentenced for the offence for which the order was made (ie under (2) above), the court must take into account the extent to which the offender complied with the requirements of the order. As to revocation following a custodial sentence, see *below*.

Substitution of conditional discharge

PCC(S)A 2000, Sched 3, Pt II, paras 12(1), 4(4)

Where a community rehabilitation order, or a community punishment and rehabilitation order is in force, and the offender or the responsible officer applies to the appropriate magistrates' court on the basis that, having regard to the circumstances which have arisen since the order was made, it would be in the interests of justice:

(1) that the order be revoked; and

(2) that an order be made discharging the offender conditionally for the offence for which the order was made,

the court may, in its discretion, grant that application, and the operational period will begin with the making of the conditional discharge and will terminate with the date on which the community rehabilitation order, or the community punishment and rehabilitation order would have ended.

Revocation following custodial sentence

PCC(S)A 2000, Sched 3, Pt II, para 13(1)

Where an offender is subject to a relevant order, and is:

(1) convicted of an offence by a magistrates' court *unconnected with* the order; and

(2) the court imposes a custodial sentence for that offence,

and, on the application of the offender or of the responsible officer, it appears that it would be in the interests of justice, having regard to the circumstances which have arisen since the order was made, the court may revoke the order.

Administrative matters

On revocation of any order, the court gives a copy of the order of revocation to the offender and to the person in charge of any institution in which he was required by the order to reside.

Amendment of orders

PCC(S)A 2000, Sched 3, Pt II, para 18

Schedule 3 provides for the amendment of relevant orders by reason of change of address, cancelling existing requirements of an order or inserting into an order new requirements which the court would have power to include if it were making the order.

The Clerk is authorised to:

JCR 1999, Schedule

(1) amend a community rehabilitation order, a community punishment order, or a community punishment and rehabilitation order by

substituting for one petty sessions area, another area in which the offender is, or is proposing to be, resident;

(2) vary an attendance centre order by either;
  (a) varying the day or time specified in the order for the offender's first attendance; or
  (b) substituting for the centre specified in the order another relevant centre reasonably accessible to the offender having regard to his age, his means of access and any other circumstances.

COMPANY OFFICER'S DISQUALIFICATION

An order may be made disqualifying an offender, who has been: CDDA 1986, s 1

(1) convicted either summarily, or on indictment of an offence;
(2) in connection with the promotion, formation, management or liquidation of a company; or
(3) connected with the receivership or management of a company's property from being:
   (a) a director, liquidator or manager of any company;
   (b) a receiver or manager of any company's property; or
   (c) in any way, whether directly or indirectly, being concerned or taking part in, the promotion, formation or management of any company,

without leave of the court.

Where the order is made by a magistrates' court, the maximum period of disqualification is five years. CDDA 1986, s 2(3)(a)(b)

Extent of order

There is no power to limit the order to one or other of the categories (1)–(3) *above*; it must contain a prohibition in respect of *all* the functions referred to in the section (*R v Seagull Manufacturing Ltd* BCLC 51), and the court should make this clear to the offender (*R v Howarth* (2001) *The Times*, 10 August).

The aim of the order is to protect the public from persons, who, whether for reasons of dishonesty, naivety or incompetence, use or abuse their role as company officer to the detriment of the public (see (*R v Millard* (1994) 15 Cr App R(S) 444; *R v Edwards* (1998) 2 Cr App R(S) 213; *R v Victory* (1998) 2 Cr App R(S) 102).

A person acting in contravention of such an order is liable, on conviction on indictment, to imprisonment for not more than two years or to a fine, or both.

'Management' defined

The words 'management of the company' refer to the management of the company's affairs. There is no reason to differentiate between internal and external affairs (*R v Crobin* (1984) 6 Cr App Rep (S) 17, *R v Austen* (1985) 7 Cr App R(S) 214, *R v Georgiou* (1988) 87 Cr App Rep 207).

The correct test, in deciding whether an offence was committed 'in connection with the management of a company' is to decide whether the offence has some relevant connection with the management, *not* whether it 'relates to the management' *nor* whether it was committed 'in the course of managing the company' (*R v Grotman* [1993] 2 All ER 789].

Compensation coupled with disqualification

While the ordinary power to order compensation applies, where there are complex financial issues involved, it is probably undesirable to couple such an order with a disqualification of this kind (*R v Holmes* (1992) 13 Cr App R(S) 29).

COMPENSATION ORDERS

Where a person is convicted of an offence, the adult court in the case of an offender aged 18 or over, and the youth court in the case of a child or young person, may, subject to certain restrictions, make an order requiring him: PCC(S)A 2000, s 130(1)(2)

(1) to pay compensation for any *personal injury, loss* or *damage* resulting from the offence, or any offence taken into consideration on sentence; or

(2) to make payments for funeral expenses or bereavement in respect of a death resulting from any such offence, other than a death due to an accident arising out of the presence of a motor vehicle on a road, and

that order may be made whether on application or otherwise.

If, on passing sentence, the court does not make an order where it has power to do so, it must give its reasons. PCC(S)A 2000, s 130(2)

Purpose of section

The powers conferred on the court to order compensation in a criminal case are intended to ensure, so far as is possible, that the offender compensates the victim for his criminal actions, and to help the victim avoid the expense and inconvenience of resorting to civil litigation to recoup damages, but:

(1) an order must not enable the offender to 'buy himself out' of the ordinary criminal penalty;

(2) the order is intended as a speedy way of dealing with simple cases in which no great amount is at stake; and

(3) an order should be made only in the plainest and most straightforward situations, and only

(4) where the offender has the means to pay (*Stamp v UDT* (1967) 131 JP 177; *R v Ferguson* [1970] 2 All ER 828); *R v Daly* (1974) 58 Cr App R 333; *R v Kneeshaw* [1974] 1 All ER 896; *R v Inwood* (1974) 60 Cr App R 70).

Compensation may sometimes be enforced without making a formal order, as where the court insists on payment of compensation before proceeding to sentence, or where sentence is deferred (see DEFERRING SENTENCE) with a view to the making of reparation.

A magistrates' court has no power to make an order on committing an offender to the Crown Court for sentence (*R v Brogan* (1975) 60 Cr App R 279).

Definitions

'Personal injury' or 'damage' include shock and anxiety directly occasioned by the offence (*Bond v Chief Constable of Kent* [1983] 1 All ER 456).

'Loss' includes the loss suffered by an innocent purchaser of stolen goods (*R v Howell* (1978) 66 Cr App R 179).

General principles

The general principles to be followed in making an order were restated in *R v Miller* (1976) 68 Cr App R 56. Those still relevant are:

(1) first and foremost, an order should be made only where the legal position is clear;

(2) the order must be precisely drawn and must be related to an offence of which the offender has been convicted, or which he has agreed to have taken into consideration;

(3) the court must have regard to the offender's means; and

(4) the order ought not to be oppressive; and

the fact that the victim to whom compensation is payable has since died does not mean that an order is inappropriate (*Holt v DPP* [1996] Crim LR 524).

Approach to making an order

Before making a compensation order the court must:

(1) satisfy itself that injury, loss or damage has resulted from the offence of which the offender has been convicted or is having taken into consideration on sentence;

(2) settle the amount of the injury, loss or damage which the offender may be required to pay; and

(3) consider the means of the offender, giving him or his representative the opportunity to be heard.

The Magistrates' Association Sentencing Guidelines (2000) set out guidelines in relation to suggested amounts of compensation for specific injuries. It is up to the court to decide what use to make of them (see *R v Broughton* (1986) 8 Cr App R(S) 379).

Causation

There must be a causal connection between the offence committed and the damage done or injury caused. The existence of civil liability is not a prerequisite to making an order in criminal proceedings (*R v Chappell* (1984) 6 Cr App R (S) 342). The court needs to ask itself whether loss or damage can fairly be said to have resulted to anyone from the offence (*R v Rowiston* (1982) 4 Cr App R (S) 85, and see *R v Taylor* (1994) 14 Cr App R (S) 276; *R v Guertjens* (1992) 14 Cr App R (S) 280; *R v Denness* [1996] 1 Cr App R(S) 15).

Real issue as to liability

Where there is a real issue as to the offender's liability to pay compensation, whether in respect of specific offences or specific victims, the question cannot be determined by argument, and the court will need to hear evidence. It is for the prosecutor to put forward evidence, so that the offender may have an opportunity to test the basis on which the order is to be made (*R v Horsham JJ, ex p Richards* [1985] 2 All ER 1114, *R v Halliwell* (1991) 12 Cr App R (S) 692).

There are cases in which the issue may be unclear, as where, eg:

(1) up-to-date medical reports, photographs, etc, need to be provided (*R v Cooper* (1982) 4 Cr App R (S) 55);

(2) questions of loss of use arise, which in civil cases are 'notoriously open to argument' (*R v Donovan* (1981) 3 Cr App R (S) 192); or

(3) matters of set-off and contribution arise, as in social security benefit frauds (*Hyde v Emery* (1984) 6 Cr App R (S) 206).

Such cases should generally be left to the civil courts or the executive to deal with.

A compensation order is not intended to be a precise evaluation of loss, such as takes place in a civil court when damages are awarded. The:

(a) power to award compensation is a fairly blunt instrument; and

(b) remedy for the victim is intended to be speedy, efficacious and cost-free

(*R v Williams* [2001] 1 Cr App R(S) 500).

Offences taken into consideration; specimen charges

Compensation may be ordered in respect of offences taken into consideration on sentence (see TICs) but the amount ordered in respect of those offences must not exceed: PCC(S)A 2000, s 131

(1) the amounts, or total amount, which is the maximum for the offence(s) of which the offender has been convicted; and

(2) the amount, or total amounts, which are in fact ordered to be paid in respect of that offence or those offences.

The fact that an offender freely admits to having made away with a certain sum does not alter the position, and does not, without the proper procedure being followed (see TICs), mean that those offences are being taken into consideration for that purpose (*R v Hose* [1995] Crim LR 259, applying *DPP v Anderson* [1978] 2 All ER 512).

Damage: Theft Act cases

In the case of an offence under TA 1968, where the property is recovered, any damage to it occurring while it was out of the owner's possession is to be PCC(S)A 2000, s 130(5) treated as having resulted from the offence, however and by whomsoever it was caused. If such property is not recovered, the presumption does not apply (*R v Ahmad* (1992) Cr App R (S) 212).

In a case of dishonest handling, where the goods are recovered, no order may be made in respect of their permanent loss (*R v Tyce* (1994) 15 Cr App R (S) 415).

Road accidents

PCC(S)A 2000, s 130(6)(7)(8)

An order may only be made in respect of injury or loss or damage (other than that suffered by a person's dependants in consequence of his death) which was due to an accident arising out of the presence of a motor vehicle on a road, if:

(1) it is in respect of damage which is treated under s 130(5) as resulting from an offence under the TA 1968; or

(2) it is in respect of injury, loss or damage for which:
   (a) the offender is uninsured in relation to the use of the vehicle (see *McDermott v DPP* [1997] RTR 474); and
   (b) compensation is not payable under any arrangements to which the Secretary of State is a party.

PCC(S)A 2000, s 130(9)(10)

Where an order is made in respect of such injury, loss or damage, the amount to be paid may include an amount representing the whole or part of any loss of, or reduction in, preferential rates of insurance attributable to the accident.

Where sums are payable by the Motor Insurers' Bureau (MIB), the compensation is limited to the amount payable by the MIB, namely £175 (*DPP v Scott* [1995] Crim LR 91).

A vehicle exempted from insurance under RTA 1988, s 144, is not 'uninsured' for this purpose, nor is a driver uninsured who merely refuses to produce details, but is, in fact, covered (*McDermott v DPP* (*above*)).

Funeral expenses

Where an order is made in respect of funeral expenses, it may be made for the benefit of anyone who incurred the expense, but an order in respect of bereavement may be made only for the benefit of a person for whose benefit a claim for damages for bereavement could be made under FAA 1976, s 1A.

The amount of compensation must not exceed that specified in s 1A(3), namely, £3,500.

Criminal Injuries Compensation Board

HO 1990

Compensation ordered by a criminal court is completely different from the compensation which victims of crime may receive from the Criminal Injuries Compensation Board under CJA 1988, Pt VII. Victims may apply to the

Board and receive compensation whether or not the offender is detected or convicted. No award is made unless the appropriate amount exceeds £1,000.

The fact that the victim may be able to get compensation from the Board should not prevent the court making an order in a proper case. Guidelines have been prepared by the Board on the range of compensation which might be payable, and are attached to Home Office Circular 85/1988, but these have not been approved by the Lord Chief Justice.

The amount of compensation payable

The court has power to order compensation up to a maximum of £5,000 for each offence. The precise extent of the injury, loss or damage does not need to be established by evidence, but:

(1) there should be some basis of evidence on which the court can consider what sum is appropriate;

(2) the amount of the compensation must be such as the court considers appropriate having regard to the evidence, and to any representation made by or on behalf of the offender or the prosecutor; and PCC(S)A 2000, s 130(4)

(3) the amount ought, in general, to be limited to the court's assessment of the amount that might have been recovered in a civil action (*R v Gateway Foodmarkets Ltd* [1997] 3 All ER 78).

A sum may be added by way of interest equivalent to what the victim would be likely to recover if he proved his claim in the civil courts (*R v Schofield* [1978] 2 All ER 705).

Where no sufficient information is available, or the evidence is unclear, the court may adjourn until that information is to hand.

Offender's means

Once the court is satisfied that injury, loss or damage of a certain amount has resulted, it is required to consider the means of the offender before deciding what sum is appropriate.

The policy of making a compensation order is subject to:

(1) the overriding limitations of PCC(S)A 2000, s 130(11) which requires the court to have regard to the means of the offender, in so far as they are known to the court, both in deciding *whether* to make an order, and in determining the amount; and

(2) the principle set out in *R v Webb* (1979) 1 Cr App R (S) 16 that an order should not be made in such an amount that the offender will have no prospect of paying it within the foreseeable future (*R v Bradburn* [1973] Crim LR 705; *R v Olliver & Olliver* [1989] Crim LR 387; *R v Yehou* [1997] 2 Cr App R (S) 48).

Offender's duty to put information before court

It is the offender's duty to put information as to his means before the court. Difficulties can be avoided:

(1) if the court indicates a provisional figure, and asks the accused's representative to provide information as to the offender's means (*R v Phillips* [1989] Crim LR 160);

(2) if his representatives carry out their duty to verify the accuracy of any information (*R v Roberts* (1987) 9 Cr App R(S) 275);

PCC(S)A 2000, s 126(1)(3)(4)

(3) before sentence, the court makes a a financial circumstances order requiring the offender to give a formal statement of his financial circumstances.

Any attempt to mislead entitles the court to infer that he has assets (*R v Bolden* (1987) 9 Cr App R (S) 83) and if he fraudulently claims to have the means to pay, he has only himself to blame if an order is made (*R v Dando* [1995] Crim LR 750).

Where the offender gives no evidence on the matter, and explanations given through his representative are 'utterly unconvincing', the court is entitled to act on the basis of any material put before it by the prosecutor, drawing appropriate inferences (*R v Maisey* & *Houghton* [2001] 1 Cr App R(S) 327).

Failure to comply with a financial circumstances order is an offence punishable with a fine on level 3 of the standard scale.

Offender without means

Where an offender is clearly without means, a compensation order should not be made on the basis of:

(1) a promise to pay; or

(2) offers by friends and relatives to pay (*R v Hunt* [1983] Crim LR 250; *R v Webb & Davis* [1979] Crim LR 466); or

(3) the proposed future sale of the matrimonial home (*R v Harrison* (1980) 2 Cr App R (S) 313; *R v Blackmore* (1984) 6 Cr App R (S) 244; *R v Butt* (1986) 8 Cr App R (S) 216; *R v Hackett* (1988) l0 Cr App R (S) 388), but

it is not unreasonable to require the offender to sell other items of property to enable him to pay the compensation (*R v Workman* (1979) 1 Cr App R (S) 335), provided the court takes steps to ascertain their value (*R v Chambers* (1981) 3 Cr App R (S) 318).

Offender sentenced to custodial sentence

If a victim is entitled to compensation, an order obviates the necessity for civil proceedings. There is no principle that an order should *not* be made against a person upon whom a custodial sentence is imposed, provided that the court bears in mind that:

(1) a custodial sentence will deprive the offender of his earning power; and

(2) it may make it difficult for him to find work when he is released; and

(3) by the time he comes out he may be in financial difficulty.

But if the offender has sufficient assets, or will have earning capacity upon his release it will often be appropriate to make an order in such a case (*R v Love* [1999] 1 Cr App R (S) 75; *R v Jorge* [1999] 2 Cr App R(S) 1).

Compensation preferred to fine

Where the court considers it appropriate both: PCC(S)A 2000, s 130(12)

(1) to impose a fine; and

(2) to make a compensation order; but

(3) the offender has insufficient means to satisfy both an appropriate fine and appropriate compensation,

preference must be given to compensation, although a fine may be imposed as well.

Payment by parent or guardian

Where the offender is a juvenile, the court *must* order his parent or guardian to pay the order, unless he is satisfied that: PCC(S)A 2000, s 137

(1) the parent or guardian cannot be found; or

(2) it would be unreasonable to so order, having regard to the circumstances of the case.

Where the offender has reached the age of 16, this provision has effect as if, instead of imposing a duty on a parent or guardian to pay, it confers a power on the court to make an order. In such a procedure it is the parent or guardian's means which need to be taken into account, not those of the juvenile.

Form of order: (1) joint orders

Where an offender is convicted of a number of offences, and:

(1) a number of different victims are involved, a separate order must be made in respect of each offence, in respect of each amount (*R v Oddy* [1974] 2 All ER 666; *R v Inwood* (1974) 60 Cr App R 70);

(2) there is only one victim, but several offences, one compendious order covering all the amounts, while not desirable, is not objectionable (*R v Wharton* [1976] Crim LR 320);

(3) the offender's means are insufficient to meet claims by a number of victims, the amount of any compensation ordered should generally be

apportioned *pro rata* among them, but there may be cases where there are good reasons for departing from this general rule (*R v Amey* [1983] 1 All ER 865).

It is technically permissible, though undesirable, to make a joint order against two or more offenders; a separate order should be made in respect of each offender.

Form of order: (2) joint orders; several offenders

An order is not an additional penalty; an order may be made against one or more co-offenders who have assets, and yet not against a third who has none (*R v Love* [1999] 1 Cr App R (S) 75).

Where two or more offenders are charged jointly and one claimant establishes a claim against them with regard to one item, each ought, in general, to be ordered to pay in equal proportions, unless one of them is shown to be more directly responsible for the offence, or their ability to pay is markedly different (*R v Grundy* [1974] 1 All ER 292).

Order made on appeal

PCC(S)A 2000, s 135

An order made on appeal from a magistrates' court is deemed to have been made by that court.

Enforcement of orders

In general, compensation is treated in the same way, for the purposes of enforcement, as a fine (see FINES AND ENFORCEMENT), save that the court has no power to remit payment of compensation.

As with fines and other money payments due to the court, there is power to allow time for payment, or to order payment by instalments.

The superior courts have said that:

(1) an order ought to be sharp in its effect and not protracted by small amounts over a long period (*R v Bradburn* (1973) 57 Cr App R 948; *R v Daly* [1974] 1 All ER 290);

(2) where the offender is sentenced at the same time to a custodial term, the court should direct the first of any instalments to be paid within a specified time of his release (*R v Bradburn* (*above*)).

Despite a number of decisions to the contrary, the Court of Appeal said in *R v Olliver* [1989] Crim LR 387, that there is no reason in principle why an order to pay a fine by instalments should not extend beyond a period of 12 months, even to a period of two or three years.

Payment under order

PCC(S)A 2000, s 132(1)(3)(5)

The person in whose favour a compensation order is made is not entitled to receive any sum(s) due to him until the possibility of an appeal on which the order could be varied or set aside, ie the 21 days under the rules, has expired; the power of the Crown Court to give leave to appeal out of time is to be disregarded.

Where an order is made in respect of an offence taken into consideration on sentence, that order ceases to have effect if the offender successfully appeals against his conviction for the substantive offence(s), or if the CACD annuls the order.

An offender may appeal against an order as if it were part of the sentence imposed in respect of the offence(s) of which he was convicted.

Compensation out of forfeited property

Where the court makes an order under PCC(S)A 2000, s 143 (see FORFEITURE, CONFISCATION AND RESTITUTION) in a case where: PCC(S)A 2000, s 145

(1) the offender has been convicted of an offence which has resulted in a person suffering personal injury, loss or damage; or

(2) any such offence is taken into consideration on sentence; and

(3) the court is satisfied that, but for the inadequacy of the offender's means, it would have made a compensation order under which he would have been required to pay compensation of an amount not less than a specified amount,

it may also order that any proceeds which arise from the disposal of the property, and which do not exceed the sum specified, be paid to that person.

Such an order will not be effective:

(a) before the expiration of six months from the date on which the forfeiture order was made; or

(b) if a successful application is made under s 1(1) of the Police (Property) Act 1897.

Review of order

At any time before the offender has paid into court the whole amount of any order made, and once there is no further possibility of an appeal, the court responsible for enforcing the order may, on the application of the offender, either discharge or reduce the amount remaining to be paid under the order if it appears that: PCC(S)A 2000, s 133

(1) the injury, loss or damage in respect of which it was made has been held in civil proceedings to be less than it was taken to be for the purposes of the order; or

(2) where the order is in respect of the loss of property, the property has been recovered by the victim; or

(3) the offender's means are insufficient to satisfy in full the compensation order and any confiscation order made in the same proceedings; or

(4) the offender has suffered a substantial reduction in his means which was not anticipated at the time the order was made, and that they are unlikely to increase for a considerable period (*R v Palmer* (1994) 15 Cr App R (S) 550),

and, where an order was made by the Crown Court, provided the consent of the Crown Court has been obtained.

CONTEMPT OF COURT

The court is not required to tolerate disturbance, interruption or obstruction of its proceedings by dissident members of the public, the accused, his relatives and 'supporters' club', and it may also take steps to punish disobedience to its orders.

A person who wilfully insults the magistrate or magistrates, any witness before, or officer of, the court, during his or their sitting or attendance in court, or in going to or returning from the court, or wilfully interrupts the proceedings of the court, or otherwise misbehaves in court, commits an offence and is liable to be committed to prison for a specified period, not exceeding one month, or a fine not exceeding level 4 on the standard scale. CCA 1981, s 12(1)(23)

Contempt in the face of the court

The modern practice to be followed in such cases is set out in *Practice Note Contempt of court: magistrates' court*) [2001] 3 All ER 94. The *Practice Note* points out that exceptional situations require exceptional treatment and while its terms ought to be followed in the generality of situations, there will be a minority of occasions where its application will not be consistent with achieving justice in the special circumstances of the particular case, and compliance should be modified as is necessary.

The court has power:

(1) to detain a person, whether the accused or some other person present in court, who willfully insults or interrupts the proceedings, or otherwise misbehaves in court (see *Bodden v MPC* [1989] 3 All ER 833; *R v Powell* (1993) *The Times*, 3 June; a threat to a witness does not amount to an insult for the purposes of this paragraph – *R v Havant JJ ex p Palmer* [1985] Crim LR 658), until the court rises: CCA 1981, s 12(1)(2)

(a) this power may be exercised to stop disruption of the proceedings, indeed detention is until the person may be conveniently dealt with without disruption of the proceedings – prior to exercising its power the offender should be warned to desist or face the prospect of being detained;

(b) in such a case the court may order any officer of the court, or a constable to take the offender into custody and detain him until the court rises; the court may, if it thinks fit, commit the offender to prison for a specified period, not exceeding one month, or impose a fine not exceeding level 4 on the standard scale;

MCA 1980, s 97

(2) to commit to custody any person attending or brought before the court who refuses without just excuse to be sworn or to give evidence, or to produce any document or thing, until the expiration of such period not exceeding one month as may be specified in the warrant or until he sooner complies, or impose upon him a fine not exceeding £2,500, or both.

In the exercise of the above power:

(a) as soon as possible, and in any event prior to an offender being proceeded against, he should be told in clear terms the conduct which is alleged to constitute his offending; and

(b) when making an order under s 12, the magistrates should state their finding as to the contempt.

In the case of an offence under s 97, unless there is good reason for dealing with the matter speedily, sentence should be adjourned to the last practicable moment (*R v Moran* (1985) 81 Cr App Rep 81; *R v Lewis* (1993) 96 Cr App R 412; *R v Montgomery* [1995] 2 All ER 28) so that the witness has a chance to reconsider his position.

It is desirable that such a person should be given the opportunity of seeking representation, although the restrictions on imposing imprisonment on an unrepresented accused do not strictly apply.

Approach to order

The court must act reasonably in committing a person to custody for contempt and must take care not to use the proverbial sledgehammer to crack what is only, after all, a nut (*R v Tamworth JJ, ex* p *Walsh* (1994) *The Times,* 3 March). Thus:

(1) in the case of a person who wilfully insults the court or interrupts proceedings, if he expresses a willingness to apologise for his misconduct, he may be brought back before the court at the earliest convenient moment in order to make the apology and to give undertakings to the court to refrain from further misbehaviour;

(2) in the majority of cases an apology and an undertaking as to future conduct should be sufficient for the court to order the offender's release; however

(3) there will be cases where the nature and seriousness of the misconduct require the court to consider exercising its powers under CCA 1981, s 12(2) to fine or order, in the case of an offender aged 18 or over, the offender's committal to custody.

Offender detained for contempt

A person detained under the provisions of either CCA 1981, s 12 or MCA 1980, s 97 should:

(1) be seen by the duty solicitor or another legal representative and be represented in the proceedings should he wish;

(2) generally be granted a representation order, and must be afforded adequate time and facilities to prepare his case;

(3) have the issue resolved on the same day if at all possible; and

(4) be brought back before the court before the magistrates conclude the business of the day.

The court should ensure that the offender understands the nature of the proceedings, including his opportunity to apologise, and in the case of an offence under s 97, to give evidence, and the alternative of its exercising its powers. Having heard from the offender's representative, the court should decide whether to take further action.

Legal representation, may, exceptionally, consist of counsel only, and any solicitor or counsel within the precincts of the court may be assigned. CCA 1981, s 12(5)

Contempt admitted

Where the offence of contempt is admitted, the court needs to decide whether it is able to proceed on the day, or whether to adjourn to allow for further reflection. If at all possible the matter ought to be dealt with on the same day, and if the matter is adjourned the offender ought ordinarily to be granted bail unless one or more of the exceptions to the right to bail (see BAIL) are made out.

When the magistrates come to sentence the offender:

(1) if his conduct was directed against them, it will not be appropriate for the same magistrates to deal with the matter; if his conduct was not directed to them it might be in order for the same magistrates to deal with him;

(2) the magistrates should ask the offender whether he has any objection to that bench dealing with him;

(3) if there is any objection to those magistrates dealing with him, a differently constituted bench should hear the proceedings.

The court dealing with the offender should then consider, taking into account any time spent on remand, and his admission of contempt, if any, and the nature and seriousness of that contempt, whether:

(a) an order for his discharge is appropriate; or

(b) in the case of an offender aged 18 or over, he should be committed, any order of committal being for the shortest period of time commensurate with the interests of preserving good order in the administration of justice.

Contempt not admitted

Where the contempt is not admitted, the magistrates' powers are limited to making arrangements for a trial to take place. They should not at that stage make findings against the offender.

In the case of a contested contempt, the trial should take place at the earliest opportunity and should be before a bench other than those magistrates before whom the alleged contempt took place.

Note that:

(1) Where possible the trial should take place on the same day (taking into account the accused's rights under ECHR Art 6);

(2) if the trial cannot take place that day, the accused should be bailed unless there are grounds under BA 1976 for remanding him in custody;

(3) at his trial the accused is entitled to call and examine witnesses where such evidence is relevant.

If the accused is found to have committed the contempt the court should again:

(a) consider whether an order for his discharge from custody is sufficient to bring proceedings to an end;

(b) allow the offender a further opportunity to apologise for his contempt or to make representations; but

if of the view, in the case of an offender aged 18 or over, that they must exercise their powers to commit to custody under CCA 1981, s 12, must take into account any time spent on remand and the nature and seriousness of the contempt before committing him for the shortest period of time commensurate with the interests of preserving good order in the administration of justice.

Strictly, a committal order under s 12(2) does not involve a 'conviction' (*R v Newberry JJ, ex p Du Pont* (1984) 148 JP 248); restrictions on the power to impose a custodial sentence on a person not legally represented do not therefore apply; nor is there any power to pass a community sentence (see *R v Palmer* [1992] 3 All ER 289).

CCA 1981, s 12(4) The court may (under (3) *above*) at any time revoke the order for committal and, if the offender is in custody, order his discharge.

Offenders aged under 18

In the case of an offender aged under 18, the general restrictions on committing persons to prison apply (*R v Selby JJ, ex p Frame* [1991] 2 All ER 344) and the power to deal with contemnors aged under 18 is very limited (*R v Byas* [1995] Crim LR 439).

Disobeying court orders

A person who disobeys the order of the court to do anything other than the payment of money, or to abstain from doing something, may be ordered to pay a sum not exceeding £50 for every day in which he is in default, or a sum not exceeding £5,000, or may be committed to custody until he has remedied his default, or for a period not exceeding two months. MCA 1980, s 63(3)

Restrictions on reporting

Where it appears necessary for avoiding a substantial risk of prejudice to the administration of justice in proceedings held in public, or any other proceedings pending or imminent, the court may order that the publication of any report of those proceedings or any part of them be postponed for such period as it thinks necessary for the purpose. CCA 1981, s 4(12)(2)

The court may also prohibit the publication of any name or other matter in connection with the proceedings before it which it has allowed to be withheld from the public. A number of points may be made (*Practice Direction (criminal: consolidated)* [2002] 3 All ER 904, para 3): CCA 1981, s 11

(1) when considering whether to make such an order there is nothing which precludes the court from hearing a representative of the press; indeed it is likely that the court will wish to do so;

(2) it is necessary to keep a permanent record of such orders for later reference;

(3) all orders made under s 4(2) must be formulated in precise terms having regard to the decision in *R v Horsham JJ, ex p Farquharson* [1983] 1 All ER 745 and orders under both sections must be committed to writing by the clerk under the court's directions;

(4) an order must state:
    (a) its precise scope,
    (b) the time at which it shall cease to have effect, if appropriate, and
    (c) the specific purpose of making the order.

The court will normally give notice to the press in some form that an order has been made under either section of the 1981 Act and the court staff should be prepared to answer any enquiry about a specific case, but it is, and will remain, the responsibility of those reporting cases, and their editors, to ensure that no breach of any orders occurs and the onus rests on them to make enquiry in any case of doubt (see further SUMMARY TRIAL, YOUTH COURT).

Tape recorders, photographs, sketches in court

CCA 1981, s 9(1)(2)(3)

It is a contempt of court to use in, or bring into court for use, any tape recorder or other instrument for recording sound, except with the leave of the court or to publish or dispose of a recording with a view to publication, or to use a recording in contravention of any leave granted.

The discretion to grant, withhold or withdraw leave or to impose conditions on their use, is unlimited. The High Court has suggested that the following factors may be relevant (*Practice Direction* [1981] 3 All ER 848):

(1) the existence of a reasonable need on the part of the applicant, whether a litigant or a person connected with the media, for the recording to be made;

(2) in a criminal case, the risk that the recording may be used to 'brief' witnesses out of court;

(3) the possibility that use of the instrument will disturb or worry witnesses or other participants.

Consideration should always be given to the imposition of conditions, should leave be granted.

CJA 1925, s 41

No person may take, or attempt to take, a photograph or make, or attempt to make any portrait or sketch, of a magistrate or party or witness to proceedings in a courtroom or in a court building or precincts or entering or leaving them.

Publication of matters exempted

CCA 1981, s 11

Where the court permits a name or other matter to be withheld from the public in proceedings before them, which should be a very rare occurrence (*R v Malvern JJ, ex p Evans* [1988] 1 All ER 371) they may give such directions prohibiting publication of that matter as appear to be necessary for the purpose for which the material was withheld (*R v Malvern JJ, ex p Evans* (*above*); *R v Evesham JJ, ex p McDonagh* [1988] 1 All ER 371; *R v Dover JJ, ex p Dover CC etc* [1992] Crim LR 371).

Note that:

(1) an application to prohibit the publication of an address should generally be heard *in camera* (*R v Tower Bridge MC, ex p Osborne* [1988] Crim LR 382);

(2) if a name or other material has already been mentioned in open court before an application is made to withhold publication, there is no power to prohibit disclosure (*R v Arundel JJ, ex p Westminster Press Ltd* [1985] 2 All ER 390).

COSTS

In a proper case the court may award costs. Whether to award costs is a matter within the discretion of the court in the light of the circumstances of the particular case. An award of costs:

(1) is intended as an indemnity and is not to be imposed as a penalty in the guise of costs (*R v Highgate JJ, ex p Petrou* [1954] 1 All ER 406);

(2) may be made to achieve a compensatory or a disciplinary purpose; and may be made to penalise inefficiency and incompetence;

(3) is not confined to actual expenses and disbursements properly incurred, but may extend to loss of time, and labour (*R v Burt, ex p Presburg* [1960] 1 All ER 424).

If the court awards an excessive amount, or takes into account irrelevant factors, the order may be quashed on judicial review (*R v Tottenham JJ, ex p Joshi* [1982] 2 All ER 507).

Power to award costs

The powers enabling a magistrates' court to award costs in criminal proceedings are primarily contained in POA 1985, Pt 11 (ss 16–21) and the regulations made under ss 19, 19A and 20 of that Act, ie the Costs in Criminal Cases (General) Regulations 1986 (SI 1986 No 1335 as amended by SI 1991 No 789). See also *Practice Note* (*criminal law: costs*) [1991] 2 All ER 924.

It must be remembered that:

(1) costs payable out of central funds and the costs of representation from public funding, are payable out of central government funds;

(2) unless an order is made under POA 1985, s 17, the costs of a private prosecutor fall on him;

(3) the costs of representation from public funding belong to the solicitor and counsel appearing under the representation order and do not cover the personal expenses of an acquitted accused;

(4) a 'defendant's costs order' (see s 16 *below*) in favour of a person represented from public funds does not include either the costs payable pursuant to the representation order or any contribution which the represented person might be liable to pay, and covers only travel and subsistence (but not loss of earnings) reasonably incurred by the accused personally.

An award of costs may be made out of central funds, or between party and party.

Costs from central funds: (1) extent

POA 1985, ss 16(7)(10), 17

Where the court orders that the costs of an accused or of a private prosecutor be paid from central funds:

(1) the order will be for such amount as the court considers reasonably sufficient to compensate the party for expenses incurred by him in the proceedings; but

(2) it will not include expenses incurred which do not directly relate to the proceedings themselves, such as loss of earnings; but

(3) may include expenses and disbursements incurred by him as a litigant (*R v Bedlington MC, ex p Wilkinson* (1999) 164 JP 156).

POA 1985, s 21(4A)(a)

Where the party in whose favour the order is made is assisted from public funding he will recover only his personal costs (see also *R v Liverpool CC, ex p The Lord Chancellor* (1993) 158 JP 821).

As to availability in the magistrates' court see the Table *below*.

Proceedings	To whom	Authority
Information not proceeded with*	Accused	POA 1985, s 16(1)(a)
Dismissal of information	Accused	POA 1985, s 16(1)(c)
Decision not to commit for trial	Accused	POA 1985, s 16(1)(b)
Proceedings in respect of indictable offence	Private prosecutor	POA 1985, s 17(1)(a)
Criminal cause or matter	Defence or private prosecution witnesses; interpreter; medical practitioner	POA 1985, s 19(3); see CC(G)R 1986
Cross-examination of vulnerable witness	Person appointed to cross-examine witness for the defence	POA 1985, s 19(3)(e)
Compensation where court refuses application for a football banning order (limited to £5,000)	Person against whom a banning notice has been given	FSA 1989; FDA 2000, Sched 1

* Includes cases which are discontinued (*DPP v Denning* [1991] 3 All ER 439).

Costs from central funds: (2) amount to be paid

POA 1985, ss 16(7)

Except where the court directs in an order for costs from central funds that only a specified sum be paid, the amount of costs to be paid is determined by the appropriate officer of the court, in which case:

(1) where the court considers it appropriate, and the person in whose favour the order is made consents, it may be specified; or

(2) in any other case, it will be determined by way of taxation by the appropriate officer, in accordance with the regulations.

The court may, however:

(a) order the disallowance of costs out of central funds not properly incurred;
(b) direct the appropriate officer to consider whether or not specified items have been properly incurred; and may
(c) make observations regarding public defence costs (for the procedure see *below*).

Where the court orders:

(i) an offender to pay costs to the prosecutor;
(ii) one party to pay costs to another;
(iii) a disallowance of, or orders a legal or other representative to meet, wasted costs,

the order for costs must specify the sum to be paid or disallowed. There is no power to award interest (*Westminster City Council v Wilgrove* [1991] 4 All ER 691).

There is nothing wrong in principle in ordering an offender to pay costs in an amount substantially in excess of any fine imposed, provided it is not grossly disproportionate, and it is for him to place before the court any appropriate information about his means (*R v Boyle* [1995] Crim LR 514).

Where the court is required to specify the amount of costs to be paid, the decision cannot be delegated. Wherever possible solicitors should provide details of costs incurred at each stage of the proceedings and the court may require the appropriate officer to make enquiries and inform the court of the costs incurred, and may adjourn, if necessary, for enquiries to be made.

Costs from central funds: (3) defence costs

Where:

POA 1985, s 16(1)

(1) an information laid before a magistrate charging a person with an offence is not proceeded with (this includes a situation where there is no jurisdiction to proceed because the information is laid outside the time limits prescribed by MCA 1980, s 127(1) (*Patel & Patel v Blakey* [1987] Crim LR 683) and cases which are discontinued (*DPP v Denning* [1991] 3 All ER 439); or
(2) a court enquiring into an either way offence determines not to commit the accused for trial in the Crown Court; or
(3) a court dealing summarily with an offence dismisses the information,

the court, or another magistrates' court subsequently dealing with the accused (*R v Liverpool MC, ex p Abiaka* (1999) 163 JP 497), may make a 'defendant's costs order'. 'Accused' may include the parent or guardian of a juvenile (CYPA 1933, s 55) and therefore, in appropriate circumstances (see p 250–251), a local authority (*R v Preston CC, ex p Lancashire CC* [1998]

3 All ER 765). An order for costs cannot be made in respect of a person who has been granted a legal representation order save for costs incurred before the grant of the order or travel and subsistence costs.

JCR 1999, Schedule

The Clerk has the power to make an order for the payment of defence costs out of central funds.

CCCGR reg 14(4)

An order may also be made in relation to breach of binding over proceedings in a magistrates' court.

Such an order should normally be made, whether or not an order for costs between parties is also made, unless there are positive reasons for not doing so.

Examples of such reasons might be:

(a) the accused's own conduct has brought suspicion on himself and has misled the prosecution into thinking that the case against him is stronger than it is;

(b) there is ample evidence to support a conviction, but the accused is acquitted on a technicality which has no merit.

On an application for a defendant's costs order, the court may rely on information from the prosecution in considering whether the accused has brought the prosecution on himself, but in order to justify refusing an order, that information must contain independent evidence supporting the truth of the allegation (*Mooney v Cardiff MC* (1999) 164 JP 220).

In the case of a person convicted of some charges but acquitted of others, the court may exercise its discretion to make an order, but may order only part of the costs incurred to be paid. Where the court considers it inappropriate that the accused recover all of the costs properly incurred, the amount must be specified in the order.

Note also that:

(i) expenses incurred by a person who is represented on public funds are to be disregarded (sums due to the Criminal Defence Service or the Lord Chancellor, are recoverable from the accused);

(ii) an accused who is a solicitor is entitled, under POA 1985, s 16(6), to compensation in respect of fees which he would otherwise have been earning on behalf of his firm, in addition to expenses actually incurred in carrying on his defence (*R v Stafford etc MC, ex p Robinson* [1988] 1 All ER 430). This is not the case with other professional persons (see *R v Stockport MC, ex p Cooper* [1984] Crim LR 233).

Costs from central funds: (4) costs of private prosecutor

The court has power in any proceedings in respect of an *indictable* offence to order payment out of central funds of such amount as it considers reasonable to compensate the prosecutor for any expenses properly incurred by him in the proceedings, but:

(1) there is no power to order the payment out of central funds of the costs of any prosecutor who is a public authority, a person acting on behalf of a public authority or acting as an official appointed by a public authority as defined in the Act; POA 1985, s 17(1)(a), (2)

(2) a 'public authority' is defined to include, amongst other bodies, the police, the CPS or any other government department and a local authority; POA 1985, s 17(6)

(3) where the conduct of the proceedings to which the costs out of central funds apply is taken over by the Crown Prosecution Service, the prosecutor who had the conduct of the proceedings before the intervention of the Service may be awarded costs in respect of the expenses incurred up to that time. POA 1985, s 17(5)

Costs from central funds: (5) approach to order

In the limited number of cases in which a prosecutor may be awarded costs out of central funds:

(1) an application must be made by the prosecution in each case; and

(2) an order should be made, save where there is good reason for not doing so, as where proceedings have been instituted or continued without good cause (see *Mooney v Cardiff MC* (1999) 164 JP 220) .

It has been said that, unless the prosecutor has misconducted himself, he ought to have his costs out of central funds where the charge is of a serious nature, even though the amount involved is trivial (*R v Esher JJ, ex p Victor Value & Co Ltd* (1967) 111 SJ 473; *R v Redbridge JJ, ex p Redbridge LBC* [1982] 3 All ER 1152). A local rule that 'it is not the practice of this court' eg to award costs in cases of shoplifting, is not an exercise of judicial discretion (*R v Lytham JJ, ex p Carter* (1975) 119 SJ 341).

Where the court makes an order, but considers that it is inappropriate that the prosecutor should recover the full amount, it may assess what amount would, in the circumstances, be just and reasonable, and specify that amount in the order. POA 1985, s 17(3)

The appropriate officer will:

(a) determine under reg 17(1)(a) whether work has been actually and properly done; and then

(b) consider what amount is reasonably sufficient to compensate the applicant for his expenses and disbursements

(*R v Leeds MC, ex p Castle* [1991] Crim LR 771.)

The amount must:

(i) be specified where the court considers it appropriate and the person in whose favour it is made agrees; or

(ii) in any other case, be determined in accordance with regulations.

Costs of witness, interpreter or medical evidence

The costs of:

(1) the attendance of a witness required by the accused, a private prosecutor or the court; or

(2) the attendance of an interpreter required because of the accused's lack of English; or

(3) compensating a duly qualified medical practitioner for the expenses properly incurred in, or incidental to, making a report:
   (a) in writing, to the court in pursuance of a request to which CJA 1967, s 32(2) (report on medical condition of offender) applies; or
   (b) otherwise than in writing, for the purposes of PCC(S)A 2000, s 11 (remand for medical examination),

are allowed out of central funds unless the court otherwise directs.

POA 1985, s 23; CC(G)R 1986, reg 16(1)

If, and only if, the court makes such a direction, the expenses of the witness may be claimed as a disbursement out of public defence funding.

A 'witness' includes any person properly attending to give evidence whether or not he gives evidence or is called, but it does not include a character witness unless the court has certified that the interests of justice so require.

Disallowance of costs out of central funds

Where the court makes an order for costs out of central funds:

(1) it *must* direct the appropriate authority to disallow the costs incurred in respect of any items if it is plain that those costs were not properly incurred; such costs are not payable under POA 1985, ss 16(6) and 17(1);

(2) it *may* direct the appropriate authority to consider or investigate on taxation any items which may not have been properly incurred.

'Costs not properly incurred'

'Costs not properly incurred' include costs in respect of work unreasonably done, eg if the case has been conducted unreasonably so as to incur unjustified expense, or costs have been wasted by failure to conduct proceedings with reasonable competence and expedition. In a plain case it will usually be more appropriate to make a 'wasted costs order' under s 19A (see *below*). The precise terms of the order for costs and of any direction must be entered on the court record. As to guidelines, see *Re a Barrister* (*Wasted Costs Order*) (*No 1 of 1991*) [1992] All ER 429.

The word 'improper' in s 19 of the Act and reg 3(1) does not denote some grave impropriety but is intended to cover an act or omission which would not have occurred if the party concerned had conducted his case properly (*DPP v Denning* [1991] 3 All ER 439).

Where the court has in mind that a direction in accordance with (1) or (2) under the heading '**Disallowance of costs out of central funds**' *above* might be given:

(a) it must inform any party whose costs might be affected, or his legal representative of its precise terms;

(b) in the case of a direction under (1) *above,* must give a reasonable opportunity to show cause why no direction should be given; and

(c) in the case of a direction under (2) *above,* should inform the party concerned of his rights to make representations to the appropriate authority

(see *R v Associated Octel Press* [1997] Crim LR 144).

This should normally be done in private at such time as the court thinks proper, though if the court decides to give a direction it may announce the decision in open court if it is of the opinion that it is in the interests of justice to do so.

The appropriate authority may consult the court on any matter touching the allowance or disallowance of costs. It is not appropriate for the court to make a direction under (1) *above* when so consulted.

Costs between parties: (1) general

A court may make an order for costs against a person convicted before it, or in dealing with a person in respect of certain orders as to sentence specified in reg 14. POA 1985, s 18(1)

It may also make such an order payable to the prosecutor, though this sum should not exceed the sum which the prosecutor has actually and reasonably incurred.

Costs between parties: (2) award against an offender

Where an offender may be said to have put the prosecutor to avoidable expense, he may be ordered to pay all or part of the sum incurred to the prosecutor; but:

(1) the offender is not to be penalised for exercising his constitutional right to defend himself;

(2) in the ordinary way, the costs should not be grossly disproportionate to any fine imposed;

(3) where the offender is under 18, the amount of any costs awarded against him must not exceed the amount of any fine imposed on him; POA 1985, s 18(5)

POA 1985, s 21(4A)(b)

(4) an order should be made where the court is satisfied that the offender or appellant has the means and ability to pay.

POA 1985, s 18(4)

Where the accused is ordered to pay a sum not exceeding £5, whether by way of fine, penalty, forfeiture or compensation, the court must not make an order for costs unless in the particular circumstances of the case it considers it right to do so.

The amount must be specified in the order. An order under s 18 includes the costs of a public defence.

Costs between parties: (3) offender's means

Costs should be awarded against an offender only *after* an enquiry into his means and as a general principle it is wrong to order an offender to pay costs of such an amount that, by reason of lack of means, he will be unable to pay within a reasonable time, and at least within 12 months (which is the period recommended by the superior courts in respect of all financial penalties) (*R v Nottingham MC, ex p Fohman* (1986) 151 JP 49; cf *R v Olliver & Olliver* [1989] Crim LR 387).

Note that:

(1) it is for the offender to disclose his means to the court (and see FINES AND ENFORCEMENT) such information as to his financial circumstances as will enable the court to assess what he can reasonably afford to pay;

(2) in the absence of such information the court is entitled to draw reasonable inferences as to his means from the evidence it has heard and from all the circumstances of the case;

(3) it is incumbent on the court to give the offender a fair opportunity to adduce any relevant financial information and to make any appropriate submissions;

(4) where the court has in mind some unusual or unconventional order potentially adverse to the offender, it must warn him and his representative of its intentions (*R v Northallerton MC, ex p Dove* [1999] Crim LR 760).

Where the offender is to serve a custodial sentence, costs should only be awarded against him if he has assets out of which the costs can be paid (*R v Baker* (1992) 14 Cr App R (S) 242).

Costs between parties: (4) cases under MCA 1980, s 12

Where an offender pleads guilty without appearing before the court in accordance with the procedure in MCA 1980, s 12 the prosecutor may claim costs provided he has notified the offender of that fact, usually by including the claim in the same document containing the statement of facts. It will be for the Clerk to bring the claim for costs to the attention of the court at the hearing (*R v Coventry MC, ex p DPP* [1990] RTR 193).

Costs between parties: (5) no award against prosecutor

There is no power, on dismissal of an information, or discharge of an accused, to order the Crown Prosecutor to pay costs; where a private prosecutor has acted spitefully, or has instituted or continued proceedings without reasonable cause, he may be ordered to pay the costs of the accused (see 'unnecessary or improper act or omission' *below*).

Unnecessary or improper act or omission

A court may order the payment of any costs incurred as a result of an unnecessary or improper act or omission by or on behalf of, any party to the proceedings as distinct from his legal representative. The court must hear the parties and may then order all or any part of the costs so incurred by one party to be paid to him by the other party. The order may be made at any time during the proceedings. POA 1985, s 19; CCC(G)R 1986

As to the meaning of 'improper' see p 161 *above*.

Before making such an order the court:

(1) must take into account any other order as to costs;
(2) must specify in the order the amount of the costs to be paid;
(3) is entitled to take such an order into account when making any other order as to costs in the proceedings. CC(G)R 1986, reg 3(2)–(4)

Note that:

(a) the order may extend to publicly funded costs incurred on behalf of any party; POA 1985, s 21(4A)(b)
(b) such an order is appropriate only where the failure is that of the accused or the prosecutor;
(c) where it is the failure of the legal representative(s), the powers of the court under s 19A (*below*) may be exercised.

Costs against legal representatives etc

The Act permits a court to disallow, or order the legal or other representative to meet the whole or any part of the wasted costs. POA 1985, s 19A

Note that:

(1) the order can be made against any person exercising a right of audience or a right to conduct litigation (in the sense of acting for a party in the proceedings);
(2) 'wasted costs' are those costs incurred by a party (which includes a party represented from public funding) as a result of any improper, POA 1985, s 19A(3)

unreasonable or negligent act or omission on the part of any representative or his employee, or which, in the light of any such act or omission occurring after they were incurred, the court considers it unreasonable to expect that party to pay.

(General guidance in the matter of wasted costs orders is given in *Ridehaigh v Horsefield* [1994] 3 All ER 848, where it was said that an order should not be made except, and to the extent, that the conduct was 'directly causative' of wasted costs.)

Procedure on wasted costs

Regulation 3B requires the court:

(1) to specify the amount of the wasted costs (see *Re a Barrister etc* [1992] 3 All ER 429); and

(2) to allow the legal or other representative and any party to the proceedings to make representations;

(3) in making the order, to take into account any other order for costs;

(4) conversely to take the wasted costs order into account when making any other order as to costs;

(5) to give reasons for making the order; and

(6) to notify any interested party (which includes the Legal Services Commission) and the appropriate officer of the determining authority, of the order and of the amount.

The court may postpone the making of an order to the end of the case if it appears more appropriate to do so, as where the likely amount is not readily available there is a possibility of conflict between legal representatives as to the apportionment of blame, or the legal representative concerned is unable to make full representations because of a possible conflict with the duty to his client.

The hearing should normally take place in private with the benefit of a note, but the court may make its order and announce its reasons for so doing in open court if it is of the opinion that it is in the interests of justice to do so. Though the court cannot delegate its decision, it may require the appropriate officer of the court to make enquiries and assess the likely amount of the costs incurred (see also *Holden & Co v CPS* [1990] 1 All ER 368, and *Practice Note* (*criminal law; costs*) (*above*).

Relevance of defence public funding

A wasted costs order should normally be made regardless of the fact that the client of the legal representative concerned is represented under public funding.

However:

(1) where the court is minded to disallow substantial public funding; and

(2) the extent and amount of the wasted costs is not clear;

it may, instead of making a wasted costs order, make observations to the determining authority that work may have been unreasonably done.

CUSTODIAL SENTENCES

Three 'custodial sentences' within the meaning of PCC(S)A 2000, s 76 are available to a magistrates' court: PCC(S)A 2000, s 76(1)(2)

(1) in the adult court, imprisonment in the case of an offender aged 21 or over (see p 176 *below*);

(2) in the adult court, detention in a young offender institution (see pp 181–183 *below*) in the case of offenders aged between 18 and 20; and

(3) in the youth court, a detention and training order for offenders aged between 12 and 17 (see pp 183–187 *below*).

In 'exceptional circumstances' a sentence of imprisonment on an adult may be suspended (see pp 177–181 *below*).

An offender's age is deemed to be that which it appears to the court to be, after considering the available evidence; it is improper for the court to adjourn after conviction for the sole purpose of allowing the offender to attain the age of 21, so that wider powers of custody may be exercised (*Arthur v Stringer* (1986) 151 JP 97).

As to detention within the precincts of the court, or at a police station, see *below*.

The adult court must, where it convicts a person under 18, remit him to a youth court for sentence unless satisfied that it can deal with him by way of: CYPA 1969, s 7(8)

(a) a referral order;

(b) an absolute or conditional discharge;

(c) a fine, or

(d) an order that a parent or guardian enter into a recognisance to take proper care of him and exercise proper control over him,

with or without any ancillary order(s) that the court has power to make when imposing an absolute or conditional discharge.

Restrictions on imposition

PCC(S)A 2000, s 76(1)(2) reserves custodial sentences for the most serious offences and restricts their imposition to cases where the offender is aged 18 or over, and:

(1) the offence(s) 'qualify' for a custodial sentence (see *below*);

(2) ordinarily, there is a pre-sentence report (see *below*); and

(3) in general, the offender is legally represented.

These restrictions do not apply to committal or attachment for contempt of court or any kindred offence, as to which see s 89(1)(a).

Pre-sentence report

PCC(S)A 2000, ss 81, 82

Before the court can impose a custodial sentence as defined in the Act, for the purpose of forming an opinion as to whether the offence(s) 'qualifies' for a custodial sentence, a written pre-sentence report must be obtained unless, in the circumstances of the case the court considers it unnecessary, and if the offender is suspected of being mentally disordered, a psychiatric report must be obtained, orally or in writing unless the court is of the opinion that it is unnecessary, and the court must consider the effect which a custodial sentence would have on the offender's mental condition and any treatment for it.

If a case needs to be adjourned for reports, a cautious bench should indicate that at that stage of the case, it is keeping all its sentencing options open, including, in the case of an either-way offence, committal to the Crown Court for sentence.

Once the court has obtained the necessary reports, it needs to consider whether the offence(s) qualify for a custodial sentence.

Legal representation

PCC(S)A 2000, s 83

The court must not pass a custodial sentence on a person who has not previously been sentenced to such a punishment unless he has had the assistance of counsel or of a solicitor to represent him in the proceedings at some time since he was found guilty and before he was sentenced, unless:

(1) having been informed of his right to apply for representation (see DEFENCE PUBLIC FUNDING) and having had the opportunity to do so, he refused or failed to apply; or

(2) he was granted a right to representation, but the right was withdrawn because of his conduct.

In such cases the offender ought to be told that the court is contemplating a custodial sentence and that he has a right to apply for representation. A breach of s 83 renders any subsequent sentence unlawful and a nullity (*R v Wilson* [1995] Crim LR 510).

Difficulties may arise where an offender 'sacks' his legal representatives between conviction and sentence. An accused granted representation has the right to be represented by solicitor and counsel of his choice who are willing to act, unless and until representation is withdrawn (*R v Harris* [1985] Crim LR 244; *R v Kirk* (1983) 76 Cr App R 194; *R v Dimech* [1991] Crim LR 846).

Qualification for custodial sentence

An offence 'qualifies' for a custodial sentence if the court is of opinion that: PCC(S)A 2000, s 79(1)(2)

(1) the offence, or the combination of the offence and one or more offences 'associated' with it, is 'so serious' that only a custodial sentence is justified for it; or

(2) if the offence is a 'violent' or 'sexual' offence, (see p 171 *below*) that only a custodial sentence would be adequate to protect the public from serious harm from the (particular) offender (*R v Jacobs & Kinsella* [1989] Crim LR 597); or

(3) the offender fails:
   (a) to express his willingness to comply with a requirement which it is proposed to include in a community rehabilitation order or a supervision order, and which requires an expression of willingness; or
   (b) to provide a sample in a drug treatment and testing order, or an order under PCC(S)A 2000, s 54(2).

The court must specifically have regard to these provisions before passing sentence, even where its attention is not drawn to them by the parties (*R v Passmore* (1985) 7 Cr App R(S) 377) and it has a duty to identify which of the statutory criteria applies (*R v Poyner* [1989] Crim LR 595).

In dealing with sentence on the breach of a former order, the fact that for the original offence only a community sentence was imposed does not prevent it qualifying for a custodial sentence, provided the offence is one which is punishable with imprisonment (*R v Bray* (1991) 12 Cr App R(S) 705, *R v Webster* (1990) 12 Cr App R(S) 760, *R v Oliver & Little* [1993] 2 All ER 9).

The court must not impose a custodial sentence merely because the offences qualify; it must still consider whether the offence is so serious that a non-custodial penalty cannot be justified and having regard to any mitigating circumstances, such a sentence remains the appropriate one.

It is wrong to impose a custodial sentence because an offender is unable to pay a substantial fine, rather than because imprisonment is merited by the offence (*R v Reeves* (1972) 56 Cr App R 366).

Spelling it out

Quite apart from any other requirements as to explaining the nature of a custodial sentence, the court *must* in passing sentence, state in open court its opinion that either (1) or (2) under the heading '**Qualification for custodial sentence**' *above* applies and why, and, in any case, must: PCC(S)A 2000, s 79(4)

(1) explain why it has come to that opinion; and

(2) explain to the offender, in ordinary language, why it is passing a custodial sentence on him.

Each offence to be considered individually

If more than one offence has been committed, each must be considered individually in determining whether an offence qualifies for a custodial sentence, and:

(1) the court must take into account aggravating and mitigating factors, such as, for example, the presence or absence of premeditation or provocation;

(2) it is not permissible to aggregate a number of minor offences to qualify an offender for a custodial sentence; though

(3) the Act allows any one or more 'associated' offences (see *below*) to be aggregated, to cover borderline cases where the instant offence may not qualify, and a community sentence is insufficient to reflect their combined seriousness.

'Associated' offences

PCC(S)A 2000, s 161(1)

An offence is 'associated' with another if the offender:

(1) is convicted of it in the proceedings in which he is convicted of the other offence, or (although convicted of it in earlier proceedings) he is sentenced for it at the same time as he is sentenced for that offence; or

(2) admits the commission of it in the proceedings in which he is sentenced for the other offence and asks the court to take it into consideration (see TICs) in sentencing him for that offence.

It follows that:

(a) an offence in respect of which a suspended sentence was passed (*R v Crawford* [1993] Crim LR 539), or a conditional discharge was made (*R v Godfrey* [1993] Crim LR 540) on a *previous occasion*; or

(b) an uncharged offence represented by a sample charge, and not taken into consideration;

(c) an order imposing 'no separate penalty' in respect of an offence for which a conditional discharge was originally ordered (*R v Godfrey* (*above*)),

is not 'associated' with the subsequent offence.

Qualification: (1) 'Seriousness'

The Act contains no definition of what a 'serious' offence is. A sensible definition is that it means the 'kind of offence which . . . would make right-thinking members of the public, knowing all the facts, feel that justice could not be done by passing any sentence other than a custodial one' (*R v Bradbourn* [1985] Crim LR 682; adopted in *R v Baverstock* [1993] Crim LR 153, *R v Cox* [1993] Crim LR 382, though this approach was deprecated in *R v Howells* [1998] Crim LR 836). The test is clearly a subjective one.

In considering the seriousness of an offence, the court:

(1) may take into account the offender's previous convictions;

(2) may take into account the prevalence of offences of a particular class and public concern about them (*R v Cunningham* [1993] Crim LR 149, *R v Cox* (*above*));

(3) *must* treat as an aggravating factor that an offence was committed on bail; PCC(S)A 2000, 151(2)

(4) *must* where the offence was racially aggravated (see RACIALLY etc AGGRAVATED OFFENCES) within the meaning of CDA 1998, s 28, treat that as a factor increasing the seriousness of the offence, and must state in open court that it was so racially aggravated.

Qualification: (2) 'sexual' and 'violent' offences

A 'sexual offence' includes: PCC(S)A 2000, s 161(2)

(1) any offence under SOA 1956 (except under ss 30, 31 or 33–36);

(2) an offence under MHA 1959, s 128;

(3) an offence under the IWCA 1960;

(4) an offence under TA 1968, s 9 (burglary with intent to commit rape);

(5) an offence under CLA 1977, s 54;

(6) an offence under the POCA 1978;

(7) an offence under SO(A)A 2000, s 3;

(8) an offence under the CLA 1977, s 1 of conspiracy to commit any of the above offences; and

(9) an offence under the Criminal Attempts Act 1981, of attempting to commit any of the above offences.

Attempted rape is also a 'sexual offence' for the purposes of these provisions (*R v Robinson* [1993] Crim LR 143). A 'violent offence' is defined in the Act as an offence which leads, or is intended or is likely to lead, to a person's death or to physical injury to a person, and includes an offence which is required to be charged as arson, whether or not it would otherwise fall within the definition.

Whether an offence is a 'violent offence' for the purposes PCC(S)A 2000, is a question of fact in each case, and depends upon the facts of the particular incident rather than on the category of the offence. The definition is narrow in its scope. An offence, other than arson which is by statutory definition such an offence, is not a 'violent offence' for the purposes of these provisions unless the terms of the charge of which the offender is convicted necessarily establish that the offence led, or was intended or likely to lead, to a person's death or to serious injury to the person (*R v Murray* [1994] Crim LR 383; *R v Cochrane* [1994] Crim LR 382).

Where offence(s) do not qualify

If none of the offences before the court qualifies for a custodial sentence, the court is restricted to imposing a community sentence (see COMMUNITY SENTENCES) or a financial penalty (see FINES AND ENFORCEMENT). Where sentence is passed in respect of offences of differing gravity, some sufficiently serious to qualify for a custodial sentence and others not, the court:

(1) is not prevented from passing a custodial sentence for the lesser offences which do not themselves qualify for custody (*Re Mussell* [1990] 2 All ER 609; *R v Oliver & Little* [1993] Crim LR 147); but

(2) ought not, in general, to pass consecutive sentences for those offences, or make the overall sentence longer by reference to them (*R v Oliver & Little* (*above*).

Where an offender has been made the subject of a community rehabilitation order by a court having full knowledge of the relevant matters, it will generally be bad sentencing practice for a court dealing with him *subsequently* for an offence committed *before* that order was made, to impose a custodial sentence (*R v Duporte* [1989] Crim LR 664).

Approach to sentence

It has been said that the court, on deciding to impose a custodial sentence, should consider imposing the minimum sentence possible which will:

(1) punish the offender for his crime;

(2) mark the disapproval of the community for the criminal acts which he has committed and be consistent with the duty to protect the interests of the public; and

(3) act as a deterrent in the future to the offender and to anyone else who might be minded to commit that sort of offence.

(*R v Bibi* [1980] Crim LR 732; *R v Hitchcock* [1982] Crim LR 541.)

Aggravating factors; antecedents

The court must, in deciding whether an offender qualifies for a custodial sentence, take into account all such information about the circumstances of the offence (including any aggravating or mitigating factors) available to it.

In considering the seriousness:

(1) of any offence, it may take into account any previous convictions of or any failure by the offender to respond to previous sentences;

(2) of any offence committed while the offender was on bail, it must treat the fact that it was committed on bail as an aggravating factor.

Note that for these purposes:

(a) a probation order or a conditional discharge made before 1 October 1992 is to be treated as a sentence;

(b) a conviction in respect of which a probation order or an order discharging the offender conditionally or absolutely is to be treated as a conviction;

(c) a conditional discharge made after 30 September 1992 is to be treated as a sentence; and

(d) a conviction, in respect of which an order discharging the offender absolutely or conditionally was made after 30 September 1992, is to be treated as a conviction.

Mitigation, discounts for plea etc

The sentencing process must be balanced by taking into account such mitigation as is available, including the age of the offender, and other considerations mentioned *below* (see DEALING WITH AN OFFENDER), and, in particular, by any recognised discount.

A tract of cases developed by the superior courts restricts a court's discretion in sentencing by giving an offender the right to expect a discount on the otherwise appropriate sentence in three circumstances, ie where:

(1) he pleads guilty or, in the case of an either-way offence has indicated a plea of guilty (*R v Barnes* [1984] Crim LR 119);

(2) there is an element of 'entrapment' by the authorities, in that the offence would not have been committed but for the activities of an informer (*R v Beaumont* [1987] Crim LR 786; *R v Chapman* [1989] Crim LR 846); or

(3) the offender gives information or assistance to the police (*R v Sinfield* (1981) 3 Cr App R(S) 258; *R v Sivan* (1988) 10 Cr App R(S) 282) early enough for it to be potentially useful (*R v Debbag & Izett* (1991) 12 Cr App R (S) 733; *R v A & B* [1988] Crim LR 757; cf *R v X* [1999] Crim LR 678),

(see generally DEALING WITH AN OFFENDER).

Time spent on remand

It is not possible, as it is in some jurisdictions, to 'backdate' a sentence. If the offender has spent time on remand before being sentenced, that time will normally count towards a sentence of imprisonment (unless he was, at the same time, in custody for other offences). Special rules apply to detention and training orders (see p 185 *below*).

Thus in respect of sentences of imprisonment, time spent on remand:

(1) counts for the purposes of calculating remission; but does not count towards the six-month period to be served before consideration of parole;

(2) does not count towards any terms of a suspended sentence subsequently activated;

(3) does not count where the offender was previously subject to a suspended sentence, a community rehabilitation order, community punishment order, or conditional discharge, in respect of any period falling before the order was made.

By CJA 1988, s 130 any period spent in custody by a juvenile in connection with the offence for which sentence is passed, or in the care of the local authority, by virtue of an order under CYPA 1969, s 23 in accommodation provided for the purpose of restricting his liberty, counts towards sentence.

Remand in foreign custody

Time spent in foreign custody pending extradition is not automatically deducted under CJA 1967, s 67, but CJA 1991, s 47 allows the court to order that all, or part, of the time spent in foreign custody should he treated as a 'relevant period' for the purposes of s 67.

It may specify such period as it considers just, in all the circumstances of the case, not exceeding the term actually spent in foreign custody.

SOME GENERAL PRINCIPLES

Length of sentence: (1) general

The term of any custodial sentence imposed by the court, apart from any aggravating or mitigating features:

(1) should be commensurate with the seriousness of the offence; and

(2) where there is more than one offence, should be commensurate with their combined seriousness; and

(3) may consist of several terms imposed concurrently or consecutively.

See *below* as to consecutive sentences, and p 182 *below* as to the minimum term in a young offender institution. Sentence may be imposed only in respect of those offences on which the offender has been convicted, or those which he has expressly asked the court to take into consideration on sentence (see TICS), where the proper procedure has been followed.

Length of sentence: (2) age of offender

The age of the offender should be taken into account on sentence. In the case of a young offender, it will almost always be appropriate to impose a shorter sentence than would be appropriate in the case of an adult, and while a deterrent sentence may be appropriate in the case of an adult, it is necessary to balance that aspect against the youth of the offender (*R v Marriott and Shepherd* [1995] Crim LR 83).

As to advanced age, see *R v W (Sentencing: Age of Defendant)* (2000) *The Times*, 26 October.

Consecutive sentences

The court may order that one custodial term commence at the end of any any other term imposed by that or any other court, bearing in mind, of course, its overall maximum powers. MCA 1980, s 133(1)

Note that:

(1) Where several offences are tried together, it is a good (but not universal) working rule, that if the offences arise out of the same transaction, the sentences ought to be concurrent (*R v Castercurn* (1972) 56 Cr App R 298); the same applies where offences form part of a series committed against the same victim over a short period of time;

(2) by statute a sentence must not be made consecutive to a term of imprisonment from which an offender has been released on licence under CJA 1991, Pt II; PCC(S)A 2000, s 84

(3) the authorities show that consecutive sentences are appropriate:
   (a) where the subsequent offence was committed while on bail awaiting trial for the former;
   (b) in the case of an assault upon a police officer in the course of an attempt to escape (*R v Castercum (above); R v Gormley* [1973] RTR 483; *R v Fitter* (1983) 5 Cr App R(S) 168), but not where the assault is part and parcel of the substantive offence, where it may be treated as aggravating the offence, and concurrent sentences ought to be passed (*R v Castercum (above); R v Wellington* (1988) 10 Cr App R(S) 384);
   (c) where a burglar assaults a householder who interrupts him, a consecutive term should be imposed for the assault.

Terms in default of payment of fines etc, imposed in addition to a sentence of imprisonment for the same offence are not subject to the same restrictions. MCA 1980, s 133(4)

Explanations for the imposition of custodial sentences

Whenever a custodial sentence is imposed on an offender the court should:

(1) in terms of its own choosing, taking care to ensure that the explanation is clear and accurate;

(2) explain the practical effect of the sentence in addition to complying with existing statutory requirements;

(3) give such explanation as is thought necessary of any ancillary orders relating to matters such as disqualification, compensation, confiscation and costs.

The sentence will be that announced by the court.

(*Practice Direction* (*criminal: consolidated*) [2002] 3 All ER 904, para 7)

In announcing sentence:

- (a) the offender should be sentenced on each charge separately;
- (b) it should be stated in his presence whether the terms are to be concurrent or consecutive;
- (c) where the offender is, at the time of sentence, already serving two or more consecutive terms of imprisonment and the court intends to increase the total period of imprisonment, it should use the expression 'consecutive to the total period of imprisonment to which you are already subject'.

Should (b) not be followed, the Clerk should ask the court, before the accused leaves court, to do so (*Practice Direction* (*criminal: consolidated*) [2002] 3 All ER 904, paras 8.1, 2).

Spelling it out

In passing a custodial sentence, the court is under a duty to:

- (1) state in open court that it is of the opinion that:
  - (a) the offence etc, is so serious that only a custodial sentence can be justified; and/or
  - (b) in the case of a violent or sexual offence, only a custodial sentence is adequate to protect the public etc; and
- (2) explain to the offender in open court and in ordinary language why it is passing a custodial sentence; and
- (3) cause the reason(s) stated by it to be specified in the warrant of commitment and entered in the register.

IMPRISONMENT

General restrictions

A number of points need to be emphasised:

- (1) no court may pass a sentence of imprisonment on an offender under 21 years of age, or commit such a person to prison for any reason, though this does not prevent the committal to prison of a person who is remanded in custody or committed in custody for trial or sentence, or transferred or sent for trial under CDA 1998, s 51;
- (2) the offender must be present when such a sentence is imposed;
- (3) legal representation must be considered (see p 168 *above*);
- (4) a pre-sentence report is normally required (see p 168 *above*).

Length of sentence

The statute creating an offence indicates whether or not imprisonment is available as a penalty, and if so, the maximum term.

The length of a term of imprisonment imposed by a magistrates' court must not: PCC(S)A 2000, s 78(1)(2)(3)(5)(6)

(1) be for less than five days, except in the case of: MCA 1980, ss 132, 133, 135, 136
   (a) a committal to prison in default of payment of a financial penalty (see p 254 *below*);
   (b) detention within the precincts of the court or at a police station (see p 260 *below*);
   (c) detention overnight of a defaulter at a police station (see p 260 *below*);
   (d) detention until the rising of the court, for contempt (see p 149 *below*);

(2) be for more than six months in respect of any one offence; and

(3) exceed 12 months overall where two or more offences triable either way are tried summarily by consent.

Where the court activates a suspended sentence (*R v Chamberlain* [1992] Crim LR 380) consecutively, or returns a prisoner on licence to serve part or the whole of his original term (*R v Worthing JJ, ex p Varley* [1997] Crim LR 688), the aggregate of sentences may exceed the term permitted above. Special rules apply to sentences imposed, whether concurrently or consecutively, for non-payment of financial penalties.

Power to suspend prison term

A sentence of imprisonment (but not any other form of detention) may be suspended for a term of not less than one year nor more than two, though the instances in which a suspended sentence is appropriate are now few and far between (*R v Robinson* [1993] 2 All ER 1). PCC(S)A 2000, s 118(1)

The effect of suspension is that the sentence will not take effect unless the offender commits another offence punishable with imprisonment within the period specified by the court. This must be explained to the offender.

It is for the court suspending the sentence to decide whether one or more terms are to run concurrently or consecutively (*Practice Direction* (*Passing of Sentence*) (*above*)). It cannot be made consecutive to another suspended sentence which is not brought into effect (*R v Blakeway* (1969) 53 Cr App R 498).

Need for exceptional circumstances

A court must not deal with an offender by means of a suspended sentence unless of the opinion that:

PCC(S)A 2000, s 118(4)

(1) the case is one in which a sentence of imprisonment would have been appropriate even without the power to suspend (*R v English* [1984] Crim LR 370; *R v Fletcher* (1991) 12 Cr App R(S) 671);

(2) the exercise of the power can be justified by the 'exceptional circumstances' of the case (*Re Okinikan* [1993] 2 All ER 5, *R v Sanderson* [1993] Crim LR 224).

The exceptional circumstances may relate either to the circumstances of the offence or of the offender (*Re Brookin* (1994) 16 Cr App R(S) 78; *R v Weston* [1995] Crim LR 900). CACD (in *R v Okinikan*) declined to lay down any definition of 'exceptional circumstances'; they will inevitably depend on the facts of each indvidual case. They did emphasise, however, that taken on their own or in combination, good character, youth and an early plea of guilty were not exceptional circumstances justifying a suspended sentence; they are common features of many cases (and see *Attorney-General's Reference (No 5 of 1993)* (1993) 15 Cr App R (S) 201; *R v Dhanji Gora Sia* [2002] 1 Cr App R (S) 356; *R v Smith* [2002] 1 Cr App R(S) 258).

Approach to sentence

The court should, in approaching its decision:

(1) first determine the length of the sentence; and then

(2) decide whether or not to suspend.

It is wrong to increase the sentence because it is being suspended (*R v Trowbridge* [1975] Crim LR 295). The court may wish to take into account the fact that the offender has spent time in custody which will not count towards the term, if it is subsequently activated (*R v Deering* [1976] Crim LR 638).

PCC(S)A 2000, s 118(7)

When imposing a suspended sentence, the effect of it must be explained to the offender. He may be told that if he commits another offence punishable with imprisonment during the operational period of the suspended sentence, the suspended term may be brought into effect.

A suspended sentence may not be expressed to be consecutive to a previous suspended sentence not brought into effect (*R v Blakeway* (1969) 133 JP 575).

Obligation to consider additional financial penalty

PCC(S)A 2000, s 118(5)

A court imposing a suspended sentence must consider whether the circumstances of the case are such as to warrant in addition the imposition of a fine or the making of a compensation order.

Improper combinations

The purpose of suspending a prison sentence is to avoid sending a person to prison; it follows therefore that:

(1) it is wrong to impose a suspended term on an offender already serving a prison sentence (*R v Hammond* [1969] Crim LR 500);

(2) it is bad sentencing practice to impose a suspended sentence on the same occasion that a community service order is made (*R v Starie* [1979] Crim LR 731);

(3) a community rehabilitation order may not be made in respect of another offence on the same occasion as a suspended sentence is imposed (*R v Percival* (1994) 15 Cr App R(S) 289). PCC(S)A 2000, s 118(6)

Activation of the sentence

Where an offender is convicted of a further offence punishable with imprisonment committed during the operational period of a suspended sentence, unless that sentence has already taken effect, the court must consider it and must deal with the offender in one of four ways, namely: PCC(S)A 2000, s 119(1)(2)(3)

(1) it must order the suspended sentence to take effect with the original term unaltered unless it is of the opinion that it would be unjust to do so in view of all the circumstances, including the facts of the subsequent offence, in which case it must state its reasons;

(2) it may order that the suspended sentence take effect with the substitution of a lesser term;

(3) it may vary the original order by substituting for the original period an operational period expiring not later than two years from the date of the variation; or

(4) it may make no order on the suspended sentence, but this last option involves a positive decision to make no order, not merely an omission to deal with the question at all; where the court makes 'no order' it must state its reasons for so doing.

Once the breach has been dealt with, no other court has power to deal again with the same breach. A difficulty may arise where the court makes 'no order' and makes a community punishment order for the subsequent offence; if the offender is brought back subsequently for failing to comply with that order, there is no power to deal with him for the suspended term (*R v Folan* [1980] 1 All ER 217; *R v Temperley* (1980) 2 Cr App R (S) 127).

It is not good sentencing practice to vary the operational period of a suspended sentence at the same time as imposing an immediate term; the suspended sentence should be activated (*R v Goodlad* [19973] 2 All ER 1200; *R v Treaves* [1981] Crim LR 511).

Meaning of 'conviction'

The court is only empowered to deal with a suspended sentence where the offender is 'convicted' of a further offence punishable with imprisonment.

It follows that:

(1) a subsequent offence dealt with by means of an absolute or conditional discharge, does not enable the court to deal with a suspended sentence (*R v Tarry* [1970] 2 All ER 185, *R v Moore* [1995] Crim LR 347);

(2) a subsequent offence for which sentence has been deferred does not operate to enable the court to deal with a suspended sentence (*R v Salmon* [1973] Crim LR 707).

Reasons for not activating sentence

As a general rule, the court dealing with a suspended sentence ought to order that it take effect, even if the subsequent offence is of a different character, but a number of decisions in the superior courts show that:

(1) the court may consider it unjust to do so where the subsequent offence is both of a different character and comparatively trivial, although the mere fact that it is of a different character is not a sufficient reason for not activating the original sentence;

(2) the fact that the subsequent offence does not warrant a custodial sentence has been said to be a strong argument for not activating the suspended term but the court has a discretion in the matter (*R v McQuillan* [1993] Crim LR 893; *R v Calladine* (1993) I5 Cr App R(S) 345; *R v Stacey* [1993] Crim LR 303);

(3) the fact that the subsequent offence is of a less serious nature may justify activating the suspended sentence with a reduced term.

It is not part of the court's function to review the propriety of the original term, but there are cases in which justice cannot be done without fitting into the pattern of events which led to the subsequent offence, the facts which led to the imposition of the original term (*R v Munday* (1971) 56 Cr App R 220).

Consecutive or concurrent

PCC(S)A 2000, s 118

Where the court orders that a suspended sentence take effect, whether with or without variation of the original term, it may order that the sentence take effect immediately, or on the expiration of another term of imprisonment passed on the offender by the court or by another court. In approaching the question of activation, the court should:

(1) first address itself to the sentence for the subsequent offence, and then to the question of activating the suspended sentence (*R v Ithell* [1969] 2 All ER 449);

(2) order the suspended sentence to take effect consecutively unless there are quite exceptional circumstances (*R v Brown* (1970) 54 Cr App R 176).

Crown Court sentences

PCC(S)A 2000, s 118

Where an offender is convicted in the magistrates' court of an offence punishable with imprisonment, and the offence was committed during the operational period of a suspended sentence passed by the Crown Court, the magistrates' court cannot deal with it, but may:

(1) if it thinks fit, commit the offender to the Crown Court, in custody or on bail; and

(2) if it does not so commit him, it must give written notice of the conviction to the Crown Court by which the suspended sentence was imposed.

The better practice in such a case is to commit the offender to the Crown Court both in respect of the fresh offence and the suspended sentence, so that the hands of the Crown Court are not tied by any action the magistrates may take (*R v Tarry* [1970] 2 All ER 185).

DETENTION IN A YOUNG OFFENDER INSTITUTION

With the exception of short local detention in court, police or customs custody, the only custodial sentence which may be passed upon an offender aged 18 but under 21 is detention in a young offender institution.

PCC(S)A 2000, s 96

Where an offender:

(1) aged at least 18 but under 21;

(2) is convicted of an offence which is punishable with imprisonment in the case of a person of 21 or over; and

(3) the court is of opinion that either or both of s 79(2)(a) and (b) apply, or the case falls within s 79(3), the sentence which the court must pass is a sentence of detention in a young offender institution.

The court must specifically have regard to these provisions before passing sentence, even where its attention is not drawn to them by the parties (*R v Passmore* (1985) 7 Cr App R(S) 377), and has a duty to identify which of the statutory criteria applies (*R v Poyner* [1989] Crim LR 595). While, in the case of several offences, the statute obliges the court to consider each offence separately (see p 170 *above*) the court is entitled, in considering whether it is satisfied that the offence was so serious that a non-custodial sentence cannot be justified, to take into account the circumstances surrounding the offence (*R v Hurren* (1989) *The Times*, 8 June; *R v Monks & Eddy* (1989) *The Times*, 27 July), including the totality of his criminal behaviour, which might include the fact that he is a persistent offender (*R v Roberts* [1987] Crim LR 581).

Length of term

PCC(S)A 2000, s 97(1)(2)(3)

The maximum terms of detention in a young offender institution that the court may impose for an offence is the same as the maximum term of imprisonment that it may impose for the offence.

A magistrates' court has no power to impose a sentence for more than six months in respect of any one offence, except in the case of two or more either-way offences, in which case a maximum of 12 months applies.

There is power to commit an offender to the Crown Court for sentence if the magistrates' court is of the opinion that the offence, or the combination of one or more offences associated with it is so serious that it merits a term of detention of more than the court has power to impose.

Except in the case of breach of a post custodial supervision requirement under CJA 1991, s 65(6) (see p 183 *below*) the minimum sentence in a young offender institution is one of 21 days.

Consecutive sentences

Subject to the statutory maxima, where an offender:

(1) is convicted of more than one offence for which he is liable to a sentence of detention in a young offender institution; or

(2) is serving a sentence of detention in a young offender institution, and is convicted of one or more further offences for which he is liable to such a sentence;

the court has the same power to pass consecutive sentences in such an institution as if they were sentences of imprisonment.

Again, where an offender:

(a) is serving a sentence of detention in a young offender institution; and

(b) is aged over 21; and

(c) is convicted of one or more further offences for which he is liable to imprisonment,

the court may pass one or more sentences of imprisonment to run consecutively upon the sentence of detention.

Supervision on release

HO 1986

Whether or not released on parole, an offender sentenced to detention in a young offender institution is subject to supervision on release. The length of the statutory supervision depends on the length of the sentence and the age of the offender. It is not normally less than three months and usually lasts from the offender's release until the end of the full period of the sentence. It is never more than 12 months, and never extends beyond the offender's 22nd birthday. On release he will be issued with a notice of supervision which sets out the requirements as specified by the Home Secretary.

Whilst under supervision the offender must comply with specified requirements, which may include requirements for securing electronic monitoring: CJA 1991, s 65(3)(4)

(1) of his compliance with other requirements; and

(2) of his whereabouts.

Where the term of detention was imposed for a 'trigger offence' a requirement may be imposed to provide samples for the purpose of ascertaining whether the offender has any specified Class A drug in his body, provided that such a requirement is imposed for the purpose of determining whether he is complying with any other specified requirement (but only at present in a pilot area). CJA 1991, s 65(5)(5A)(5B)

An offender who, without reasonable excuse, fails to comply with any requirement is liable on summary conviction to:

(1) a fine not exceeding level 3 on the standard scale; or

(2) imprisonment if he is aged 21 when convicted, or detention in a young offender institution if he is not, for a period not exceeding 30 days.

Although he is not liable to a further term of supervision at the end of that sentence, the previous term continues until the end of the period.

(Note: this form of detention is to be abolished (CJCSA 2000) from a date to be appointed; the age for a term of imprisonment will also be reduced to 18.)

DETENTION AND TRAINING ORDER

Subject to PCC(S)A 2000, ss 90 and 91, a detention and training order which provides a period of detention and training, followed by a period of supervision, may be passed by the youth court on a person aged under 18 where: PCC(S)A 2000, ss 100(1)(2)(3), 102, 103

(1) he is convicted of an offence which is punishable with imprisonment in the case of a person aged 21 or over; and

(2) the court is of opinion that either or both of PCC(S)A 2000, s 79 2(a) and (b) apply (see p 169 *above*) or the case falls within s 79(3) (see p 169 *above*), provided that an order is not to be made:

   (a) in the case of an offender under the age of 15 at the time of his conviction, unless the court is of opinion that he is a persistent offender;

   (b) in the case of an offender under the age of 12 at that time, unless:

(i) the court is of opinion that only a custodial sentence would be adequate to protect the public from his further offending; and

(ii) the offence was committed on or after such date as the Home Secretary may appoint (as yet no date has been appointed).

An order may be imposed on an offender who was aged 17 at the date he committed an offence, even though he has attained the age of 18 by the date on which sentence is imposed (*Aldis v DPP* [2002] Crim LR 434).

Spelling it out

PCC(S)A 2000, s 100(4)

In making an order, where PCC(S)A 2000, s. 100(2) applies, the court must, in addition to the duty imposed by s 79(4), state in open court that it is of the opinion mentioned in paras (a) and (b) of s 79(2), p 169 *above*.

What amounts to a 'persistent offender'

The superior courts have said that 'persistent offender' is not to be defined for these purposes in terms of the Inter-departmental circular *Tackling the Youth Justice System* 1997, but that the currently understood meaning of the words 'persistent offender' should be applied to the facts of the case (*R v AS* [2001] 1 Cr App R (S) 62 (series of offences committed over two days); see also *R v B* [2001] Crim LR 80). The application of the test is best left to the good sense of the court (*R v Dexter* [2001] 1 Cr App R(S) 389).

Note that:

(1) it is not necessary, to come within the definition that the offender should have previous convictions (*R v Smith* [2001] 1 Cr App R(S) 62) or that he should have committed a string of offences of the same or a similar character (*R v B* (*above*));

(2) it is not necessary that his failure to address his offending behaviour arises from failure to comply with previous orders (*ibid*); and

(3) account may be taken of offences in respect of which he has been cautioned (*R v D* [2001] Crim LR 864).

Custodial Sentences

Term of order

PCC(S)A 2000, s 100(3)

The order (which is a custodial sentence for the purposes of PCC(S)A 2000, s 76 (and ss 79–84 apply accordingly) is an order that the offender shall be subject, for the term specified in the order, to a period of detention and training, followed by a period of supervision.

The term of such an order must:

(1) be for 4, 6, 8, 10, 12, 18 or 24 months; and

PCC(S)A 2000, s 101(1)(2)(3)(5)(8)

(2) not exceed 24 months, taking into account any period for which the offender has been remanded in custody in connection with the

offence, or any other offence the charge for which was founded on the same facts or evidence; and

(3) not exceed the maximum term of imprisonment that the Crown Court could, in the case of an offender aged 21 or over, impose for the offence.

It is not permissible to pass a number of shorter terms and aggregate them into a term of four months (*R v Kent YC, ex p Kingwell* [1999] Crim LR 168).

Time spent in custody

The court must, in fixing the term of the order, take into account any time spent in custody in connection with the offence. It should indicate its intention to make an order, so that it can be informed of any period spent in custody or on remand before considering the appropriate length of the term (*R v Haringey YC, ex p A* (2000) *The Times*, 30 May; *R v Davis* (2000) *The Times*, 20 December).

In relation to this type of order (as opposed to a sentence of imprisonment, (see pp 173, 174 *above*): the court is not bound to reflect mathematically all such time in the sentence passed:

(1) it is neither appropriate nor desirable that a precise reflection should be given for a day or two spent in custody (*R v ILCC, ex p N & S* [2000] Crim LR 871); but

(2) if a significant time has been spent in custody, a matter of weeks or months, the proper approach is to reduce the otherwise appropriate term to reflect that period.

The period reflected in the term imposed will depend on the circumstances, including the apparent impact, if any, of the period of custody on the offender, the length of time spent in custody and the relationship between the period spent in custody and the period of detention and training contemplated (*R v Fieldhouse & Watts* [2000] Crim LR 1020).

In *Fieldhouse* it was said that while no rule of general application could be devised where, for instance, one month has been spent in custody, this is the equivalent of a two month term, thus if the term otherwise contemplated is

(a) four months, such a period may result in a non-custodial sentence being passed;

(b) up to 12 months, the period spent in custody may result in the imposition of a term at the next level down;

(c) 18–24 months, the period spent on remand may have no effect.

References to 'remand in custody'

PCC(S)A 2000, s 133(3)

The reference in s 101(8) to an offender being remanded in custody, is a reference to his being held in a police station, being remanded in or committed to custody by an order of the court, being remanded or committed to local authority accommodation under CYPA 1969, s 23, and placed and kept in secure accommodation or detained in a secure training centre or being remanded, admitted or removed to hospital under MHA 1983, ss 35, 36, 38 or 48.

A person is in 'police detention' for the purposes of subs (7) where he is in police detention at any time under PACE 1984, or at any time when he is detained under s 14 of the Prevention of Terrorism (Temporary Provisions) Act 1989.

Consecutive terms

PCC(S)A 2000, s 101(3)(7)

Where the offender:

(1) is convicted of more than one offence for which he is liable to an order; or

(2) is already subject to such an order and is convicted of one or more further offences for which he is liable to an order,

the court has the same power to pass consecutive terms as if they were sentences of imprisonment, save that, while there is no requirement that the total term add up to one of the periods specified in s 101(1) (*R v Norris* [2000] Crim LR 48):

(a) an order must not be made in respect of an offender the effect of which would be that he would be subject to detention and training orders for an aggregate which exceeds 24 months; and

(b) if the aggregate term to which he would otherwise be subject does exceed 24 months, the excess will be treated as remitted.

The court may, when imposing consecutive detention and training orders whose individual terms are taken from the list in subs (1), fix an aggregate term taken from the list, ie any even number of months between 4 and 24. This gives the court a measure of discretion in arriving at terms which reflect the varying culpability of different offenders involved in the same case (*R v B* [2001] Crim LR 80).

Supervision

On release from a term of detention and training, the offender is liable to supervision. Breaches of that supervision are dealt with by the youth court.

New offences during currency of the order

PCC(S)A 2000, s 105

Where:

(1) after his release and before the date on which the term of the order ends, the offender commits an offence punishable with imprison ment in the case of a person aged 21 or over; and

(2) whether before or after that date he is convicted of that 'new offence' the court by or before which he is convicted may, whether or not it passes any other sentence on him, order him to be detained in such secure accommodation as the Home Secretary may determine for the whole or any part of the period which:

   (a) begins with the date of the court's order; and
   (b) is equal in length to the period between the date on which the new offence was committed, or the last of the days if it was committed over several, and the date on which the order would end,

the term will, as the court directs, be served either before and be followed by, or concurrently with, any sentence imposed for the offence, and in either case will be disregarded in determining the appropriate length of that sentence for a single offence.

CUSTODY TIME LIMITS

POA 1985 and the Regulations made thereunder (SI 1987, No 299, amended by SI 1999, No 2744, SI 1999, No 2743) prescribe time limits during which an accused may be held in custody (and 'custody' includes remand, or committal to local authority accommodation) of the court in relation to specified stages of the proceedings.

The purpose of these provisions is:

(1) to ensure that the periods for which unconvicted persons are held in custody are as short as possible;

(2) to oblige the prosecutor to prepare his case for trial with all due diligence and expedition, and

(3) to invest the court with a power and duty to control any extension of the maximum period for which a person may be held in custody pending trial.

These are very important objectives and the court must be careful to give weight to all three (*R v Manchester CC* [*ex p McDonald* 1999] 1 Cr App R 409).

Magistrates' courts limits

The maximum periods during which a person accused of an offence in the magistrates' court may be in the custody of that court are: CTLR 1987, reg 4(1)(4)

(1) in the case of an *indictable only* offence, between first appearance and the time when the court decides whether to send him to the Crown Court under s 51 – 70 days;

(2) in the case of an offence triable *either way*, between first appearance and the start of the summary trial, or as the case may be, the time when the court decides to commit him to the Crown Court for trial – 70 days; but

(3) if, in such a case, before the expiry of 56 days following the accused's first appearance, the court decides to proceed to summary trial under MCA 1980, ss 19–24, the maximum period between the accused's first appearance and the start of the summary trial – 56 days;

(4) in the case of an offence triable only on indictment, between first appearance and the time the court decides whether or not to send him for trial – 70 days;

(5) in the case of a summary offence, between the accused' s first appearance and the start of the trial – 56 days.

(Additional limits apply in the case of persons under 18 but only in pilot areas (see YOUTH COURT – 'Relevant courts').)

References to 'commit for trial' include in the case of an 'old-style' committal, the day the court begins to hear evidence, and in a case where a transfer notice was given, the date on which it was given. Proceedings for an offence are taken to commence when the accused is charged or, as the case may be, when an information is laid charging him with the offence.

The Regulations are directed towards the offence and not the offender. 'Offence' in reg 4(1) is not to be read as 'offences'; each offence attracts its own time limit (*R v Waltham Forest MC, ex p Lee* [1993] Crim LR 522; *R v Wolverhampton MC and Stafford CC, ex p Uppal* [1995] Crim LR 223; see also *R v Maidstone CC, ex p Clark* [1995] 3 All ER 513; *R v Peterborough CC, ex p L* [2000] Crim LR 470; and *R v Leeds CC, ex p Wardle* (2001) *The Times*, 13 March (HL) (where compatibility with ECHR is considered)).

The 'maximum period'

CTLR 1987, reg 2(5); SI 1999/2743, reg 2

The 'maximum period' laid down does not include the day on which custody commenced, and a custody time limit which would otherwise expire on a Saturday, Sunday, Christmas Day, Good Friday or a bank holiday, is treated as expiring on the nearest preceeding day which is not one of those days.

Where the limits do not apply

Where a person:

POA 1985, s 22(5)(6)(6A)

(1) escapes from the custody of a magistrates' court or the Crown Court before the expiry of a limit which applies to his case; or
(2) having been released on bail in consequence of the expiry of a custody time limit, fails to surrender at the appointed time, or is arrested for breach of bail, and is accordingly at large:
    (a) the period for which the person is unlawfully at large, and
    (b) such additional period (if any) as the court may direct, having regard to the disruption of the prosecution occasioned by:
        (i) the person's escape or failure to surrender; and
        (ii) the length of the period mentioned in (a) above must be disregarded so far as the offence in question is concerned, for the purposes of the overall time limit which applies in his case in relation to the stage which the proceedings have reached at the time of the escape or, as the case may be, at the appointed time.

The fact that the accused is in custody for other matters does not prevent the time limit running (*R v Peterborough CC, ex p L* (*above*)). Where, following the initial charge(s) on which the accused first appeared before the magistrates, another charge is added, then, irrespective of its nature, or when it was added, subject only to the accused being able to show abuse of process, a new custody time limit is created (*R v Leeds CC, ex p Stubley* [1999] Crim LR 822; *R v Leeds CC, ex p Wardle* [2001] 2 Cr App Rep 301 HL).

Effect of expiry of limit

On being notified that:

(1) an accused who is in custody pending trial; CTLR 1987, reg 6(6)

(2) has the benefit of a custody time limit under reg 5, and

(3) the time limit is about to expire,

the court must grant that person bail in accordance with BA 1976 as modified for the purpose (see BAIL), with effect from the expiry of the limit, subject to a duty appear before the court for trial.

Where this situation arises, the prosecution will need to decide *before* the expiry of the limit, whether:

(1) to apply for an extension, or further extension, of the time limit; or

(2) to apply for conditions to be attached to the bail granted to the accused.

Application for extension

An application by the prosecution for the extension, or further extension, of a time limit may be made orally or in writing: CTLR 1987, reg 7

(1) *before* the relevant time limit has expired (*R v Peterborough CC, ex p L* (*above*));

(2) by giving, not less than five days before making the application, notice in writing to the accused or his representative, and to the court, of his intention to make the application; unless

(3) the accused or his representative informs the prosecutor that he does not require such notice; or

(4) the court is satisfied on a balance of probabilities (*Re Craig* (1991) 91 Cr App R 7) that it is not practicable for the prosecution to comply and directs either that the prosecution need not comply, or specifies a lesser minimum period.

The Clerk may, with the consent of the accused, extend an overall time limit under POA 1985, s 22. JCR 1999, Schedule

In the case of an application based on the length and complexity of the case, though CCR 1982, r 7 does not require it, it is good practice to give the grounds in the notice (*R v CCC, ex p Marotta* 10 Arch News 2).

Successive applications

It is not:

(1) normally permissible, when an application is refused, for an application to be made to a second bench on the same grounds, but see *R v*

Bradford CC, ex p Crossling, etc [2000] 1 Cr App R 463 (where the first court may have acted on misleading information);

(2) permissible, where the High Court has reviewed a court's decision, for a further application to be made to a another court (*R v Peterborough CC, ex p L* (*above*); cf *R v Leeds CC, ex p Stubley* [1999] Crim LR 822).

Grounds for extension of period

POA 1985, s 22(3)

A time limit may be extended or further extended by the court at any time before its expiry (*R v Croydon CC, ex p Commrs of Customs & Excise* [1997] 8 Arch News 1, DC), but not unless it is satisfied on a balance of probabilities:

(1) that the need for the extension is due to:
  (a) the illness or absence of the accused, a necessary witness, or a member of the court;
  (b) a postponement which is occasioned by the ordering by the court of separate trials in the case of two or more accused or two or more offences; or
  (c) some other good and sufficient cause; and

(2) that the prosecution has acted with all due diligence and expedition (*R v Norwich CC, ex p Parker* [1992) Crim LR 500).

'Good and sufficient cause', and 'due diligence and expedition' are two distinct issues, and require both separate consideration and a separate ruling. 'Good cause' will not avail the prosecutor if he has not acted with 'due expedition' (*R v CCC, ex p Bennett* (1999) *The Times*, 25 January).

'Good and sufficient cause' interpreted

The words are not susceptible of a precise definition (*R v Norwich CC, ex p Ricketts* [1990] Crim LR 715). It will be a matter of fact in each case (*McKay White v DPP* [1989] Crim LR 375).

Thus:

(1) An almost infinite number of matters may, depending on the facts, constitute such cause, though, eg:
  (a) the seriousness of the offence, or
  (b) the need to protect the public, or
  (c) the fact that the extension sought is only a short one,

  are not amongst them (*R v Manchester CC, ex p McDonald, etc* [1999] 1 All ER 805); and

(2) matters relevant to the granting or refusing of bail cannot of themselves provide good and sufficient cause for extending a time limit (*R v Sheffield CC, ex p Headley* (*above*).

The unavailability of a bench or courtroom, may, in special cases and on appropriate facts, amount to such a cause, see *below* under 'Listing difficulties'.

'Due diligence and expedition'

'Due diligence' is not the same as 'due expedition'. To fulfil the test of 'due expedition' it is not enough to show that the prosecuting authorities 'are doing their best'. The test needs to be measured against some yardstick, or the object of the Act is defeated (*R v Southampton CC, ex p Roddie* [1991] Crim LR 619; *R v Sheffield MC, ex p Turner* (1991) 93 Cr App R 180).

'All due expedition' requires the diligence and expedition which would be shown by a competent prosecutor conscious of his duty to bring the case to trial as quickly and as reasonably and fairly as possible (*R v Manchester CC, etc* (*above*)).

Note that:

(1) delay on the part of an independent forensic laboratory is irrelevant to the question whether the prosecutor has acted with 'due expedition', although he should do everything possible to ensure that evidence is available on time (*R v CCC, ex p Johnson*, [1999] 2 Cr App R 51);

(2) the reference to the prosecutor having acted 'with all due expedition' refers to the time up to the making of the application to extend the limit, not to the issue of whether future delay may be caused by acceding to the application (*R v Woolwich CC, ex p. Gilligan* (*above*);

(3) lack of due diligence and expedition will not be fatal if it has no causal connection with the need for an extension (*R v Kingston CC, ex p Bell* 164 JP 633).

Listing difficulties

The courts have held, though reluctantly (*R v Manchester CC* (*above*)) that the unavailability of a bench or courtroom in which to try an accused in custody, is capable of amounting to 'good and sufficient cause' for extending the time limits (*R v CCC, ex p Abu-Wadeh* [1997] 1 All ER 159), though such factors are less likely to be worthy of consideration where the trial is not expected to be long or complex, or one in which the convenience of witnesses has to be taken into account (*R v Leeds CC, ex p Wilson* [1999] Crim LR 738), but:

(1) the court should approach such grounds with great caution, as there is obviously a danger that the purposes of the statute will be undermined by too readily granting extensions on this basis;

(2) the fact that witnesses are professional investigators does not make their convenience, particularly with regard to other duties, irrelevant;

(3) where the application is made on the basis that the case clashes with another the prosecutor will need to show why the other case requires priority (*R v Croydon YC, ex p C* [2001] Crim LR 40).

(4) many of the problems which arise in this area can be obviated by fixing an early date for the trial.

Fixing a date

In *R v Worcester CC, ex p Norman* 164 JP 201, it was said that there is a joint duty on the prosecutor and on the court to make early arrangements for the fixing of a trial date within the custody time limits:

(1) ideally, the date should be fixed at an early administrative hearing, where the timetable can be tailored to the date that has been fixed;

(2) if it is impossible to fix a date at that time the court should direct that the date be fixed on a date before the expiration of the custody time limit and that the matter should be re-listed in the event of a failure to agree a date;

(3) if the fixing of a date within the custody time limit is impossible, this should be appreciated at an early date and an application to extend made sooner rather than later, thereby enhancing the prospect of a date being fixed as soon as possible after the expiry of the limit;

(4) if the court, or the Clerk, fails to take the initiative, it is for the prosecutor to press for a date within the time limit, the duty on the defence being to provide the names of witnesses required so that their availability can be ascertained.

The hearing of the application to extend

Bearing in mind the overriding purposes of the legislation (see p 189 *above*) a court considering an application for an extension:

(1) needs to be satisfied, on a balance of probabilities, that both the conditions in s 22(3) are made out, before exercising its discretion;

(2) must not abdicate its responsibility to address the issues by granting the application 'on the nod', because the parties agree, or because there is no objection to this course;

(3) should consider all matters directly and genuinely bearing on the preparation of the case for trial, bearing in mind that;
   (a) the time limit is a maximum not a target; and
   (b) the prosecutor is not obliged to show that each stage has been completed as quickly and efficiently as is humanly possible; though
   (c) no attention should be paid to excuses such as staff shortages, sickness, etc;

(4) may need to hear evidence, or may, according to the circumstances of the case, be able to rely on information supplied by the parties;

(5) may, if, but only if, it is so satisfied, exercise its discretion to extend the time limit. If it is not satisfied it may not, but, if it is satisfied it may, but need not, extend the time limit (*R v Manchester CC* (*above*)); and

(6) should give brief reasons for its ruling, indicating the way in which it has reached its conclusions (*R v Leeds CC, ex p Briggs* [1998] Crim LR 744).

Conditions of bail

An application by the prosecutor for conditions to be attached to the bail to be granted an accused where the time limits have expired is made: CTLR 1987, reg 6(1)(2)(3)(4)(5)

(1) by giving notice in writing not less than five days before the expiry of the time limit, to the court and to the accused or his representative;

(2) stating whether or not he intends to ask the court to impose conditions, and, if he does, the nature of the conditions sought; and

(3) making arrangements for the accused to be brought before the court within the period of two days preceding the expiry of the time limit.

The prosecutor need not comply with (1) *above* if he has given notice of his intention to apply for an extension, or further extension, of the time limit; he need not comply with (2) if the court so directs. If the court is satisfied that it is not practicable, in all the circumstances, for the prosecution to comply with (1) it may so direct, or specify a lesser minimum period.

On receiving notice that the prosecutor intends to ask the court to impose conditions on the grant of bail, the accused or his representative must:

(a) give notice in writing to the court and to the prosecutor, that the accused wishes to be represented at the hearing of the application; or

(b) give notice to the court and to the prosecutor, stating that the accused does not wish to oppose the application; or

(c) give to the court, for its consideration, a written statement of the accused's reasons for opposing the application, sending a copy of the statement, at the same time, to the prosecutor.

Appeal to the Crown Court

An appeal brought: CTLR 1987, reg 27A(1)(2)

(1) by an accused under POA 1985, s 22(7) against a decision of the magistrates' court to extend, or further extend, a time limit imposed by the 1987 Regulations; or

(2) by the prosecutor under POA 1985, s 22(8) against a decision refusing to extend or further extend such a time limit,

is commenced by the appellant's giving notice in writing of appeal:

(a) to the Clerk of the magistrates' court which took the decision;

(b) if the appeal is brought by the accused, to the prosecutor, and if the prosecution is being carried on by the CPS, to the appropriate Crown Prosecutor;

(c) if the appeal is brought by the prosecutor, to the accused; and
(d) to the appropriate officer of the Crown Court.

Contents of notice

CTLR 1987, reg 27A(1)(3)

The notice of appeal must state:

(1) the date on which the time limit applicable to the case is due to expire; and
(2) if the appeal is brought by the accused under POA 1985, s 22(7), the date on which the time limit would have expired had the magistrates' court decided not to extend, or further extend, the time limit.

CTLR 1987, reg 27A(1)(4)

On receiving the notice of appeal, the appropriate officer of the Crown Court will enter the appeal, and give notice of the time and place of the hearing to the appellant, the other party to the appeal and the clerk to the magistrates' court which took the decision.

Abandonment

CTLR 1987, reg 27A(1)(5)

Without prejudice to the power of the Crown Court to give leave for an appeal to be abandoned (see APPEALS), an appellant may abandon an appeal under these provisions by giving notice in writing to any person to whom the notice of appeal was required to be given, not later than the third day preceding the day fixed for the hearing of the appeal (disregarding any Saturday, Sunday or bank holiday).

Effect of successful appeal

Where:

(1) the prosecutor successfully appeals a grant of bail by the magistrates'court, the judge will stipulate a date (within the powers of the magistrates under MCA 1980, ss 128, 128A and 129) as a remand date on which the accused is to be brought before the magistrates' court (*R v Manchester MC, ex p Geza Szakal* [2000] Crim LR 47);

BA 1976, s 3(1)

(2) the accused successfully appeals, and is admitted to bail by reason of the expiry of the custody time limit, the judge's powers to impose conditions on the grant are restricted:
   (a) there is no power to require a surety for his surrender,
   (b) there is no power to require the accused to give security for his surrender under BA 1976, s 3(4)(5).

He may be required, however, after (not before) his release, to comply with any other conditions of bail appropriate under s 3(6).

Re-institution of proceedings

In certain circumstances, proceedings which have stayed owing to the expiry of the custody time limits may be re-instituted by laying a fresh information within three months or such longer period as the court may allow. POA 1985, s 22B

DEALING WITH AN OFFENDER

This section covers the situation following SUMMARY TRIAL, that is, after conviction or finding of guilt, and before, and leading up to, sentence.

PROCEDURE AFTER CONVICTION

As a general rule, the court must sentence an offender for every separate offence of which he is convicted. He need not be dealt with on the day of conviction, nor in every case by the court which convicted him. The following options are available to the adult court (as to juveniles see YOUTH COURT):

(1) to remit a juvenile offender to a youth court, in an appropriate case (see *below* p 399);

(2) to refer a juvenile offender to a youth offender panel (see *below* p 399);

(3) to remit an offender to another magistrates' court, under MCA 1980, s 39 (see pp 399, 400 *below*);

(4) to adjourn for enquiries and a report (see ADJOURNMENT AND REMAND);

(5) to adjourn for other purposes, such as the production of a driving licence (see DISQUALIFICATION AND ENDORSEMENT), or the payment of compensation (see COMPENSATION);

(6) to adjourn for medical examination and a report (see MENTALLY DISORDERED OFFENDERS);

(7) to defer sentence (see DEFERMENT OF SENTENCE); or

(8) to commit an offender convicted summarily of an either-way offence to the Crown Court for sentence or to be dealt with (see COMMITTAL FOR SENTENCE).

REMITTING THE OFFENDER TO ANOTHER COURT

The adult court *must*, after convicting a juvenile, remit him to a youth court for sentence *unless* satisfied that it can deal with him by way of: PCC(S)A 2000, s 8

(1) a referral order (see YOUTH COURT); or

(2) an absolute or conditional discharge;

(3) a fine; or

(4) an order that a parent or guardian enter into a recognisance to take proper care of him and exercise proper control over him,

with or without any ancillary order(s) that the court has power to make when imposing an absolute or conditional discharge (see SUMMARY TRIAL).

PCC(S)A 2000, s 10(1)(2)

Where the court has convicted an offender who has attained the age of 18 of an offence punishable with imprisonment, or one in respect of which it has a power or a duty to disqualify him from driving under RTOA 1988, ss 34, 35 or 36, it may, in certain circumstances remit him to another magistrates' court to be dealt with (see SUMMARY TRIAL).

PRELIMINARIES

Adjournment for reports – *R v Gillam*: a potential trap

In many cases, before reaching a decision as to the appropriate sentencing option, it will be necessary for the court to adjourn for reports to be provided or enquiries made. In *R v Gillam* [1981] Crim LR 85, and the numerous cases which have followed it, it has been emphasised that where the court adjourns after conviction in order to obtain a report as to the offender's suitability for, eg, community punishment:

(1) the court must be careful not to create in the offender's mind any expectation that it will take such a course if reports are favourable; but

(2) should state expressly that it is 'keeping its options open', and that in the case of an either-way offence it includes the option to commit to the Crown Court for sentence; otherwise

(3) if it does not, a sense of injustice, real or imagined, may be created in the offender's mind, and the superior courts have indicated that they will intervene.

JCR 1999, Schedule

Following a plea of guilty, the Clerk may request a pre-sentence report but may *not* give any indication as to the seriousness of the offence.

Where bail is granted pending the preparation of a pre-sentence report, it is sensible to inform the offender that the grant of bail does not indicate the sentence which the magistrates have in mind (*R v Renan* [1994] Crim LR 379), but failure to warn the offender that the court is considering a custodial sentence does not vitiate the subsequent sentence (*R v Woodin* [1994] Crim LR 72).

Medical report

JCR 1999, Schedule

The Clerk may request a medical report and, for this purpose, remand the accused on bail on the same conditions as those, if any, previously imposed, or, with the consent of both parties, on other conditions.

Bail or custody

There is no general presumption in favour of bail after conviction, though it may be granted, (subject to CJPOA 1994, s 25), where:

(1) the offender appears or is brought before the court to be dealt with for breach of the requirements of a community rehabilitation order or a community punishment order; or

(2) the offender's case is adjourned for the purpose of enabling enquiries and a report to be made, to assist the court in dealing with him for the offence.

Where an offender's case is adjourned for enquiries or reports, and the offence or one of the offences, of which he is convicted in the proceedings is punishable with imprisonment, he need not be granted bail if it appears that it would be impracticable to complete the enquiries or to make the report without keeping him in custody.

BA 1976, s 4(1) Sched 1, Pt I

DEALING WITH SENTENCE

The *means* of dealing with an offender include:

(1) imposing any sentence which the court has power to impose; or

(2) committing him to the Crown Court for sentence or to be dealt with; and

(3) unless he is being committed for sentence to the Crown Court, making any ancillary order in addition to any sentence imposed.

The *manner* in which the court deals with the offender will depend upon the views of the bench. In formulating its view, the court will need to take into account:

(a) the nature, circumstances and seriousness of the offence, and any facts surrounding its commission, as to which see 'Factual basis for sentence' pp 204, 205 *below*;

(b) the sentencing options available, which are dealt with in the sections of this book;

(c) the age of the offender (see AGE OF OFFENDER);

(d) in the case of financial penalties, the offender's means (see FINES AND ENFORCEMENT); and

(e) the options appropriate to the offender's personal circumstances and previous record,

bearing in mind the relevant statutory provisions and any guidance given to magistrates by the superior courts, particularly in relation to

(i) qualification for a custodial sentence (see CUSTODIAL SENTENCES);

(ii) qualification for a community sentence (see COMMUNITY SENTENCES); and

(iii) the means of the offender in the case of any financial penalty, including costs.

Where several offenders fall to be sentenced, it is desirable that they should all be sentenced by the same court. Where one pleads not guilty and his case is adjourned for trial, sentences on those who plead guilty should be adjourned to the conclusion of his trial (*R v Weekes & Others* (1982) 74 Cr App R 161).

APPROACH TO SENTENCING

It has been suggested that a proper approach might be for the court to:

(1) consider the offence, and assess its seriousness;

(2) determine what the public interest requires as a punishment in a case of that kind;

(3) consider any aggravating or mitigating features; and

(4) if the crime is not so grave that he ought to be punished for it, consider what might be in the interests of the offender.

Those matters have now been embraced in a formal sentencing structure.

The CJA 1991 established a sentencing structure for all offences which reasserted the principle of 'just desserts': that any sentence of the court must reflect the seriousness of the offence that has been committed and the personal circumstances of the offender. The structure requires the court to determine:

(1) is an absolute discharge or a conditional discharge appropriate?

(2) is a fine appropriate?

(3) is the offence 'serious enough' for a community penalty?

(4) is the offence 'so serious' that only a custodial sentence is appropriate and, in the case of an either-way offence, are the magistrates' court powers of punishment sufficient?

The fact that the magistrates express a 'tentative view' in open court before retiring does not preclude them from coming to a different view after deliberating (*R v Kingston-upon-Thames Justices, ex p Aplaslam* [1983] Crim LR 112), but see *R v Gillam (above)*.

PURPOSE OF SENTENCING

The form of sentence imposed on an offender will depend upon the factors outlined above, bearing in mind any restrictions placed upon its use, in particular by PCC(S)A 2000.

The options available may be classified as:

(1) **nominal**, the obvious example being an absolute discharge, though small fines may also qualify;

(2) **preventive** or **conditional**, of which there may be said to be three distinct types of order:
   (a) a bind-over, where breach involves forfeiture of a specific sum;
   (b) a conditional discharge, which permits a court to act on a breach, but does not involve a specific sentence on the breach; and
   (c) a suspended sentence of imprisonment in the case of an offender aged 21 or over;

(3) **rehabilitative**, such as an attendance centre, most community orders such as a community rehabilitation order in the case of a person aged 16 or over, a community punishment order, which though intended to be rehabilitative, also has, as its name implies, a punitive element, or an order combining a community punishment order with a community rehabilitation order, a drug testing and treatment order or a curfew order;

(4) **reformatory**, the obvious examples being an attendance centre, or a detention and training order, the latter, though punitive, being intended to have a regime which is, at the same time, 'constructive,' with an emphasis on discipline and education;

(5) **remedial**, such as hospital and guardianship orders, or, again, a drug testing and treatment order; and finally,

(6) **punitive**, such as a fine or a custodial sentence.

A good working rule is not to mix sentences which fall into established and different categories (*R v McElhorne* [1983] Crim LR 487).

The Magistrates' Association has produced Magistrates' Courts Sentencing Guidelines (1 September 2000) which include many of the offences which come before the court on a frequent and regular basis. The Guidelines provide a structure for assessing the seriousness of the particular offence and for determining the appropriate sentence for that offence and the particular offender. In supporting the Guidelines, the Lord Chancellor and a former Lord Chief Justice have said of them:

(1) they are only guidelines and do not curtail a court's discretion in imposing the sentence it considers appropriate;

(2) they may be considered as a notional starting point;

(3) they exist to help in arriving at the appropriate sentence and to give more information in that process;

(4) they help to assist in maintaining an overall consistency of approach in sentencing.

MATTERS TO BE CONSIDERED

Factual basis for sentence

It is important that any sentence imposed on an offender should have a sound factual basis, whether he pleaded guilty or whether there has been a trial. On the trial of an information the court forms its own view of the facts and must deal with him on those facts. Where the accused pleads guilty, or a different court deals with sentence, the prosecutor will summarise the facts in open court, informing the court of the factual basis on which sentence ought to be based, and enabling the accused to challenge anything with which he does not agree.

Note that:

(1) information relating to the offender's antecedents and character is provided by the prosecutor; it ought to be sufficiently particularised to make it possible it to be challenged, and ought to be first-hand information, wherever possible, without reliance on hearsay or records; (*R v Wilkins* (1978) 66 Cr App R 49; *R v Robinson* [1969] Crim LR 314);

(2) submissions in mitigation which, though relevant to sentence, are not immediately connected with the facts of the offence should be considered as part of the sentencing process;

(3) mitigating circumstances, if not admitted by the prosecutor, ought to be established by the accused, on a balance of probabilities (*R v Odey* (1984) 6 Cr App R(S) 318; *R v Council* (1983) 5 Cr App R(S) 366).

Resolution of disputed facts: 'Newton hearing'

Where:

(1) it appears that a plea of guilty involves a clear admission of the whole of the ingredients of the offence charged, the court is entitled to accept that plea;

(2) there is any area of dispute as to facts which go not to the ingredients of the offence but the dispute between the prosecution and the defence is such to have a potentially significant effect on the level of sentence, the court must give consideration to holding a 'Newton hearing' to resolve the issue (*R v Newton* [1983] Crim LR 198). A 'Newton hearing' should only be held where the difference on facts is material to sentence (*R v Sweeting* [1988] Crim LR 131);

(3) the defendant, having pleaded guilty, puts forward an account of the offence which the prosecution does not, or feels it cannot challenge, but which the court feels unable to accept either because it conflicts with the prosecution's facts or because it is inherently incredible and defies common sense, it is desirable that the court makes it clear that

it does not accept the defence version and why (*R v Tolera* [1998] Crim LR 425);

(4) the court has decided upon summary trial, it should hear evidence upon any disputed facts and resolve any dispute itself, proceeding to sentence in the light of the facts found (*R v Telford MC, ex p Darlington* (1987) 152 JP 215);

(5) the court decides not to hear evidence, but to deal with sentence in the light of any submissions made by counsel, then if there is any substantial dispute between prosecutor and accused, the version put forward by the accused must be accepted (*R v Smith* [1986] Crim LR 640).

There is no need to hold a hearing of this nature where the version put forward by the accused is patently absurd (*R v Hawkins* [1986] Crim LR 194; *R v McKenzie* [1986] Crim LR 346; *R v Bilinski* (1988) 86 Cr App R 146), or in a case where the prosecutor's version is not disputed but new material is put forward to offset the gravity of the allegation (*R v Hopkins* [1987] Crim LR 204; *R v Ogunti* [1987] Crim LR 836).

Where there is a dispute as to relevant facts affecting sentence, the defence should make the matter clear to the prosecutor at the outset of the hearing (*R v Gardener* [1994] Crim LR 301).

The initiative for holding a 'Newton hearing' must be with the court and it is not dependant on the prosecution or defence asking for it (*R v Beswick* [1996] Crim LR 62).

Antecedents: administrative matters

Antecedents will be prepared by the police and submitted to the CPS with the case file. Five copies of the antecedents will be prepared in respect of each defendant and provided to the CPS who will be responsible for distributing them to others at the sentencing hearing. Normally two copies will be provided to the court, one to the defence and one to the probation service when appropriate.

Where, following conviction, a custodial order is made, one of the court's copies will be attached to the order sent to the prison. In instances where antecedents have been provided to the court some time before the hearing the police will, if requested to do so by the CPS, check the record of convictions.

Details of any additional convictions will be provided using the standard format above. These will be provided as above and attached to the documents already supplied. Details of any additional outstanding cases will also be provided at this stage. These apply unless there is a local agreement between the CPS and the court that alters that arrangement (*Practice Direction* (*criminal: consolidated*) [2002] 3 All ER 904, para 27).

Offences taken into consideration

The offender may, at this stage, admit other offences, and may ask for them to be taken into consideration. The procedure outlined in TICs (see pp 403, 404) must be carefully followed.

Discount for plea of guilty

PCC(S)A 2000, s 152

A court is required by statute to take into account, in deciding on sentence, both the stage at which the offender indicated his intention to plead guilty, and the circumstances in which the indication was given; and the court, where it imposes a sentence which is less severe than it would otherwise have been, must state that fact in open court (*R v Hastings* [1966] RTR 331).

A plea of guilty may be taken as an indication of remorse, and there is a public policy aspect in encouraging it. The superior courts have developed a policy by which:

(1) a discount must be given for a plea of guilty, depending on when it is entered; and

(2) a discount must not be refused (*R v Costen* [1989] Crim LR 601) unless the case falls within a limited range, as where the offender is a danger to the public and the need to protect the public outweighs the usual policy.

The accused must be made aware that he will have a discount if he pleads guilty, and that if he waits until the last moment before doing so, that discount will be reduced. He must thereafter see the discount clearly reflected in his sentence (*R v Okee* [1988] 2 Cr App R(S) 199).

Mathematical calculations, such as those suggested by the superior courts for Crown Court sentences (*R v Hoult* [1990] Crim LR 664; *R v Buffrey* [1993] Crim LR 319) are of little value in the magistrates' courts; but certain points may be valid, such as:

(a) where the plea is clearly a tactical one no discount, or only a minimal one, need be given;

(b) where the plea is delayed until the last minute a minimal discount may be given (*R v Okee* (*above*));

(c) a greater discount should be given to an offender who pleads guilty at the first opportunity, than to one who leaves it to a later stage (*R v Rafferty* [1998] Crim LR 433, *R v Barber* [2002] 1 Cr App R(S) 386); and

(d) where the offender is caught red-handed and a plea of guilty is virtually inevitable (*R v Morris* (1988)10 Cr App R (S) 216), no discount need be given.

Where committal to the Crown Court for sentence (see COMMITTAL FOR SENTENCE) is applicable, the offender may have his discount by not being committed.

In the case of juvenile offenders, a discount should be given on the usual principles (summarised in *R v Sharkev and Daniels* [1994] Crim LR 866).

Assistance to the authorities

Offenders need to know that it is worth their while, in so far as sentence is concerned, disclosing the criminal activities of others, for the benefit of the law-abiding public in general (*R v Sivan* [1988] Crim LR 771). Cases of this sort are more likely to arise in the Crown Court, but the principles governing them are similar.

Any relevant information should be put before the court in the form of a document by a senior police officer or a member of any other law-enforcement agency. It should not be heard in private by the court.

Note that:

(1) it should be shown to the offender and his consent should be obtained to its being tendered;

(2) if the offender disagrees with its contents it is not appropriate to permit cross-examination of the person who presented it – he is not a witness for the prosecutor; the offender may ask for an adjournment for another document to be prepared;

If the offender objects to its contents, the court should disregard it (*R v X* [1999] Crim LR 678).

OTHER FACTORS RELEVANT TO SENTENCE

Prison overcrowding.

Courts are encouraged, when considering a comparatively short sentence, to consider whether an even shorter one might not be equally effective in protecting the public interest and punishing and deterring the offender (*R v Ollerenshaw* [1998] Crim LR 515, updating *R v Bibi* [1980] 1 WLR 1193). This approach is no less valid in the light of prison overcrowding, a matter of grave concern. Imprisonment is to be imposed when necessary and for no longer than is necessary (*R v Kefford* [2002] Crim LR 432).

In *R v Lipton* (1980) 71 Cr App R 102), it was said that this approach applied:

(1) 'not only to the obvious case of the first offender for whom any prison sentence, however short, might be an adequate punishment and deterrent'; but also

(2) to certain other comparatively less serious offences; but

(3) *not* to 'most robberies, most offences of violence, the use of a weapon to wound, or to burglary of private dwelling houses' (as to such, see further MODE OF TRIAL; **Burglary: Dwelling house**).

Views of victim

The damaging and distressing effects of a crime on the victim clearly represent an important factor in the sentencing decision, and those effects may include the anguish and emotional suffering of the victim or, in a case of death, the surviving close family (*R v Nunn* [1996] Crim LR 210), but:

(1) the sentence imposed by the court cannot *depend* upon the views of the victim of the offence; it is for the court to assess the impact of the offence on the particular victim though where:
   (a) the sentence passed may actually aggravate the victim's distress, this may be a consideration; and
   (b) the victim's forgiveness may be treated as showing that the harm done by the offender is less than would otherwise be the case (see *R v Roche* [1999] Crim LR 339);

(2) the court needs to balance the victim's views with the nature of the offence and the particular facts of the case (*R v Nunn* [1996] Crim LR 210, *R v Hayes* (1999) *The Times*, 5 April; *R v Roche* (*above*)); and

(3) the court is entitled to receive evidence of the psychological effects of the offence on the victim.

On the other hand, the opinions of the victim or the surviving members of his family about the appropriate level of sentence do not provide any sound basis for an assessment (*R v Nunn* (*above*)).

Victims' personal statements

A scheme, which started on 1 October 2001, gives victims a more formal opportunity to say how a crime has affected them. It may help to identify whether they have a particular need for information, support and protection. It will also enable the court to take the statement into account when determining sentence.

When a police officer takes a statement from a victim the victim is told about the scheme and given the chance to make a victim personal statement. Such a statement may be made or updated at any time prior to the disposal of the case. The decision about whether or not to make such a statement is entirely for the victim.

If the court is presented with a victim personal statement the following approach should be adopted:

(1) the victim personal statement and any evidence in support should be considered and taken into account by the court prior to passing sentence;

(2) evidence of the effects of an offence on the victim contained in the victim personal statement or other statement, must be in proper form, ie made under CJA 1967, s 9, or an expert's report, and served upon the defence solicitor or the accused if he is not represented, prior to sentence;

(3) except where inferences can properly be drawn from the nature of or circumstances surrounding the offence, the court must not make assumptions unsupported by evidence about the effects of an offence on the victim;

(4) the court must pass what it judges to be the appropriate sentence having regard to the circumstances of the offence and of the offender, taking into account, so far as the court considers it appropriate, the consequences to the victim;

(5) the court should consider whether it is desirable in announcing sentence to refer to the evidence provided on behalf of the victim.

The opinions of the victim or the victim's close relatives as to what the sentence should be are therefore not relevant, unlike the consequence of the offence on them. Victims should be advised of this. If, despite the advice, opinions as to sentence are included in the statement, the court should pay no attention to them (*Practice Direction* (*criminal: consolidated*) [2002] 3 All ER 904, para 28).

The totality principle

When the court deals with an offender in respect of two or more offences and has calculated the sentence in respect of each offence, it should then review the aggregate sentence and decide whether the total sentence is just and appropriate (*R v Hewitt* [1980] Crim LR 116). Where, however, the court is considering community or custodial sentences the court must from the outset be aware of the seriousness of the offence and the criteria which must be satisfied in respect of such sentences.

If a court is imposing fines in respect of a number of offences it must review the total sum and ensure that it remains proportionate to the totality of the offending and that it is within the offender's capacity to pay (*R v Chelmsford CC, ex p Birchall* [1990] Crim LR 352).

No separate penalty

Where an offender has been convicted of a number of offences the court may deal with some by ordering 'no separate penalty' provided that no additional penalty is considered appropriate because of the number and nature of the offences or because the principal sentence is not available for all the offences being dealt with (see *R v Fairhurst* [1987] Crim LR 60).

THE MACHINERY OF SENTENCE

Presence of offender

The offender must be physically present in court where:

MCA 1980, s 11(3) (1) he is sentenced to a custodial sentence; or

MCA 1980, s 11(4) (2) a road traffic disqualification is imposed on him, unless, in this latter case:
   (a) the court has adjourned after conviction; and
   (b) he has been notified of the time and place for the resumption of the hearing, and the reason for the adjournment; and he fails to appear.

Representation

In general the offender should be present when sentence is announced, in particular:

(1) it is essential that that the offender or his legal representative has the opportunity to address the court in mitigation of sentence (*R v Billericay JJ, ex p Rumsay* [1978] Crim LR 306); and

(2) he must be present when a custodial sentence or a disqualification is imposed.

The court may proceed in the absence of the accused in accordance with such provisions of MCA 1980, ss 19–22 as are applicable in the circumstances, if the court considers that by reason of his 'disorderly conduct' it is not practicable for the proceedings to be conducted in his presence.

Spelling it out

Albeit the practical effects of a sentence are almost wholly governed by statutory provisions, it is desirable for the magistrates to ensure that the practical effects of the sentence are understood, not only by the offender, but by the victim and by any members of the public who are present in court or who read a fuller account of the proceedings in the newspapers.

As in the case of the finding, any explanation should be in terms of the magistrate(s) own choosing, taking care to ensure that the explanation is clear and accurate; it is a duty which cannot be delegated.

By statute, the court must:

(1) explain when passing a custodial sentence why PCC(S)A 2000, s 79 (2)(a) or (b) applies (see pp 169, 170);

(2) explain when passing a custodial term for a longer period than is commensurate with the offence (PCC(S)A 2000, s 83) to give its reasons;

(3) cause the reason for passing a custodial sentence to be entered in the warrant of commitment and recorded in the court register (see p 176);

(4) give reasons for not activating a suspended sentence in full (see p 180); and

(5) give its reasons for not making a compensation order (see p 139).

PROCEDURE AFTER SENTENCE

Suspending sentence pending appeal

There is no obligation on a court to suspend the operation of any sentence or order where an offender gives notice of appeal, but:

(1) it is the usual practice not to enforce a fine pending the result of any appeal;

(2) there is a power, but no obligation, to suspend a disqualification from driving; RTA 1988, s 39; MCA 1980, s 113(1)

(3) there is a power but no obligation, to grant bail to a person sentenced to a custodial term;

(4) a compensation order (see COMPENSATION), and, in some circumstances a restitution order (see FORFEITURE, CONFISCATION AND RESTITUTION), is suspended until the expiration of the time for appeal has expired, or, where notice is given, until the determination of the appeal.

Varying or rescinding a sentence

The court may subsequently vary or rescind a sentence or other order imposed or made when dealing with an offender if it appears that it would be in the interests of justice to do so. This power extends to replace a sentence or order which for any reason appears to be invalid. The power may be exercised at any time and by a court not necessarily composed of the original magistrates who imposed the sentence or made the order. MCA 1980, s 142

Derogatory assertions: publication

Where an accused has been convicted of an offence, and a speech in mitigation is made by him or on his behalf before the court determining in respect of the offence, or deciding whether he should be committed to the Crown Court for sentence and there are substantial grounds for believing: CPIA 1996, s 58

(1) that an assertion forming part of the speech or submission is derogatory to a person's character because it suggests that his conduct is, or has been, criminal, immoral or improper; and

(2) that the assertion is false, or that the facts asserted are irrelevant to the sentence; and

(3) the assertion was not made at the trial at which the person was convicted of the offence, or during any other proceedings relating to the offence,

the court may, as soon as is reasonably practicable after making the determination on sentence, make an order under s 58(8) in relation to the assertion, prohibiting its publication. Where it appears to the court that there is a real possibility of such an order being made, an order may be made at a time before the court has made its determination on sentence, under s 58(7).

An order under s 58(7), made in anticipation of an order under s 58(8) being made, may be revoked at any time, and in any event ceases to have effect when the court makes a determination with regard to sentencing. An order under s 58(8) may be made whether or not one under s 58(7) was made. An order under s 58(8) may also be revoked at any time, and in any event ceases to have effect at the end of a period of 12 months beginning with the day on which it was made.

DEFENCE PUBLIC FUNDING

LAA 1988 (and the LA (General) Regulations 1989 made under it) is repealed by AJA 1999 which establishes a Legal Service Commission having functions in relation to the Community Legal Service and the Criminal Defence Service which it sets up. The Commission is under a duty to establish, maintain and develop the Criminal Defence Service for the purpose of securing that individuals involved in criminal investigations or criminal proceedings have access to such advice, assistance and representation as the interests of justice require. AJA 1999, s 12(2)

The Criminal Defence Service (Funding) Order 2001 (SI 2001 No 855) (see p 221 *below*) makes provision for the funding and remuneration of services provided as part of the Criminal Defence Service.

'Criminal proceedings' defined

'Criminal proceedings' are proceedings:

(1) before any court for dealing with an individual accused of an offence;

(2) before any court for dealing with an individual convicted of an offence (including proceedings in respect of a sentence or order);

(3) for dealing with an individual under the Extradition Act 1989, s 9, Sched 6, para 6;

(4) for binding an individual over to keep the peace under MCA 1980, s 115 and for dealing with an individual who fails to comply with an order under that section;

(5) for contempt committed, or alleged to have been committed, by an individual in the face of the court; and

(6) concerning an individual before any such court or body as may be prescribed (other than the above).

Prescribed proceedings – s 12(2)(g)

The following have been prescribed as 'criminal proceedings' for the purposes of AJA 1999, s 12(2)(g): GR 2001, reg 3(2)(3)(4)

(1) civil proceedings in a magistrates' court arising from failure to pay a sum due or to obey an order of that court where such failure carries the risk of imprisonment;

(2) proceedings under CDA 1998, ss 1, 2 and 4 relating to anti-social behaviour orders or sex offender orders;

(3) proceedings under the CDA 1998, s 8(1)(b) relating to parenting orders made where an anti-social behaviour order or a sex offender order is made in respect of a child;

(4) proceedings under the CDA 1998, s 8(1)(c) relating to parenting orders made on conviction of a child;

(5) proceedings under CDA 1998, s 9(5) to discharge or vary a parenting order as mentioned in (3) and (4) *above*;

(6) proceedings under CDA 1998, s 10 to appeal against a parenting order made as mentioned in (3) or (4) *above*; and

(7) proceedings under FSA 1989, as amended, ss 14B, 14D, 14G, 14H, 21B and 21D (banning orders and references to a court).

Availability of representation

AJA 1999, s 14(1), Sched 3, para 1

A right to representation for the purposes of any kind of criminal procceedings may be granted to an individual such as is mentioned in relation to that kind of proceedings in s 12(2) of the Act (see *above*). Representation may also be granted to an individual to enable him to resist an appeal to the Crown Court otherwise than in an official capacity.

General power to grant representation

GR 2001, reg 5

Whether or not an application has been made for a representation order, the court may at any stage of proceedings, in the circumstances provided for under GR 1, grant such an order.

'Court' here includes any body before which criminal proceedings take place.

Grant of right by court

AJA 1999, s 14 Sched 3, para 2; GR 2001, reg 3(4)

A court before which any criminal proceedings take place, or are to take place, may grant a right to representation in the interests of justice:

(1) in respect of those proceedings;

(2) for the purpose of any related bail proceedings;

(3) for the purpose of any preliminary or incidental proceedings; and

(4) for the purpose of criminal proceedings before another court.

Applications for judicial review or *habeas corpus* relating to any criminal investigations or proceedings are not to be regarded as incidental to such criminal investigations or proceedings.

Contempt cases

AJA 1999, s 12(2)(f)

In any proceedings for contempt committed, or alleged to have been committed by an individual in the face of the court, the court may order that the person concerned be granted representation for the purposes of the proceedings, if it appears desirable in the interests of justice.

Statutory criteria

Any question as to whether a right to representation should be granted must be determined according to the interests of justice. In deciding what the interests of justice are in relation to any individual, the following factors, now statutory, but identical with those obtained in the light of the authorities decided on the previous legislation (but which may be added to or varied by the Lord Chancellor) are to be taken into account. AJA 1999, s 14, Sched 3, para 5

They are whether:

(1) the individual would, if any matter arising in the proceedings is decided against him, be likely to lose his liberty or livelihood or suffer serious damage to his reputation;

(2) the determination of any matter arising in the proceedings may involve consideration of a substantial question of law;

(3) the individual may be unable to understand the proceedings or to state his case;

(4) the proceedings may involve tracing, interviewing or expert cross-examination of witnesses on his behalf; and

(5) it is in the interests of another person that the applicant be represented.

A right to representation must always be granted in such circumstances as may be prescribed.

Applying for representation

'Representation' here, means representation for the purposes of proceedings and includes the assistance which is usually given by a representative in the steps preliminary or incidental to any proceedings and, subject to any time limits which may be prescribed, advice and assistance as to any appeal. AJA 1999, s 26

An application for a representation order in respect of proceedings in a magistrates' court is made either to the appropriate officer of the court in Form A or: GR 2001, regs 4, 7

(1) orally to the court;

(2) where a notice of transfer for trial under CJA 187, s 4 (serious fraud cases) has been given, to the appropriate officer of the court;

(3) orally or in writing to the court enquiring into the offence as examining justices or sending for trial under CDA 1998, s 51;

(4) in the case of an appeal to the Crown Court, to the appropriate officer of that court;

(5) where the applicant was granted a representation order for proceedings in a magistrates' court and was committed for trial in the Crown Court under MCA 1980, s 6(2), to the appropriate officer of the magistrates' court ordering the committal,

and the appropriate officer of the relevant court, or the relevant court, may grant or refuse the application. A statement of means in Form B is not ordinarily required since a magistrates' court has no power to order any contribution, or to make a recovery of defence costs order, but is required for the purposes of the Crown Court when an accused is sent for trial under CDA 1998, s 51.

Where application is made orally to the court, the court may refer it to the proper officer for determination.

The appropriate officer of each court keeps a record of every application to that court for a representation order, and of its outcome.

Where an application is refused, the appropriate officer will deliver to the applicant written reasons for the refusal and the details of the appeal process.

Applying to the Commission: regulation 3(2) cases

GR 2001, reg 4(3)

Any application for the grant of a representation order in respect of those criminal proceedings set out in GR 2001, 3(2) for the purposes of AJA 1999, s 12 (2)(g) (ie those listed at p 213 (*above*)) must be made on Form A and must be made to the Commission, and may only be granted by the Commission or a person acting on behalf of the Commission where such function has been delegated in accordance with AJA 1999, s 3(4). Where such an application is refused, the applicant will be provided by the Commission with written reasons for the refusal and details of the appeal process.

Selecting a representative

AJA 1999, s 15; GR 2000, regs 9, 11

An individual who has been granted a representation order may select any representative(s) willing to act for him. Where he does so, the the Commission (under AJA 1999, s 14(1)) will fund such representation, provided the representative selected is:

(1) employed by the Commission to provide such representation; or

(2) authorised to provide such representation under a crime franchise contract with the Commission, which commences on or after 2 April 2001 and specifies the rate of remuneration for such representation.

Representation in magistrates' courts etc

GR 2001, regs 9, 10

In relation to any criminal proceedings in a magistrates' court, any proceedings in the Crown Court coming within regs 3(2), 9–10 (*above*) and any proceedings preliminary or incidental thereto (but not proceedings for contempt in the face of the court), representation is restricted to a representative:

(1) employed by the Commission to provide such representation; or

(2) authorised to provide such representation under a crime franchise contract with the Commission which commences on or after 2 April 2000, and specifies the rate of remuneration for such representation.

An order may include representation by an advocate in a magistrates' court only in the case of an indictable offence, including one triable either way, or proceedings under the Extradition Act 1989, s 9, or Sched 1, para 6.

An 'advocate' in this context is a barrister or a solicitor who has obtained a higher advocacy qualification in accordance with regulations and the rules of the Law Society.

Where, however, the court is of the opinion that circumstances make the proceedings unusually grave or difficult, it may grant representation by both a solicitor and an advocate, if it considers it would be desirable.

Representation in the Crown Court

GR 2000, reg 11

Representation under a representation order in respect of any proceedings in the Crown Court (other than those mentioned in reg 3(2)) (see pp 213, 214 *above*)) is exercisable only in relation to those representatives who are:

(1) employed by the Commission to provide such representation;

(2) authorised to provide such representation under a crime franchise contract with the Commission; or

(3) involved in a 'very high cost' serious fraud case, where representation is limited to a current member of the Serious Fraud Panel.

Note that:

(a) a 'very high cost' case is one where the trial is likely to last for 25 days or more, or specific costs are likely to amount to £150,000 or more; and

(b) the 'Serious Fraud Panel' is a panel of solicitors appointed under arrangements made by the Commission to deal with such cases.

Such a case is one in which the offence charged is primarily or substantially founded on allegations of fraud or other serious financial impropriety, or involves complex financial transactions. The regulation does not apply to any proceedings referred to in AJA 1999, s. 12(2)(f) (proceedings for contempt in the face of the court).

Representation in very high cost cases

VHCCR 2001, reg 3(1)(2)

Where a representation order has been granted in relation to a very high cost case and the Commission proposes to enter into an individual contract for the provision of funded services in relation to that case, and either:

(1) it serves notice that it does not propose to enter into such a contract with any or all of the current representatives; or

(2) any or all of those representatives serves notice that they do not propose to enter into such a contract,

then the Commission is no longer required to fund representation by the relevant current representative. The person in whose favour the representation order was made may select a different representative chosen in accordance with GR 2001, and the representation order may be amended accordingly.

Amendment and revocation

GR 2001, reg 3(1)(2)

Where a representation order has been granted by a relevant court or in the relevant circumstances by the Commission, it may be amended or withdrawn, whether by the relevant court or by the Commission. If legal representatives withdraw during the trial, fresh solicitors and counsel must be assigned unless the order is revoked (*R v Harris* [1985] Crim LR 244; *R v Chambers* [1989] Crim LR 367; *R v Dimech* [1991] Crim LR 846).

In some circumstances the court may have to conduct an enquiry as to why an accused has dispensed with his legal representatives (*R v Seale* [1997] Crim LR 899).

Renewal of application

ROAR 2001, reg 4

An applicant whose application for a representation order has been refused by the court is entitled to renew his application either orally or in writing to the same court, or in writing to the appropriate officer of that court.

Where an application is renewed:

(1) to the appropriate officer, he may either grant it or refer it to a magistrate; or

(2) to the court, the court may grant it, refuse it or refer it to the appropriate officer, in which case the latter may grant it or refer it to a magistrate.

A magistrate of the court to whom an application is referred may grant or refuse the application, giving reasons for that refusal, and where the application is in writing, reasons must be given in writing.

ROAR 2001, reg 6

A person whose application for a grant of a representation order has been refused by the Commission is also entitled to renew it, in writing to the Funding Review Committee, which may grant or refuse it, giving reasons in writing for any refusal.

Withdrawal of representation

GR 2001, reg 15

The court before which proceedings are heard, or, in respect of any proceedings mentioned in regulation 3(2), the Commission, must consider whether to withdraw the representation order:

(1) where any charge or proceedings against the assisted person are varied, the court or the Commission as appropriate, must consider whether the interests of justice continue to require that he be represented in respect of the varied charge or the proceedings;

(2) where the assisted person declines to accept a representation order in the terms which are offered;

(3) at the request of the assisted person; or

(4) where the representative named on the representation order declines to continue to represent the assisted person.

Where representation is withdrawn, the appropriate officer or the Commission, as appropriate, will provide written notification to the assisted person and to the solicitor (or, where there was no solicitor assigned, to the advocate), who must inform any assigned advocate (or, where notification is given to the advocate, any other assigned advocate).

If there is a subsequent application by the assisted person for a representation order in respect of the same proceedings, he must declare the previous withdrawal of representation and the reason for it.

Where a representation order has been withdrawn, appeal lies against such withdrawal on one occasion only, to the body which withdrew the order. Regulations 4 to 6 (*above*) apply to such appeals. ROAR 2001, reg 7

An appeal in writing must be in such form as is from time to time specified.

Magistrates' assignment of Queen's Counsel in Crown Court

A magistrates' court has power to grant a representation order for Queen's Counsel only in the following circumstances: GR 2001, reg 12(14)

(1) for Queen's Counsel alone on a committal, transfer or sending for trial for murder; or

(2) for Queen's Counsel with one junior counsel, upon receiving a notice of transfer under CJA 1987, s 4, where the prosecution is brought by the Serious Fraud Office.

Change of representatives

The court may grant or refuse an application for a change of representative. GR 2001, reg 14 The application may be made to the court before which proceedings are heard to select a representative in place of a representative previously selected. The application must state the grounds on which it is made.

The court may grant the application where:

(1) the representative considers himself under a duty to withdraw from the case in accordance with his professional rules of conduct and, in

such a case, the representative must provide details of the nature of such duty;

(2) there is a breakdown in the relationship between the assisted person and the representative such that effective representation can no longer be provided and, in such a case, the representative must provide details of the nature of the breakdown;

(3) through circumstances beyond his control, the representative is no longer able to represent the assisted person; or

(4) some other substantial compelling reason exists.

Authorisation of expenditure

GR 2001, reg 17

Where it appears necessary for the proper conduct of proceedings for costs to be incurred under a representation order by taking any of the following steps:

(1) obtaining the written report of one or more experts;

(2) employing any other person to provide a written report or opinion (otherwise than as an expert);

(3) obtaining any transcripts or recordings; or

(4) doing anything which is unusual in its nature or requires unusually large expenditure,

the solicitor may apply to the Costs Committee (as formerly one applied to the Legal Aid Area Committee) for prior authority to do so.

Travelling and accommodation expenses

GR 2001, reg 18

A representative assigned to an assisted person may apply to the court for prior authority for the incurring of travelling and accommodation expenses in order to attend at the trial or other proceedings.

Transfer of documents

GR 2001, reg 16

Where an accused is committed or sent for trial by a lower court to a higher court, or appeals from a lower court to a higher court, the appropriate officer of the lower court must send to the appropriate officer of the higher court:

(1) a copy of any representation order previously made in respect of the same proceedings; and

(2) a copy of any application for a representation order which has been refused.

Notification of very high costs cases

GR 2001, reg 21

Any solicitor who has conduct of a funded very high cost case (see pp 217, 218 (*above*)) must notify the Commission as soon as practicable. If he fails to do so without good reason, and as a result there is a loss to public funds, the court or Commission, as appropriate, may refuse payment of his costs up to the extent of such loss. However, such payment must not be refused without the solicitor being given a reasonable opportunity to show why it should not be refused.

Duty to report abuse

Where a representative for an applicant or assisted person knows or suspects that a person: GR 2001, reg 22

(1) has intentionally failed to comply with any provision of regulations made under AJA 1999 concerning the information to be provided by him; or

(2) in furnishing such information, has knowingly made a false statement or false representation,

the representative must immediately report the circumstances to the Commission. This duty is notwithstanding the relationship between, or the rights of a representative and client, or any privilege arising out of such a relationship.

Funding

The Criminal Defence Service (Funding) Order 2001 (SI 2001 No 855) makes provison for the funding and remuneration of services provided as part of the Criminal Defence Service until 4 April 2005. AJA 1999, ss 13(3), 14(3), 105, Sched

It is further provided that the Commission may only fund services as part of the Criminal Defence Service by making payments in respect of the provision of representation in contempt proceedings.

For contract services, remuneration is limited to the rates set out in Part E of the specfication to the Commission's General Criminal Contract. Special maximum rates are provided for services in high cost cases, funded by the Lord Chancellor or under individual contracts.

DEFERRING SENTENCE

Where the court is satisfied, having regard to the nature of the offence and to the character and antecedents of the offender, that it would be in the interests of justice so to do; it may defer passing sentence on an offender until such date as it may specify, not being more than six months after the date of the deferment is announced, for the purpose of enabling the court, in dealing with him to have regard to: PCC(S)A 2000, s 1(1)(2)(3)

(1) his conduct after conviction (including, where appropriate his making reparation for his offence); or

(2) any change in his circumstances.

Deferment in this manner does not imply that the offence or offences 'were not so serious that a non-custodial sentence cannot be justified'; the court may think that a custodial sentence is justified and still defer, having regard to the offender's circumstances (*R v Bray* (1991) 12 Cr App R(S) 705).

Where the passing of sentence is deferred under these provisions, it may not be deferred again by the magistrates' court under the same provisions. PCC(S)A 2000, ss 1(2)(3)(7)

Objects of deferment

Deferment may be appropriate where:

(1) the conduct of the offender is not sufficiently specific to be made the subject of a condition imposed as part of a community rehabilitation order; or

(2) where the steps to be taken by the offender could not, of themselves, be the subject of a condition, for example where he is to make reparation, or at least demonstrate a real intention and capacity to do so.

Deferring sentence: the procedure

The legislature and the superior courts have hedged around with difficulties what should have been a very simple provision. In order to avoid the problems that can arise from the exercise of the power to defer, the court should note that:

(1) if it intends to exercise the power under s 1, the word 'defer', should be expressly used; if it intends merely to adjourn, the word should be avoided altogether (*R v Fairhead* [1975] 2 All ER 737);

(2) sentence can be deferred under s 1 only with the offender's consent, and he should be asked expressly if he consents (*R v McQuaide* [1975] Crim LR 246);

(3) it should be made clear to the offender what the particular purpose of the deferment is, and what conduct is expected of him during the period, and, ideally, he should be given notice of the terms in writing (*R v George* [1984] 3 All ER 13);

(4) a district judge who sits regularly at a particular location should reserve to himself the duty of dealing with the case on the date to which it is deferred, a bench of magistrates ought to leave a note of their reasoning to be available on that day (*R v Jacobs* (1976) 62 Cr App R 116);

(5) only a district judge who is sure that he will deal with the case on the date to which sentence is deferred should give any hint as to the probable outcome of the case (*R v Johnson* (1981) 145 JP 491).

Ancillary orders; RT disqualification

Deferment being, in effect, a species of adjournment, there is no power to make any order other than:

(1) a restitution order (see FORFEITURE); or

(2) a road traffic disqualification (see DISQUALIFICATION AND ENDORSEMENT).

(*R v Dwyer* (1975) 60 Cr App R 39); nor is there power to attach conditions to the deferment, such as medical treatment (*R v Skelton* [1983] Crim LR 686).

When deferring sentence, there is no power to remand, and therefore no questions as to bail can arise (see *R v Ross* (1988) 86 Cr App R 337).

Process to compel appearance

PCC(S)A 2000, s 2(4)

Where sentence has been deferred upon an offender and the court proposes to sentence him, whether on the date originally specified, or before that date in consequence of a further conviction, or where the offender does not appear on the date specified, a summons, or in an appropriate case a warrant, may be issued to bring him before the court.

Passing sentence on the deferred date

PCC(S)A 2000, s 1(5)

Where sentence has been deferred, the offender falls to be sentenced:

(1) on the date to which sentence was deferred, or on any date to which that hearing has been adjourned or postponed; or

(2) if, before the expiration of the period of deferment, he is convicted in Great Britain of any offence.

The power to deal with an offender in a case where the passing of sentence has been deferred includes power to deal with him in any way in which the court which deferred sentence could have dealt with him, and includes the power conferred by PCC(S)A 2000, s 3, to commit him to the Crown Court for sentence.

It should be noted that;

(a) it is not necessary that the offender be dealt with exactly on the date originally specified; there is nothing to prevent the court adjourning or postponing the hearing of the matter, provided it does not defer again under s 1(*R v Ingle* [1974] 3 All ER 811); but

(b) if sentence is deferred to a date after the expiry of the six month period, the court is deprived of its jurisdiction to sentence (*R v W London Stipendiary Magistrate, ex p Watts* (1987) *The Times*, 30 May);

(c) counsel who represented the offender on the earlier occasion should, if possible appear for him on the date when sentence is to be passed (*R v Ryan* [1976] Crim LR 508).

The purpose of deferment must be ascertained from the available information, and the court needs to determine if the offender has substantially conformed, or attempted to conform, with the proper expectations of the court which deferred sentence. If he has, then he may legitimately expect that an immediate custodial sentence will not be imposed. If he has not, the court should be careful to state with precision in what respects he has failed (*R v George* (*above*). It should not be influenced by other proceedings which are pending but incomplete (*R v Aquilina* [1990] Crim LR 134).

Sentence after further conviction

PCC(S)A 2000, s 2(2)(3)

Where an offender, in respect of whom a court has deferred sentence is, during the period, convicted in England and Wales of a subsequent offence, then, without prejudice to s 1(1), and whether or not the offender is sentenced for the later offence during the period of deferment, the court which passes sentence on him for the subsequent offence may also, if this has not already been done, pass sentence on him for the offences for which sentence was deferred.

Nature of sentence on deferred date

On the day on which the sentence originally deferred is dealt with, the court is bound to approach the matter on a fair consideration of the offender's progress, if any, during the period of deferment. Thus:

(1) it would be wrong to imprison the offender if he has fulfilled that which was required of him (*R v Gilby* [1975] 2 All ER 743; *R v Head* [1976] Crim LR 157; *R v Smith* [1979] Crim LR 251); and

(2) if the report made to the court is not unfavourable, a substantial custodial sentence is probably not appropriate.

He should not be sentenced, on the date to which the sentence is deferred, on the basis of 'extraneous' matters, such as failure to report to the police on another matter under investigation, or failure to pay outstanding fines in respect of other offences (*R v Benstead* (1979) 1 Cr App R (S) 32).

DISQUALIFICATION AND ENDORSEMENT

An offender convicted of one of the more serious offences involving motor vehicles may be disqualified from driving a motor vehicle and from holding or obtaining a driving licence. HO 1990

Disqualification:

(1) to some extent serves a basic public protection purpose, where the offender's conduct has proved a danger to other road users; and

(2) in most cases, is intended to punish misuse, or careless use, of vehicles and to deter both the offender and others from indulging in it.

Disqualification is part of the basic penalty imposed by the court for the offence, but it is an ancillary order and must always be attached to the sentence; it cannot stand alone.

The court should not give partial judgment by, eg, fining an offender on one occasion and imposing an order of disqualification on another. The whole of the sentence should be imposed at one time (*R v Talgarth JJ, ex p Bithell* [1973] 2 All ER 717), but see *R v Annesley* [1976] 1 All ER 589, and '**Interim disqualification**' (p 229 *below*).

Length of disqualification

The law provides no limit to the length of a disqualification beyond any minimum prescribed, but the superior courts have advised against the use of very long periods unless the offender is a menace to other road users (*R v Rickard* [1975] RTR 104; *R v Davitt* [1974] Crim LR 719). An offender disqualified for a very long period is particularly likely to commit further offences of driving whilst disqualified which he might not, were the term shorter.

There is no rule that an offender who is sent to prison and also disqualified has the right to have the period of disqualification coincide, more or less automatically, with the period he has to serve. The nature of the offence, his antecedents, and the extent to which he will be handicapped by not being able to drive on his release, are all matters which need to be taken into consideration (*R v Hansel* (1982) 4 Cr App R(S) 368).

All disqualifications run from the date of imposition; there cannot be consecutive periods.

As to disqualification for life, see *R v Buckley* [1994] Crim LR 387.

Situations in which disqualification arises

RTOA 1988, s 34

An offender may be disqualified:

(1) where the offence of which he is convicted attracts obligatory or discretionary disqualification; or

RTOA 1988, s 35

(2) where he has committed repeated offences attracting such disqualification under the 'totting-up' provisions;

PCC(S)A 2000, s 147

(3) where a vehicle has been used for the purpose of an assault (ie in a non-road traffic situation); and

PCC(S)A 2000, s 146(1)(2)(3)

(4) in addition to dealing with him in any other way.

The various systems run parallel to each other, and are not mutually exclusive.

Where the court proposes to impose a discretionary disqualification, it should draw this to the attention of the offender or his legal representative, so that he may deal with the point specifically (*R v Powell & Carvell* [1985] Crim LR 330).

RTOA 1988, s 44

The particulars of all offences involving obligatory or discretionary disqualification must be endorsed on the offender's licence:

(1) unless there are special reasons for not doing so, irrespective of whether he is disqualified or not; or

(2) in the case of exemption from disqualification and endorsement for certain construction and use offences, where a person is convicted of an offence under RTA 1988:
   (a) under s 40A (using a vehicle in a dangerous condition etc) the court must not order him to be disqualified, or order any particulars of penalty points to be endorsed, if he proves, on a balance of probabilities, that he did not know and had no reasonable cause to suspect that use of the vehicle involved the danger of injury to any person; and
   (b) under s 41A (breach of requirement as to brakes, steering gear or tyres) the court must not order him to be disqualified, or order any particulars of penalty points to be endorsed, if he proves, on a balance of probabilities, that he did not know and had no reasonable cause to suspect that the offence would be committed.

RTOA 1988, ss 29, 31

The court, in deciding whether or not to exercise its powers of discretionary disqualification may take into account particulars of:

(i) previous convictions endorsed on the counterpart of the offender's licence, or are revealed on a printout of the offender's driving record from DVLA; and

(ii) any penalty points which are to be taken into account in considering the totting-up' provisions (see pp 234–236 *below*).

Absolute and conditional discharge

Where the court makes an order of conditional or absolute discharge in respect of an offence carrying obligatory or discretionary disqualification or compulsory endorsement, it may exercise any power of discretionary disqualification, and *must* exercise any duty of obligatory disqualification. RTOA 1988, s 46(1)

Interim disqualification

The court may impose an interim disqualification in respect of an offender convicted of an offence involving obligatory or discretionary disqualification where it:

(1) commits him to the Crown Court for sentence (see COMMITTAL FOR SENTENCE) under PCC(S)A 2000, s 6 or any enactment mentioned in s 6(4) to which that section applies; RTOA 1988, s 26

(2) remits him to another magistrates' court, under MCA 1980, s 39 (see DEALING WITH AN OFFENDER);

(3) defers passing sentence on him (see DEFERMENT OF SENTENCE); or

(4) adjourns his case after conviction but before dealing with him (see ADJOURNMENT AND REMAND),

the interim disqualification to have effect until the offender has been dealt with in respect of the offence.

There is no need to specify a period, only to order disqualification. If the offender is not sentenced before the expiry of six months from the date of the order, the disqualification lapses. If the sentencing court subsequently imposes a disqualification, that disqualification will be treated as running from the date on which he was disqualified under the interim order.

The offender must produce his licence and any counterpart for endorsement; he commits an offence if he fails to do so, unless:

(a) he can satisfy the court that he has applied for a new licence and it has not yet been received; or

(b) he surrenders a receipt for his licence and its counterpart showing that it has been taken out of his possession under the fixed penalty system (as to which see p 234 *below*), and produces the licence and its counterpart to the court immediately after their return.

The licence is not endorsed at this stage but the order is notified to the Secretary of State, as is any order of the sentencing court not disqualifying the offender.

Where an interim disqualification is imposed ('the first order') no other court may make a further order in respect of the same offence, or of any offence in respect of which the first order could have been made.

Production of the licence; suspension

RTOA 1988, s 27

Apart from any question of interim disqualification, in order to decide whether or not to exercise any of its powers of disqualification, the court must, unless it has already received them, require the offender's licence and its counterpart to be produced.

Where the offender has not done so, unless:

(1) he has produced a current receipt for it and its counterpart (issued under s 56) not later than the day before the appointed date for the hearing; or

(2) has posted it in the proper manner to the court; or

(3) produces it at the hearing,

he is guilty of an offence, and the licence is suspended from the date when its production was required until it is produced, together with its counterpart to the court, during which time it ceases to have effect.

1. OBLIGATORY DISQUALIFICATION FOR SERIOUS OFFENCES

On conviction of any of the offences (1)–(6) set out below, an offender *must* be disqualified, in the absence of special reasons (see pp 239–244 *below*), for *not less than 12 months*. On conviction of an offence of dangerous driving a re-test must be ordered, which in this case is an extended driving test, and he remains disqualified until he has passed the test.

RTOA 1988, s 34(1)

(1) dangerous driving (RTA 1988, s 2; RTA 1991, s 1) – DD3O;

(2) driving or attempting to drive whilst unfit through drink or drugs (RTA 1988, s 4(1)) – DR20;

(3) driving or attempting to drive with excess alcohol concentration (RTA 1988, s 5(1)(a)) – DR10;

(4) failing, without reasonable excuse, when driving or attempting to drive, to supply an evidential specimen (RTA 1988, s 7(6)) – DR30;

(5) motor racing and speed trials on public ways (RTA 1988, s 12) – MS50;

(6) aggravated vehicle taking (TA 1968, s 12A; AVTA 1992, s 3). The fact that the offender did not drive the vehicle is not to be regarded as a special reason either for not disqualifying or not endorsing;

RTOA 1988, s 34(4)

Where an offender, convicted of an offence carrying the obligatory disqualification, has, in the three years preceding that offence, been disqualified on two or more occasions for at least 56 days, the minimum period of disqualification for the offence must be two years.

On conviction of any of the offences under (2) (3) or (4), where the offender, in the 10 years immediately preceding the commission of that offence was convicted of a like offence, the court must disqualify him for *not less than* 3 years, unless for special reasons it thinks fit to order him: RTOA 1988, s 34(3)(4)

(a) *not* to be disqualified; or

(b) to be disqualified for a shorter period.

The grounds for that decision must be stated in open court and recorded in the register. RTOA 1988, s 47(1)

If on conviction of any of the above offences the court finds special reasons and does not disqualify, the licence must be endorsed with the number of points set out in RTA 1988, Sched 2 (see pp 233, 234).

Courses for drink/drive offenders

Where an offender is convicted of: RTOA 1988, s 36A

(1) driving or being in charge when under the influence of drink or drugs;

(2) driving or being in charge with excess alcohol; or

(3) failing to provide a specimen for analysis;

and is disqualified under RTOA 1988, s 34 for a period of not less than 12 months, the court may order that the period of disqualification under s 34 be reduced if the offender satisfactorily completes, by a specified date, a specified approved course, provided the reduction is not less than three months and does not exceed one quarter of the unreduced period.

Such an order is not to be made unless:

(a) the court is satisfied that a place on the specified course is available;

(b) the offender appears to the court to be of or over the age of 17;

(c) the effect of the course is explained in ordinary language to the offender and he is told of the fees, and the necessity of his paying them before the course begins; and

(d) the offender agrees to the order being made.

The date by which the course is to be completed must be at least two months before the last day of the disqualification as reduced; the order must specify the petty sessions area, or in the case of an order made by a district judge the commission area in which the offender resides, or will reside.

Completion of course; certificate

An offender will be regarded as having completed a course satisfactorily only if a certificate to that effect is received by the Clerk of the supervising court before the end of the disqualification imposed. If it is received after the end of RTOA 1988, s 34B, 34C the period as it would have been reduced, the order has effect as if the reduced period ended with the date on which it was received.

Where the course organiser declines to give a certificate, redress is given to an aggrieved offender, who may apply to the supervising court for relief.

2. OFFENCES CARRYING DISCRETIONARY DISQUALIFICATION

HO 1990

Discretionary disqualification and obligatory endorsement (RTOA 1988, ss 34(2),44; RTA 1991, s 29) apply to road traffic offences which are not, like those carrying obligatory disqualification, invariably grave matters, but which may still be serious enough to justify a period of disqualification.

Where the court does not exercise its power of disqualification, it *must,* in the absence of special reasons, endorse the licence with the appropriate number of penalty points.

These offences are:

No	Code	Offence	Statute	Max penalty	Pts
(7)	CD10 CD20 CD30	Careless driving Driving without reasonable consideration	RTA 1988 s 3	Level 4	3–9
(8)	SP10 SP20 SP30	Speeding	RTRA 1984 s 89(1)	Level 3	3–6, or 3 if fixed penalty
(9)	DR50	In charge, whilst unfit through drink or drugs	RTA 1988, s 4(2)	3 m and/or level 4	10
(10)	DR40	In charge, with excess alcohol	RTA 1988, s 5(1)(b)	3 m and/or level 4	10
(11)	DR70	Refusing roadside test	RTA 1988, s 6(4)	Level 3	4
(12)	DR60	Failure to provide specimen, otherwise than in (11) above	RTA 1988, s 7(6)	3 m and/or level 4	10
(13)	MS20	Carrying passenger on motorcycle	RTA1988, s 23	Level 3	3
(14)		Failure to comply with traffic directions including: TS10 (a) signals TS20 (b) double white lines; TS30 (c) stop sign TS40 (d) directions of constable TS50 (e) others	RTA 1988, s 35	Level 3	3
(15)	MS10	Dangerous position	RTA 1988, s 22	Level 3	3

No	Code	Offence	Statute	Max penalty	Pts
(16)	MW10	Contravention of temporary prohibition or restriction	RTRA 1984, s 16(1)	Level 3	3–6 or 3 if fixed penalty
		Special roads regulations (except stopping)	RTRA 1884, s 17(4)	Level 4	3–6, or 3 if committed in in respect of speed restriction, 3 in any other case
(17)	PC10 PC20 PC30	Pedestrian crossing offences	RTRA 1984, s 25(5)	Level 3	3
(18)	TS60	School crossing patrol offence	RTRA 1984, s 28(3)	Level 3	3
(19)	CU20 CU50 CU60	Dangerous condition etc	RTA 1988 s 40A	Level 5 (goods vehicles) otherwise level 4	3
(20)	CU10 CU30 CU40	Breach of requirement as to brakes, steering gear or tyres	RTA 1988, s 41A	Level 5 (goods vehicles) otherwise level 4	3
(21)	CU50	Load likely to cause danger because of its insecurity or position	RTA 1988, s 40A	No disqualification where offender proves that he did not know, and had no reasonable cause to suspect, that use of vehicle involved a danger of injury to any person	3
(22)	AC10	Failing to stop and give particulars	RTA 1988, s 107(4)	6 m and/or level 5	5–10
(23)	AC20	Failing to report accident	RTA 1988, s 107(4)	6 m and/or level 5	5–10
(24)	LC10	Driving otherwise than in accordance with licence	RTA 1988, s 87(1)	Level 3	3–6
(25)	LC30	Driving after making false declaration as to physical fitness	RTA 1988, s 92(1)	Level 4	3–6
(26)	LC40	Driving after such failure	RTA 1988, s 94(3A)	Level 3	3–6
(27)	LC5	Driving after refusal or revocation of licence	RTA 1988, ss 92(3),94A	6 m and/or level 5	3–6
(28)	IN10	No insurance	RTA 1988, s 43	Level 5	6–8
(29)	MS40	Driving with uncorrected defective eyesight	RTA 1988, s 96	Level 3	3
(30)	MS40	Refusing to submit to eye test	RTA 1988, s 96(3)	Level 3	3
(31)	BA10	Driving whilst disqualified	RTA 1988, s 103(1)(b)	6 m and/or Level 5	6

No	Code	Offence	Statute	Max penalty	Pts
(32)		Failure of vehicle keeper etc to give information as to identity of driver	RTA 1988, s 172	Level 3	3
(33)	UT10	Taking or attempting w/o consent	TA 1968, s 12	6 m and/or Level 5	
(34)	UT20	Stealing or attempting to steal vehicle	RTOA 1988 Sch 2, Pt 2	6 m and/or £5,000	
(35)	MS30	Playstreet offences	RTRA 1984 ss 29(3), 30(6)	Level 3	2
(36)	UT30	Going equipped for theft etc	TA 1968, s 25	6 m and/or Level 5	10
(37)		Aiding and abetting, etc obligatorily disqualifiable offence	RTOA 1988, s 28(1)(b)		

[1] Now an arrestable offence, Police Reform Act 2002.
[2] The High Court of Justiciary has held that an accused's reply in response to a police requirement for information as to the driver's identity under s 172(2), is inadmissible to prove that the accused was the driver on the occasion in question, because any other construction of the sub-section is incompatible with ECHR Art 6(1), and in particular, the protection against self-incrimination (*Brown v Procurator Fiscal* (2000) *The Times*, 4 February).

3. REPEATED OFFENCES – THE PENALTY POINTS SYSTEM

Penalty points

Under the penalty points system, an offender who commits a series of offences within a period of three years *must* be disqualified because of his repeated offending, whether or not the particular offence before the court would, in itself, justify disqualification.

It should be noted that:

RTOA 1988, s 5(1A)(5A)

(1) the system applies only to offences carrying obligatory or discretionary disqualification (as set out *above*);

(2) it applies in relation to an offence committed by aiding and abetting etc. the commission of an offence such as is described in (1) above as if the offence involved discretionary disqualification;

RTOA 1988, s 44(1)(a)

(3) if the court disqualifies the offender for his offence, *no penalty points* fall to be endorsed on his licence; if he is not disqualified they are, unless there are special reasons for not doing so;

RTOA 1988, s 28(4)

(4) if the offender is convicted, whether on the same occasion or not, of two or more offences committed on the same occasion and involving obligatory endorsement, the total number of penalty points to be attributed to them is the number that would be attributed on a conviction for one of them. Thus if the convictions are on separate

occasions, the number to be attributed on later occasions is thereby restricted; but

(5) if (4) above would ordinarily apply to two or more offences the court may still, if it thinks fit, decide that it will not apply to the offences, but must state its reasons for so doing in open court and enter those reasons in the register; RTOA 1988, s 28(5)

(6) once an offender is disqualified under RTOA 1988, s 35, the 'slate is wiped clean' of all penalty points accumulated up to the time of disqualification.

Disqualification

Disqualification under the penalty points system arises where the offender has, as a result of offences committed within the three-year period, accumulated a total of 12 or more penalty points, including those to be endorsed on the instant occasion, commonly known as 'totting'. HO 1990

The following points should be noted:

(1) if, taking the current offence into account, but disregarding any offence for which he is disqualified under RTOA 1988, s 34, the number of penalty points over the three-year period comes to 12 or more, the disqualification is obligatory unless there are 'mitigating circumstances'; RTOA 1988, s 35

(2) the qualifying date for both the earlier and the current offences is the *date of the offence,* not the date of conviction;

(3) where the offender is convicted on the same occasion of more than one offence involving obligatory or discretionary disqualification, not more than one 'totting up' disqualification may be imposed;

(4) the *minimum period* for which such a person is to be disqualified varies according to whether he has been previously disqualified during the three years preceding the commission of the latest offence in respect of which penalty points are being taken into account. If:
   (a) there are no such disqualifications, the minimum period is six months;
   (b) there is one – 12 months; and
   (c) there are two or more, the minimum period is two years.

Disqualification by the Crown Court under PCC(S)A 2000, s 147, or interim disqualifications pending committal to the Crown Court (RTOA 1988, s 26; RTA 1991, s 25) and disqualifications imposed in respect of stealing a vehicle (TA 1968, ss 12 and 25) or attempting to do so, are not included. PCC(S)A 2000, s 147

Disqualification and Endorsement

Mitigating circumstances

The court may disqualify such an offender under the 'totting' provisions for a period below the minimum required under the system, or may decide not to disqualify at all, where it is satisfied that there are grounds for mitigating the normal consequences of conviction, but may *not* do so where the offence is one carrying obligatory disqualification (see also *R v Thomas* [1983] 3 All ER 756).

'Mitigating circumstances' are not to be equated with 'special reasons' (see p 239 *below*). The former will, in the ordinary way, largely be circumstances pertaining to the offender, and concerned not with the gravity of the offence, but with the repetition of offences within a comparatively short period.

The statute expressly excludes from consideration, any circumstances:

(1) that are alleged to make the offence(s) not serious; or
(2) that show hardship, short of 'exceptional hardship';
(3) which have been taken into consideration already on another occasion within the three years immediately preceding the conviction.

The test of 'exceptional hardship' is not the same as that for 'special reasons'. The court does not need to hear sworn evidence, although obviously it will usually be desirable to do so (*Owen v Jones* [1988] RTR 102). Where an offender seeks to contend that mitigating grounds which he is putting forward are other and different from those put forward to some other court within the three year period, it is for him to prove that they are different, by reference to that court's record or by calling evidence (*R v Sandbach JJ, ex* p *Perscud* (1985) 5 Cr App R(S) 177).

New drivers

The Road Traffic (New Drivers) Act 1995 provides for the revocation of the driving licence of a new driver who accumulates six or more penalty points within a probationary period of two years after he first qualifies. A driver whose licence is revoked under these provisions must take a further test to regain his entitlement to drive.

Disqualification and Endorsement

4. DISQUALIFICATION UNTIL TEST PASSED

RTOA 1988, s 36(4)(6)

Where an offender is convicted of an offence involving obligatory endorsement the court, may, having regard to the safety of road users generally order him to be disqualified until he passes an appropriate driving test (whether or not he has previously passed a test).

RTOA 1988, s 36(5)

An 'appropriate driving test' includes:

(1) an 'extended driving test' where an offender is convicted of an offence involving obligatory disqualification, or is disqualified under RTOA 1988, s 35; and

(2) a test of competence to drive prescribed by virtue of RTA 1988, s 89(3).

The superior courts have emphasised on a number of occasions (see eg *R v Peat* [1985] Crim LR 110, *R v Lazzari* (1984) 6 Cr App R(S) 83) that such an order is *not* intended as a punishment, but to protect the public against incompetent drivers. Unless the making of an order is obligatory, the power should be exercised only where there is reason to doubt the offender's competence to drive, whether through age, infirmity or the circumstances of the offence. RTOA 1988, s 36(4) provides that in deciding whether to make an order, the court must have regard to the safety of road users.

Where a person is disqualified until he passes an extended driving test, any earlier order under RTOA 1988, s 36 ceases to have effect and no further order is to be made by a court under s 36 while he is so disqualified. RTOA 1988, s 36(7)

A disqualification under s 36 expires only when proof of the passing of the test is delivered to the Secretary of State. An order of disqualification under s 36 places the offender in the category of a provisional licence holder and should he drive otherwise than in accordance with the terms of the provisional licence he will be guilty of driving whilst disqualified.

5. DISQUALIFICATION WHERE VEHICLE USED FOR CRIME

(1) Assaults etc

Where: a person is convicted of common assault, or of any other offence involving an assault (including an offence of aiding, abetting, counselling, procuring or inciting the commission of an assault), and the court is satisfied that the assault was committed by driving a motor vehicle, it may order the person convicted to be disqualified for holding or obtaining a driving licence for such period as it thinks fit. PCC(S)A 2000, s 147(2)(4)(5)

The offender must be required to produce his driving licence and its counterpart, where he holds a licence, and where he holds a Community licence, that licence and its counterpart.

(2) Any offence

The court before whom a person is convicted of any offence, and *which has been notified by the Home Secretary that the power is exercisable,* may, in addition to dealing with an offender in any other way, order him to be disqualified for holding or obtaining a driving licence for such period as it thinks fit. PCC(S)A 2000, s 146

6. NOTIFICATION OF DISEASE ETC

RTOA 1988, s 22

Where, in any proceedings for an offence committed in respect of a motor vehicle, it appears to the court that the accused may be suffering from any disability, or prospective disability, as is likely to cause his driving of a vehicle to be a source of danger to the public, it must notify the Secretary of State, but there must be sufficient evidence before the court, even if it comes from the defence, that the accused is suffering from such a disability or prospective disability before it is appropriate to do so (*R v Chichester JJ, ex p Crouch* (1982) 146 JP 26).

Where there is evidence that an offender is liable to recurring bouts of an illness, such as hypomania, but is otherwise competent to drive, this is the course to take rather than to make a driving test order (*Hughes v Challes* [1984] RTR 283).

7. PROCEEDINGS AFTER DISQUALIFICATION; SUSPENSION; REMOVAL

The giving of notice of appeal from the magistrates' court does not operate to suspend an order of disqualification. If the order is to be suspended, it must be suspended by judicial act.

Where an offender gives notice of appeal, or of his intention to apply for judicial review:

RTOA 1988, ss 39, 40

(1) the magistrates' court may, if it thinks fit, suspend any disqualification pending appeal;
(2) any disqualification, whether obligatory or discretionary, may be suspended:
    (a) by the Crown Court, where the offender appeals to it against conviction or sentence;
    (b) by the High Court, where the offender applies to the magistrates to state a case under MCA 1980, s 87; [RTOA 1988, s 40(1)(4)(7)]
    (c) by the High Court, where the offender applies, or applies for permission to claim a quashing order under CPR 1998, r 54 in respect of the proceedings before the magistrates' court. [RTOA 1988, s 40(1)(5)(7)]

RTOA 1988, s 42

A person disqualified by order of the court may apply to the court which made the order to remove it, provided that:

(1) two years have elapsed, if the disqualification was for less than four years; or
(2) half the period has elapsed, if the disqualification was for not less than four and not more than ten years; or

Disqualification and Endorsement

(3) five years have elapsed in any other case.

The court, as it thinks fit, having regard to the character of the applicant and his subsequent conduct, the nature of the offence and any other circumstances:

(a) may, by order, remove the disqualification from such date as it may specify; or

(b) may refuse the application; but

(c) must *not* add to it any conditions or additional requirements (*R v Bentham* (1981) 3 Cr App R(S) 229).

If the application is granted, the applicant may be ordered to pay the whole or any part of the costs. Where the application is refused, a further three months must elapse before another is entertained. RTOA 1988, s 42(5)(b)

These provisions do not differentiate between discretionary and obligatory disqualification, and subject to the above-mentioned prescribed periods, there is nothing in law to prevent the court removing an obligatory disqualification although, if it thinks fit, the court may regard it as one which it is somewhat less ready to remove than a discretionary disqualification (*Darmer v Davison* [1976] RTR 45).

The provisions of RTOA 1988, s 42 do not apply to disqualifications under RTOA 1988, s 36. RTOA 1988, s 42(6)

8. SPECIAL REASONS

Special reasons may allow the court to reduce the period of any disqualification ordered, or justfy the court not disqualifying at all, or in certain circumstances not endorsing a conviction on an offender's licence. The law was reviewed in *DPP v O'Connor etc* [1992] RTR 55. The court is required to go through a two-stage process. First it must determine whether there are special reasons, and then it must ask itself whether, in its discretion, having regard to the special reasons, it ought not to disqualify, or ought to disqualify for a shorter period.

To constitute a special reason, four conditions must be fulfilled. These are that the facts advanced:

(1) must amount to mitigating or extenuating circumstances;

(2) must *not* amount to a defence to the charge;

(3) must be directly connected with the commission of the offence; and

(4) must be matters which can properly be taken into account when imposing punishment (*R v Wickins* (1958) 42 Cr App R 236).

RTOA 1988, s 47(1)

The court is required to state openly any grounds for finding that special reasons exist for mitigating the statutory penalty, and enter those grounds in the register. The mere fact that the circumstances disclose a special reason does not, of itself, mean that the offender is entitled, as a matter of course, to escape disqualification.

There is a serious burden on a court to decide, in its discretion, whether to refrain from disqualifying (*Taylor v Rajan* [1974] 1 All ER 1087). The power should be exercised only in clear and compelling circumstances (*Taylor v Rajan* (*above*); *Vaughan v Dunn* [1984] Crim LR 365; *DPP v Bristow* [1998] RTR 106).

Even where the above conditions are fulfilled, there may be some overriding factor which precludes the court from regarding as 'special reasons' some circumstance which at first appeared to fall within the scope of the four preconditions (*Delaroy-Hall v Tadman* [1969] 1 All ER 25; and see *R v St Albans CC, ex p Donovan* [2000] 1 Cr App R (S) 344 DC).

The court is concerned not with the special reason that caused the offender to take his car onto the road, but with the special reason for not disqualifying or for imposing a lesser disqualification.

Special to the offence

The need for the facts to be directly connected with the commission of the offence means that the fact put forward as a special reason must be 'special', in contrast with those that are general, and special to the *offence* rather than to the offender. It is for this reason that special reasons are not to be found in, eg, the following circumstances where:

(1) the offender is a professional driver (*Whittall v Kirby* [1946] 2 All ER 552), or has been driving for many years without complaint (*Hersom v Lines* [1951] 2 All ER 650), or is a careful person who would never have risked driving had he realised his condition (*Newnham v Trigg* [1970] RTR 107);

(2) the offender is disabled and had no other means of getting home (*Mullarkey v Prescott* [1970] RTR 296), or relies on his vehicle for transport (*R v Jackson, R v Hart* [1969] 2 All ER 535), or that disqualification will cause him serious hardship and/or hardship to his family (*Knowler v Rennison* [1947] 1 All ER 302; *Taylor v Austin* [1969] 1 All ER 544; *Reynolds v Roche* [1972] RTR 282); *East v Blayden* [1987] RTR 291);

(3) the offender is a doctor, and the medical services in his area will deteriorate by reason of his being unable to drive (*Holroyd v Berry* [1973] RTR 145), or a soldier on active service who must be in a position to drive (*Gordon v Smith* [1971] RTR 52), or that the offender is a detec-

tive engaged in 'undercover' activities which involve visiting public houses (*Vaughan v Dunn* [1984] RTR 376);

(4) the offender has an idiosyncratic medical condition or diabetes (*R v Wickens* (1958) 42 Cr App R 236; *R v Jackson, R v Hart* [1969] 2 All ER 453; *Jarvis v DPP* (2000) 165 JP 15);

(5) the offender has to drive because of his domestic situation (*Reynolds v Roche* (*above*)).

Even less is it any sort of special reason that the court considers the penalty of disqualification too severe (*Williamson v Wilson* [1947] 1 All ER 306) or unfair (*Bolliston v Gibbons* [1985] RTR 176). The fact that the offence is a trivial one is not a special reason for not *endorsing*, but the court is always entitled to take account of the minor nature of the offence, and the fact that any breach was unintentional (*Hawkins v Roots, Hawkins v Smith* [1976] RTR 49; *Marks v West Midlands Police* [1981] RTR 471; *Bobin v DPP* [1999] RTR 375).

Excess alcohol offences

The vast majority of cases in which offenders seek to put forward special reasons are those relating to excess alcohol. The views of the superior courts over a number of years, when analysed, are that in relation to such offences:

(1) in cases under RTA 1988, ss 4, 5, and 7(6), it must be borne in mind that a person who deliberately drives, knowing that he has consumed a considerable quantity of alcohol, presents a potential danger to the public, which no private crisis can lightly excuse;

(2) in a case under s 5, the amount of excess, however small, is not capable of amounting to a special reason – the Act lays down the prescribed statutory limit (*Delaroy-Hall v Tadman* [1969] 1 All ER 25);

(3) the effect of lack of food, or the effect of drink on an empty stomach, is not capable of amounting to a special reason, whether under s 4 or s 5 (*Archer v Woodward* [1959] Crim LR 46; *Knight v Baxter* [1971] RTR 270);

(4) the fact that an offender, unknown to him, was suffering from a disease which produced a greater degree of unfitness than would be present in a normal person, might amount to a special reason under s 5 (*R v Wickens* (1958) 42 Cr App R 236), as might the fact that he had inhaled industrial fumes at work (*Bremer v Metropolitan Police Commissioner* (1969) 133 JP 185), but such features are irrelevant on a conviction under s 5 (*Goldsmith v Laver* [1970] RTR 163);

(5) the court should rarely, if ever, exercise its discretion in favour of an offender where the alcohol content exceeded 100 mg per 100 ml of blood (*Taylor v Rajan* [1974] RTR 304; *Vaughan v Dunn* [1984] RTR 376);

(6) the fact that the offender offered a specimen of urine when blood was required of him, cannot be taken into account as a special reason (*Grix v Chief Constable of Kent* [1987] RTR 193);

(7) it is difficult to conceive of a special reason in relation to a contravention of s 7(6) (*R v Jackson* [1969] 2 All ER 453).

Sudden emergencies

A sudden emergency may amount to a special reason in cases under ss 4 and 5, as where an unexpected situation arises in which a person who has been drinking but not intending to drive is impelled to do so by a sudden medical necessity, or in answering an emergency call (*Aichroth v Cottee* (1954) 118 JP 499; *Brown v Dyerson* [1968] 3 All ER 39; *R v Lundt-Smith* [1964] 3 All ER 225; *R v O'Toole* (1971) 55 Cr App R 206).

A burglary at club premises where the driver was a key holder has been held to be an emergency sufficient to justify a finding of special reasons (*DPP v Cox* [1996] RTR 123 DC; see also *DPP v Enston* [1996] RTR 324; *R v Whittle* [1996] RTR 154).

In dealing with such cases, the superior courts have said that the whole of the circumstances should be considered, including the nature and degree of the crisis or emergency which caused the offender to take his car onto the road, and also:

(1) whether the emergency was sufficiently acute to justify the offender taking out his car;

(2) whether there were alternative means of transport available, or alternative means of dealing with the crisis;

(3) the manner of the offender's driving, the commission of traffic offences may be a consideration telling against exercise of the court's discretion; and

(4) whether the offender otherwise acted responsibly and reasonably.

These matters need to be considered objectively and it is not for the court to put itself into the offender's position in assessing 'reasonableness'.

A driver complaining of dizziness and blurred vision did not constitute a medical emergency sufficient to justify a finding of special reasons where the passenger, her husband, who was affected by drink, decided to take over the driving (*DPP v Whittle* (*above*)).

There is a difference in a situation presented to a driver on the outward journey and that on the homeward journey after the emergency has been dealt with (*DPP v Waller* [1989] RTR 112).

It is unlikely that merely travelling to a near relative because of some emotional need will ever be able to amount to a special reason (*Thompson v Diamond* [1985] RTR 316).

'Laced drinks' cases

It is often put forward in excess alcohol cases, that the offender's drink had been 'laced' by a third party, in order to found a special reason on the ground that the drink which the offender consumed was stronger or more potent than he had anticipated. It is not enough to show that the drink was stronger than he thought.

To be capable of amounting to a special reason, there must be an element of intervention or misleading by a third party, whereby the offender was induced to take stronger drink than he would normally have done by someone who misled him, or gave him false information.

It must be shown (*Pugsley v Hunter* [1973] RTR 254; *Smith v Geraghty* [1986] RTR 222), and the burden is on the offender to show, by relevant and admissible evidence (not hearsay – *James v Morgan* [1988] RTR 85), that the quantity of alcohol in his blood in excess of the prescribed limit:

(1) is attributable to additional drink; and

(2) was put into his glass without his knowledge.

The court must decide, firstly, whether the facts are capable of amounting to a special reason, and additionally, whether the offender should have realised, when he came to drive, that he was not fit to do so by reason of the alcohol present in his body (*Pridige v Gant* [1985] RTR 196; *DPP v Barker* [1990] RTR 1; *Donahue v DPP* [1993] RTR 156).

The defence is one which the court should always examine with care. Expert evidence will be highly relevant, though it is not a requirement.

It is undesirable for the court to let itself be drawn into detailed scientific calculations, even where these are put before it by expert witnesses (*Smith v Geraghty* [1986] RTR 222).

Factors to be considered

It was suggested in *Chatters v Burke* [1986] RTR 396, that there were seven factors to be considered and taken into account when deciding whether there were special reasons for mitigating the normal consequences of a conviction, namely:

(1) how far was the vehicle driven?

(2) in what manner was it driven?

(3) the state of the vehicle;

(4) whether it was the offender's intention to go further;

(5) the conditions of road and traffic prevailing;
(6) the reason for the car being driven;
(7) most importantly of all, whether there was a danger of the offender coming into contact with pedestrians or other road users.

The mere fact that the offence occurred late at night, at a time and place where there were not many people about, or that the offender was merely re-parking, is not of itself capable of amounting to a special reason for not disqualifying. It might, however, amount to a special reason to show that the offender drove only a few yards in circumstances where his manoeuvres were unlikely to bring him into contact with other road users (*Mullarkey v Prescott* [1970] RTR 296; *Coombs v Kehoe* [1972] 2 All ER 55; cf *Haime v Walklet* [1983] RTR 512; *Redmond v Parry* [1986] RTR 146; *DPP v Humphries* [2000] RTR 52).

Proof of special reasons

The burden of proving circumstances amounting to a special reason lies upon the offender; the standard is that of a 'balance of probabilities'. The court should take into account:

(1) any relevant admissible evidence, given on oath;
(2) any admissions made in accordance with CJA 1967, s 10;
(3) any 'expert reports' tendered and admissible by virtue of CJA 1988, s 30; and
(4) any submissions made by the prosecutor and/or the offender's legal representative.

Hearsay evidence given by the accused, as to what he has heard since the incident, does not qualify (*James v Morgan* [1988] RTR 85).

Construction and use: exceptions to endorsement

RTOA 1988, s 48

Where a person is convicted of an offence under the Construction and Use Regulations which carries mandatory endorsement, such as an offence under RTA 1988, s 40A (using a vehicle in a dangerous condition etc) the court must *not* order him to be disqualified or order any particulars of penalty points to be endorsed if he proves, on a balance of probabilities, that he did not know and had no reasonable cause to suspect that the use of the vehicle involved a danger of injury to any person.

Where the conviction is for an offence under RTA 1988, s 41, a breach of a requirement as to brakes, steering gear or tyres, the court must *not* order disqualification or endorsement of penalty points if he proves, on a balance of probabilities, that he did not know and had no reasonable cause to suspect that the offence would be committed.

EUROPEAN COURT REFERENCE

Under Art 177 of the EEC Treaty, the European Court of Justice has jurisdiction, among other things, to give preliminary rulings concerning the interpretation of the EEC Treaty, the validity or interpretation of Acts of the institutions of the Community, and the interpretation of the statutes of bodies established by an act of the Council, where these statutes so provide.

Where a question of this nature is raised before any court or tribunal of a member state, it may, if it considers that a decision on a question of law is necessary to enable it to give judgment, request the Court of Justice to give a ruling on it.

Though such cases are likely to be rare, a magistrates' court in England and Wales is a court or tribunal falling within Art 177, which has a discretion to refer a question if it considers it 'necessary' to enable it to give judgment.

Courses open to the court

Community law is ordinarily to be applied like any domestic law. The European Communities Act 1972 requires Community law to be treated as a question of law, not one of fact which requires proof by a skilled witness.

If a difficult question of interpretation arises and the court, advised by its clerk, is satisfied that there is a real doubt as to the law, which must be settled before the case is decided, three courses are open:

(1) in most cases, it will be appropriate for the court to decide the question, leaving an appellate court, most suitably the High Court, to refer any question to the European Court;

(2) to state a case under MCA 1980, s 108, in the ordinary way, for the opinion of the High Court, leaving that court to refer any question to the European Court; or

(3) the magistrates' court may itself refer the matter to the European Court.

This last option is in no way an appeal. The European Court does not decide the case; it gives a ruling, binding on all courts within the Community.

Approach to question

Ordinarily:

(1) the court should exercise considerable caution before referring a question;

(2) the court should decide questions of Community law itself; if its decision is wrong, a higher court, which will usually be the more suitable forum to make the reference, can do so, being in a better position to assess the appropriateness of, and to formulate, the question to be referred;

(3) it is highly undesirable to make a reference until all the evidence has been called and the court is satisfied that there cannot be an acquittal on the facts.

(*R v Plymouth JJ, ex p Rogers* [1982] 2 All ER 452)

FINES AND ENFORCEMENT

A fine is the most frequently used disposal in a magistrates' court; statistics show that a fine is imposed in some 95 per cent of summary cases. In many cases no alternative penalty is available. Where there is a choice between a fine and other penalties, the court will need to consider whether a financial penalty is:

(1) the suitable or only permitted disposal in the circumstances of the offence;

(2) justified, given the circumstances of the offence, or whether the offender qualifies for a custodial or community sentence, and

if a fine is appropriate, ensure that the amount, together with any compensation or costs imposed, is related to the offender's means, otherwise an attempt to avoid a custodial penalty will have failed.

Limitation on amount

The amount of a fine is limited by the maximum fine for the offence, the age and means of the offender. It is also important to observe the 'totality principle', in that the total amount of fines imposed for different offences does not exceed what is appropriate for the whole of the conduct being punished (see, eg, *R v Chelmsford CC, ex* p *Birchall* [1990] Crim LR 352).

Where no maximum is provided by the statute creating the offence, the following maxima apply:

(1) Levels of fine on the 'standard scale': CJA 1988, s 37
   (a) Level 1 – £200
   (b) Level 2 – £500
   (c) Level 3 – £1,000
   (d) Level 4 – £2,500
   (e) Level 5 – £5,000

(2) Either way offence triable summarily – £5,000 MCA 1980, ss 32(9), 36(1)(2)

(3) Summary offence, where statute provides no express power to fine – fine at level 3

(4) Schedule 2 MCA 1980 offence tried summarily – fine at level 4

(5) Refusal to give evidence – £2,500

(6) Contempt of court (CCA 1981, s 12(2)) – £2,500

(7) Young offenders: PCC(S)A 2000, s 135
   (a) under 14 – £250
   (b) 14–17 – £1,000

Approach to fine

PCC(S)A 2000, s 128(1)(2)(3)(4)

The amount of any fine imposed must be such as, in the court's opinion, reflects the seriousness of the offence, but in fixing the amount, whether that has the effect of increasing or reducing the amount, the court:

(1) must enquire into the offender's financial circumstances; and

(2) may take into account the circumstances of the case, including amongst other things;

(3) the financial circumstances of the offender (whether an individual or other person) so far as they are known to the court.

Ability to pay: means

One of the overriding principles in relation to the imposition of a fine is that it should be within the offender's ability to pay. Once the fine has been assessed on the principles stated above, but only then, should the offender's means be assessed (*R v Rizvi* (1979) 1 Cr App R (S) 307; *R v Charalambous* [1985) Crim LR 328).

It should be remembered that:

(1) it is wrong to impose a fine upon an offender of substantial means for an offence for which one of lesser means would go to prison (*R v Lewis* [1965] Crim LR 121); conversely;

(2) it is wrong to imprison an offender because he is unable to pay a substantial fine (*R v Reeves* [1972] Crim LR 194):

(3) it is wrong to scale up a fine in the case of an unusually affluent offender (*R v Fairbairn* (1980) 2 Cr App R (S) 315);

(4) it may be necessary to scale down an otherwise appropriate fine if the sum is more than the offender can be fairly required to pay within a reasonable time; and

(5) despite a number of pronouncements to the contrary, *R v Olliver* [1989] Crim LR 387 held that there was no reason in principle why an order to pay a fine by monthly instalments should not extend for two or even three years.

A fine should not, of course, be imposed on the basis that someone other than the offender is going to pay it on his behalf (*R v Baxter* [1974] Crim LR 611) let alone on the basis that the public should be reimbursed for any possible claim made on the Criminal Injuries Compensation Board (*R v Roberts* [1980] Crim LR 507).

Where an offender has spent some time in custody before sentence, the court should reflect some credit for that period in the amount of the fine (*R v Warden* [1996] Crim LR 443).

Financial circumstances order

Before sentencing an individual the court may make a financial circumstances order in respect of him, requiring him to give such statement of his financial circumstances as the court requires, within a specified period. PCC(S)A 2000, s 126

The court has a similar power to order a financial circumstances statement from the parent or guardian of a juvenile where it is contemplating an order against such a person under PCC(S)A 2000, s 137. PCC(S)A 2000, s 136

Where an offender has: PCC(S)A 2000, s 128(5)

(1) been convicted in his absence under MCA 1980, ss 11, 12; or

(2) failed to comply with a financial circumstances order; or

(3) otherwise failed to cooperate with the court in its enquiry into his financial circumstances,

and the court considers that it has insufficient information to make a proper determination of his financial circumstances, it may make such determination as it thinks fit.

If the offender declines to provide proper information about his means, the court is entitled to assume that he is being evasive, and that he has sufficient means to pay the fine, and may act accordingly (*R v Higgins* [1998] Crim LR 777).

If, in fixing the amount of a fine, the court has determined the offender's financial circumstances under s 128(5), and on enquiring subsequently is satisfied that had it had the results of that enquiry when sentencing it would not have imposed a fine, or would have imposed a smaller amount, it may remit the whole or part of it. PCC(S)A 2000, s 129

Combination with other penalties

A fine is a purely punitive measure which enables the court to demonstrate society's disapproval in a case where punishment short of custody or a community penalty is the appropriate response. Being punitive, it cannot be combined for the same offence for which is imposed : HO 1990

(1) an absolute or conditional discharge (*R v McClelland* (1951) 115 JP 159).

(2) a community rehabilitation order; or

(3) a community punishment order.

Where an offender has made a substantial profit from his offence, it may be proper to impose a fine in addition to a period of custody or a suspended sentence (see CUSTODIAL SENTENCES).

'The totality principle'

As in any other field of sentencing, where fines are imposed for a number of offences, it is important for the court to bear in mind the 'totality principle', namely that culpability should be considered as a whole and fines be apportioned accordingly (*R v Chelmsford CC, ex p Birchall* [1990] Crim LR 353). Where the court imposes a fine in respect of a principal offence and there are other offences for which it considers that any additional penalty is not appropriate, they may deal with them by ordering 'no separate penalty' on that offence,

Payment by parent or guardian: (1) general

PCC(S)A 2000, s 137(1)(3)(5)

Since few juveniles are likely to have the money available to pay fines, compensation or costs, where a person aged under 18 is convicted of an offence for which a fine, or an order for costs may be imposed or a compensation order made, and the court is of the opinion that the case would best be met by such an order, whether with or without any other punishment, the court:

(1) must, in the case of an offender under 16; and

(2) may, in the case of an offender aged 16–17,

order the fine (compensation or costs) to be paid by the offender's parent or guardian unless:

(a) that person cannot be found; or

(b) it would be unreasonable, having regard to the circumstances, to make such an order.

PCC(S)A 2000, s 137(3)

A similar provision applies in a case where the court is minded to impose a fine in respect of the breach of certain community and other orders.

An order should not be made unless the parent or guardian has been given an opportunity of being heard, or has been required to attend and has failed to do so.

Payment by parent or guardian: (2) purpose of s 137

In considering whether to make an order under these provisions, it was said under the previous legislation (CYPA 1933, s 55(l)) that the court should have regard to the purpose of the section, which is that:

(1) parents should take some responsibility for their childrens' activities and they should take their duties seriously;

(2) they cannot be held vicariously liable for every act of their child (*Lenihan v West Yorkshire Met Police* (1981) 3 Cr App R (S) 42); and

(3) it is unreasonable to make an order where a parent has done the best he or she can to keep their child from criminal ways (*R v Sheffield CC, ex p Clarkson* (1986) 8 Cr App R (S) 454) and is in no position to control it (*TA v DPP* [1996] Crim LR 606).

Payment by parent or guardian: (3) local authority as 'parent or guardian'

References to a parent or guardian are to be construed as references to a local authority where the child or young person is: PCC(S)A 2000, s 137(4)(5)

(1) one for whom that authority has parental authority; and
(2) in their care; or
(3) provided with accommodation by them in the exercise of any function (in particular those under the Children Act 1989) which stands referred to their social services committee under the Local Authority Social Services Act 1970.

An order remanding a young person into local authority accommodation does not confer parental responsibility (*North Yorkshire County Council v Selby Youth Court JJ* [1994] 1 All ER 991, and see *Marlowe Child & Family Services Ltd v DPP* [1998] Crim LR 594).

Payment by parent or guardian: (4) orders against local authorities

The power of a local authority to restrain an offender in its care might be less than that of a parent. It has the same right to assert the unreasonableness of an order as has a parent or guardian.

Where the authority has done everything it reasonably and properly can to protect the public from the offender, it is unreasonable to make an order against it (*D v DPP* [1995] Crim LR 748).

Where the authority stands *in loco parentis* and the accused juvenile is acquitted, the authority is entitled to a defence costs order where it would be appropriate in the case of the accused (*R v Preston CC, ex p Lancashire CC* [1998] 3 All ER 765).

Payment by parent or guardian: (5) fixing the quantum

Similar provisions apply to an order against a parent or guardian as apply to financial orders in respect of offenders, and a parent or guardian, other than a local authority, may be required to comply with a financial circumstances order. PCC(S)A 2000, s 138

Payment by parent or guardian: (6) appeals

A parent or guardian may appeal to the Crown Court against an order made under these provisions. PCC(S)A 2000, s 137(6)

ENFORCEMENT OF FINANCIAL PENALTIES

The principal methods of enforcement are set out below. Unless otherwise stated, for enforcement purposes a 'fine' includes any pecuniary penalty payable on conviction.

(1) Search

MCA 1980, s 80

Where the court has adjudged a person to pay a sum on conviction:

(1) the court may order him to be searched; and

(2) any money found on him may be applied to the payment of any fine or costs.

Money found on him at the time of his arrest, or on being taken to prison or any other place of detention may be applied in the same manner.

(2) Immediate payment; time to pay; instalments

MCA 1980, s 75 (1)(2)

The court may:

(1) require immediate payment of any fine; or

(2) allow time for payment; or

(3) order payment by instalments of weekly or monthly amounts which can be adjusted to the offender's circumstances.

JCR 1999, Schedule

Where the court has allowed time for payment it (or the Clerk) may, on application by or on behalf of the person liable to pay, allow further time or allow payment by instalments.

MCA 1980, s 85A, JCR 1999, Schedule

Where the court has ordered payment by instalments, it (or the Clerk) may, on application by the person liable to pay, vary the number of instalments payable, the amount of any instalment and the date on which any instalment becomes payable.

Note that:

MCR 1981, r 65(1)

(a) where time is allowed or instalments are ordered, an entry must be made to that effect in the court register, or a separate record kept for the purpose;

MCA 1980, s 86(1)(1A)(1B), JCR 1999, Schedule

(b) where time is allowed or instalments are ordered, the court (or the Clerk) may, either then or later, fix a day on which, if any part of the sum remains unpaid, the defaulter must appear in person to enable a means enquiry to be held, or a hearing prior to the issue of a warrant of commitment;

(c) whilst monetary penalties ought to be capable of payment within 12 months, there is nothing wrong in principle, in an appropriate case, with the period of payment being longer (*R v Olliver & Olliver* [1989] Crim LR 387);

MCA 1980, s 75(3)

(d) where payment by instalments is ordered, and default is made in the payment of any one instalment, proceedings may be taken as if default had been made in all.

(3) Warrant of distress

Where default is made in paying any fine adjudged payable on conviction by a magistrates' court, the court (or the Clerk) may issue a warrant of distress for the purpose of levying the sum. MCA 1980, s 76(1), JCR 1999, Schedule

The distress warrant is authority for a constable or other authorised person to take any money or goods of the defaulter, save for the clothing or bedding of the defaulter or his family, or the tools, books, vehicles or other equipment that he personally needs to use in his employment, business or vocation. MCR 1981, r 54(2)(4)

A distress warrant is of limited effectiveness where a defaulter has few possessions or claims those which he has to be the property, eg of friends or relatives, or subject to hire purchase.

Fines and Enforcement

Note that:

(1) if the court considers that there is a reasonable likelihood of the defaulter having available assets to pay the sums due it should enforce payment by distress warrant (*R v Birmingham JJ, ex p Bennett* [1983] 1 WLR 114);

(2) a policy to issue distress warrants for fines in excess of £25 which have not been paid after a final demand for payment has been made,was described in *R v Hereford & Worcester MC, ex p McRae* (1998)163 JP 433 as 'both laudable and commendable';

(3) where the court has power to issue a distress warrant, if expedient to do so, it may postpone its issue until such time, and on such conditions, as it thinks fit, the time and conditions being capable of variation if the court thinks it just to do so. MCA 1980, s 77(1)

Any goods so taken must be sold by public auction or in such manner as the defaulter in writing may allow. After payment of the costs and charges of the distress, any money which remains is paid to the Clerk who applies it toward payment of the fine. MCR 1981, r 54(6)

If it appears from the return to a distress warrant that the defaulter's property will be insufficient to satisfy the sum due, the court may issue a warrant of commitment. MCA 1980, s 76(2)

It is only when considering issuing a warrant of commitment that a means enquiry need be held (*R v Hereford & Worcester MC, ex p MacRae* (*above*)), though if the court, whilst conducting a means enquiry in respect of an unrepresented defaulter, has it in mind to issue a distress warrant, it should give notice to the defaulter, and give him an opportunity to make representations (*R v Guildford JJ, ex p Rich* (1996) 160 JP 645).

(4) Imprisonment in default

MCA 1980, s 76(1)(3)

Where default is made in paying any fine adjudged payable on conviction by a magistrates' court, the court may, subject to the restrictions set out below, issue a warrant committing the defaulter, if aged 18 or over (see p 261 *below* for defaulters under 18), to prison.

The period of imprisonment or detention must not be for less than five days, and while consecutive terms may be imposed in respect of fines owing for separate offences, the maximum must not exceed the relevant period set out in MCA 1980, Sched 4 (see p 256 *below*). Where the total sum exceeds the statutory maximum, separate warrants ought to be issued (*R v Midhurst JJ, ex p Seymour* (1983) 147 JP 266).

In deciding whether to make terms of imprisonment in default concurrent or consecutive, the court should adopt a similar approach as in terms imposed for offences (see p 175 *above*) (*R v Southampton JJ, ex p Davies* [1981] 1 All ER 722).

Warrant of commitment: (1) postponement

MCA 1980, s 77(1)(2)

If the court considers it expedient, it may postpone the issue of a warrant of commitment until such time, and upon such conditions, as it thinks just, and, more importantly, may:

(1) fix a term of imprisonment or detention; and

(2) postpone the issue of the warrant of commitment until such time, and upon such conditions, as it thinks just.

Having done so, the court may, at any time thereafter:

(a) direct the issue of the warrant to be postponed to a different time from that to which it was previously postponed; and/or

(b) vary any of the conditions on which issue of the warrant was postponed,

but only if it thinks it just to do so, having regard to any change of circumstances since postponement was ordered, or since the court last exercised one or both of these powers.

MCA 1980, s 77(5)(6)(7)

If, on the application of the person to whom a postponed warrant relates, it appears to a justice acting for the same petty sessions area that, since the warrant was postponed, or the powers above were exercised, there has been a change of circumstances which make it just for the court to exercise its powers, he may refer the application to the court, whereupon the Clerk is required to:

(i) fix a time and place for the application to be heard; and

(ii) give notice to the applicant of that time and place.

If notice is given, but the applicant fails to appear at the time and place specified, the court may proceed to hear the application in his absence.

If, before the application has been heard, the warrant of commitment has been issued, the court has power to order that it cease to have effect, and that the applicant, if he has already been arrested on the warrant, be released, provided that the court is satisfied that the change in circumstances on which the applicant relies was not put before the court when it determined whether to issue the warrant. MCA 1980, s 77(8)

Warrant of commitment: (2) immediate default sentence

The court is empowered to issue a warrant of commitment on the occasion of convicting an offender (without holding a means enquiry) only where: MCA 1980, s 82

(1) in the case of an offence punishable with imprisonment, the offender appears to have sufficient means to pay forthwith; or

(2) it appears that the offender is unlikely to remain long enough at an abode in the UK to enable payment to be enforced by other methods; or

(3) on the occasion of that conviction, the court sentences the offender to a term of imprisonment for another offence; or

(4) the offender is already serving such a sentence.

The court cannot fix a default sentence in advance of issuing the warrant of commitment except where it has power to issue a warrant forthwith.

Warrant of commitment: (3) default sentence after conviction

Where, on the occasion of the offender's conviction, the court does not issue a warrant of commitment, and does not fix a default sentence under s 77(2), it may not issue a warrant of commitment thereafter, unless: MCA 1980, s 82(3)

(1) the defaulter is serving a sentence of imprisonment; or

(2) since conviction, the court has held a means enquiry in his presence, on at least one occasion.

Where a means enquiry is required, the court may not, on the occasion of that enquiry or thereafter, issue a warrant of commitment unless:

(a) in the case of an offence punishable with imprisonment, it appears that he has sufficient means to pay; or

(b) the court is satisfied that that default is due to the offender's wilful refusal or culpable neglect, and the court has tried or considered all other methods of enforcing payment (see s 82(4A)) and it appears that they are inappropriate or unsuccessful.

The court must consider, or try, all other methods of enforcement; there is no discretion to do otherwise (*R v Norwich MC, ex p Lilly* (1987) 151 JP

689). If a warrant of commitment is issued the court must be able to show that it has, in fact, considered all other alternative methods of enforcement and found them to be inappropriate or that they have tried them and been unsuccessful. These matters must be shown in detail on the warrant of commitment and in the court register. In addition where a defaulter is under 21 a warrant of commitment to detention cannot be issued unless he has been placed under supervision in respect of the sum due to be paid or the court is satisfied that it is undesirable or impracticable to place him under supervision. Where the court is so satisfied the grounds on which it is so satisfied must be entered on the warrant and in the court register (*R v Norwich MC, ex p Lilly* (*above*); *R v Oldham JJ and another, ex p Cawley* [1996] 1 All ER 464).

MCA 1980, s 82(6)

Where the defaulter is in prison and the court seeks to initiate proceedings, it is prudent for it to make enquiry to see whether or not the police are holding property which might belong to the defaulter, before deciding whether to proceed by way of distress or by way of warrant of commitment.

Where the court is considering the imposition of imprisonment in default of payment or the activation of a suspended default sentence after further default has been made, the defaulter is entitled to be legally represented at the means enquiry and may apply for a legal representation order for that purpose.

Maximum periods of imprisonment in default

MCA 1980, Sched 4, para 1

An amount not exceeding £200	7 days
An amount exceeding £200 but not £500	14 days
An amount exceeding £500 but not £1,000	28 days
An amount exceeding £1,000 but not £2,500	45 days
An amount exceeding £2,500 but not £5,000	3 months
An amount exceeding £5,000 but not £10,000	6 months
An amount exceeding £10,000	12 months

Presence of defaulter

MCA 1980, s 82(5)

After the occasion of an offender's conviction, the court must not issue a warrant of commitment for a default except at a hearing at which the offender is present unless:

(1) it has previously fixed a term in default under s 77(2); or

(2) the offender is serving a custodial sentence.

MCA 1980, s 82(5A)–(5F)

In any event, the court must not issue a warrant in either situation at a hearing at which the defaulter is not present unless:

(a) the Clerk has first served notice in writing on the defaulter, stating that the court intends to hold a hearing to consider whether to issue a warrant; and

(b) the notice states the reason(s) why the court so intends.

The notice must state the time and place appointed for the hearing and inform the defaulter that if he considers there are grounds why the warrant should not be issued, he may make representations to the court in person or in writing.

The court may, however, exercise its power to issue the warrant whether or not he makes representations.

The notice is deemed to be served if it is sent by registered post or recorded delivery service, addressed to the defaulter at his last known address, notwithstanding that the notice is returned undelivered or is, for any reason, not received by him.

At such a hearing, the court must consider such information about the defaulter's means as is available, unless it has previously enquired into his means and postponed the issue of the warrant of commitment under MCA 1980, s 77(2).

Where the court exercises its power under MCA 1980, s 77(2) to postpone issue of the warrant, it may, at the same hearing issue a notice in writing under s 82(5A), the time stated in the notice being a time on any day following the end of the period for which the issue of the warrant was postponed. In any other case, the time stated in the notice must be not earlier than 21 days after the notice is issued.

Defaulters already serving sentence

Where the effect of imposing a default sentence to be served consecutively to an existing prison sentence is to reduce disproportionately the prisoner's entitlement to remission on that sentence, unpaid fines should not be dealt with until the offender is released from the existing sentence (*R v Ipswich JJ, ex p Smith* (1992) 156 JP 787).

Means enquiry

If a fine or other sum is not paid within the time allowed, the defaulter is brought before the court for a means enquiry. This enquiry, required by MCA 1980, ss 82(3) and 86(1) takes the form of putting the defaulter on oath or affirmation and questioning him about the reasons for his failure to pay, and the state of his means since the imposition of the fine or other penalty. HO 1990

The Clerk may fix or vary the date for the holding of a means enquiry. JCR 1999, Sched; PCC(S)A 2000, s 126; JCR 1999, Sched

A summons or warrant may be issued to bring him before the court, and the court (or the Clerk) may, either before or after enquiring into his means, make an order requiring him to furnish, within a specified period, a statement of his financial circumstances.

PCC(S)A 2000, s 126(4)(5)

If the defaulter, without reasonable cause, fails to comply with a financial circumstances order he is liable on summary conviction to a fine on level 3.

If, in providing the statement in compliance with the court order he:

(1) makes a statement which he knows to be false in a material particular; or

(2) recklessly furnishes a statement which is false in a material particular; or

(3) knowingly fails to disclose any material fact,

he is liable, on summary conviction to three months imprisonment, a fine on level 4 or to both.

Role of legal adviser

The role of the legal adviser in fine default proceedings or any other proceedings for the enforcement of financial orders, obligations or penalties is to assist the court. He must not act in an adversarial or partisan manner.

He may:

(1) with the express or implied request of the magistrates ask questions of the defaulter to elicit information which the magistrates will require to make an adjudication, for example to facilitate his explanation for the default (*R v Corby JJ, ex p Mort* (1998) 162 JP 310);

(2) advise the magistrates in the normal way as to the options open to them in dealing with the case.

He must not, however, set out to establish wilful refusal or neglect or any other type of culpable behaviour, to offer an opinion on the facts, or to urge a particular course of action upon the magistrates.

The duty of impartiality is the paramount consideration for the legal adviser at all times, and this takes precedence over any role he may have as a collecting officer.

(5) **Deductions from income support**

CJA 1991, s 24; DISR 1992

Where an offender is entitled to income support the court may apply to the Secretary of State for the deduction of sums from income support to satisfy payment of a fine or compensation.

The weekly amount deducted to pay off fines may not exceed five per cent of the personal allowance payable to someone over 25, nor may the total deduction (along with those for arrears of housing, fuel and water) exceed 15 per cent. Deductions are made at source and the DSS determine whether there is sufficient income support to allow the deductions to be made. An application may be made by the court after a means enquiry. The court may also apply in respect of a Crown Court order.

The Clerk is authorised to make or withdraw an application for the deduction from an offender's income support to satisfy a financial penalty, and do such other things as are required or permitted to be done by a magistrates' court under the DISR 1992. JCR 1999, Sched

(6) Money payment supervision order

Where the court does not commit a defaulter to prison forthwith, in default of payment of any sum adjudged to be paid on conviction, it may, either on the occasion of his conviction, or on a subsequent occasion, order him to be placed under the supervision of such person as the court may appoint, until the fine is paid. MCA 1980, s 88

Note that:

(1) the order is designed to minimise committals in default, and is not, in any sense, a community rehabilitation order;

(2) an ancillary worker employed by the probation and after care service, or a fines enforcement officer employed by the court, is usually appointed for the purpose;

(3) the order remains in force so long as the defaulter is still liable to pay any part of the sum, unless the court decides otherwise, or makes a transfer of fine order (see p 260 *below*) without prejudice, in either case, to making a new order

Where such an order is in force, the court must not commit the defaulter to prison in default or for want of distress, unless it has taken such steps as may be reasonably practicable to obtain an oral or written report from the supervisor as to the defaulter's means and conduct and has considered it.

(7) Enforcement by civil courts

A cumbersome procedure is provided by MCA 1980, s 87 as amended, by which sums adjudged to be paid on conviction may be enforced by the High Court or a county court (see, eg, *Gooch v Ewing* [1986] 3 All ER 654).

Enforcement action may not be taken until after a means enquiry under s 82 and where it appears to the court that the defaulter has sufficient means to pay forthwith.

(8) Attachment of earnings

The court may make an attachment of earnings order to secure the payment of any sum, and this without the need for an application where the offender consents: AEA 1971, s 1(3), AER 1971

(1) adjudged to be paid on conviction, or treated as so adjudged to be paid; or

(2) required to be paid by any contribution order,

either on the application of the offender, or, of its own motion where he has failed to make one or more of the payments required.

Such an order requires the offender's employer to make periodical payments from the offender's earnings to the clerk of the court. Where there is any possibility of the offender losing his job because of the making of the order, the court may consider it preferable to adopt other means of enforcement.

The order served on the employer specifies:

(a) the total amount to be paid;

(b) the 'normal deduction rate'; and

(c) a 'protected earnings rate' below which the court thinks it would not be reasonable to reduce the earnings.

Thus the full amount of the normal deduction rate is not taken if to do so would be to cause the offender's earnings to fall below the protected earnings rate.

If the offender changes his employer a new order must be made or the old order must be directed to the new employer.

(9) Detention for one day

MCA 1980, s 135

Where the court would have power, but for MCA 1980, ss 82 or 88, to commit a person to prison in default of payment, it may order him to be detained within the precincts of the courthouse or a police station, until such hour, not later than 8 pm of the same day as it may specify, unless such an order would deprive the offender of an opportunity of returning home on the day of the order.

(10) Overnight custody

MCA 1980, s 136

Where the same conditions are fulfilled as in (9) above, the court may issue a warrant for the defaulter's arrest and detention in a police station. On arrest the defaulter will be detained until 8 am the following day, or if he is arrested between midnight and 8 am, until 8 am on the day on which he is arrested. He may be released within four hours of that time if the officer in charge of the police station thinks it expedient to do so in order to enable him to go to work, or for any other sufficient reason.

(11) Attendance Centre Order

(see COMMUNITY SENTENCES).

(12) Transfer of fine order

MCA 1980, s 89, JCR 1999, Schedule

Where it imposes a fine, and the offender lives in another petty sessions area, the court (or the Clerk) may make an order transferring the fine to a court acting for that area, in which case the responsibility for collection enforcement lies with that court.

(13) Defaulters under 18

Where the court, were it not for the provisions of PCC(S)A 2000, s 89, would have power to commit to prison a person under 18 for default, in failing to pay, or want of sufficient distress to satisfy, a sum adjudged to be paid on conviction, it may, subject to certain conditions: MCA 1980, s 81

(1) order the defaulter's parent or guardian, if he consents to enter into a recognisance to ensure that the defaulter pays as much of the sum as remains unpaid; or

(2) order that so much of the sum as remains unpaid to be paid by the parent or guardian, if such a course seems reasonable in all the circumstances of the case,

provided in the latter case that the parent or guardian has been given an opportunity to be heard, unless having been required to attend has failed to do so. But:

(a) no such order, nor an attendance centre order under PCC(S)A 2000, s 60, may be made in respect of a defaulter under 18, unless the court, has since the conviction held a means enquiry in his presence on at least one occasion; and

(b) no order under (1) or (2) above may be made unless the court is satisfied that the defaulter has, or has had since the date on which the sum was adjudged to be paid, the means to pay the sum or any instalment of it on which he has defaulted, and refuses or neglects, or has refused or neglected, to pay it.

Remission of fines

Powers of remission do not extend to monetary penalties other than fines. MCA 1980, s 85

Where the court has imposed a fine on conviction it may at any time remit the whole or any part of the fine, if it thinks it just to do so, having regard to any change of circumstances which have occurred since the date of conviction, or since any postponement of the issue of the warrant of commitment. Where a person has been convicted of an offence in his absence or has failed to comply with a financial circumstances order or has failed to co-operate with the court's enquiry into his financial circumstances, the court may make a determination as it thinks fit in respect of that person's means. If subsequently, when enquiring into that person's financial circumstances the court is satisfied that had it had the results of that enquiry when sentence was passed it would: PCC(S)A 2000, s 129

(a) have fixed a smaller amount; or

(b) not have fined him,

it may remit the fine in whole or in part.

When enforcing a fine imposed by the Crown Court, no part of it may be remitted without the consent of that court.

Fines and Enforcement

STATUTORY POWERS AND PROVISIONS FOR THE ENFORCEMENT OF FINANCIAL PENALTIES

Remission of fine	MCA 1985, s 85; PCC(S)A 2000, s 129	p 261
General power to re-open cases	MCA 1980, s 142	p 400, 401

FOOTBALL BANNING ORDER

Part II of the Football Spectators Act 1989, as amended by the Football (Disorder) Act 2000, and the Football (Disorder)(Amendment) Act 2002 enables a court dealing with an offender convicted of certain types of offence, to make a banning order for a specified period, by which the offender is required to report himself to a designated police station at a time when a specified football match is taking place outside England and Wales. Parallel powers under the Public Order Act 1986 have been repealed.

As to the powers and functions of the 'enforcing authority', see s 19, and as to the 'exempting authority' s 20.

Banning order

Where an offender is: FSA 1989, s 14A(1)(2)(5)

(1) convicted of a 'relevant' offence (see Sched 1), ie one of those offences for which the court may make a declaration of relevance for the purpose of a banning order; and

(2) the court is satisfied that there are reasonable grounds to believe that making a banning order would help to prevent violence or disorder in connection with any regulated football matches (as defined in SI 2000, No 2126),

the court must make such an order in respect of the offender. If it does not make an order, it must state that fact in open court, and give its reasons.

Such an order may only be made:

(a) in addition to any sentence imposed in respect of the offence, or

(b) in addition to an order discharging him conditionally,

the latter, in spite of anything in PCC(S)A 2000, ss 12, 14, relating to conditional discharges and their effect (see ABSOLUTE AND CONDITIONAL DISCHARGE).

A banning order may also be made on complaint, under ss 14B–14D.

Declaration of relevance

The court may not make a declaration of relevance unless:

(1) the prosecutor gave notice to the accused five days before the first day of the trial that it was proposed to show that the offence with which he was charged related to a football match; or FSA 1989, s 23

(2) the accused consents to waive that requirement; or

(3) the court is satisfied that the interests of justice do not require more notice to be given.

Effect of banning order

FSA 1989, s 14

A banning order:

(1) in so far as matches in England and Wales are concerned, prohibits the person subject to the order from entering premises for the purpose of attending such matches; and

(2) in so far as matches outside England and Wales are concerned, requires that person to report at a police station in accordance with the Act.

'Football matches' include matches played, or intended to be played.

The period relevant to a football match is the period:

(a) beginning two hours before the start; or

(b) beginning two hours before the advertised start; or

(c) the time when the spectators are first admitted to the ground, whichever is the earliest; and

(d) finishing one hour after the end of the match.

FSA 1989, FSA s 14 s 14E(2)(5)(6)

The order will require the person subject to it to report initially at a police station specified in the order within five days of the order being made, unless he is detained in legal custody, in which case, if:

(i) he is released more than five days before the expiry of the period for which the order has effect; and

(ii) he was precluded by his being in custody from reporting initially,

the order has effect as if it required him to report initially at the police station within the five days beginning with the date of his release.

FSA 1989, s 14J

A person subject to an order who fails to comply with a requirement imposed by the order, or a requirement imposed under s 19(2B) or (2C) below, is guilty of an offence, and is liable on summary conviction to six months imprisonment, or to a fine not exceeding level 5 (see FINES AND ENFORCEMENT) or to both.

Surrender of passport

FSA 1989, s 14E(3)(4)

A banning order must, unless it appears to the court that there are exceptional circumstances, require the surrender of the passport of the person subject to the order in connection with regulated football matches outside the United Kingdom.

If the court finds such exceptional circumstances, it must state in open court what they are.

Period of restriction

A banning order has effect for a period beginning with the day on which it is made, and where: FSA 1989, s 14F

(1) it is made in addition to a sentence of imprisonment taking immediate effect, the maximum period is ten years and the minimum period is six years;

(2) it is made in any other case (apart from cases made on complaint) the maximum is five years, and the minimum is three years.

The period imposed must not be longer than the maximum nor shorter than the minimum.

Additional requirements

A banning order may, if the court making the order thinks fit, impose additional requirements. The order may be varied by that court, or by another court acting for the same petty sessions area, to impose, replace or omit such additional requirements. FSA 1989, s 14G

Photograph order

On the application by or on behalf of the prosecutor in respect of the offence for which the banning order was made, the court by which a banning order is made, may also make an order requiring: PorA 1986, s 35

(1) a constable to take, or cause to be taken, a photograph of the person to whom the order relates; and

(2) the offender to go to a police station specified in the order, not later than seven days after the order is made, at a specified time or times, to have his photograph taken.

A person failing to comply is liable to arrest without warrant for his photograph to be taken.

Administrative provisions

The order must specify the police station at which the offender is to report initially; the order must be explained in ordinary language to him. FSA 1989, s 14E(1)

A copy of the order will be given to the offender, and as soon as is reasonably practicable, a copy of it will be sent to the enforcing authority, and to the officer responsible for the police station at which the offender is to report initially. If the offender is sentenced to, or is serving, a custodial sentence, a copy will be sent to the governor of the prison or other person to whose custody he is committed.

Termination of order

If a banning order has had effect for at least two thirds of the period imposed, the person subject to it may apply to the court which made it, or another FSA 1989, s 14H magistrates'court sitting for the same petty sessions area, to terminate it, and the court may either terminate it or refuse the application.

In exercising its powers, the court may:

(1) have regard to the offender's character, his conduct since the order was made, the nature of the offence or conduct which led to it, and any other circumstances which appear to be relevant;

(2) the court may order the offender to pay all or any part of the costs of the application;

(3) if the application is refused, the court will not entertain a further application in respect of the order within a period of six months beginning with the date of the refusal.

Again, copies of any order will be sent to those persons to whom copies of the the original order were sent (see *above*).

FORFEITURE, CONFISCATION, AND RESTITUTION

FORFEITURE (DEPRIVATION ORDER)

The general power of forfeiture or 'deprivation', as it is called in the Act applies to all criminal offences. It overlaps the narrower specific powers provided by various statutes, to which reference should be made if appropriate. It serves a dual purpose, namely the removal from circulation of an article which has been used for the purposes of committing or facilitating the commission of an offence, and as part of the punishment inflicted on an offender.

The general power: s 143

Subject to certain restriction (see *below*) a general power is given to the court to deprive a convicted offender of his rights in property where: PCC(S)A 2000, s 143

(1) the court is satisfied that any property which:
  (a) has been lawfully seized from him; or
  (b) was in his possession, or under his control at the time when he was apprehended for the offence, or when the summons in respect of it was issued;
    (i) has been used for the purpose of committing, or facilitating the commission of, any offence; or
    (ii) was intended by him for that purpose; or

(2) the offence (or an offence which the court has taken into consideration) consists of unlawful possession of property which:
  (a) has been lawfully seized from him; or
  (b) was in his possession, or under his control at the time when he was apprehended for the offence, or when the summons in respect of it was issued.

'Facilitating the commission of an offence' includes, for this purpose, the taking of any steps after it has been committed, for the purpose of disposing of any property to which it relates or of avoiding apprehension or detection. PCC(S)A 2000, s 143(8)

Such an order may be made whether or not the court also deals with the offender in any other way in respect of the offence of which he has been convicted, and without regard to any restrictions on forfeiture in any enactment contained in an Act passed before 29 July 1988. PCC(S)A 2000, s 143(4)

Restrictions on use of s 143

PCC(S)A 2000, s 143(5)

As forfeited property has some financial value, the court must, in considering whether to make an order, have regard to:

(1) the value of the property; and

(2) the likely financial and other effects on the offender (taken together with any other order the court contemplates making).

Note also that:

(a) the power applies to all offences, including those to which a narrower specific statutory power applies (eg drugs and firearms, as to which see *below*) (*R v O'Farrell* [1988] Crim LR 387);

(b) the power cannot be used to deprive an offender of his rights in real property (*R v Khan* [1982] 3 All ER 969);

(c) the order is confined to the use, etc. of the property by the offender, not, eg by a person to whom drugs are supplied (*R v Slater* [1986] 3 All ER 786);

(d) the order is punitive in nature, and must be looked on as part of the sentence. The 'totality principle' therefore applies and it may be necessary to adjust other parts of the sentence (*R v Priestley* [1996] Crim LR 356).

Procedure and evidence

An order may be made only:

(1) where the prosecutor proves that the requirements of the section are fulfilled (*R v Kingston-upon-Hull JJ, ex p Hartung* [1981] Crim LR 42; *R v Pemberton* [1983] Crim LR 121); or

(2) on an admission by the accused or a specific finding by the court (*R v Troth* [1980] Crim LR 249);

(3) in the most straightforward cases and where a prior opportunity is given for representations to be made (*R v Powell* [1985] Crim LR 330); and

(4) in the case of a number of joint offenders, against all rather than against one only (*R v Ottey* [1984] Crim LR 506).

Straightforward cases only

An order should be made only in the most straightforward of cases, and only upon the offender's admission, or on a specific finding by the court (*R v Troth* (*above*)). There may be cases where the order will have a disproportionately severe effect on an offender and should not be made (*R v Taverner* [1976] RTR 242).

Where a number of offenders are equally guilty, it is wrong to make an order in relation to one accused only (*R v Ottey* (*above*)) but it may be fair and proper to reflect the differing levels of participation (*R v Burgess* [2001] 2 Cr App R (S) 5).

On making such an order, the court should make an express finding on the basis on which it is made (*R v Ranasinghe* [1999] 2 Cr App R (S) 366).

Serious road traffic offences

Where a person commits an offence under RTA 1988 which is punishable with imprisonment, by: PCC(S)A 2000, s 143(6)(7)

(1) driving, attempting to drive or being in charge of a vehicle; or
(2) failing to comply with a requirement under RTA 1988, s 7 (failure to provide specimen for analysis or for a laboratory test) in the course of an investigation into whether the offender had committed an offence while driving, attempting to drive or in charge of a vehicle; or
(3) failing, as the driver of a vehicle, to comply with RTA 1988, s 170(2)(3) (duty to stop and give information or to report accident),

the vehicle is said to be regarded for the purposes of s 143(1), above, and s 144(l)(b), below, as used for the purpose of committing the offence, and for committing any offence of aiding, abetting, counselling or procuring the commission of the offence.

Application for benefit of victim

Where the court makes an order in a case where: PCC(S)A 2000, s 52(1)

(1) the offender has been convicted of an offence which has resulted in any person suffering personal injury, loss or damage; or
(2) any such offence is taken into consideration on sentence; and but for the inadequacy of the offender's means it would have made a compensation order under which he would have been required to pay not less than a specified amount,

it may also order that any proceeds which arise from the disposal of the property and which do not exceed a sum he specifies, shall be paid to that person.

An order of this kind is not effective:

(a) before the end of the period specified in s 144(l)(a) above; or
(b) where a successful application under the P(P)A 1897 s 1(1) has been made.

Effect of order

The effect of an order is that, apart from depriving the offender of his rights, if any, in the property, it enables the property to be taken into the custody of PCC(S)A 2000, ss 143(3), 144

Forfeiture, Confiscation, and Restitution

the police, if not already in their possession, and the P(P)A 1897, s 69 then applies, with certain modifications, leaving any third party or other claimant to make a claim within the six months under the Act.

Firearms offences

FA 1968, s 52(1)

An order as to the forfeiture or disposal of a firearm or ammunition found in the possession of an offender may be made, where the offender:

(1) is convicted of an offence under FA 1968 (other than one under s 23(3) or an offence relating specifically to air weapons); or

(2) is convicted of an offence for which he is sentenced to imprisonment; or

(3) has been ordered to enter into a recognisance to keep the peace, a condition of which was that he should not carry a firearm (but see *R v Randall* (1986) Cr App R(S) 433); or

(4) is subject to a community rehabilitation order containing a requirement that he shall not possess, use or carry a firearm.

FA 1968, s 52(3)

Where a firearm is forfeited, it may be seized and detained by a constable.

Drugs offences

Where a person is convicted of:

MDA 1971, s 27(1)(2)

(1) an offence under MDA 1971; or

(2) a 'drug trafficking offence' within the meaning of DTA 1986, s 36(1),

and anything is shown to the satisfaction of the court to relate to the offence, the court may order it to be forfeited and either destroyed or dealt with in such other manner as it may order. If a person claiming to be the owner, or to be otherwise interested in the property, applies to be heard, an order must not be made unless an opportunity is given to him to be heard.

A number of broad principles were laid down in the cases of *R v Cuthbertson* [1980] 2 All ER 401; *R v Ribeyre* [1982] Crim LR 538; *R v Marland & Jones* (1986) 82 Cr App R 134; *R v Churcher* (1986) 8 Cr App R(S) 94; *R v Cox* (1986) 132 JP 162; *R v Llewellyn* [1985] Crim LR 750, thus:

(a) the order is concerned with forfeiture and not with restitution, compensation or the redress of unlawful enrichment;

(b) the order is designed to deal only with things which are tangible in the sense that physical possession may be taken of them by order of the court; 'anything' includes money (*R v Beard* [1974] 1 WLR 1549);

(c) it is necessary to connect the specific thing forfeited with a particular offence to which it relates (see *R v Morgan* [1977] Crim LR 488); working capital for future deals may be forfeited under the general power in PCC(S)A 2000, s 143 (*R v O'Farrell* [1988] Crim LR 387); and

(d) the offender ought to be permitted to adduce any material tending to show that the thing in question is not related to the offence.

Seizure and detention of exported or imported cash

A customs officer or a constable may, in certain circumstances, seize cash being imported into or exported from the UK. Such cash may not be detained for more than 48 hours unless its continued detention is authorised by an order made by a magistrate, who is satisfied that: CJ(IC)A 1990, ss 25, 26

(1) there are reasonable grounds for suspecting that it directly or indirectly represents any person's proceeds of, or is intended by any person for use in, drug trafficking; and

(2) continued detention is justified while its origin or derivation is further investigated, or consideration is given to the institution of criminal proceedings.

No order may be for more than three months at a time, and the total period must not exceed two years from the date of the original order.

DTCFR 1991 provide for the making of the relevant applications in respect of such cash, and its forfeiture.

Public Order Act 1986

A court by which a person is convicted of an offence under PorA 1986, ss 19, 21 or 23 in relation to racial hatred, or under s 18 relating to the display of racially offensive written material, must order to be forfeited any written material or recording (as defined in s 29) produced and shown to be written material or a recording to which the offence relates. PorA 1986, s 23

The order does not take effect until the ordinary time for appeal has expired, or, if an appeal is initiated, until it is finally determined or abandoned.

Game Act 1831

CJPOA 1994, Sched 9, para 4 contains provisions for forfeiting vehicles in the possession or under the control of poachers.

CONFISCATION UNDER PROCEEDS OF CRIME ACT 2002

The Proceeds of Crime Act 2002, Pt 1 establishes the Assets Recovery Agency and its Director, charged with providing for confiscation in relation to persons who benefit from criminal conduct. When Pt 2 of the Act comes into force, magistrates' courts will no longer have any jurisdiction to make a confiscation order of the kind made under CJA 1988, Pt VI; only the Crown Court will be empowered to make such an order where an offender is:

PCA 2002, s 6

(1) convicted of certain offences in proceedings before it;
(2) committed to it by a magistrates' court for sentence in respect of an offence or offences, under PCC(S)A 2000, ss 3, 4 or 6; or
(3) committed to it by a magistates' court in respect of an offence or offences, under PCA 2002, with a view to a confiscation order being considered (see COMMITTAL FOR SENTENCE).

Committal with a view to a confiscation order

PCA 2002, s 70

Where an offender is convicted of an offence by a magistrates' court and the prosecutor asks the court to commit him to the Crown Court with a view to a confiscation order under the Act being considered, the court:

(1) *must* commit him to the Crown Court in respect of the offence; and
(2) *may* commit him to the Crown Court in respect of any other offence of which he has been convicted by that magistrates' court or any other court, and the magistrates' court has power to deal with him for it, in custody or on bail, and the powers of the Crown Court under PCA 2002, s 6 apply.

If a committal under these provisions is made in respect of an offence for which the magistrates would (apart from s 70) have committed the offender for sentence under PCC(S)A 2000, s 3(2) (see COMMITTALS FOR SENTENCE) the magistrates must state that fact.

CONFISCATION UNDER CJA 1988, PT VI

The aim of the confiscation provisions enacted by CJA 1988, amended by the Proceeds of Crime Act 1995, is to deprive an offender of any benefit he may have received from his crimes, and at the same time to deprive any other person of any benefit derived through him. An order may be made by a magistrates' court in addition to any other disposal, and does not prevent the court dealing with the offender in any other way. The provisions are not penal in nature; their purpose is to deprive the offender of what is not rightfully his. CJA 1988 is printed as amended by PCA 1995.

The provisions will be repealed on the coming into force of PCA 2002, Sched 12.

These provisions have been amended to take account of the position after amendment by PCA 1995, which came into force on 1 November 1995. Care must be taken, in considering the case before the court, to pinpoint which of three stages in the legislation is applicable – CJA 1988 as amended by CJA 1993, CJA 1988 as further amended by CJPOA 1994 or CJA 1988 as further amended by PCA 1995.

Application

Part VI of PCA 1995 in relation to confiscation orders, CJA 1988, applies to any offence which is listed in Sched 4 to the Act, or, if not so listed, is an indictable offence, other than a drug trafficking offence (as defined in DTA 1994), or an offence under Pt III of the Prevention of Terrorism (Temporary Provisions) Act 1989. CJA 1988, s 71(9)(c)

Obligation to make enquiry

Where an offender is convicted in any proceedings before a magistrates' court, of an offence of a relevant description, the court must, where either: CJA 1988, s 71(1)–(3)

(1) the prosecutor has given written notice to the court that he considers it would be appropriate for the court to proceed under the section, or

(2) the court considers, even though it has not been given notice, that it would be appropriate to do so,

proceed, before sentencing or otherwise dealing with the offender in respect of that offence or any other relevant conduct, in the way set out below:

(a) the court must first determine whether the offender has benefited from any relevant criminal conduct; CJA 1988, s 71(1A)(1B)(1C)

(b) if it determines that he has so benefited, it must then:
  (i) determine in accordance with s 71(6) the amount to be recovered in his case by virtue of the section, and
  (ii) order the offender, under s 71, to pay that amount, unless

(c) it is satisfied that the victim of any relevant criminal conduct has instituted, or intends to institute, civil proceedings against the offender in respect of loss, injury or damage sustained in connection with that conduct.

In this last case, the court may, though it is not bound to do so, make an order, but s 71(6) (*below*) does not apply for determining the amount, and if the court does make an order, it must be of such an amount, not exceeding that which would apply by virtue of s 71 (6), as the court thinks fit.

Definitions

'Relevant criminal conduct' (introduced by PCA 1995), in relation to a person convicted of an offence, means, subject to s 72AA(6), that offence taken together with any other offences of 'a relevant description' which are either offences of which he is convicted in the same proceedings or offences which the court will be taking into consideration on sentence. CJA 1988, s 1(1D)(1E)

An offence is 'an offence of a relevant description' in the case of an offence of which an offender is convicted in any proceedings before the court or which is or will be taken into consideration by it, if it is an offence to which Pt VI applies.

CJA 1988, s 71(4)(5)

A person 'benefits from an offence' if he obtains property as a result of, or in connection with, its commission. His benefit is the value received. Where a person derives a pecuniary advantage as a result of or in connection with the commission of an offence, he is to be treated as if he had obtained as a result of or in connection with the commission of the offence, a sum of money equal to the value of the pecuniary advantage.

Procedure

The court is not empowered to make an order unless the prosecutor gives written notice to the court that it appears to him that the court would be able to make an order requiring the offender to pay at least the minimum amount (£10,000). If such notice is given:

CJA 1988, s 72(2)

(1) the court must determine whether it ought to make an order, taking into account any information placed before it showing that the victim of an offence to which the procedure relates has initiated, or intends to initiate, criminal proceedings against the accused, in respect of loss, injury or damage sustained in connection with the offence;
(2) if the court determines to make an order, it must:
   (a) before sentencing or otherwise dealing with the offender in respect of the offence or any of the offences,
   (b) determine the amount to be recovered in his case, and
   (c) make a confiscation order for that amount, specifying the offence or offences;

CJA 1988, s 72(5)

(3) account must be taken of the order *before*:
   (a) imposing a fine;
   (b) making any order involving payment by him (other than a compensation order (see COMPENSATION);
   (c) making a forfeiture order under PCC(S)A 2000, s 143 or MDA 1971, s 27.

Subject to that, the order will be left out of account in determining the sentence or other order which is appropriate.

The court is not restricted by any other enactment from making an order (see below for postponed determinations).

Evidence: (1) information by prosecutor

CJA 1988, s 73(1)(1A)

Where the offender has been convicted of an offence of a relevant description and the court is proceeding either as a result of written notice given by the prosecutor or of its own motion, and requires a statement from the prosecutor, the latter must, within such a period as the court directs, tender a statement as to any matters relevant to:

(1) determining whether the offender has benefited from any relevant criminal conduct; and

(2) assessing the value of that benefit,

and where the case is one in which the prosecutor has made a declaration that the case is one appropriate for the procedure to be followed (ie under s 72AA(l)(b)) such a statement must set forth all such information available as to the application of the statutory assumptions under s 72AA(4)(5)(b) or (c).

The prosecutor is entitled at any time to tender a further statement, and the court may require one, and may vary the time within which it requires any statement to be tendered. CJA 1998, s 73(1)(1B)(7)

If the accused accepts to any extent any allegation in the statement, the court may treat his acceptance as conclusive of the matters to which it relates.

For this purpose the court, if satisfied that a copy of the statement has been served on him, may require the accused to indicate to what extent he does accept such allegations, and, so far as he does not, to indicate any matters on which he proposes to rely.

Evidence: (2) accused's failure to comply

If the accused fails to comply in any respect with a requirement to indicate his acceptance or non-acceptance of the prosecutor's allegations, he may be treated as accepting every allegation in the statement apart from: CJA 1988, s 73(3)

(1) any allegation in respect of which he *has* complied; or

(2) any allegation that he has benefited from an offence, or that property was obtained by him as a result of, or in connection with, the commission of an offence (which must be proved by the prosecutor).

Evidence: (3) accused's statement

In the same class of proceedings, for the purpose of obtaining, information to assist it in carrying out its function, the court may order the offender to give it such information as may be specified in the order, in such manner and before such date as it may specify.

Again, if he fails, without reasonable cause, to comply with the order, the court may draw such inferences as it considers appropriate. If the prosecutor accepts to any extent any allegation made by the offender, the court may treat that acceptance as conclusive of the matters to which it relates.

Evidence: (4) manner of acceptance

An allegation may be 'accepted' or a matter 'indicated' either: CJA 1983, s 73(5)

(1) orally before the court; or

(2) in writing, in accordance with rules of court.

Burden of proof

CJA 1988, s 71(7A) The standard of proof required to determine any question arising under Part VI of the Act as to:

(1) whether a person has benefited from any offence; or

(2) the amount to be recovered in his case,

is that applicable to civil proceedings.

Statutory assumptions: s 72AA

CJA 1988, s 72AA(1)(2)(7) This section applies where in any proceedings before a magistrates' court an offender is convicted of a qualifying offence, that is an offence in relation to which all the following conditions are satisfied:

(1) it is an offence to which Part VI applies (see p 275 *above*);

(2) it is an offence which was committed after the commencement of PCA 1995, s 2; and

(3) the court is satisfied that it is an offence from which the offender has benefited,

which is an offence of a relevant description (see p 275 *above*), and:

(a) the prosecutor gives written notice (for the purposes of s 71(1)(a)),

(b) containing a declaration that the case is, in his opinion, in which it is appropriate for the provisions of this section to be applied; and

(c) the offender is convicted in those proceedings of at least two qualifying offences (including the offence in question), or has been convicted of a qualifying offence on at least one previous occasion during 'the relevant period' (ie six years ending when the proceedings in question were instituted against the offender).

CJA 1988, s 72AA(3)–(7) In such circumstances, when proceeding under s 71 in pursuance of the prosecutor's notice, the court may, if it thinks fit, act on three statutory assumptions in similar terms to those contained in DTA 1994, s 4(3), in similar circumstances, and subject to similar exceptions, in determining whether the offender has benefited from relevant criminal conduct and, if he has, in assessing the value.

Where the statutory assumptions are made in any case, the offences from which, in accordance with those assumptions, the offender is assumed to have benefited, are to be treated as if they were comprised for the purpose of Part VI, in the conduct which is to be treated, in that case, as relevant criminal conduct in relation to the offender.

Certificate of opinion

Where the court is satisfied as to any matter relevant for determining the amount that might be realised at the time an order is made, it:

(1) may issue a certificate giving its opinion as to the matters concerned; and

(2) shall issue a certificate, if satisfied that the amount that might be realised at the time the order is made is less than the amount the court assesses to be the value of the accused's benefit from the offence(s).

Sum ordered to be paid

(Subject to s 71(IC)) the sum which the order requires the offender to pay shall be equal to the benefit in respect of which it is made, or the amount appearing to be the amount that might be realised at the time the order is made, whichever is the less. CJA 1988, s 71(6)

Combination of confiscation and compensation

Where the court makes both a confiscation order and a compensation order (see COMPENSATION): CJA 1988, s 72(7)

(1) against the same person, and

(2) in the same proceedings,

and it appears that he will not have sufficient means to satisfy both orders in full, the court *must* direct that so much of the compensation order as will not be recovered because of the insufficiency of means shall be paid out of any sum recovered under the confiscation order.

Postponed determination

Where the court considers that it needs further information before: CJA 1988, s 72A(1)–(3)(6)(11)

(1) determining whether the offender has benefited from any relevant criminal conduct; or

(2) determining the amount to be recovered in his case,

it may, for the purpose of enabling that information to be obtained, on application by the offender or the prosecutor, or of its own motion, postpone making the determination for such period as it may specify. More than one postponement may be made, but unless the court is satisfied that they are exceptional circumstances it must not specify a period which, by itself or when taken together with earlier postponements, exceeds six months beginning with the date of conviction, that is:

(a) the date on which the offender was convicted of the offence concerned, or

(b) where he was convicted in the same proceedings, but on different dates, of two or more offences which are comprised in relevant criminal conduct, the date of the earlier conviction.

No need for postponement of sentence

CJA 1998, s 72A(7)–(9)

Where the court exercises its powers to postpone or extend the period for dealing with the making of a determination it may nevertheless proceed to sentence or otherwise deal with the offender in respect of the offence(s).

Appeal against conviction

CJA 1988, s 72A(4)(6)

Where the offender appeals against his conviction (which includes an appeal by way of case stated), the court may:

(1) postpone making a determination for such period as it may specify; or

(2) where it has already postponed a determination, extend the specified period,

but unless there are exceptional circumstances the postponement or extension must not exceed a period of three months after the determination or disposal of the appeal.

The postponement or extension may be made as in s 72A(5) (*above*).

Enforcement

CJA 1988, s 75(2)(3)(4)

An amount ordered to be paid under an order is treated as a fine for the purposes of MCA 1980, s 31(3).

Where:

(1) a warrant of commitment is issued for a default in the payment of an amount ordered to be paid under an order in respect of an offence; and

(2) at the time of the issue of the warrant the offender is liable to serve a term of custody in respect of the offence,

the term of imprisonment to be served in default of payment will not begin to run until after the substantive term under (2) above.

CJA 1988, s 75(5A)

Where the offender serves a term of imprisonment in default of paying any amount due under an order, his serving that term does not prevent the confiscation order from continuing to have effect, so far as other methods of enforcement are concerned.

REVIEW, REVISION, AND REASSESSMENT

Certain of the court's decisions or orders may be reviewed or revised at a later date.

(1) Review

Where, in an appropriate case:

(1) the prosecutor did not give the required notice, and either

(2) the court decided not to proceed under s 71, or no determination was made,

(3) and the prosecutor comes into possession of evidence which was not then available, and which, in his opinion, would have led the court to determine that the offender had benefited from relevant criminal conduct,

he may apply to any magistrates' court for the same area, within six years of the offender's conviction, to consider it. If it does, and it is satisfied that it is appropriate, in all the circumstances to do so, it may proceed under s 71, as if it were doing so before sentence, and may, though it is not bound to, make a confiscation order.

Certain restrictions apply to the nature of the evidence to be considered (s 74A(5)–(9)).

(2) Revision

Where, in an appropriate case:

(1) there was originally a determination that the offender had not benefited from any relevant criminal conduct, and

(2) the prosecutor comes into possession of evidence not considered by the court which, in his opinion would have led the court to determine that the offender had done so,

he may apply to any magistrates' court for the same area, within six years of the offender's conviction, to consider it. If it does so, and it is satisfied that it is appropriate, in all the circumstances to do so, it may proceed under s 71, as if it were doing so before sentence, and may, though it is not bound to, make a confiscation order.

Again, certain restrictions apply to the nature of the evidence to be considered (s 74B(5)–(9)).

(3) Reassessment

Where, in an appropriate case:

(1) there was a determination of a sum to be paid under a confiscation order, and

(2) the prosecutor is of the opinion that the value of the offender's benefit was greater than the benefit assessed by the court,

he may apply to any magistrates' court for the same area, within six years of the offender's conviction, to consider it. If, after doing so, the court is satisfied that the offender's benefit was greater than that originally assessed, it must make a fresh determination, as if it were proceeding under s 71 before sentence.

Again, certain restrictions apply to the nature of the evidence to be considered (s 74C(4)–(7)).

POLICE (PROPERTY) ACT 1897

The Act provides that where property comes into the possession of the police in connection with a criminal charge, or in the execution of a search warrant, a magistrates' court may, on the application of the police or a claimant, make an order for its delivery to the person who appears to be its owner, or if the owner cannot be ascertained, make such other order as it thinks fit.

The procedure under this Act should only be used in straightforward cases (*Raymond Lyons & Co v Metropolitan Police Commissioner* [1975] 1 All ER 335).

MAGISTRATES' COURTS ACT 1980, S 48

Where:

MCA 1980, s 48

(1) a summons or warrant has been issued requiring a person to appear or be brought before the court to answer an information; or

(2) a person has been arrested without warrant for an offence; and

(3) property has been taken from him after the issue of the summons or warrant, or the arrest without warrant,

the police must report the taking of the property, with particulars of it, to the magistrates' court dealing with the offence.

Where the court is of the opinion that:

(a) consistently with the interests of justice and the safe custody of the accused,

(b) the whole or any part of the property may be returned to him,

it may direct that the property, or such part of it as it directs, be returned to him or to such other person as he requires.

The section does not apply to property or documents taken from premises on or after arrest (see *R v Southampton MC, ex p Newman* [1988] 3 All ER 669).

RESTITUTION ORDER

A restitution order restores to the person entitled property or goods which have been 'stolen'. It should be made only where the title to property is abundantly clear; in any other case, an applicant should be left to seek his remedies under the Police (Property) Act 1897, or in the civil courts (*R v Ferguson* (1970) 54 Cr App R 410).

An order maybe made where: PCC(S)A 2000, s 148

(1) goods have been stolen and a person is convicted with reference to the theft (whether or not stealing is the gist of the offence); or
(2) the court takes such an offence into consideration on determining sentence.

The words 'stolen' and 'theft' refer as well to offences of obtaining property by deception, blackmail, and handling property obtained by deception and blackmail. TA 1968, s 24(4)(8)

'Goods' includes all kinds of property except land, and includes things severed from the land by stealing. PCC(S)A 2000, s 148(10)

Power to make order

The court may make an order: PCC(S)A 2000, s 148(2)

(1) ordering any person having possession of the goods to restore them to a person entitled to recover them from him;
(2) on the application of a person entitled to recover from the offender *any other goods,* directly or indirectly representing those in (1) *above,* as being the proceeds of any disposal or realisation of the whole or part, or of goods representing them, that those *other goods* be delivered or transferred to the applicant;
(3) that a sum not exceeding the value of the goods in (1) *above* be paid out of any money of the offender, *taken out of his possession on apprehension,* to any person who, if the goods were in the possession of the offender, would be entitled to recover them from him.

Where an order is made under (1) *above,* and it appears that the offender has sold the goods to another who acted in good faith, or has borrowed money from that other on their security, the court may order to be paid to that person, out of the money of the offender *taken from his possession on apprehension,* a sum not exceeding the price paid or the amount owed. No application is necessary. PCC(S)A 2000, s 148(4)

Orders under (2) and (3) *above* may be combined provided the total does not exceed the value of the goods.

An order may be made whether or not the passing of sentence is deferred in other respects.

Procedure

No order should be made unless, in the court's opinion the relevant facts appear from: PCC(S)A 2000, s 148(5)(6)

(1) evidence given at the trial, or the 'available documents'; together with
(2) any admissions made by or on behalf of any person in connection with the proposed exercise of the court's powers.

'The available documents' include any written statements or admissions which were made for use, and would have been admissible, as evidence at the trial, the depositions taken at any committal proceedings, and any written statements or admissions used as evidence in those proceedings. Evidence given after sentence is not 'evidence given at the trial' (*R v Church* (1970) 55 Cr App R 65).

A representation order ought to be given where complex matters of restitution fall to be decided.

The court has no power to make a restitution order when committing an offender to the Crown Court for sentence (*R v Blackpool JJ, ex p Charlson* [1972] 3 All ER 854).

Suspension pending appeal

Unless there is no dispute and the court so directs, a restitution order is suspended pending appeal:

(1) in any case for 21 days, ie until the expiration of the period for giving notice of appeal to the Crown Court; or
(2) where notice of appeal is given *within time,* until the determination of the appeal.

INFORMATION, SUMMONS, AND WARRANT

Criminal proceedings in a magistrates' court are activated by arrest, charge and production before the court, or by the issue of a summons or warrant following the laying of an information.

The information

The court is informed of the alleged commission of an offence by an information being laid before it.

Generally:

(1) there is no time limit for laying an information in respect of an indictable offence (*Kemp v Liebherr GB Ltd* [1987] 1 All ER 885); but

(2) magistrates cannot try an information in respect of a summary offence unless it was laid within six months from the time the offence was committed or some other specific period prescribed for the particular offence; and MCA 1980, s 127

(3) in computing that period, the day on which the offence was committed is to be excluded.

(*Marren v Dawson Bentley & Co Ltd* [1961] 2 All ER 270.)

Laying the information

An information:

(1) in writing, is laid when it is received in the office of the Clerk (*Hill v Anderton* [1982] 2 All ER 963); there is no need for personal consideration, either by the Clerk or a magistrate at that stage; it is the issue of process which is the judicial act;

(2) may be laid orally, before a magistrate, the Clerk, or a member of the Clerk's staff who has been specifically authorised for the purpose (see ROLE OF CLERK) (*R v Gateshead JJ, ex p Smith* (1985) 149 JP 681);

(3) may be laid by computer link between the police station and the court, even though it is not printed out until a later date (*R v Pontypridd JC, ex p B* [1988] Crim LR 842).

Contents

An information: MCA 1980; MCR 1981, r 4(1)(2); s 100(1); MC(F)R 1981, Form 1

(1) describes the offence with which the accused is charged in ordinary language;

(2) may be laid by the prosecutor in person, or by his counsel or solicitor or other person authorised in that behalf;

(3) need not be in writing or on oath unless specifically provided by law;

(4) may be laid before the Clerk unless it needs to be substantiated on oath;

(5) need not be laid in the presence of the accused.

It may still be laid properly within the time limit even though it is not in the prescribed form (*R v Kennet JJ, ex p Humphrey & Wyatt* [1993] Crim LR 787). Any defect in process is cured by the accused's appearance (*Re Akomolede* [1995] Crim LR 161).

Duplicity

A vital rule which applies alike to the contents of a charge or summons is that it should not charge more than a single offence. Thus:

MCR 1981, r 12(1)

(1) a magistrates' court may not try an information which charges more than one offence;

(2) if an information charges more than one offence it is bad for duplicity, and the court cannot convict upon it (*Hargraves v Alderson* [1964] 26B 159).

The remedy is for the prosecution to seek to amend at the outset, proceeding on the single offence in the amended summons.

A charge or summons is 'duplicitous' where it alleges more than one activity (see *Ware v Fox* [1967] 1 All ER 100). Where the statute forbids the doing of an act in one of two ways, it creates two offences, but where it creates a duty to do either one of two acts, it creates a single offence (*North v Gerrish* (1959) 123 JP 313). It is not duplicitous to set out being in charge of a motor vehicle 'while under the influence of drink or a drug' (*Thompson v Knights* [1947] 1 All ER 112), for this is a single activity, as is driving 'at a speed and in a manner dangerous to the public' (*R v Clow* [1963] 2 All ER 216); see also *Newton Ltd v Smith etc* [1962] 2 All ER 19 ('wilfully or negligently').

Defect in information

There are three types of defect which can occur in an information and a summons based on it:

(1) an error so fundamental that it cannot be remedied by any appropriate and reasonable amendment, thus causing the prosecution to fail;

(2) an error which is substantial enough to require amendment which the magistrate may allow; an adjournment should be granted if the defence are placed at any disadvantage;

(3) an error so trivial that the defence have not been misled as to the true basis of the information (*New Southgate Metals Ltd v Islington LBC* [1996] Crim LR 334). See also MCA 1980, s 123, (*Garfield v Maddocks* [1973] 2 All ER 303).

As a general rule no objection will be allowed to any defect in the form of any information, complaint, summons or warrant, nor may objection be taken if there is a variation between the contents of the information, summons or warrant and the evidence adduced at the hearing. MCA 1980, s 123

The judicial act

Upon an information being laid showing that a person has committed, or is suspected of committing, an offence, a summons may be issued, directed to him, requiring him to appear before the court. MCA 1980, s 1(1)

The issue of process is a judicial act. If the person issuing it exercises that discretion wrongfully and refuses to issue process, mandatory order (*mandamus*) may issue. There is nothing to prevent batches of informations being put before one magistrate or the Clerk (*R v Gateshead JJ, ex p Tesco Stores Ltd* [1981] 1 All ER 1027). If the Clerk, exercising the powers of a single magistrate for this purpose, refuses to issue process, the court is not entitled to review that decision.

There is no question of any preliminary hearing; the magistrate, or the Clerk need only be satisfied that it *is* a proper case to issue process. There is no obligation on him to make an enquiry into the matter (*R v Clerk to the Bradford JJ ex p Sykes* [1999] Crim LR 748). The accused has no right to be heard on the matter, though the magistrate may hear him, if he thinks fit (*R v W London JJ, ex p Klahn* [1979] 2 All ER 221).

If the information is substantiated on oath, a magistrate may issue a warrant for his arrest.

The power to issue process

The power to issue process arises where: MCA 1980, s 1(2)

(1) the offence was committed, or is suspected to have been committed, within the court's area;

(2) it appears necessary or expedient, with a view to the better administration of justice, either that the person should be tried jointly with, or in the same place as, some other person who is charged with an offence and is in custody, or is, or is to be within the area (see also *R v Abergavenny JJ, ex p Barratt* [1993] Crim LR 785);

(3) the accused resides, or is believed to reside, within the area;

(4) a court for the area has jurisdiction under some enactment; or

(5) the offence was committed outside England and Wales, and is punishable exclusively on summary conviction, if a court for the area would have jurisdiction if he were before it; and

(6) in respect of a summary offence the information is laid within time (*R v Blackburn JJ, ex p Holmes* [2000] Crim LR 300).

The jurisdiction of the magistrates is based on the facts of the case rather than on the form of process, and the fact that the information wrongly states the offence to have been committed outside the court's area does not deprive them of jurisdiction if the offences were in fact committed within the area (*R v Ormskirk MC, ex p Battistini* [1990] Crim LR 591).

Form of summons

MCA 1980, s 1(7); JCR 1999; MCR 1981, r 98(1); MC(F)R 1981, Forms 2, 3 CJ(IC)AR 1991

A summons may be issued by a single magistrate, the Clerk or other authorised person. Where it is issued by a named magistrate it ought to be signed by him, or state his name, and be authenticated by the Clerk's signature.

It should state shortly the matter of the information, and the time and place at which the accused is required to appear.

As to the service of a summons outside the United Kingdom, see CJ(IC)AR 1990.

Issue of warrant

MCA 1980, s 1(4); MC(F)R 1981, Form 4

A warrant may be issued:

(1) initially, instead of a summons, where:
   (a) the accused has attained the age of 18 and the offence is indictable or is punishable with imprisonment; or
   (b) the accused's address is not sufficiently established to enable a summons to be served; or

MCA 1980, s 13(1),(3)

(2) in the course of proceedings, where the accused fails to appear at a hearing or an adjourned hearing, and the court decides not to proceed in his absence, provided:
   (a) he has attained the age of 18; and
   (b) the offence is punishable with imprisonment, or after conviction, the court proposes to disqualify him from driving,

MCA 1980, s 13(2)(2A)

provided that where a summons has been issued, a warrant must not be issued thereafter under this provision, unless the court is satisfied on oath or in the prescribed manner, that:
   (i) the summons was served on the accused within what appears to the court to be a reasonable time before the trial or the adjourned trial, or
   (ii) the adjournment now being made is a second or subsequent adjournment of the trial, and the accused was present at the last or

only occasion when the trial was adjourned, and on that occasion the court fixed the date for the adjourned hearing; or

(3) where the court adjourns the trial after having received evidence, or having convicted the accused on his plea of guilty under MCA 1980, s 9(3), or after having, on a previous occasion convicted him under s 12(2), if it considers it undesirable, by reason of the gravity of the offence, to continue the trial in his absence; or MCA 1980, s 13(5)

(4) where the accused has been released on bail, and, being under a duty to surrender in criminal proceedings, fails to do so at the time and place appointed, or, having surrendered, absents himself; or

(5) in certain circumstances, in connection with proceedings for the determination of mode of trial (see MODE OF TRIAL).

Note that:

(a) a warrant cannot be issued by the Clerk; MCA 1980, ss 1(3), 11(2), 13(3)(3A); JCR 1999

(b) a warrant cannot be issued unless the information has been substantiated on oath and, in the case of a first instance warrant, the information is in writing;

(c) a first instance warrant ought not to be issued where a summons would be equally effective unless the charge is a serious one (*Dumbell v Roberts* (1944) 108 JP 139).

The Clerk may, where there is no objection on behalf of the accused, issue a warrant, whether or not backed for bail, for failure to surrender bail. JCR 1999, Schedule

Backing for bail

A warrant may be 'backed' for bail, by endorsing it with a direction: MCA 1980, s 117

(1) in the case of criminal proceedings, that the person arrested be released on bail subject to a duty to appear at a specified court and time; and

(2) in the case of bail *otherwise* than in 'criminal proceedings', that he be released on entering into recognisances, with or without sureties, for his appearance.

The amounts in which any surety, and in (2) the principal, are to be bound, must be endorsed on the warrant.

Witness summons/warrant

Where a justice, the Clerk or other authorised person is satisfied that a person in England or Wales, or even outside the British Islands: MCA1980, s 97(1)(2A)

(1) is likely to be able to give material evidence, or to produce any document or thing likely to be material evidence in transfer proceedings or a summary trial; and

(2) will not attend voluntarily as a witness, or voluntarily produce the document or thing,

a summons must be issued requiring that person to attend at the time specified in the summons to give evidence or to produce the document or thing (see *R v Reading JJ, ex p Berkshire County Council* [1996] Crim LR 347 for the principles as to what documents are 'likely' to be material evidence).

MCA 1980, s 97(2)(2A)

If that person fails to attend court in answer to the summons, the court may issue a warrant for him to be brought before the court at the time and place specified in the warrant, provided that in such a case:

(a) the court is satisfied by evidence on oath that (1) *above* is made out, and that that person is in England or Wales;

(b) it is proved on oath or in such manner as is provided, that he was duly served with the summons and that a reasonable sum has been tendered to him in respect of costs and expenses; and

(c) it appears to the court that there is no just excuse for his failure to attend.

MCA 1980, s 97(2B)(2C)

A magistrate may, however, refuse to issue a summons in relation to the summary trial of an information if he is not satisfied that an application for the summons was made by a party to the case as soon as reasonably practicable after the accused pleaded not guilty.

Where an accused seeks witness warrants to secure the attendance of witnesses who will not come voluntarily, the court is bound to issue them where the evidence of the witnesses is critical to the case (*R v Bradford JJ, ex p Wilkinson* [1990] 2 All ER 833; *R v Bristol MC, ex p Rootes* [1994] RTR 40). The fact that the accused is represented, and that that representative could, therefore, put the accused's case before the court is an irrelevant consideration (*R v Nottingham JJ, ex p Fraser* (1995) 159 JP 612).

If a witness chooses to ignore a summons he will be in contempt of court and can expect to be punished: his failure is likely to disrupt the trial process or undermine it entirely (*R v Young* (2000)) *The Times*, 6 May.

Role of the Clerk

JCR 1999, Schedule

The Clerk may:

(1) issue a summons, including a witness summons;

(2) mark an information as withdrawn; and

(3) where no evidence is offered by the prosecutor, dismiss an information or discharge the accused in respect of an information .

JURISDICTION AND INITIAL PROCEDURE

The principal function of magistrates' courts today is to try summarily, that is without a jury, such offences as are allocated to their jurisdiction by law. While they have powers to augment the investigation of offences by, for example, the issue of search and access warrants, and some supervision of police detention, their functions as examining magistrates have been reduced to little more than a formality. They also have important functions in relation to the collection of fines imposed by all criminal courts and the enforcement and supervision of community sentences. While the great majority of criminal cases are tried and dealt with in magistrates' courts, the powers of such courts both to try and to punish offenders are limited. They are entitled to take cognisance of an offence only where, and to the extent that jurisdiction is conferred upon them.

Limitations on jurisdiction

Jurisdiction may be limited by:

(1) the age of the accused (see *below*);

(2) the limits of the court's territory (see p 294 *below*);

(3) the category of offence forming the subject matter of the charge (see p 295 below);

(4) any time limits or consents required by statute (see pp 295, 296 below); and, finally

(5) disqualification, in relation to any particular member of the bench (see pp 296–298 below).

Distinctions may need to be made between the 'adult' court and the youth court (see YOUTH COURTS).

1. AGE OF ACCUSED

The absence of any power in the adult court to impose a detention and training order indicates that, in general, Parliament considered that a non-custodial sentence should be passed in respect of juveniles, and that wherever possible, children and young persons, should be dealt with in the youth court (see further *R (W) v Southampton Youth Court* [2002] Crim LR 750).

The general rule

CYPA 1933, s 46(1)

No charge against a person under 18, and no application, the hearing of which is assigned to a youth court (see YOUTH COURT), may be heard by the 'adult' court. There are, however, three exceptions to this general rule:

CYPA 1933, s 18

(1) a charge made jointly against a juvenile and an adult must be heard by CYPA 1963, the adult court;

MCA 1980, s 29(1)

(2) a juvenile may be tried in the adult court where a person of 18 or over is charged at the same time with aiding, abetting, procuring, allowing or permitting the juvenile's offence;

(3) a juvenile may be tried in the adult court where he is charged with aiding and abetting an offence by a person of 18 or over, or where his offence arises out of circumstances which are the same as, or are connected with, those in relation to which the adult is charged at the same time.

CYPA 1933, s 45(IA)

The fact that in the course of the proceedings it appears that the accused is a juvenile does not prevent the adult court from continuing the proceedings up to their determination; nor is there anything to prevent the adult court from dealing with remand and bail, and it is entitled to hear evidence for these purposes.

Where notification is received that an accused wishes to plead guilty in writing in accordance with MCA 1980, s 12, and the court has no reason to believe that he is a juvenile, he is deemed to have attained the age of 18 for the purposes of the proceedings.

Plea of guilty by older accused

MCA 1980, s 29(1)(2)

Where a juvenile appears, or is brought before the adult court on an information charging him with an offence jointly with one or more others, any of whom are 18 or over, then if:

(1) the court proceeds to summary trial of the information, and the older accused, or one of them, pleads guilty; or

MCA 1980, s 29(1)(2)(3)

(2) the court:
   (a) proceeds with a view to committal for trial in the case of the older or each of the older accused; and
   (b) in the case of the juvenile, proceeds to summary trial of the information;

then, in either situation, if the juvenile pleads not guilty, the court may, before any evidence is called in his case, remit him for trial by a youth court acting for the same place as the remitting court, or for the place where he habitually resides. He will then be brought before that court to be tried.

MCA 1980, s 29(4)

There is no right of appeal against an order of remittal. The remitting court may give such directions as appear necessary with respect to custody or bail until he can be brought before the youth court.

Remittal to youth court for sentence

Where a juvenile is found guilty in the adult court of any offence, that court must, unless satisfied that it would be undesirable to do so, remit him to a youth court sitting either for the place where the remitting court sits, or for the place where he habitually resides, for sentence, and that court may deal with him in any way in which it could have dealt with him if he had been tried and convicted there. CYPA 1933, s 56

The receiving court has all the powers of jurisdiction that it would have had in the first place and could, for example, accept a change of a plea of guilty to not guilty during the course of proceedings. (*R v Stratford Youth Court, ex p Conde* [1997] 1 WLR 113).

In particular, the 'adult' court must remit a juvenile offender to the youth court for sentence unless it is of the opinion that his case can properly be dealt with by: or

(1) a conditional or absolute discharge; or

(2) a fine; or

(3) an order requiring his parent or guardian to enter into recognisances to take proper care and control of him; or

(4) a referral order PCC(S)A 2000, s 16

with or without any ancillary order, which the court has power to make on an absolute or conditional discharge.The adult court will give such directions as are necessary in relation to custody or bail, and will send to the youth court a certificate of remittal setting out the relevant matters.

The juvenile has no right of appeal against the remittal, although he has the ordinary rights of appeal against any order made by the youth court as if he had been found guilty by it.

Right to trial on indictment

A person under the age of 18 appearing or being brought before a magistrates' court, whether the adult court or a youth court, on an information charging him with an indictable offence other than homicide, has no right of trial on indictment, and must be tried summarily, unless: MCA 1980, ss 6(2), 24(1)(2)

(1) the offence is such as is mentioned in PCC(S)A 2000, s 91(1) or (2) under which young persons convicted on indictment of certain grave crimes may be sentenced to be detained for long periods and the court considers that if he is found guilty of the offence it ought to be possible (for the Crown Court) to sentence him in pursuance of s 91(3); or

(2) he is charged jointly with a person who has attained the age of 18 (even though that person is the subject of a separate committal, see

R v Coventry City MC, ex p M (1992) 156 JP 809), and the court considers it necessary in the interests of justice to commit both of them for trial.

In these two circumstances the court must commit the juvenile for trial on indictment, provided the provisions of MCA 1980, s 6 are fulfilled (see *R (C and Another) v Sheffield Youth Court*; *R (N) v Sheffield Youth Court* (2003) *The Times*, 23 January).

In a case under (2) *above,* the court may also commit the juvenile for trial in respect of any other offence with which he is charged at the same time, whether jointly with the adult or not, if that offence arises out of circumstances which are the same as, or are connected with, those giving rise to the first-mentioned offence.

Determination of age

The date on which to determine whether the accused has attained the age of 18 or not, is the date on which he appears before the court on the occasion when it makes the decision as to mode of trial (*Re Daley* [1982] 2 All ER 974; *R v Vale of Glamorgan Juvenile JJ, ex p Beattie* (1984) 149 JP 120).

Juveniles and publicity

CYPA 1933, s 39

In any proceedings, the court may direct that no newspaper report of the proceedings shall reveal the name, address or school, or include any particulars calculated to lead to the identification of any juvenile concerned in the proceedings.

The terms of such an order must be clear. Where there is doubt as to which of several children the order relates, they should be clearly identified.

A written copy should be drawn up as soon as is practicable after the oral order is pronounced, and should be made available in the court office for inspection by representatives of the press. The fact that an order has been made should be notified in the daily court list *(R v CCC, ex p Crook and Godwin* [1995] Crim LR 509).

2. Territorial jurisdiction

MCA 1980, ss 2, 17

Apart from any special rules governing offences committed on journeys or those committed on boundaries between two or more areas, the court has jurisdiction:

(1) to try all summary offences committed within the county or other area;

(2) to try all summary offences for which a person is brought before the court in answer to a summons, or on the execution of a warrant;

(3) to proceed with a view to committal for trial, where the offence charged was committed by a person who appears, or is brought before, the court, whether or not the offence was committed in that area;

(4) to try any either-way offence summarily, where it would have had power to proceed with a view to transfer for trial; and

(5) to try any summary offence for which a person could be tried by a court in any other area, if he is being tried for another offence within the jurisdiction of the court.

The responsibility for determining the issue of jurisdiction falls upon the magistrate or Clerk issuing process, and an information should state as clearly as possible the place at which the alleged offence occurred and the name and address of the accused (*R v Abergavenny JJ, ex p Barratt* [1993] Crim LR 785).

Offenders remitted for sentence

The court has power to impose sentence upon an offender remitted to it from another magistrates' court under MCA 1980, s 39 (see DEALING WITH OFFENDER).

3. CATEGORY OF OFFENCE

Criminal offences are grouped into three categories, namely:

(1) the most serious, triable only on indictment;

(2) those triable either way, that is either on indictment or, with the consent of the accused, summarily; and

(3) those triable summarily only.

Criminal damage (a so-called 'schedule offence') is a special case to which special rules apply (see MODE OF TRIAL).

4. TIME LIMITS; CONSENT; OUSTER

A magistrates court may not try a summary offence unless the information was laid within six months of the time when the offence was allegedly committed unless an enactment expressly permits a longer period. In the case of a continuing offence, the period runs from the time when the offence ceased to be committed (*BT v Nottinghamshire CC* [1999] Crim LR 217). There is no time limit in the case of offences triable on indictment only or either way. MCA 1980, s 127

Certain other statutes lay down specific time limits within which a prosecution must be brought. Where not otherwise stated, the magistrates must not try an information or complaint unless it was laid or made within six months from the time when the offence was committed or the cause of complaint arose (see INFORMATION, SUMMONS AND WARRANT). This rule does not apply to indictable offences.

A statute may require the consent of the DPP, the Attorney-General, a minister or other person or body, before a prosecution may be brought. In such a case unless that consent is signified the court has no jurisdiction.

In certain rare cases the jurisdiction of the magistrates' court may be ousted by statute or under common law.

Where a 'criminal proceedings order' or an 'all proceedings order' is made in the High Court, no information may be laid before a magistrate by the person against whom the order is made, without leave of the High Court.

5. DISQUALIFICATION OF MAGISTRATE

ECHR Art 6(1) confers a right to a hearing by an independent and impartial tribunal. An individual magistrate may be disqualified from acting in a judicial capacity on grounds of an interest or bias in the proceedings, or because of some factor in the antecedents of the accused. There is obviously a distinction to be drawn between dealing with adjournments, formal remands, bail applications and pleas of guilty on the one hand, and cases in which he is required to adjudicate on whether guilt is made out.

The general principle on which such conditions are based were stated thus in *R v Liverpool JJ, ex p Topping* [1983] 1 All ER 490: 'Would a reasonable and fair-minded person sitting in court and knowing all the relevant facts, have a reasonable suspicion that a fair trial was not possible?'

Disqualification: (1) statutory prohibitions

Statute forbids the participation of a magistrate who:

JPA 1979, s 64
(1) is a member of a local authority from sitting in any proceedings (there are exceptions) brought by or against that authority; and

MCA 1980, s 42
(2) in the course of the same proceedings, has been informed that the accused has one or more previous convictions for the purpose of determining whether or not he should have bail; proceedings before the court on an application for dismissal of a charge under the new transfer proceedings (MCA 1980, s 6 as amended) from which the summary trial arose are to be treated as part of the trial.

Disqualification: (2) interest in the proceedings

A magistrate should disqualify himself from trying a case:

(1) where he has an active connection with a party to the proceedings (*R v Altrincham JJ, ex p Pennington* [1975] 2 All ER 78, 304, see also *R v Bow Street Metropolitan Stipendiary Magistrate, ex p Pinochet Ugarte (No 2)* [1999] 1 All 577 HL);

(2) where he has a direct pecuniary or proprietary interest, however small, in the outcome of the case (*R v Cambourne JJ, ex p Pearce* [1954] 2 All ER 850),

or should, at any rate, bring the matter to the attention of the parties before the case is opened and find out whether there is any objection to his participating (*Metropolitan Properties Co Ltd v Lannon* [1968] 3 All ER 304).

The test is whether, having regard to all the relevant circumstances, there is a real danger of bias, in the sense that he might unfairly regard, or unfairly look upon with favour or disfavour, the cause of a party to the issue under consideration (*R v Gough* [1993] 3 All ER 724).

Disqualification: (3) accused's previous convictions

Where a magistrate has been concerned with an accused on another occasion, apart from the statutory prohibition relating to bail applications:

(1) he is not entitled to take part in the determination of the accused's guilt on a summary trial where he dealt with an application for a representation order which included information as to previous convictions (*R v Blyth Valley JC, ex p S* (1987) 151 JP 805);

(2) he is not disqualified by the mere fact that has been concerned with the accused in other proceedings, although it is desirable, if practicable to do so, to have the case heard by another bench (*R v McElligott, ex p Gallagher & Searle* [1972] Crim LR 332).

Where a magistrate who is about to try a case discovers that there are other unrelated charges against the accused, he has a discretion whether to continue; the test is whether, in the circumstances, there would be an appearance of, rather than actual, bias on his part, if he were to proceed (*R v Liverpool JJ, ex p Topping* [1983] 1 All ER 490). If, in the course of the trial of an information, he becomes aware, from a source other than the evidence given in court, that the accused has one or more previous convictions it is his duty to disclose the fact forthwith, even if it means starting the trial afresh before another bench (*R v Birmingham MC, ex p Robinson* (1986) 15O JP 1).

Disqualification: (4) circumstances arising

Magistrates should take care, during the proceedings, that they do not express support for one party or the other (see eg *R v Highgate JJ, ex p Riley* [1996] RTR 150) and should show that they are giving 'actual and apparent' attention to the matters in hand. See eg *R v Weston-Super-Mare JJ, ex p*

Taylor [1981] Crim LR 179 (magistrate apparently asleep), *R v Marylebone MC, ex p Perry* [1992] Crim LR 514 (signing warrants while accused speaking); *R v S Westminster JJ, ex p Daniels* (1996) 161 JP 121 (magistrate browsing through sentencing guidelines during hearing) and see *R v Romsey JJ, ex p Gale* (1991) 156 JP 567.

A magistrate is not otherwise disqualified from continuing through having decided some interlocutory matter in the course of the proceedings (*R v Norfolk Stipendiary Magistrate ex p Taylor* [1998] Crim LR 276 (evidence); *DPP v Acton Youth Court* [2001] 1 WLR 1828 (public interest immunity), *KL & LK v DPP* (2002) 166 JP 369 (special measures direction)).

Disqualification: (5) time for raising issue

If a magistrate thinks that he may be disqualified from hearing a case, he ought to raise the matter himself (*R v Downham Market JJ, ex p Nudd* [1989] Crim LR 147), as he should if he becomes aware of something during the trial (*R v Birmingham MC, ex p Robinson* (1985) 150 JP 1). If a ground of objection becomes apparent to a party, it should be raised at the first opportunity, since, for instance, a pecuniary interest cannot form the subject matter of an appeal, unless objection is taken at the trial.

It is for the magistrate(s) to decide, as in other matters of law, whether he, or they, are disqualified (*R v Weston-super-Mare JJ, ex p Shaw* [1987] 1 All ER 255. A magistrate is not bound to disqualify himself where an objection is raised; if he satisfies himself that the principle in *Topping* (p 296 *above*) is not infringed, he may continue to act (*R v Tooke* (1898) 154 JP 661).

6. INITIAL PROCEDURE

Early administrative hearing

CDA 1998, s 50(1)(2)

Where an accused has been charged with an offence at a police station, the court before which he appears or is brought for the first time in relation to that charge, unless he is to be dealt with under CDA 1998, s 51 (SENDING FOR TRIAL s 51) may consist of a single magistrate, who may, at an early administrative hearing:

(1) ask the accused whether he wishes to receive public funding (see DEFENCE PUBLIC FUNDING);

(2) determine his eligibility for it, if he does wish it; and

(3) if it is determined that he is eligible, arrange for the necessary grant.

CDA 1998, s 50(3)(4)

In addition, he may exercise, subject to the above, any of the powers of a single magistrate (see CDA 1998, s 49) as he thinks fit, and may remand the accused in custody or on bail (see ADJOURNMENT AND REMAND).

Where the hearing is being conducted by the Clerk, acting as a single magistrate, he may not:

(a) remand the accused in custody; or

(b) without the consent of the prosecutor and the accused remand the accused on bail on conditions other than those, if any, that were previously imposed.

The Clerk may, however, in matters preceding trial: JCR 1999, Schedule

(1) fix or set aside the date, time and place for the trial of an information;

(2) give, vary or revoke any directions for the conduct of a criminal trial, including directions as to the:
   (a) timetable for proceedings;
   (b) attendance of the parties;
   (c) service of documents relied on by the parties; and
   (d) manner in which evidence is to be given;

(3) with the consent of both parties, give, vary or revoke any order for separate or joint trials in the case of two or more accused and/or two or more informations.

Classification of offences

In the case of offences triable summarily only, or in the case of an adult, those offences triable only on indictment, the mode of trial is prescribed by law. There are, however, three classes of case in which a magistrates' court is required to make a judicial determination as to the mode of trial.

These are cases where there appears or is brought before the court, a person:

(1) who has attained the age of 18, on an information charging him with an offence triable either way (other than a 'schedule offence'); MCA 1980, s 18

(2) who has attained the age of 18, charged with a 'schedule offence' (ie one of those under the CDA 1971 listed in MCA 1980, Sched 2); or MCA 1980, s 22

(3) who is under the age of 18, on an information charging him with an indictable offence other than homicide. MCA 1980, s 24

The relevant date for deciding whether a right of trial by jury exists by reason of such an accused having attained the age of 18 is at the moment the court decides which mode of trial to adopt (*Re Daley* [1982] 2 All ER 974; *R v Lewes JC, ex p Turner* (1985) 149 JP 186; *R v Vale of Glamorgan Juvenile JJ, ex p Beattie* (1984) 149 JP 120; *R v Nottingham JJ, ex p Taylor* [1991] 4 All ER 860).

While it is desirable that an accused should, as far as possible, know from the outset the charge or charges that he has to meet, in many cases it may be necessary to add or to substitute fresh charges for those already preferred.

At the stage when the court is required to consider mode of trial, consideration will be given to the charges which are then preferred and to any submissions made by the prosecutor or the defence. If the prosecution wish to add or substitute new charges, either to ensure that the case is tried summarily, or to ensure that it is tried on indictment, that is not a ground for refusing a summons applied for, provided the court is satisfied that, on the facts disclosed, the course proposed is a proper one and is appropriate (*R v Redbridge JJ, ex p Whitehouse* (1991) 156 JP 293).

'Either-way offences'

MCA 1980, s 32(1)(9)

An offence triable 'either way' means an offence which, if committed by a person who has attained the age of 18, is triable either summarily or on indictment.

Intention as to plea: MCA 1980, ss 17A–17C

MCA 1980, s 17A

Where a person aged 18 or over appears or is brought before the court on an information charging him with an offence triable either way, then, in his presence:

(1) the charge must be written down, if this has not already been done, and must be read to him; and

(2) the court must then explain to him in ordinary language that he may indicate whether (if the offence were to proceed to trial) he would plead guilty or not guilty, and that if he indicates that he would plead guilty:
   (a) the proceedings will constitute from the beginning a summary trial of the information, and
   (b) the court will be empowered to commit him to the Crown Court for sentence, if appropriate, under PCC(S)A 2000, s 3;

(3) the court must then ask him whether he would plead guilty or not guilty, though no part of this procedure is to be taken to constitute the taking of a plea.

MCA 1980, 17B

Where such an accused is absent but is legally represented, and it is a case where the court considers that by reason of his disorderly conduct before the court, it is not practicable to conduct this procedure in his presence, and that it should proceed in his absence, then:

(1) the charge must be written down, if this has not already been done, and read to his representative; and

(2) the court must ask that representative whether the accused would plead guilty or not guilty.

Effect of accused's intention to plead

If the accused, or in a case under s 17B his representative:

MCA 1980, s 17A(6)(7)(8), 17B(3)(4)

(1) indicates that he would plead guilty, then the the court will proceed as if:

(a) from the beginning the proceedings constituted the summary trial of the information; and
(b) MCA 1980, s 9(1) was complied with and the accused pleaded guilty under it;

(2) indicates that he would plead not guilty, then the court will proceed under s 18 (*below*);

(3) fails to indicate how he would plead he shall be taken to indicate that a plea of not guilty would be entered.

Adjournment

The court may adjourn the 'intention to plead' proceedings at any time and when doing so may remand the accused, if present. The accused must be remanded if: MCA 1980, s 17C

(1) on the first occasion he appeared or was brought before the court he was in custody, or having been released on bail, surrendered to the custody of the court; or

(2) he has been remanded at any time in the course of proceedings on the information,

and the usual rules as to remand apply.

JUSTICES' CLERK/LEGAL ADVISER

The Justices' Clerk must be a barrister or solicitor who has a five-year magistrates' court qualification (CLSA 1990, s 71).

It is impracticable for the Justices' Clerk to act as legal adviser at every sitting of the court, and in general he will have one or more deputies and legal advisers to perform that function, each of whom will be qualified for the purpose, being either barristers or solicitors, or being qualified in terms of the Justices' Clerks (Qualification of Assistants) Rules 1979.

Functions

The Clerk is responsible for:

(1) the legal advice tendered to the magistrates;

(2) the performance of any of the functions set out below by any member of his staff acting as legal adviser;

(3) ensuring that competent advice is available to magistrates when he is not personally present in court; and

(4) the effective delivery of case management and the reduction of unnecessary delay.

(*Practice Direction* (*criminal: consolidated*) [2002] 3 All ER 904, para 55.1)

Legal advisers

Where a person other than the Clerk – a legal adviser – is authorised to perform any of the functions of the Clerk, he will have the same responsibilities as the Clerk.

A legal adviser may consult the Clerk or any other person authorised by the Clerk for the purpose, before tendering advice to the bench.

If the Clerk or that authorised person gives advice directly to the bench, he must give the parties, or their advocates, an opportunity of repeating any relevant submissions prior to the advice being given.

(*Practice Direction* (*criminal: consolidated*) [2002] 3 All ER 904, para 55.1)

Responsibilities of legal advisers

A legal adviser is responsible for:

(1) providing the magistrates with any advice they require properly to perform their functions, *whether or not they have requested that advice*, on:

(a) questions of law (including European Court of Human Rights jurisprudence and those matters set out in s 2(1) of the Human Rights Act 1998);
(b) questions of mixed law and fact;
(c) matters of practice and procedure;
(d) the range of penalties available;
(e) any relevant decisions of the superior courts or other guidelines;
(f) other issues relevant to the matter before the court;
(g) the appropriate decision-making structure to be applied in any given case;
(h) assisting the court, where appropriate, as to the formulation of reasons and the recording of those reasons;

(2) ensuring that every case is conducted fairly; and

(3) assisting unrepresented parties to present their case.

(*Practice Direction* (*criminal: consolidated*) [2002] 3 All ER 904, para 55.2, 3.)

General conduct of the proceedings

The general conduct of proceedings in the courtroom is a matter for agreement between the bench and the legal adviser (*Hobby v Hobby* [1954] 2 All ER 365, *R v Consett JJ, ex p Postal Bingo* [1967] 1 All ER 605). It will vary from court to court according to the views of the presiding magistrate and the Clerk or legal adviser. The overall conduct of proceedings is the responsibility of the presiding magistrate, but the efficiency of the court will generally depend on a delicate balance of functions between the two.

Restrictions on their role

Neither the Clerk, nor a legal adviser may play any part in making findings of fact, but he:

(1) may assist the bench by reminding them of the evidence, using any notes of the proceedings for this purpose;

(2) may ask questions of witnesses and the parties in order to clarify the evidence and any issues in the case.

When advising the magistrates, the Clerk or legal adviser, whether or not he has been previously in court, should:

(a) ensure that he is aware of the relevant facts; and

(b) provide the parties with the information necessary to enable the parties to make any representations they wish as to the advice before it is given.

While he has a specific duty to assist an unrepresented party, he must take care, in rendering that assistance, not to appear to become an advocate for the party concerned (*Practice Direction* (*criminal: consolidated*) [2002] 3 All ER 904, para 55.4, 5, 6).

Tendering advice

At any time, the magistrates are entitled to receive advice to assist them in discharging their responsibilities. If they are in any doubt as to the evidence which has been given, they should seek the aid of their legal adviser, referring to his notes as necessary.

Such advice should ordinarily be given in open court. Where they request their adviser to join them in the retiring room;

(1) the request should be made in the presence of the parties in court;
(2) any legal advice given to them other than in open court should be clearly stated to be provisional, and the adviser should subsequently repeat the substance of the advice in open court and give the parties an opportunity to make any representations they wish on that provisional advice;
(3) the legal adviser should then state in open court whether the provisional advice is confirmed or, if it is varied, the nature of the variation.

(*Practice Direction* (*criminal: consolidated*) [2002] 3 All ER 904, para 55.7, ss 8)

There is no legal requirement that the magistrates should accept and act upon the advice of their legal adviser on matters of law. In practice, however, it is accepted that they ought to do so; magistrates who fail to do so on a point of law may find themselves being ordered to pay the costs of any appeal which follows (*Jones v Nicks* [1977] Crim LR 365).

The performance of a legal adviser may be appraised by a person authorised by the magistrates' courts committee to do so. For this purpose the appraiser may be present in the magistrates' retiring room. The content of the appraisal is confidential, but the fact that an appraisal has taken place, and the presence of the appraiser in the retiring room, should be briefly explained in open court.

Assisting the parties

The legal adviser is under a duty to assist unrepresented parties to present their case, but must do so without appearing to become an advocate for the party concerned (*Practice Direction* (*criminal: consolidated*) [2002] 3 All ER 904, para 55.9).

In the case of an unrepresented accused, it is his duty to explain to him in simple language the substance of the charge. Where the accused, instead of putting questions to a witness, makes assertions, the legal adviser must assist him, by putting such questions to the witness as seem necessary. This will inevitably involve questioning the accused in order to elucidate the points he is seeking to make. This will usually be the legal adviser's function (*R v Richmond & Gilling West MC, ex p Steel* [1993] Crim LR 711). As to apparent bias on the part of legal adviser, and the risk of its 'infecting' the magistrates, see *R v Gough* [1993] 2 All ER 724.

Pleas of guilty by letter: s 12

Where a person has been served with a summons and, in accordance with the provisions of MCA 1980, s 12, submits a written plea of guilty in respect of the subject matter of the summons, it falls to the Clerk to read aloud to the court:

(1) the notification that the accused wishes to plead guilty;
(2) any submission received with that notification which the accused wishes to be brought to the attention of the court with a view to mitigation of sentence; as well as
(3) the statement of the facts of the offence which is relied on by the prosecutor.

Where the procedure under s 12 is followed, a claim for costs by the prosecutor against the accused may be notified in the document containing the statement of facts. If the prosecutor is not present at the hearing, the claim for costs must be brought to the attention of the court by the Clerk so that the magistrates may decide whether to order payment of costs (*R v Coventry MC, ex p DPP* [1990] 3 All ER 277).

Fine default proceedings

The role of the legal adviser in fine default proceedings or any other proceedings for the enforcement of financial orders, obligations or penalties is to assist the court. He must not act in an adversarial or partisan manner. He may:

(1) with the agreement of the magistrates ask questions of the defaulter to elicit information which the magistrates will require to make an adjudication, for example to facilitate his explanation for the default;
(2) advise the magistrates in the normal way as to the options open to them in dealing with the case.

He must not, however, set out to establish wilful refusal or neglect or any other type of culpable behaviour, to offer an opinion on the facts, or to urge a particular course of action upon the magistrates.

The duty of impartiality is the paramount consideration for the legal adviser at all times, and this takes precedence over any role he may have as a collecting officer.

The appointment of other staff to 'prosecute' the case for the collecting officer is not essential to ensure compliance with the law, including the Human Rights Act 1998. Whether to make such appointments is a matter for the justices' chief executive (*Practice Direction* (*criminal: consolidated*) [2002] 3 All ER 904, para 55.10).

Notes of evidence

While in summary proceedings there is no *statutory duty* imposed on the Clerk or legal adviser to take a note of the evidence, if he is to be able to fulfil his duties and obligations under the *Practice Direction,* a note of the evidence will almost certainly need to be taken.

On the other hand:

(1) the High Court has no power, where a note has been taken, to direct that a copy be provided for the use of the Crown Court on an appeal (*R v Clerk to the Lancaster JJ, ex p Hill* (1984) 148 JP 65);

(2) where a request for a copy of the notes is made by the solicitor representing an appellant on an appeal to the Crown Court, it has been said that the Clerk or legal adviser ought to 'look sympathetically' on such request (*R v Clerk to Highbury Corner JJ, ex p Hussein* [1986] 1 WLR 1266);

(3) where an appellant is in receipt of a representation order, a copy of the notes must be supplied to his solicitor if he requests them; and

(4) the High Court has also suggested (*Hill v Wilson* (1984) 149 JP 252; *R v Clerk to Highbury Corner JJ,* (*above*)) that notes should be supplied to privately represented appellants.

The Clerk is required to provide notes of the evidence to:

(a) the Crown Court when an offender is committed for sentence; MCR 1981, r 17(1)(b)

(b) the Crown Court when an offender is committed with a view to the making of a hospital order accompanied by an order under MHA 1983, s 41 restricting discharge; and

(c) the other magistrates' court when an offender is remitted there for sentence under MCA 1980, s 39.

Insofar as bail applications are concerned, the Clerk or legal adviser is required, where the court hears full argument, to make a note of that argument.

Judicial functions: Justices' Clerks Rules 1999

The Justices Clerks Rules 1999, SI 1999, No 2784 specify those things, set out below, authorised to be done by, or before, a single magistrate for a petty sessions area, which may also be done by, or before, a Justices' Clerk for that area.

Note that:

(1) they may also be done by, or before, a person appointed by a Magistrates' Courts Committee, to assist the Clerk, provided that that person has been specifically authorised by the Clerk for that purpose, and any reference to a 'Justices' Clerk' in the Rules is to be taken as a reference to that person;

(2) in relation to the powers which may be exercised at an early administrative hearing under CDA 1998, s 50 (see pp 298, 299), any such authorisation by the Clerk must be recorded *in writing* at the time the authority is given, or as soon as practicable thereafter;

(3) where a magistrate or magistrates exercise his or their discretion to refuse an application, such as a refusal to issue a summons, the Clerk, or other authorised person cannot be required to reconsider that refusal.

The Clerk or other authorised person should always be in a position to give reasons for his decision.

SPECIFIC POWERS

Process

The Clerk may;

(1) issue a summons, including a witness summons;

(2) where there is no objection on behalf of the accused, issue a warrant, whether or not backed for bail, for failure to surrender to bail;

(3) mark an information as withdrawn;

(4) where no evidence is offered by the prosecutor, dismiss an information or discharge the accused in respect of an information.

Costs

The Clerk, exercising the powers of a single magistrate, may make an order for the payment of defence costs out of central funds.

Adjournment, remand, and bail

The Clerk may:

(1) where the parties consent, adjourn the hearing of a complaint;

(2) extend bail on the same conditions, if any, previously imposed, or with the consent of both parties, impose or vary the conditions;

(3) where there is no objection by the prosecutor, further adjourn criminal proceedings, and remand the accused, where the accused, having

been remanded on bail on the previous adjournment, is remanded on bail, in his absence, on the like terms and conditions;

(4) with the consent of both parties, further adjourn criminal proceedings, but only where:
   (a) the accused, not having been remanded on the previous adjournment, is not remanded on the further adjournment; or
   (b) the accused having been remanded on the previous adjournment, is remanded on bail on like terms and conditions, or with the consent of both parties, on other terms and conditions;

(5) where the prosecutor appeals against a decision of a magistrate to grant bail, give a direction under MCR 1981, r 93A(7) or (8) for the release of an accused on bail with or without conditions as directed by the court.

Police bail

In the case of bail granted by the police under PACE 1984, the Clerk may:

(1) appoint a later time at which a person under a duty to appear at the magistrates' court, is to appear, and, provided there is no objection by the prosecutor, enlarge the recognisances of any sureties under MCA 1980, s 4(1);

(2) appoint an earlier time for the appearance of such a person at the magistrates' court.

Crown Court cases

The Clerk may:

(1) commit an accused on bail for trial in accordance with MCA 1980, s 6(2) and (3)(b) where, having been remanded on bail on the previous adjournment, he is released on bail on the like terms and conditions;

(2) where an accused is to be tried on indictment, grant a representation order for the purpose of the proceedings in the Crown Court.

Pleas

The Clerk may, after having stated the substance of an information laid against an accused, ask him whether he pleads 'guilty' or 'not guilty' to the charge(s).

Pre-trial matters

The Clerk may, in matters preceding trial:

(1) fix or set aside the date, time and place for the trial of an information;

(2) give, vary, or revoke any directions for the conduct of a criminal trial, including directions as to the:

(a) timetable for proceedings;
(b) attendance of the parties;
(c) service of documents relied on by the parties; and
(d) manner in which evidence is to be given;

(3) with the consent of both parties, give, vary, or revoke any order for separate or joint trials in the case of two or more accused and/or two or more informations;

(4) with the consent of the accused, extend an overall time limit

under POA 1985, s 22 as and when that provision is brought into force.

Pre-sentence matters

The Clerk may, in relation to sentence:

(1) following a plea of guilty, request a pre-sentence report, but may *not* give any indication as to the seriousness of the offence;

(2) request a medical report and, for this purpose, remand the accused on bail on the same conditions as those, if any, previously imposed, or, with the consent of both parties, on other conditions;

(3) remit the offender to another court for sentence;

(4) make an order for an offender to produce his driving licence and its counterpart;

(5) give consent for another magistrates' court to deal with the breach of a conditional discharge.

Community orders

In relation to community orders, the Clerk may:

(1) amend a community rehabilitation order, a community punishment order, or a community punishment and rehabilitation order by substituting for one petty sessions area, another area in which the offender is, or is proposing to be, resident;

(2) vary an attendance centre order by either;
   (a) varying the day or time specified in the order for the offender's first attendance; or
   (b) substituting for the centre specified in the order another relevant centre reasonably accessible to the offender having regard to his age, his means of access and any other circumstances;

(3) sign the certificate given to the Crown Court under PCC(S)A 2000, s 16(4) as to non-compliance with a community order imposed by the Crown Court.

Statutory declaration s 14

The Clerk may accept service of a statutory declaration made under MCA 1980, s 14.

Enforcement of financial penalties

In relation to the enforcement of financial penalties, the Clerk may:

(1) issue a distress warrant;

(2) allow further time for the payment of any sum enforceable by a magistrates' court;

(3) where the court has ordered payment of an enforceable sum by instalments, vary the number and amounts of instalments;

(4) make a transfer of fine order;

(5) make an order in relation to a statement of means;

(6) fix or vary the date for the holding of a means enquiry;

(7) make or withdraw an application for the deduction from an offender's income support to satisfy a financial penalty, and do such other things as are required or permitted to be done by a magistrates' court under the Fines (Deduction from Income Support) Regulations 1992.

LICENSED PREMISES EXCLUSION ORDERS

Where an offender is convicted of an offence committed on licensed premises and the court is satisfied that, in committing the offence: LP(E)A 1980, s 1(1)(3)

(1) he resorted to violence; or

(2) offered or threatened to resort to violence,

it may make an exclusion order for not less than three months; and not more than two years, prohibiting him from entering those premises or any other premises specified in the order, without the express consent of the licensee, his servant or agent. The order is designed for, and justified in, cases of those persons who make a nuisance of themselves in public houses,and who qualify for being debarred from going to those premises, to the annoyance of other customers and possible danger to the licensee (*R v Grady* [1990] Crim LR 608).

It is not possible to make an order excluding the offender from all licensed premises in a specified county or petty sessions area but the order may include the name of more than one set of premises (*R v Penn* [1996] Crim LR 360).

Such an order may be:

(1) made *in addition to* any sentence imposed in respect of the offence of which the offender is convicted; or LP(E)A 1980, s 1(2)

(2) notwithstanding the provisions of PCC(S)A 2000, ss 12, 14, in addition to an order of conditional or absolute discharge.

The order can be made on application, or by the court of its own motion (*R v Penn,* (*above*)).

A person entering premises in breach of the order is liable to a fine not exceeding level 3 on the standard scale or imprisonment not exceeding one month or both. LP(E)A 1980, s 2(1)(2)

The order is not affected by a breach, save that the court may consider whether or not the order should continue in force and may, if it thinks fit, terminate it, or vary it by deleting the name of any specific premises.

The Clerk will send a copy of the order to the licensee(s) of all the premises to which the order relates, (*R v Arrowsmith* [2003] 3 *Archbold News* 3).

MENTALLY DISORDERED OFFENDERS

The courts are given a variety of powers to deal with persons who are not so mentally disordered as to be absolved from criminal responsibility for their actions, but are nevertheless in need of psychiatric treatment. It is seldom that a magistrates' court will need to deal with insanity raised as a question of unfitness to plead or as a defence in law. In the case of offences triable summarily only, a prosecutor is unlikely to insist on proceeding (see *R v Metropolitan Stipendiary Magistrate, ex p Aniifowosi* (1985) 144 JP at p 752 *per* Woolf J), and indeed it is not improper, in such a case, for the court to suggest to the prosecutor that he might choose to withdraw the charge. In the case of indictable only offences, and those triable either way, the accused will be sent, or should be committed to the Crown Court for trial, where the issue can be determined by a jury. HO 1990

A magistrates' court may:

(1) if the offence is one punishable on summary conviction with imprisonment make a hospital order *without convicting* the accused, but it must first be satisfied that he did the act or made the omission with which he is charged;

(2) *after conviction*, when making a community rehabilitation order, add a requirement that the offender undergo treatment for a mental condition;

(3) remand a person, when considering an order under (1)(2) or (4) to hospital for examination and report; and

(4) *after conviction* of an offence punishable on summary conviction with imprisonment make a hospital order or a guardianship order, or send a person to hospital under an interim hospital order.

The magistrates' court cannot conjoin a hospital order with a restriction order; only the Crown Court can do that.

It should be noted that:

(a) the psychiatric facilities which the court may use for its purposes are the same as those provided by the NHS for the treatment of non-offending patients;

(b) where the court has in mind the making of a hospital order or an interim hospital order, Regional Health Authorities are required to assist in identifying an appropriate hospital for a particular offender;

(c) different hospitals specialise in the treatment of different forms of mental disorder, so that in respect of any one catchment area there are likely to be at least two hospitals, one providing treatment for mental illness and one providing treatment for mental handicap; for this reason the consent of the hospital is required before the court may order admission.

Remand for medical examination without convicting

PCC(S)A 2000, s 11

Where on the trial of an offence punishable on summary conviction with imprisonment, the magistrates' court is satisfied that the accused did the act or made the omission charged, but is of the opinion that an enquiry ought to be made into his physical or mental condition before the method of dealing with him is determined, it *must* adjourn to enable an examination and report to be made, and must remand him.

Where he is remanded in custody, an adjournment must not exceed 3 weeks at a time; if he is remanded on bail it must not exceed 4 weeks at a time.

Bail, if granted, *must* be conditional, and *must* include requirements that the accused:

(1) undergo medical examination by a qualified medical practitioner or if the enquiry is into his mental condition and the court so directs, two medical practitioners; and

(2) attend for that purpose at such institution or place, or on such practitioner as the court directs; and

(3) if the enquiry is into his mental condition, comply with any other directions which may be given to him.

BA 1976, s 24(1)(2)

In the exceptional case in which the court grants bail to a person accused, of *murder* unless it considers satisfactory reports on his mental condition have already been obtained, the court *must* order that he:

(a) undergo examination by two medical practitioners for the purpose of enabling such reports to be made; and

(b) attend for that purpose at such institution or place as the court directs and complies with any directions given to him.

At least one of the medical practitioners must be one approved for the purposes of MHA 1983, s 12 (see *below*).

Remand to hospital for reports: s 35

MHA 1983, s 35(1)(2b)(3)(4)

The court may remand to hospital, for reports on his mental condition, a person who:

(1) has been convicted by it of an offence punishable on summary conviction with imprisonment; or

(2) is charged with such an offence, if it is satisfied that he did the act or made the omission charged; or

(3) consents to such exercise of the court's powers.

Before doing so, however, the court must be:

(a) satisfied on the written or oral evidence of a medical practitioner (approved for the purposes of s 12) that there is reason to suspect that the accused is suffering from mental illness, psychopathic disorder, mental impairment or severe mental impairment; and

(b) of opinion that it is impracticable for such a report to be made if the accused is remanded on bail; and

(c) satisfied on the written or oral evidence of the medical practitioner who would be responsible for making the report, or of a representative of the hospital managers, that arrangements have been made for admission within seven days from the date of the remand.

Where so satisfied, the court may, pending his admission, give directions for his conveyance to, and detention in, a place of safety. The exercise of this power is likely to be rare, and should be adopted only with the consent of the accused's legal representatives (*R v Lincoln (Kesteven) JJ, ex p O'Connor* [1983] 1 All ER 901).

He will be conveyed to the specified hospital by a constable or other person directed by the court; the hospital is bound to admit and detains him. MHA 1983,35(9)

An accused remanded to hospital under MHA 1983, s 35, is entitled to obtain, *at his own expense,* an independent report of his mental condition, from a medical practitioner chosen by him and to apply to the court on the basis of that report, for his remand to be terminated. MHA 1983, s 35(8)

Further remand; reports not complete

The court, having exercised its powers under s 35, may further remand such person where it appears on the oral or written report of the medical practitioner making the report that it is necessary for completing the assessment of his mental condition, and: MHA 1983, s 35(5)–(7)

(1) the power may be exercised without that person being before the court, provided he is represented by counsel or a solicitor who is given an opportunity to be heard; but

(2) the remand or further remand may not be for more than 28 days at a time, or for more than 12 weeks in all; and

(3) the court may terminate the remand if it appears appropriate to do so.

Absconder from detention

If a person remanded under s *35* absconds from hospital or while being conveyed to or from hospital, he may be arrested without warrant and brought before the court which remanded him. The court may then terminate the remand and deal with him in any way in which it could have dealt with him had he not been remanded. MHA 1983, s 35(1)

Hospital order after conviction

MHA 1983, s 37

Where a person is convicted of an offence punishable on summary conviction with imprisonment, the adult court in the case of an offender aged 18 or over, and the youth court in the case of a juvenile (*R v Barking YC* [2002] Crim LR 657), may make a hospital order, authorising the offender's admission to, and detention in, a hospital specified in the order. Such an order allows him to be taken to the hospital specified and detained there until he is discharged by the hospital authorities or by a Mental Health Review Tribunal.

It seems that an order may be made under this section, even where the accused elects trial by jury in the case of an either way offence (*R v Ramsgate JJ ex p Kazmarek* (1985) 149 JP 16), or where he was unable to to consent to summary trial (*R v Lincoln (Kesteven JJ,* (*above*)) on the basis that he is still before the court.

Preconditions for hospital order

MHA 1983, s 37(1),(3)

Before a hospital order can be made, the court must be:

(1) dealing with a person for an imprisonable offence;

MHA 1983, s 37(2)

(2) satisfied on the written or oral evidence of two medical practitioners (at least one of whom is approved for the purposes of s 12), that:
   (a) the person concerned is suffering from mental illness, psychopathic disorder, mental impairment or severe mental impairment; and
   (b) the mental disorder from which he is suffering is of a nature or degree which makes it appropriate for him to be detained in a hospital for medical treatment;
   (c) in the case of a psychopathic disorder or mental impairment, the treatment is likely to alleviate or prevent the deterioration of his condition;

MHA 1983, s 37(4)

(3) satisfied there is a place available for him at the hospital to be specified in the order, and arrangements have been made for his admission within 28 days; and

(4) of opinion, having regard to all the circumstances including the nature of the offence, and the character and antecedents of the person concerned, and to other available methods of dealing with him, that the most suitable method of disposing of his case is by means of a hospital order.

An accused should always be represented where the court is considering making such an order (*R v Blackwood* [1974] Crim LR 437).

MHA 1983, s 37(6)

The order must specify the form(s) of mental disorder from which, on the evidence the accused is found to be suffering, and an order cannot be made unless both doctors find the same form(s) of disorder.

Hospital order without convicting

Where a person is charged before the court with an offence, and it would have power on convicting him of the offence to make a hospital order, as being a person suffering from mental illness or mental impairment, then: MHA 1983, s 37(3)

(1) if the court is satisfied that he did the act or made the omission,

(2) it may, if it thinks fit, make a hospital order without convicting him.

Since, where such a procedure is followed no trial is called for, the circumstances in which it is adopted are bound to be rare, and will usually require the consent of those acting for the accused (*R v Lincoln (Kesteven) JJ, ex p O'Connor* [1983] 1 All ER 901). The power may be exercised even where the accused has elected trial by jury (*R v Ramsgate JJ, ex p Kazmarek* (1984) 149 JP 16). But there is no jurisdiction to make a hospital order in respect of a person charged with an offence triable on indictment only (*R v Chippenham Magistrates' Court, ex p Thompson* (1995) 160 JP 207).

The accused has the same right of appeal to the Crown Court as if the order had been made on conviction. MHA 1983, s 45

Interim hospital order: s 38

Where a person is convicted of an offence punishable on summary conviction with imprisonment and the court is satisfied that the pre-conditions for a hospital order exist, so that there is reason to suppose that it may be appropriate for a hospital order to be made, the court may, before making a hospital order, or dealing with him in any other way, make an 'interim' hospital order. MHA 1983, s 38

An 'interim' order remains in force for such period, not exceeding 12 weeks, as the court specifies when making it, and may be renewed for as further periods of 28 days at a time if it appears on the written or oral evidence of the responsible medical officer that the continuation is warranted, but: MHA 1983, s 38(5)(6)

(1) no 'interim' order may be continued in force for more than six months in all;

(2) the court must terminate the 'interim' order where it makes a full order, or if, after considering the evidence it decides to deal with the offender in some other way.

An interim order may be renewed without the offender being brought before the court, provided he is represented by counsel or a solicitor who is given an opportunity of being heard.

Restriction order: MHA 1983, s 41

A restriction order is one which accompanies a hospital order in cases where the court considers that, for the protection of the public from serious harm, the offender should not be released from hospital without careful HO 1990 consideration by either the Secretary of State or the Mental Health Review Tribunal. The order prevents the offender from being discharged, granted leave of absence or being transferred to another hospital without the approval of the Home Secretary.

MHA 1983, s 43(1)

A magistrates' court has no power to make a restriction order, but if:

(1) a person of 14 years or over is convicted of an offence punishable on summary conviction with imprisonment; and

(2) the conditions for making a hospital order are fulfilled; but

MHA 1983, s 43(2)

(3) it appears, having regard to the nature of the offence, the antecedents of the offender and the risk of his committing further offences if set at large, that if a hospital order is made a restriction order ought also to be made,

the court may, instead of dealing with him in any other manner, commit him to the Crown Court to be dealt with in respect of the offence.

MHA 1983, s 43(4)

The Crown Court in such a situation is limited to either making a hospital order, with or without a restriction order, or dealing with the offender in any other manner in which the magistrates' court could have dealt with him. It may, therefore, be appropriate to commit such an offender at the same time, under PCC(S)A 2000 s 3 (see COMMITTAL FOR SENTENCE), if of opinion that greater punishment should be awarded than the magistrates' court has power to impose.

'Psychiatric' community order

There will be cases where the court considers that a hospital order is not warranted, and that it would be more appropriate to deal with the offender by means of a community rehabilitation order, or, in the case of a juvenile, a supervision order, with an additional requirement of medical treatment (see COMMUNITY SENTENCES).

Guardianship order: MHA 1983, s 37

A guardianship order may be made by the adult court in the case of an offender aged 18 or over, and by the youth court in the case of an offender

HO 1990

aged 16 or 17. Such an order places the offender under the guardianship of either the local authority social services department or of some person (such as a relative) approved by the local authority.

An order may not be made unless:

MHA 1983, s 37(1)(2)(4)

(1) the offender has attained the age of 16; and

(2) the authority or person concerned is willing to receive him into guardianship.

The effect of the order is to give the guardian power to require the offender to live at a specified place, to attend specified places at specified times for medical treatment, occupation, education or training, and to allow access to a doctor, approved social worker or other specified person. In this way it enables a relative or social worker to help the offender to manage in his own home or a hostel.

There is no sanction available in the event of non-compliance, as there is with a community rehabilitation order.

Improper combinations

The court may not, where a hospital order or a guardianship order is made, in respect of the offence: MHA 1983, s 60(6)

(1) pass a sentence of imprisonment;

(2) impose a fine; or

(3) make a community rehabilitation order.

'Imprisonment' here includes any sentence or order for detention.

There is nothing to prevent the court making any other order which it has power to make.

Information from Health Authority

MHA 1983, s 39

The court, if minded to make a hospital order, or an 'interim' order, may request:

(1) the Health Authority, for the region in which the offender resides or last resided; or

(2) any other Health Authority which appears to be appropriate,

to furnish it with such information as the authority has or can obtain, with respect to the hospital or hospitals in its area, if any, at which arrangements could be made for admission. The Authority is bound to comply with the request.

Requirements as to medical reports

Special procedural requirements govern the reception of medical evidence in relation to hospital orders: MHA 1983, s 54

(1) Of the medical practitioners whose evidence is taken into consideration, at least one must be approved for the purposes of s 12, as having special experience in the diagnosis of treatment of mental disorder;

(2) a reporting in writing required from such a medical practitioner or from a person representing the hospital managers, may be received in evidence without proof of the signature, qualification, authority or description of that person, but the court may always require him to attend to give oral evidence;

(3) where a report is tendered otherwise than by the accused, a copy of it must be given to his legal representative, or, if he is not represented, the substance of it must be disclosed to him, or if he is a child or young person, to his parent or guardian if in court, unless it relates merely to arrangements for his admission;

(4) the accused may require the signatory of the report to attend and give oral evidence; and

(5) evidence to rebut the contents of the report may be called by him or on his behalf.

Accused subject to 'transfer direction'

MHA 1983, s 52(1)(3)

The power of remanding an accused under MCA 1980, s 128 (see ADJOURNMENT AND REMAND) may be exercised by the court without his being brought to court, if he is subject to a transfer direction under MHA 1983, s 48, that is, he has been removed from prison to hospital by reason of mental disorder.

MHA 1983, s 52 (4)(5)

Special provisions apply in such a case, as follows:

(1) if he is further remanded in custody, the period of remand is deemed not to have expired;

(2) he may not be remanded in his absence unless he has appeared before the court within the previous six months;

(3) the court may direct that the transfer direction shall cease to have effect, notwithstanding that the remand period has not expired, or that the accused is committed to the Crown Court, if satisfied, on the written or oral evidence of the responsible medical officer, that:
   (a) the accused no longer requires treatment in hospital for mental disorder; or
   (b) no effective treatment can be given for the disorder in the hospital to which he has been removed;

(4) a transfer direction ceases to have effect on the expiration of the period of remand, unless the accused is transferred to the Crown Court for trial, or to be otherwise dealt with. If he is transferred to the Crown Court and the direction has not ceased to have effect (under s 52(5)) it is treated as if it were given under s 51.

MODE OF TRIAL

Where a person: MCA 1980, ss 18(1)(2), 19(1)(3)

(1) who has attained the age of 18;

(2) appears or is brought before the court;

(3) on an information charging him with an offence triable either way (other than a 'schedule offence'); and

(4) he, or in his absence, his representative indicated, under the initial procedure (see pp 298–301 *above*) that he would plead not guilty, or

(5) no plea is indicated,

the court (unless the case is being carried on by a law officer, or the court has power to make a hospital order under MHA 1983, s 37(3) without convicting the accused (*R v Lincoln (Kesteven) JJ, ex* p *O'Connor* [1983] 1 All ER 901) *must*:

(a) before any evidence is called,

(b) having regard to any representations made by the prosecutor or each accused,

determine whether the offence appears to be more suitable for summary trial or for trial on indictment, bearing in mind:

(i) the nature of the charge;

(ii) whether the circumstances of it make the offence one of a serious character;

(iii) whether the punishment which the magistrates' court could inflict would be adequate; and

(iv) any other circumstances which make it more suitable for trial in one way or another.

If the prosecution is being carried on by one of the law officers and he applies for MCA 1980 the offence to be tried on indictment, the court is deprived of its discretion and s 19(4) *must* proceed with a view to committing the accused to the Crown Court for trial. MCA 1980, s 19(4)

Special rules apply to criminal damage, (see pp 331–334 *below*).

Preliminary procedure

Before making its determination, the court must ensure that: MCA 1980, ss 18(1)(2), 19(1)(2)

(1) each accused is identified, and the charge is read to him;

(2) each accused is asked whether he knows that he is entitled to ask the prosecutor for a summary or a copy of the statements in his case, and if not, or if he has not yet made a request, or it has not been complied with, whether he wants an adjournment (see ADVANCE INFORMATION);

(3) the prosecutor and each of the accused are given an opportunity to give their views on where the case should be tried.

These functions, which are mandatory (*R v Tottenham JJ, ex p Arthur's Transport Services* [1981] Crim LR 180) may be discharged by a single magistrate.

Special procedures apply where the accused is absent but legally represented (see pp 331–334 *below*).

Relevant considerations; national guidelines

It is important for the court to inform itself fully at the preliminary stage of the seriousness of the offence alleged, since its powers to alter the mode of proceedings at a later stage and subsequently to commit to the Crown Court for a more severe sentence (see COMMITTAL FOR SENTENCE), could be restricted.

Certain important general principles apply, namely that:

(1) one starts with the proposition that serious offences should be tried by the Crown Court *(R v South Greenhoe JJ , ex p DPP* [1950] 2 All ER 42, *R v Coe* [1969] 1 All ER 65);

(2) both sides must be given an opportunity to make representations *(R v Horseferry Road JJ, ex p Constable* [1981] Crim LR 405);

(3) once the court has acted on the relevant information, a differently constituted bench is *not* entitled to come to a different conclusion on the same information (*R v Liverpool JJ, ex p CPS* [1989] Crim LR 655), though it may exercise its power under MCA 1980, s 25 (see *below)* to change from summary trial to commmital proceedings and *vice versa* in a proper case.

In *Practice Direction* (*criminal: consolidated*) [2002] 3 All ER 904, para 51, the High Court observed that:

(a) the court should never make its decision on the grounds of convenience or expedition (and see *R v lpswich JJ, ex p Callaghan* (1995) 159 JP 748);

(b) it should assume for the purpose of deciding mode of trial that the prosecution version of the facts is correct;

(c) the accused's antecedents and any personal mitigation are irrelevant for the purposes of deciding mode of trial (indeed the court is not entitled at this stage to know of the accused's previous convictions (*R v Colchester JJ, ex p N Essex Building Co Ltd* [1977] 3 All ER 567);

(d) the fact that the offences are alleged to be specimens is a relevant consideration; the fact that the accused will be asking for other offences to be taken into consideration, if convicted, is not;

(e) where a case involves complex questions of fact or difficult questions of law, including difficult issues of disclosure of sensitive material the magistrates should consider committing for trial;

(f) where two or more accused are jointly charged with an offence each has an individual right to elect his mode of trial.

It is not appropriate for the magistrate(s) to base their decision on the fact that one or more of the accused have indicated an intention to elect trial by jury (*R v Ipswich MC ex p Callaghan, above*).

Individual offences

The *Practice Direction* of 2002 makes it clear that in general, unless otherwise stated, either way offences should be tried summarily unless the court considers that:

(1) the particular case has one or more of the features set out below; *and*

(2) its sentencing powers are insufficient (*R v Flax Bourton MC, ex p Commissioners of Customs & Excise* [1996] Crim LR 907).

The magistrates should also consider their power to commit an offender for sentence under PCC(S)A 2000, ss 3 and 4, if information emerges during the course of the hearing which leads them to conclude that the offence is so serious, or the offender such a risk to the public, that their powers to sentence him are inadequate. This means that committal for sentence is no longer determined by reference to the character and antecedents of the accused.

Features relevant to individual offences

The High Court suggests that in considering individual offences, the magistrates may be helped in deciding whether or not to commit an accused for trial by having regard to the considerations below.

It is recognised that the guidelines are offered by way of assistance and not as directions, nor are they intended to impinge upon the magistrates' duty to consider each case individually. The guidelines apply to all persons aged 18 or over charged with an either-way offence.

Burglary: Dwelling house

Cases should be tried summarily unless the court considers that one or more of the following features is present in the case *and* that its sentencing powers are insufficient. Magistrates should take account of their powers under PCC(S)A 2000, ss 3 and 4 to commit for sentence:

(1) entry in the daytime when the occupier (or another) is present;

(2) entry at night of a house which is normally occupied, whether or not the occupier (or another) is present;

(3) the offence is alleged to be one of a series of similar offences;

(4) when soiling, ransacking, damage or vandalism occurs;

(5) the offence has professional hallmarks;

(6) the unrecovered property is of high value (see *below* for definition of high value);

(7) the offence is racially motivated.

Note: attention is drawn to MCA 1980, Sched 1, para 28(c) by which offences of burglary in a dwelling cannot be tried summarily if any person in the dwelling was subjected to violence or the threat of violence.

Burglary: Non-dwellings

Cases should be tried summarily unless the court considers that one or more of the following features is present in the case and that its sentencing powers are insufficient. Magistrates should take account of their powers under PCC(S)A 2000, ss 3 and 4:

(1) entry of a pharmacy or doctor's surgery;

(2) fear is caused or violence is done to anyone lawfully on the premises (eg night-watchman, security guard);

(3) the offence has professional hallmarks;

(4) vandalism on a substantial scale;

(5) the unrecovered property is of high value: (see *below* for definition of high value);

(6) the offence is racially motivated.

These factors will now need to be considered further as the result of the judgment of the CA (CD) *R v McInerney and R v Keating* ([2002] EWCA Crim 303). The Court defined offences of domestic burglary and the variant levels of aggravating factors in those offences. The Court gave guidance on the mode of trial for offenders with previous convictions for domestic burglary.

Irrespective of that guidance, where a person is:

PCC(S)A 2000, s 111

(a) charged with a domestic burglary which is alleged to have been committed after 30 November 1999; and

(b) at the time of the burglary was alleged to have been committed:

    (i) he was aged 18 or over; and

(ii) he had been convicted in England and Wales of two other domestic burglaries; and

(c) one of those other burglaries was committed after he had been convicted of the other; and

(d) both of them were committed after 30 November 1999, CDA 1998, s 51(1)

the new charge must be treated as an indictable only offence and the person must be sent to the Crown Court for trial.

Theft and fraud

Cases should be tried summarily unless the court considers that one or more of the following features is present in the case *and* that its sentencing powers are insufficient. Magistrates should take account of their powers under PCC(S)A 2000, ss 3 and 4 to commit for sentence,:

(1) breach of trust by a person in a position of substantial authority, or in whom a high degree of trust is placed;

(2) theft or fraud which has been committed or disguised in a sophisticated manner;

(4) theft or fraud committed by an organised gang;

(5) the victim is particularly vulnerable to theft or fraud, eg the elderly or infirm;

(6) the unrecovered property is of high value (see *below* for definition of high value).

Handling stolen goods

Cases should be tried summarily unless the court considers that one or more of the following features is present in the case *and* that its sentencing powers are insufficient. Magistrates should take account of their powers under PCC(S)A 2000, ss 3 and 4 to commit for sentence, see para 51.3(g):

(1) dishonest handling of stolen property by a receiver who has commissioned the theft;

(2) the offence has professional hallmarks;

(3) the property is of high value: (see *below* for definition of high value).

Social security frauds

Cases should be tried summarily unless the court considers that one or more of the following features is present in the case *and* that its sentencing powers are insufficient. Magistrates should take account of their powers under PCC(S)A 2000, ss 3 and 4 to commit for sentence, see para 51.3(g):

(a) organised fraud on a large scale;

(b) the frauds are substantial and carried out over a long period of time.

OAPA 1861, ss 20 and 47

Violence

Cases should be tried summarily unless the court considers that one or more of the following features is present in the case *and* that its sentencing powers are insufficient. Magistrates should take account of their powers under PCC(S)A 2000, ss 3 and 4 to commit for sentence:

(1) the use of a weapon of a kind likely to cause serious injury;

(2) a weapon is used and serious injury is caused;

(3) more than minor injury is caused by kicking or head-butting;

(4) serious violence is caused to those whose work has to be done in contact with the public or are likely to face violence in the course of their work;

(5) violence to vulnerable people, eg the elderly and infirm;

(6) the offence has clear racial motivation.

Note: the same considerations apply to cases of domestic violence.

Public Order Act offences

Cases should be tried summarily unless the court considers that one or more of the following features is present in the case *and* that its sentencing powers are insufficient. Magistrates should take account of their powers under PCC(S)A 2000, ss 3 and 4 to commit for sentence:

(1) cases of *violent disorder* should generally be committed for trial;

(2) *affray;*
   (a) organised violence or use of weapons;
   (b) significant injury or substantial damage;
   (c) the offence has clear racial motivation;
   (d) an attack on police officers, ambulance staff, fire-fighters and the like.

Violence to and neglect of children

Cases should be tried summarily unless the court considers that one or more of the following features is present in the case *and* that its sentencing powers are insufficient. Magistrates should take account of their powers under PCC(S)A 2000, ss 3 and 4 to commit for sentence:

(1) substantial injury;

(2) repeated violence or serious neglect, even if the physical harm is slight;

(3) sadistic violence, eg deliberate burning or scalding.

Indecent assault

Cases should be tried summarily unless the court considers that one or more of the following features is present in the case *and* that its sentencing powers are insufficient. Magistrates should take account of their powers under PCC(S)A 2000, ss 3 and 4:

(1) substantial disparity in age between victim and accused, and a more serious assault;

(2) violence or threats of violence;

(3) relationship of trust or responsibility between accused and victim;

(4) several more serious similar offences;

(5) the victim is particularly vulnerable;

(6) serious nature of the assault.

Unlawful sexual intercourse

Cases should be tried summarily unless the court considers that one or more of the following features is present in the case *and* that its sentencing powers are insufficient. Magistrates should take account of their powers under PCC(S)A 2000, ss 3 and 4 to commit for sentence:

(1) wide disparity of age;

(2) breach of position of trust;

(3) the victim is particularly vulnerable.

Note: unlawful sexual intercourse with a girl *under* 13 is triable only on indictment.

Drugs

Class A:

(1) supply; possession with intent to supply: these cases should be committed for trial;

(2) possession: should be committed for trial unless the amount is consistent only with personal use.

Class B:

(1) supply; possession with intent to supply: should be committed for trial unless there is only small scale supply for no payment:

(2) possession: should be committed for trial when the quantity is substantial and not consistent only with personal use.

Dangerous driving and aggravated vehicle taking

Cases should be tried summarily unless the court considers that one or more of the following features is present in the case *and* that its sentencing powers are insufficient. Magistrates should take account of their powers under PCC(S)A 2000, ss 3 and 4 to commit for sentence:

(1) alcohol or drugs contributing to the dangerous driving;

(2) grossly excessive speed;

(3) racing;
(4) prolonged course of dangerous driving;
(5) other related offences;
(6) significant injury or damage sustained.

Criminal damage

Cases should be tried summarily unless the court considers that one or more of the following features is present in the case *and* that its sentencing powers are insufficient. Magistrates should take account of their powers under PCC(S)A 2000, ss 3 and 4 to commit for sentence:

(1) deliberate fire-raising;
(2) committed by a group;
(3) damage of a high value;
(4) the offence has clear racial motivation.

Note: offences set out in MCA 1980, Sched 2 (which includes offences of criminal damage which do not amount to arson) *must* be tried summarily if the value of the property damaged or destroyed is £5,000 or less.

Meaning of high value

This means at least twice the amount of the limit imposed by statute on a magistrates' court when making a compensation order (currently £5,000).

If magistrates are uncertain as to the normal level of sentencing for offences which have mode of trial guideline characteristics, they should seek advice as to the level of sentence set by the Court of Appeal (*R v Northampton MC, ex p Customs & Excise Commissioners* [1994] Crim LR *598*).

Summary trial more suitable; the accused's election

MCA 1980, s 20

If, after following the above procedure, the court considers the offence is more suitable for summary trial:

(1) each accused must be told in ordinary language that the court:
  (a) considers it more suitable for him to be tried summarily for the offence;
  (b) he may either consent to be tried summarily, or, if he wishes, he may elect to be tried by a jury;
  (c) if he is tried summarily and convicted and the court is of the opinion:
    (i) that the offence or the combination of the offence and other offences associated with it were so serious that greater punishment should be inflicted for the offence than the court has power to impose; or

(ii) in the case of a violent or sexual offence that a sentence of imprisonment for a term longer than the court has power to impose is necessary to protect the public from serious harm from him;

(2) each accused must be asked whether he consents to be tried summarily or elects to be tried by a jury.

If an accused consents to be tried summarily, the court proceeds to summary trial; if he does not, the court proceeds with a view to committal to the Crown Court for trial.

Failure to follow this procedure is fatal to any subsequent summary trial (*R v Tottenham JJ, ex p Arthur's Transport* [1981] Crim LR 180, and see *R v Cardiff MC, ex p Cardiff City Council* (1987) *The Times*, 4 February). The magistrates must ensure that the accused understands the 'nature and significance of the choice' put to him (*R v Birmingham JJ, ex p Hodgson* [1985] 2 All ER 193).

Multiple accused

In a case where:

(1) two or more accused are jointly charged with an offence triable either way and the court considers the offence to be more suitable for summary trial;

(2) the right of election is given to each accused individually, not to all the accused collectively,

it follows that where some accused elect for summary trial and others elect for trial on indictment, the magistrates must try the former summarily, and proceed with a view to committal proceedings in respect of the latter (*R v Brentwood JJ, ex p Nicholls* [1991] 3 All ER 359, HL; *R v Wigan MC, ex p Leyland* [1995] Crim LR 892).

Procedure where trial on indictment more suitable

If, after following the above procedure, the offence appears more suitable for trial on indictment, the accused must be told of this, and the court will then proceed with a view to committal for trial (see COMMITTAL PROCEEDINGS). MCA 1980, s 21

Criminal damage: MCA 1980, Sched 2

Where an accused is charged with damaging or destroying property (or with attempting, aiding and abetting, or inciting such an offence) under CDA 1971, s 4, a special procedure applies by which, if it is clear that the value involved does not exceed £5,000, he must be tried summarily. The court is concerned with the value of the property itself, not with any consequential losses which may ensue (*R v Colchester MC, ex p Abbott* [2001] Crim LR 564). MCA 1980, ss 22(1)(10)

Where such an offence is tried summarily and the accused is convicted, the court's powers of punishment are limited to a fine of £1,000 and three months' imprisonment, and this is important, there is no power to commit the offender to the Crown Court for sentence under PCC(S)A 2000, s 3.

Where:

MCA 1980, s 22(11)

(1) the accused is charged on the same occasion with two or more such offences and it appears to the court that they constitute or form parts of a series of two or more offences of the same or a similar character; or

(2) the offence charged consists in incitement to commit two or more such offences,

the value involved will be taken to be an aggregate of the values involved.

Determination of value

MCA 1980, s 22(1)(10)

Where the value is not clear the court must consider, having regard to any representations made by the prosecutor or the accused, whether the value involved (see the value indicated in the second column of the schedule) exceeds £5,000.

It should be noted that:

(1) the court is not obliged to hear evidence, though it may if it thinks fit; it is obliged only to have regard to representations (*R v Canterbury etc, JJ, ex p Klisiak* [1981] 2 All ER 129); but

(2) where difficulties arise in establishing the value involved, the prosecutor is entitled to seek to prove the minimum amount of damage (*R v Salisbury JJ, ex p Mastin* [1986] Crim LR 454).

MCA 1980, s 22(8)

Where an accused person is convicted of such an offence, no right of appeal lies to the Crown Court on the ground that the decision on value was mistaken.

Result of determination

MCA 1980, s 22(2)–(6)

Where, as a result of the court's determination on value it appears:

(1) clear that for the offence charged, the value involved does not exceed the prescribed amount, no question of trial on indictment arises, and the court proceeds as if the offence(s) were triable summarily only;

(2) clear that for the offence charged, the value involved does exceed the prescribed amount, the offence(s) cease to be the subject of the special procedure, and the ordinary rules governing mode of trial apply;

(3) for any reason, not to be clear whether, for the offence(s) charged, the value exceeds the prescribed amount, the procedure is as follows:
   (a) the charge is read to the accused;

(b) he is asked whether he knows that he is entitled to ask the prose cutor for a summary or copy of the statements in the case, and if not, or if he has not made a request, or if he has and it has not been complied with, whether he wants an adjournment;
(c) he must be told that he may consent to be tried summarily for the offence, and that if he does so, he will be tried summarily; and
(d) he is told that if he is tried summarily for the offence and he is convicted, the court may not impose on him a sentence of more than three months' imprisonment or a fine of more than £1,000;
(e) he must then be asked whether he consents to be tried summarily.

If the accused consents to be tried summarily, the court will proceed to summary trial. If he does not, it will adopt the normal procedure for determining the mode of trial.

Proceeding in the absence of the accused

In general, the proceedings for determining mode of trial, whether the ordinary procedure or the special procedure under s 22 is adopted, will take place in the presence of the accused. The court may, however proceed to deal with such matters in the absence of the accused, provided:

(1) the accused is represented by counsel or a solicitor who, in the absence of the accused, signifies his consent to those matters being conducted in his absence; and
(2) the court is satisfied that there is good reason for so doing.

In such a case, if the court considers summary trial appropriate and the accused's consent to summary trial is signified, the court will proceed to summary trial of the information. It may, of course always direct his attendance (see *below*).

In the case of criminal damage, and the special procedure involved there, if:

(a) the accused is absent; and
(b) it is not clear whether the value exceeds £5,000 or not,

the court cannot proceed under s 22(5). Instead:

(i) if the accused's consent has been given, or is signified by his legal representative, the court miust proceed as if the offence were triable summarily only; and
(ii) if consent has not been given, and is not signified, the court will proceed to determine the suitability of the offence for trial one way or the other.

The court may always proceed in the absence of the accused if it considers that by reason of his disorderly conduct before the court, it is not practicable for the proceedings to be conducted in his presence. In such a situation the court may proceed without giving the explanation of his rights (ordinarily required by s 20) and, if his consent to summary trial has not been given or is not signified, the explanation required by s 20 is not necessary and the court will proceed with a view to committal for trial, adjourning the hearing if appropriate, without remanding the accused.

Where it appears to the court that the offence is more suitable for trial on indictment, the statement of this fact required by s 21 is not applicable, and the court will prepare to proceed with a view to committal for trial, adjourning the hearing, if appropriate, without remanding the accused.

Adjournments

MCA 1980, s 18(4)

Mode of trial proceedings may be adjourned at any time, and the court, on doing so on any occasion when the accused is present may remand him. He *must* be remanded, in custody or on bail where:

(1) on the occasion on which he first appeared or was brought before the court to answer the information, he was in custody, or having been released on bail, surrendered to the custody of the court; or

(2) he has been remanded at any time in the course of the proceedings on the information.

Where the court remands the accused he must appear, or be brought before the court at the time fixed for the resumption of the proceedings.

Absence of accused; direction to appear

MCA 1980, s 26

Where the court is not satisfied that there is good reason for proceeding in the absence of the accused, the magistrate, or any of the magistrates of which the court is composed, may issue a summons directed to the accused requiring his presence; and if the accused is not present at the time and place appointed for the proceedings under MCA 1980, ss 19(1) or 22(1), as the case may be, the court may issue a warrant for his arrest.

Altering mode of trial

MCA 1980, s 25(1)(2)

Where:

(1) the court has 'begun to try' an adult summarily (other than the summary trial of criminal damage) it may:
   (a) at any time before the conclusion of the evidence for the prosecution,
   (b) discontinue the summary trial and proceed with a view to committal for trial, and, on doing so, may adjourn the hearing without remanding the accused.

Note that:

(i) if the accused pleads guilty, there is no trial, and no evidence for the prosecution (*W Midlands Chief Constable v Gillard* [1985] 3 WLR 936); *R v Hammersmith JC, ex p 0* [1987] Crim LR 639);

(ii) the trial process does not only begin with the giving of evidence: it may begin after a plea of not guilty where eg the court hears submissions on a preliminary ruling of law (*R v Horseferry Road MC, ex p K* [1996] 3 All ER 719); but

(iii) a court remanding an accused does not thereby 'begin to try' him (*R v St Helens JJ, ex p Critchley* (1988) 152 JP 102, *R v Southend MC ex p Woods* (1988) 152 JP 970);

(2) on an application for dismissal of a charge under MCA 1980, s 6, the court has begun to consider the evidence and any representations per mitted under that section, then: MCA 1980, s 25(3)

(a) if at any time during its consideration,

(b) it appears, having regard to the evidence or representations, and to the nature of the case,

(c) that the offence is after all more suitable for summary trial, the court may:

(i) if the accused is present, after complying with s 25(4) (see *below*) ask him whether he consents to be tried summarily and, if he so consents, may, subject to s (3A), proceed to try the information summarily (see *R v McLean ex p MPC* [1975] Crim LR 289); or

(ii) in the absence of the accused, if the accused's consent is signified by the person representing him, proceed to try the information summarily, or, if consent is not signified, adjourn the proceedings without remanding the accused, and fix the time and place of the next hearing at which the accused is to appear.

Before asking for his consent, it must be explained to the accused that although it appears to the court more suitable for him to be tried summarily, this can only be done if he consents; and unless this has already been done, explain to him that he may, in appropriate circumstances be committed to the Crown Court for sentence under MCA 1980, s 38. MCA 1980, s 25(4)

This power can only be exercised in accordance with s 25; there is no power independent of that section which entitles the court to alter mode of trial, as, for example where there has been a change of circumstances, or where there are circumstances which were not drawn to the attention of the court on the earlier occasion (*R v St Helens MC, ex p Critchley* (*above*); *R v Liverpool JJ, ex p CPS* [1989] Crim LR 655) but see *R v Horseferry Road MC ex p K* [1996] 3 All ER 719).

In particular the power is not available where an unequivocal plea of guilty has been accepted (*R v Dudley JJ, ex p Gillard* (1984) 148 JP 577), nor to overcome the decision in *R v Brentwood JJ* (*above*) thus preventing trials at different venues (*R v W Norfolk JJ, ex p McMullen* (1992) 157 JP 461).

Accused seeking to change election

Where, having elected summary trial in respect of an either-way offence, the accused seeks to elect trial by jury, the court may, in a proper case, grant such an application but is not bound to do so.

While an accused should not lightly be deprived of his right to trial by jury (*R v Craske, ex p MPC* [1957] 2 All ER 792) the court is not bound to allow a change:

(1) merely because the accused was not represented at the hearing when he made his election (*R v Lambeth Metropolitan Stipendiary Magistrate, ex p Wright* [1974] Crim LR 444); or

(2) where the accused keeps changing his mind (*R v W Bromwich JJ, ex p Pearson* 1981] Crim LR 709).

The test is whether the accused properly understood the nature and significance of his choice when he originally made his election, a crucial factor being, of course, whether he believed he had a defence, something which he might not know until he has had legal advice (*R v Birmingham JJ, ex p Hodgson and Wiseman* [1985] 2 All ER 193; *R v Highbury Corner Metropolitan Stipendiary Magistrate, ex p Weekes* [1985] 2 WLR 643).

The fact that a previous application has been made and refused is no ground for refusing to consider a fresh application.

Where the court allows a plea of guilty to be withdrawn, the accused ought to be allowed to reconsider whether he consents to summary trial (*R v Bow St Magistrate, ex p Welcombe* (1992) 156 JP 609).

POLICE DETENTION

PACE 1984, Pt IV, together with Code DTQ made under it, provide a comprehensive scheme applying to all persons in police detention after arrest. Absolute limits are set on the detention of persons without charge, and the external scrutiny of police detention is entrusted to the court.

Limitation of detention without charge

A suspect is not to be detained at a police station for more than 24 hours from the 'relevant time' as defined in the Act. If not charged within that time, he must be released or his further detention must be authorised: PACE 1984, ss 41–43

(1) by the superintendent responsible for the police station, on specified grounds, for up to 36 hours after the 'relevant time'; and

(2) on the expiry of those 36 hours, by a warrant issued by a magistrates' court.

Warrant for further detention

An application for a warrant of further detention is made by a constable, on oath or affirmation supported by an information, to a court consisting of two or more magistrates sitting otherwise than in open court, provided that the person to whom the application relates: PACE 1984, ss 43(1), 45(1)

(1) has been furnished with a copy of the information; and

(2) has been brought before the court for the hearing.

Contents of the information

The information in support of a warrant for further detention must state: PACE 1984, s 43(14)

(1) the *nature of the offence* for which the suspect has been arrested;

(2) the general *nature of the evidence* on which he was arrested;

(3) what enquiries have been made and what further enquiries relating to the offence are proposed;

(4) the *reasons* for believing that the continued detention of the suspect is necessary for the purposes of those further enquiries.

Time for making the application

An application may be made at any time before the expiry of 36 hours after the 'relevant time' or, in the case where: PACE 1984, s 43(5)

(1) it is not practicable for the court to hear the application at that time, but

(2) the court will sit during the six hours following the end of that period,

at any time before the expiry of those six hours.

PACE 1984, s 43(6)

In the latter case, the suspect may be kept in police detention until the application is heard and the custody officer will make a note of that fact on the custody record, and the reason why he was kept.

Legal representation

PACE 1984, s 43(3)

The suspect is entitled to be legally represented at the hearing, and if he is not, but wishes to be, the court must adjourn to enable him to obtains representation, and he may be kept in police detention during the adjournment.

Considering the application

Where:

PACE 1984, s 43(7)

(1) the application is made *after* the expiry of 30 hours, and it appears to the court that it would have been reasonable for the police to make it *before* the expiry of that period, the application *must* be dismissed;

PACE 1984, s 43(4)

(2) the court has reasonable grounds for believing that:
   (a) detention without charge is necessary to secure or to preserve evidence relating to an offence for which the suspect is under arrest, or to obtain evidence by questioning him;
   (b) an offence for which he is under arrest is a *serious arrestable offence;* and
   (c) the investigation is being conducted diligently and expeditiously;

it may issue a warrant for further detention authorising the police to keep him in detention;

PACE 1984, s 43(8)

(3) the court is *not* satisfied that the above grounds exist, it *must* refuse the application or adjourn the hearing until a time not later than 36 hours after the 'relevant time'; the suspect will be kept in police detention during the adjournment.

PACE 1984, s 43(13)

If it is proposed to transfer the suspect to a police area other than the one in which he is detained when the application is made, the court is bound to have regard to the distance and time involved in the journey.

Refusal of application

PACE 1984, s 43(15)

Where an application is refused, the suspect must be charged forthwith or released on bail, though he need not be released before the expiry of the 24 hour period after the 'relevant time' or the expiry of any period of continued detention authorised by the superintendent.

PACE 1984, s 43(17)

No further application may be made in respect of the suspect unless supported by evidence which has come to hand since the court's refusal.

Granting of application: warrant

Where the court is satisfied that further detention is justified on the above grounds, a warrant may be issued authorising the suspect to be kept in police detention, and stating: PACE 1984, s 43(1)(10)

(1) the time at which it was issued;
(2) the name of the suspect and the period authorised, being such period:
    (a) as the court thinks fit having regard to the evidence before it, but
    (b) not for longer than 36 hours.

The suspect must be released from police detention either on bail or without bail, upon or before the expiry of the warrant, unless he is charged. He may not be re-arrested without a warrant for the offence for which he was previously arrested unless new evidence justifying a further arrest has come to light since his release. PACE 1984, s 43 (18)(19)

Extension of the warrant

A court may extend a warrant for further detention issued under s 43 for a further 36 hours but not for longer than 96 hours after the 'relevant time'. PACE 1984, s 44

The procedure and the criteria are similar to those under s 43.

PRE-TRIAL DISCLOSURE

A new emphasis has been given, with the adoption of ECHR, particularly by the 'equality of arms' provisions of Art 6, to the prosecutor's duty to give advance information of material in his possession, and to disclose material which might undermine his case (see *Edwards v UK* (1992) 15 EHRR 417, *Rowe & Davis v UK* (2000) EHRR 1, and *R v Stratford JJ ex p Imbert* (1999) 163 JP 693).

EITHER-WAY OFFENCES: ADVANCE INFORMATION

Advance information: (1) prosecutor's duty

As soon as practicable after a person has been charged with an offence *triable either way,* or a summons has been served on a person in connection with such an offence, the prosecutor must provide him with a notice in writing explaining the effect of the provisions below and setting out the address at which a request under them may be made. AIR 1985, rr 1, 2, 3

If, in any proceedings: AIR 1985, r 4

(1) in respect of a person who has been charged with an offence, triable either way before the court considers whether the offence appears to be more suitable for summary trial or trial on indictment (see MODE OF TRIAL); or,

(2) where the accused has not attained the age of 18 years when he appears or is brought before the court, before he is asked whether he pleads guilty or not guilty (see p 300),

the accused or a person representing the accused requests the prosecutor to furnish him with advance information, the prosecutor must, (subject to Rule 5 *below*) furnish him as soon as practicable with either:

(a) a copy of those parts of every written statement which contain information as to the facts and matters of which the prosecutor proposes to adduce evidence in the proceedings, or

(b) a summary of the facts and matters of which the prosecutor proposes to adduce evidence in the proceedings.

(See *R v Calderdale MC, ex p Donaghue & Anor* [2001] Crim LR 145)

A 'written statement' here means a statement made by a person on whose evidence the prosecutor proposes to rely in the proceedings and, where such a person has made more than one written statement one of which contains information as to all the facts and matters in relation to which the prosecutor proposes to rely on the evidence of that person only that statement is a written statement for purposes of paragraph (a) above.

Where in any part of a written statement or in a summary furnished under paragraph (a) reference is made to a document on which the prosecutor proposes to rely, he must, (subject again to Rule 5 *below*), when furnishing the part of the written statement or the summary, also furnish either a copy of the document or such information as may be necessary to enable the person making the request to inspect the document or a copy of it. A 'document' includes a video tape (*R v N Essex JJ, ex p Lloyds* [2001] Crim LR 145).

Advance information: (2) exemption under r 5

AIR 1985, r 5

The exemption in Rule 5 permits the prosecutor, if he is of the opinion that the disclosure of any particular fact or matter in compliance with the above requirements might lead to any person on whose evidence he proposes to rely in the proceedings being intimidated, to an attempt to intimidate him being made or otherwise to the course of justice being interfered with, he is not obliged to comply with those requirements in relation to that fact or matter.

Where the prosecutor considers that he is not obliged to comply with the requirements imposed in relation to any particular fact or matter, he will give notice in writing to the person who made the request to the effect that certain advance information is being withheld by virtue of that paragraph.

Advance information: (3) court's function

AIR 1985, rr 6, 7

Where:

(1) an accused appears or is brought before the court in proceedings in respect of which these provisions apply, the court must:
   (a) before it considers whether the offence appears to be more suitable for summary trial or trial indictment (see MODE OF TRIAL);
   (b) satisfy itself that the accused is aware of the requirements which may be imposed on the prosecutor under Rule 4; and

(2) where the accused has not attained the age of 18 years when he appears or is before the court in proceedings in respect of which these provisions apply, the court must, before he is asked whether he pleads guilty or not guilty, satisfy itself that he is aware of the requirements which may be imposed on the prosecutor under Rule 4 (*above*).

If, in any proceedings in respect of which these provisions apply, the court is satisfied that a request under Rule 4 having been made to the prosecutor by or on behalf of the accused, a requirement imposed on the prosecutor by that Rule has not been complied with, it cannot order the prosecution to comply (*R v Dunmow JJ, ex p Nash* (1993) 157 JP 1153) but *must* (*King v Kucharz* (1989)153 JP 336) adjourn the proceedings pending compliance with the requirement unless it is satisfied that the conduct of the case for the accused will not be substantially prejudiced by non-compliance with the requirement. There is no power to dismiss the proceedings for abuse of proceedings on the basis that these rules have not been complied with (*AP, MD & JS v Leeds Youth Court* (2001) 165 JP 684).

Where, in those circumstances the court decides not to adjourn the proceedings, a record of that decision, and of the reasons why the court was satisfied that the conduct of the case for the accused would not be substantially prejudiced by non-compliance with the requirement must be entered in the register.

DISCLOSURE

Disclosure of Expert Evidence

The Magistrates' Courts (Advance Notice of Expert Evidence) Rules 1997 provide for disclosure to the other party of any expert evidence which it is intended to adduce.

Disclosure under CPIA 1996

Where a person:

(1) is charged with a *summary offence* in respect of which a court proceeds to summary trial and in respect of which he pleads guilty; or CPIA 1996, s 1

(2) who has attained the age of 18 is charged with an offence which is *triable either way*, in respect of which a court proceeds to summary trial, and in respect of which he pleads not guilty; or

(3) under the age of 18 is charged with *an indictable offence* in respect of which a court proceeds to summary trial and in respect of which he pleads not guilty,

ss 3 *et seq* provide for disclosure by both prosecutor and defence of material of all kinds, in particular, information and objects of all descriptions.

Primary disclosure by prosecutor

The prosecutor must, within the prescribed time limit: CPIA 1996, ss 3(1)(2)(8), 12

(1) disclose to each accused any prosecution material which has not previously been disclosed to him and which in the prosecutor's opinion might undermine the case for the prosecution against the accused; or

(2) give to each accused a written statement that there is no material of such a description.

'Prosecution material' is defined for these purposes as material: CPIA 1996, s 3(3)

(a) which is in the prosecutor's possession and came into his possession in connection with the case for the prosecution against the accused; or

(b) which, in pursuance of a code operative under CPIA 1996, Pt II, he has inspected in connection with the case for the prosecution against the accused.

(Part II of the CPIA 1996 provides for codes of practice to be prepared by the Secretary of State governing criminal investigations dealing, amongst other things, with the recording and disclosure of information, having an effect on the proceedings, similar to that of codes of practice under PACE.)

Manner of disclosure

CPIA 1996, s 3(3)

Where material consists of information which:

(1) has been recorded in any form, the prosecutor discloses it for these purposes:
   (a) by securing that a copy is made of it and that a copy is given to each accused; or
   (b) if, in the prosecutor's opinion, that is not practicable or desirable, by allowing each accused to inspect it at a reasonable time and at a reasonable place or by taking steps to secure that he is allowed to do so;

   and a copy may be in such form as the prosecutor thinks fit and need not be in the same form as that in which the information has already been recorded;

CPIA 1996, s 3(4)

(2) has not been recorded, the prosecutor discloses it for, these purposes by securing that it is recorded in such form as he thinks fit and:
   (a) by securing that a copy is made of it and that a copy is given to each accused; or
   (b) if, in the prosecutor's opinion that is not practicable or desirable, by allowing each accused to inspect it at a reasonable time and at a reasonable place or by taking steps to secure that he is allowed to do so.

CPIA 1996, s 3(5)

Where material does not consist of information, the prosecutor discloses it for these purposes by allowing each accused to inspect it at a reasonable time and a reasonable place or by taking steps to secure that he is allowed to do so.

Document received under code

CPIA 1996, s 4

Where the prosecutor acts to disclose material, and before doing so he was given a document in pursuance of a provision included in a code under Pt II of the Act, he must give the document to each accused when he makes disclosure.

Public interest immunity

CPIA 1996, s 3(6)(7)

Material must not be disclosed under these provisions to the extent that the court, on an application by the prosecutor, concludes that it is not in the public interest to disclose it and orders accordingly. In particular, material must not be disclosed under these provisions where:

(1) it has been intercepted in obedience to a warrant issued under ICA 1985, s 2; or

(2) it indicates that such a warrant has been issued or that material has been intercepted in obedience to such a warrant.

See also Magistrates' Courts (Criminal Procedure and Investigation Act 1996)(Disclosure) Rules 1997, r 2.

Prosecutor's continuing duty

CPIA 1996 imposes on the prosecutor a continuing duty to disclose, after he complies with s 3 or purports to do so, right up to the time the accused is acquitted or convicted or the prosecutor decides not to proceed with the case concerned. CPIA 1996, s 9

He is bound to keep under review throughout whether at any given time there is prosecution material which:

(a) in his opinion, might undermine the case for the prosecution against the accused, and which has not been disclosed; or

(b) might be reasonably expected to assist the accused's defence as disclosed by the defence statement,

and if there is must disclose it as soon as is reasonably practicable, subject, of course, to restrictions applying to sensitive material.

Prosecutor's failure to observe time limits

The fact that the prosecutor purports to act under ss 3 or 7 after the end of the relevant period under s 12 does not on its own constitute grounds for staying the proceedings for abuse of process, though it may if the failure involves such delay by the prosecutor that the accused is denied a fair trial. CPIA 1996, s 10

Voluntary disclosure by accused

Where, in magistrates' courts' proceedings, the prosecutor complies with the above provisions or purports to do so, the accused *may* give a defence statement to the prosecutor, and if he does do so, must also give such a statement to the court. If he gives a defence statement, he must do so within the prescribed time limit. CPIA 1996, ss 6, 12

A 'defence statement' for these purposes is a written statement setting out in general terms the nature of the accused's defence:

(1) indicating the matters on which he takes issue with the prosecution; and

(2) setting out, in the case or each such matter, the reason why he takes issue with the prosecution.

On committal to the Crown Court a defence statement is *required* in terms of the CPIA 1996 (Defence Disclosure Time Limits) Regulations 1997.

Alibi

CPIA 1996, ss 5(7)(8), 6(3)

If the defence statement discloses an alibi the accused must give particulars of the alibi in the statement, including:

(1) the name and address of any witness the accused believes is able to give evidence in support of the alibi, if the name and address are known to the accused when the statement is given;

(2) any information in the accused's possession which might be of material assistance in finding any such witness, if his name or address is not known to the accused when the statement is given.

Evidence in support of an alibi is evidence tending to show that by reason of his presence at a particular place or in a particular area at a particular time, the accused was not, or was unlikely to have been, at the place where the offence is alleged to have been committed at the time of its alleged commission.

Secondary disclosure by prosecutor

CPIA 1996, s 7

Where the accused gives a defence statement under ss 5 or 6 the prosecutor must, within the prescribed time limits:

(1) disclose to the accused any prosecution material which has not

(2) previously been disclosed to the accused and which might be

(3) reasonably expected to assist the accused's defence as disclosed by the statement given to the prosecutor under ss 5 or 6; or

(4) which, in pursuance of a code operative under CPIA 1996, Pt II, he has inspected in connection with the case against the accused.

The same method of disclosure applies as under s 3(3)–(5), and the same restrictions on sensitive material apply.

Application by accused for disclosure

CPIA 1996, s 8

Where the accused gives a defence statement under ss 5 or 6, and the prosecutor complies with s 7, or purports to do so, or fails to comply with it, and the accused has at any time reasonable cause to believe that there is prosecution material which might be reasonably expected to assist his defence as disclosed in the statement given to the prosecutor under ss 5 or 6, and the material has not been disclosed to him, he may apply to the court for an order requiring the prosecutor to disclose such material to him.

The 'relevant material' is material:

(1) which is in the prosecutor's possession, and came into his possession

in connection with the case for the prosecution against the accused; or

(2) which in pursuance of a code operative under CPIA 1996, Pt II he has inspected in connection with the case for the prosecution against the accused; or

(3) if, in pursuance of a code operative under Pt II, the prosecutor must, if he asks for it, be given a copy of it or be allowed to inspect it in connection with the case for the prosecution against the accused.

The usual rules as to the disclosure of sensitive material apply.

Public interest

CPIA 1996 makes it clear under ss 3(6), 7(5), 8(5) and 9(8), that a court may make an order on the application of the prosecutor that sensitive material be withheld from disclosure. In proceedings in the magistrates' court, at any time before he is convicted, or the prosecutor decides not to proceed with the case, the accused may apply to the court for a review of the question, whether it is still not in the public interest to disclose material affected by the order. In such a case the court must review the question and, if it concludes that it is in the public interest to disclose material to any extent, order accordingly and take steps to inform the prosecutor of its order. CPIA 1996, s 14

Third party interests

Where an application is made under ss 3(6), 7(5), 8(5), 9(8), 13(2) or 14(4), a person claiming to have an interest in the material may apply to the court, and if he shows that he was involved (whether alone or with others and directly or indirectly) in the prosecutor's attention being brought to the material, the court must not make an order unless the applicant has been given an opportunity to be heard. CPIA 1996, s 15

Confidentiality of disclosed documents

If the accused is given, or allowed to inspect, a document or other object under ss 3, 4, 7, 9, 13, or 14, or an order under s 8, he may use it or disclose information recorded in it, only for the limited purpose, to the extent that it has been displayed or communicated to the public in court: CPIA 1996, s 16

(1) in connection with the proceedings for the purposes of which he was given it or allowed to inspect it;

(2) with a view to taking further criminal proceedings (for instance by way of appeal) with regard to the matter giving rise to the proceedings in (1); or

(3) in connection with the proceedings in (2).

An accused may apply to the court for an order granting permission to use or disclose the object or information, and may use or disclose it to the extent ordered by the court, after the prosecutor or any third party has had an opportunity of being heard.

CPIA 1996, s 17

It is a contempt of court for a person knowingly to use or to disclose an object or information recorded in it, in contravention of s 16.

PRISONER ON EARLY RELEASE

A prisoner serving a sentence imposed by a court may be released on licence, under which he is required to comply with certain conditions including a requirement as to supervision. The commission of a further offence during that probationary period shows that he is not taking advantage of the opportunity to live a law-abiding existence instead of remaining in prison for the full term (see *R v Blades* (1999) TLR 688). In certain circumstances a magistrates' court may return such an offender to prison, but the more appropriate course, if there is a significant period of the original sentence unexpired, or the fresh offence is of any seriousness is to commit him to the Crown Court for sentence (*R v Harrow JJ, ex p Jordan* [1997] 2 All ER 344).

When power exercisable

Where a prisoner released on licence, (not an escapee from prison (*R v Matthews & Jacobs* [2000] EWCA Crim 677)) other than a person committed for contempt of court or any kindred offence): PCC(S)A 2000, s 116

(1) before the date on which, but for his release on licence, he would have served his sentence in full, *commits* an offence punishable with imprisonment; and

(2) before or after that date, is *convicted* of that fresh offence, the court before whom he is convicted may, whether or not it passes any other sentence on him, order him to be returned to prison for the whole or any part of the period which:

 (a) begins with the date of the order; and

 (b) is equal in length to the period between the date on which the fresh offence was committed and the date on which he would otherwise have served his sentence in full,

 or commit him to the Crown Court for sentence.

The power should not be exercised where the prisoner's licence has been revoked (*R v Governor of HM Prison Elmley etc* [1999] Crim LR 333, *R v Cawthorne* [2001] 1 Cr App R(S) 136).

The court should identify those matters which, in its opinion, give rise to an order under s 116 (*R v Divers* [1999] Crim LR 843).

Approach to order

Before contemplating the making of such an order, the court will need to establish:

(1) the period of the sentence originally imposed; and

(2) the date on which the offender was released, in order to determine whether the later offence was committed within the full term of the original sentence; and

(3) the *quantum* remaining from the original sentence on the date of the fresh offence.

Having established that it has the power, the court may then decide whether, in its discretion, it will make an order, bearing in mind:

(a) any progress made by the offender since his release;

(b) the nature and gravity of the fresh offence, and whether it calls for a sentence of imprisonment; and

(c) the totality of the sentence,

or will commit the offender to the Crown Court for sentence on *both* offences (*R v Taylor* [1998] 1 All ER 357, and see the approach in *R v Home Secretary, ex p Probyn* [1988] 1 All ER 357).

Having decided to make an order, the court must decide whether the term under s 116 should be served:

(i) concurrently with the term for the fresh offence; or

(ii) *before* the term for the fresh offence commences.

The term under s 116 cannot be ordered to be served *consecutively* to that for the fresh offence but the term for the fresh offence may be ordered to run consecutively to the term under s 116 (*R v Clerkenwell MC, ex p Feeley* [1996] Crim LR 525).

RACIALLY ETC. AGGRAVATED OFFENCES

Under recent legislation, certain offences carry an enhanced penalty where they are racially or religiously aggravated, and in sentencing an offender for any offence, the fact that it was racially or religiously aggravated (as defined) is to be taken as a factor aggravating the offence.

Specifically aggravated offences:

(1) assaults

Offences of malicious wounding or grievous bodily harm (OAPA 1861, s 20), actual bodily harm (s 47), or common assault which are racially or religiously aggravated are triable either way, and on summary conviction are punishable with a maximum of six months imprisonment, a fine not exceeding the statutory maximum (£5,000), or both (NB – attracts 'grave crimes' procedure for juveniles). CDA 1998, s 29(1)(2)

(2) criminal damage

An offence of destroying or damaging property belonging to another (CDA 1971, s 1(1)) which is racially or religiously aggravated, is triable either way, and on summary conviction is punishable with a maximum of six months imprisonment, a fine not exceeding the statutory maximum (£5,000), or both; CDA 1998, s 30(1)(2)

(3) public order offences

(a) Offences of causing fear of, or provocation of violence, intentional harassment, alarm or distress (POSA 1986, ss 4, 44) which are racially or religiouslys aggravated are triable either way, and on summary conviction are punishable with a maximum of six months imprisonment, a fine not exceeding the statutory maximum (£5,000), or both. CDA 1998, s 29(1)(2)

(b) An offence of harassment, alarm, or distress (POSA 1985, s 5) is a summary offence, punishable by a fine not exceeding level 4 on the standard scale.

(4) harassment

Offences of harassment and putting people in fear of violence (PHA 1997, ss 2, 4) which are racially or religiously aggravated are triable either way, and on summary conviction are punishable with a maximum of six months imprisonment, a fine not exceeding the statutory maximum (£5,000), or both. CDA 1998, s 32

Aggravating factor in other offences

PCC(S)(A) 2000, s 153(1)

If the court is considering the seriousness of an offence in relation to sentence, and the offence is not one of the above offences (ie an offence under CDA 1998, ss 29–32) and that offence is racially or religiously aggravated, the court must:

(1) treat that fact as an aggravating factor, increasing the seriousness of the offence; and

(2) state in open court that the offence was so aggravated.

Meaning of 'racially or religiously aggravated'

CDA 1998, s 28(a)(b); PCC(S)(A) 2000, s 153

An offence is racially or religiously aggravated if:

(1) at the time of committing it, or immediately before or after doing so, the offender demonstrates towards the victim of the offence hostility based on the victim's membership, or presumed membership, of a racial or religious group; or

(2) the offence is motivated, wholly or partly, by hostility towards members of a racial or religious group based on their membership of that group.

CDA 1998, s 28(4)(5)

'Racial group' means a group of persons defined by reference to race, colour, nationality (including citizenship), or ethnic or national origins; 'religious group' means a group of persons defined by reference to religious belief or lack of religous belief.

Note that:

CDA 1998, s 28(2)

(a) 'membership' includes association with members of that group;
(b) 'presumed' means presumed by the offender,

CDA 1998, s 28(3)

and for the purposes of the above it is immaterial whether or not the offender's hostility is also based, to any extent, on any other factor.

RECOMMENDATION FOR DEPORTATION

Subject to certain limitations, a court sentencing an offender aged 17 or over who is not a British citizen within the meaning of the British Nationality Act 1981, for an offence punishable with imprisonment, may add a recommendation to the Home Secretary that the offender be deported from the UK. Such a recommendation is ancillary to any other sentence imposed for the offence. HO 1990

In making a recommendation, the court is indicating that it is to the detriment of this country for the offender to remain here. The final decision is taken by the Home Secretary who may take into account the offender's personal circumstances and the political situation in the country to which he will go if an order is made (*R v Nazari* [1980] 3 All ER 880).

Limitations: (1) Commonwealth citizens

A British citizen, or any person having the 'right of abode' in the UK (IA 1971, s 2) may not be deported. In addition, exemption is given to a citizen of a Commonwealth country, or of the Republic of Ireland, where the court is satisfied that the offender: IA 1971, s 7(1)

(1) was such on 1 January 1973; and

(2) was ordinarily resident in this country at that time; and

(3) has been ordinarily resident here for the five years immediately preceding his conviction, although

(4) any part of that five years during which he was undergoing imprisonment or detention by virtue of a sentence passed in the UK, Channel Islands or the Isle of Man, and for which he was imprisoned etc for six months or more, is excluded from the period.

'Ordinary residence' is a matter of fact and degree. Mere temporary absence will not create a gap; illegal residence from the start cannot amount to 'ordinary' residence (*R v Bangoo* [1976] Crim LR 746). Since many of the above matters are peculiarly within the knowledge of the offender, he is entitled, and should be invited, to give evidence about them (*R v Edgehill* [1963] 1 All ER 181).

A Commonwealth citizen who is a first offender is seldom deported unless his offence was particularly grave, he asked for a number of offences to be taken into consideration, or he was admitted to the country only temporarily and has been convicted of 'overstaying'. HO 1990

Limitations: (2) EC Nationals

HO 1990

EC nationals who are in this country exercising their right of free movement under the Treaty of Rome, as in the course of their employment, or as dependants of someone who is here in the course of their employment, may be deported only where the requirements of Community law, as interpreted by the Court of Justice are satisfied (*R v Home Secretary, ex p Santillo* [1981] 2 All ER 897).

A court considering whether to make such a recommendation may act:

(1) where the offender's record taken together with the offence committed indicates that it is likely that he will offend again (this is a very important consideration); the existence of a previous conviction is not, by itself, a sufficient basis for making a recommendation;

(2) where it is satisfied that the offender's continued presence in the country represents a 'genuine and sufficiently serious threat to the requirements of public policy affecting one of the fundamental interests of society' (*R v Escauriaza* [1988] Crim LR 252, *R v Soura* (1988) 10 Cr App R(S) 376).

No recommendation ought to be made without full enquiry, and reasons for the recommendation must be given, both to the Home Secretary and to the offender (*R v Kraus* (1982) 4 Cr App R(S) 113; *R v Secretary of State for Home Affairs Ex p Dannenberg* [1984] 2 All ER 481; *R v Frank* (1992) 13 Cr App R(S) 500).

Irrelevant considerations

The court is not concerned with the political systems which operate in other countries. It is inappropriate for a magistrates' court to express a view about the matter where it has no knowledge beyond common knowledge, which may be wrong. These are matters for the Home Secretary (*R v Altawel* (1981) 3 Cr App R(S) 28).

Preconditions for recommendation

IA 1971, s 6(1)(2)(3)

Before making a recommendation, the court must be satisfied that:

(1) the offender is 17 or over;

(2) the offender has no right of abode;

(3) the offence is punishable with imprisonment;

(4) the offender has been given not less than seven clear days' notice in writing of the court's intention; and

(5) the court considers it appropriate to make a recommendation, bearing in mind the nature of the offence, the offender's record and the potential detriment to this country of his remaining.

(*R v Caird* [1970] Crim LR 656; *R v Nazari, above*)

Approach: (1) immigration legislation

Where there has been a deliberate flouting of the immigration legislation (*R v Baidoo* (1971) 55 Cr App R 253) it may be said that as a matter of practice, unless a recommendation is made, the matter may never come to the attention of the Home Secretary. The fact of the recommendation puts the matter fairly and squarely before him. He is not bound to make an order, and is likely to take into consideration matters different from, or additional to those considered by the court, including the length of time the offender has been in the country, the strength of his connections with it, his personal history, domestic circumstances, and any other mitigating feature.

Approach: (2) other criminal cases

Where the offence is properly a criminal one, in which case the accused's immigration status is not relevant (*Miller v Lenton* (1981) 3 Cr App R (S) 171; *R v Nunu* [1991] Crim LR 653), the superior courts have made a number of observations on the approach to be adopted in considering whether the continued presence of an offender in this country is to its detriment (see *R v Nazari* [1980] 3 All ER 880); *R v Ariquat* (1981) 3 Cr App R(S) 83; *R v Altawel* (1981) 3 Cr App R(S) 28; *Miller v Lenton (above)*; *R v Tschuma* (1981) 3 Cr App R(S) 171; *R v Audi Bali* [2001] 2 Cr App R(S) 461). Thus:

(1) in examining 'detriment', the court should look at the offence and at the likelihood of its being repeated, or of other offences being committed, on the broad picture and the evidence available;

(2) the court ought also to consider the effect of a recommendation on those who are innocent and not before it, such as the offender's family;

(3) this calls for a delicate balancing exercise between the possibility that the offender will commit further offences in this country, and the harm that may be done to innocent persons if he is to be deported (*R v Carvioto* (1990) 12 Cr App R(S) 71; *R v Odendaal* [1992] Crim LR 378; *R v Shittu* (1993) 14 Cr App R(S) 283);

(4) the fact that an offender is subject to mental instability connected with, or resulting in, the commission of a serious criminal offence, is a good reason for making a recommendation.

The court should give its reasons in detail.

Procedure

In considering whether to make, or in making a recommendation, the court should:

(1) deal first with the offence on its merits, and then proceed to consider whether or not to make a recommendation (*R v Edgehill* [1963] 1 All ER 181);

(2) conduct a full enquiry into the circumstances, hearing counsel specifically on that issue (*R v Antypas* (1972) 57 Cr App R 207);

(3) grant a representation order where such a course is otherwise appropriate, for the purpose of making submissions (*R v Edgehill*, (*above*));

(4) ensure, before making any recommendation, that the requisite notice has been served in Form 1M3; it may be necessary to adjourn for that to be done;

(5) give its reasons for making a recommendation in open court, and these should be committed to writing and be signed by the magistrates. Copies should be sent together with the recommendation to the Home Secretary, and to the offender. If reasons are not given the recommendation will be quashed (*Dannenberg v Home Secretary* (1984) 148 JP 321; *R v Rodney* [1996] Crim LR 357).

It is not proper for the court to postpone sentence in order to see whether the Home Secretary will act upon the recommendation.

Effect of deportation order

A deportation order made by the Home Secretary remains in force until it is revoked or ceases to have effect by reason of a conviction for illegal entry. There is no jurisdiction to make a fresh recommendation while that order is in force (*R v Kelly* (1966) 47 Cr App R 352).

Detention or release after recommendation

IA 1971, Sched 3, para 2(1)

Unless the court otherwise directs, an offender in respect of whom a recommendation is made, if not detained in pursuance of the sentence of a court or released on bail, will be detained pending the Home Secretary's decision.

The court may, however, direct him to be released subject to such directions as to residence and reporting to the police as it may specify. There is, of course, no power to take sureties (see also *R v Ofori & Tackie* [1994] Crim LR 822).

IA 1971, Sched 3, paras 4, 5, 6(1)

Further, on application to the court by the offender or by a constable or immigration officer, restrictions may be imposed where they were not imposed before. Any restrictions which were imposed may be annulled or varied and any further directions given.

IA 1971, Sched 3, para 10

Where such a person is arrested and brought before the court (or a magistrate), which forms the opinion that he is contravening, or is likely to contravene, any restriction imposed it (or he) may direct either that that person be detained, or that he be released subject to restrictions. If so satisfied it must release him without altering any restrictions previously imposed.

SEARCH, ACCESS, ETC.

A magistrate has certain powers in relation to the investigation of criminal offences, at once assisting the police by the issue of a warrant where their powers are lacking or restricted, and at the same time acting as a check on the exercise of those powers. The police and some other investigators (eg the Customs and Excise, Immigration Officers) have powers under a number of statutes to search premises. The Police and Criminal Evidence Act 1984 provides a standard procedure for applications for search warrants under all Acts of Parliament, but removes from the jurisdiction of a magistrates' court certain potentially sensitive matters.

THE POLICE AND CRIMINAL EVIDENCE ACT 1984

Entry and search of premises; application for warrant

On the application of a constable, made on oath or on affirmation, a magistrate may issue a warrant to enter and search premises, if satisfied that there are reasonable grounds for believing that: PACE 1984 s 8

(1) a serious arrestable offence (or a relevant offence under the Immigration Act s 29D); and

(2) there is material on specified premises which is likely to be of substantial value (whether of itself or together with other material); and

(3) that material does *not* consist of, or include material subject to legal privilege, excluded material or special procedure material, and

(4) any of the following conditions apply, namely that:
   (a) it is not practicable to communicate with a person entitled to grant entry to the *premises*;
   (b) it is not practicable to communicate with a person entitled to grant access to the *evidence*;
   (c) entry will not be granted unless a warrant is produced;
   (d) the purposes of the search may be frustrated, or seriously prejudiced unless the searching officers are able to gain immediate access.

Seach, Access, etc.

Material excluded from magistrate's jurisdiction

The Act excludes from the ambit of search warrants issued by a magistrates' court, searches for:

(1) items subject to legal privilege, as defined in s 10;

(2) 'excluded material', being personal records, human tissue or tissue fluid, or 'journalistic material' as defined in ss 11–13; and

(3) 'special procedure material' as defined in s 14.

In cases arising under (2) and (3) above, application must be made to a circuit judge under Sched 1. The magistrates have no jurisdiction.

'Legal privilege'

Legal privilege is defined in the Act to mean:

PACE 1984 s 10

(1) communications between a professional legal adviser and his client or a person representing his client, made in connection with the giving of legal advice to the client (as to conveyancing material, see *R v ILCC ex p Baines & Baines* [1987] 3 All ER 1025);

(2) communications between such persons or any other persons, made in contemplation of, and for the purposes of, legal proceedings (including an application for defence public funding: (*R v Snaresbrook CC ex p DPP* [1988] 1 All ER 315); and

(3) items enclosed with, or referred to, in such communications, and made in connection with the giving of advice, or the contemplation of, and for the purposes of legal proceedings (see as to a blood sample obtained in relation to a breathalyser offence, *R v R* [1994] 4 All ER 260),

so long as they are in the possession of a person entitled to them. Items held with the intention of furthering a criminal purpose are not items subject to legal privilege (*R v Leeds MC, ex p Dumbleton* [1993] Crim LR 866, *R v CCC, ex p Francis & Francis* [1988] 1 All ER 677).

'Excluded material'

Excluded material is defined to include three categories of material:

PACE 1984 s 11

(1) personal records which a person has acquired or created in the course of any trade, business, professional or other occupation, or for the purposes of any paid or unpaid office, which he holds in confidence;

(2) human tissue or tissue fluid which has been taken for the purposes of diagnosis or medical treatment, and which a person holds in confidence; and

(3) journalistic material which a person holds in confidence and which consists of documents or records.

'Personal records' are defined as documentary and other records covering an individual who can be identified from them, relating to his physical or mental health, and any spiritual counselling or assistance given to him, or to be given to him, by any voluntary organisation or by an individual who, by reason of his office etc has responsibilities for his personal welfare, or, by reason of a court order, has responsibilities for his supervision.

'Journalistic material' means material acquired or created for the purposes of journalism, but only if it is in the possession of the person who so acquired or created it. Such a person holds it in confidence if he holds it subject to an undertaking, restriction, or obligation.

'Special procedure material'

'Special procedure material' is defined to include: PACE 1984 s 14

(1) material other than that subject to legal privilege or excluded material, in the possession of a person who has acquired or created it in the course of a trade, business etc, or for the purposes of his office, and holds it either subject to an express or implied undertaking to hold it in confidence, or subject to a restriction on disclosure or obligation of secrecy contained in any enactment; and

(2) journalistic material other than excluded material.

Application for warrant: safeguards

Where a constable applies to the court for a search warrant, whatever the statute under which the application is made, the application is made *ex parte* supported by an information: PCA 1984 s 15(1)–(4)

(1) stating the *ground* on which the application is made, and the enactment under which the warrant is sought;

(2) specifying the *premises* which it is desired to enter and search;

(3) identifying, as far as is practicable, the *articles* or *persons sought.*

The constable may need to answer on oath or affirmation any questions put to him by the court.

The magistrate has a duty to consider the criteria set out in s 8 above, and must in particular, where the constable is not forthcoming on the matter, enquire expressly as to the nature of the material sought, and whether it consists of or includes material subject to privilege (*R v Chesterfield JJ ex p Bramley* [2000] Crim LR 385). He has no jurisdiction over such material, and unless he can satisfy himself that no such material is involved, he must refuse the application, and leave the police to rely on their powers under PACE 1984, s 9 (*R v Guildhall MC, ex p Primlake Holdings etc* [1990] 2 WLR 841).

As to applications for search warrants in respect of overseas investigations, see CJ(IC)A 1990, s 7.

The warrant

The warrant, when issued, authorises entry on *one occasion only.* It must specify the name of the applicant, the date of issue, the enactment under which it is issued, the premises to be searched, and, as far as is *practicable,* the articles or persons sought. PACE 1984 s 15(5)–(8)

Two copies must be made and clearly certified as such. Entry and search under the warrant must take place within one month of the date of issue.

BANKERS' BOOKS EVIDENCE ACT 1879

BBEA 1879 ss 3–9 A copy of any entry in a banker's book (which includes records kept on microfilm, magnetic tape or any other form of mechanical or electronics data retrieval mechanism) is admissible in evidence as *prima facie* evidence of the entry.

BBEA 1879, s 7 On the application of any party to legal proceedings the court may order that such party be at liberty to inspect and take copies of any entry in a banker's book for any of the purposes of such proceedings.

An order may be made without summoning the bank or other party, but must be served on the bank three clear days before the order is to be obeyed, unless the court otherwise orders.

Note that:

(1) before making an order, the court should be satisfied that legal proceedings have begun and that the application is not just a 'fishing expedition' to find evidence on which to hang a charge, and that the prosecutor, who normally makes such an application, has other evidence supporting the charge against the accused (*Williams v Summerfield* [1972] 2 All ER 1334);

(2) the application is normally made *ex parte,* but there is much to be said for adjourning it and directing that notice be given to the other party (*R v Marlborough St Magistrate, ex p Simpson* (1980) 70 Cr App R 291, *R v Nottingham JJ, ex p Lynn* (1994) Cr App R 288);

(3) the order ought to be limited to a certain specific period, and ought not to be oppressive (*R v Marlborough St Magistrate, ex p Simpson,* (*above*));

(4) the mere fact that the accused has given notice of his intention to plead guilty is not a reason for refusing an order (*Owen v Sambrook* [1981] Crim LR 239).

Where the court is faced with a difficult case, in which it is in doubt as to whether or not its jurisdiction should be exercised, it may refuse to make an order, stating that it should be made to the High Court (*Williams v Summerfield, above*).

Letters of request

CJA 1988, s 29(1)–(4) Where, on an application made to him, it appears to a magistrate that criminal proceedings:

(1) have been instituted; or

(2) are likely to be instituted if evidence is obtained for the purpose,

he may order that a letter of request be issued to a court or tribunal, or appropriate authority specified in the order and exercising jurisdiction in a place outside the United Kingdom, requesting it to assist in obtaining, for the purposes of the proceedings, evidence specified in the letter. A prosecuting authority may make such an application, and if proceedings have already been instituted, so may any person charged with an offence in the proceedings.

An application is made *ex parte* in accordance with MC(CJIC)R 1996.

Value Added Tax Act 1994

Where in the course of an investigation into suspected value added tax offences, Customs and Excise officials apply to a magistrate for an order of production of documents, the application should normally be made *inter partes unless* there was a real reason to believe that an application or notice might result in the loss of material valuable to the investigation. If it is decided to proceed *inter partes* it is normally appropriate to give notice of the application to: VATA 1994, Sched 11, para 11

(1) those from whom access was sought; and

(2) others who are obviously likely to be directly affected by the order (eg the suspects under investigation) (*R v City of London MC, ex p Asif & others* [1996] Crim LR 725).

SENDING FOR TRIAL S 51

The Crime and Disorder Act 1998, s 51 makes provision for adults who are charged with an indictable only offence to be sent directly to the Crown Court for trial, following a preliminary hearing in the magistrates' court; committal proceedings are retained only for offences triable either way, which are not related to an indictable only offence.

Offences triable only on indictment

Included with those offences ordinarily triable only on indictment are those which, in prescribed circumstances, are to be treated as indictable only for the purposes of trial, which include:

(1) Class A drug trafficking where the accused has two previous convictions for such an offence (PCC(S)A 2000, s 110); and

(2) an either-way offence charged together with an offence under FA 1968, s 17 (possessing a firearm while committing an offence specified in the Schedule).

Adults to be dealt with under s 51

Where a person aged 18 or over, appears or is brought before a magistrates' court, charged with an offence which is: CDA 1998, s 51(1)(2)

(1) triable only on indictment; or

(2) an either way offence related to an indictable offence; or

(3) a summary offence which is punishable with imprisonment or carries RT disqualification, and is related to an indictable offence; or

(4) an either-way offence with which he is charged jointly with another accused who is sent to the Crown Court in respect of a related indictable-only offence,

he must be sent forthwith to the Crown Court to be tried in respect of those offences.

As to juveniles, see *below*.

'Related offences'

A 'related offence' is CDA 1998, s 51(12)

(1) an either-way offence, but only if it could be joined in the same indictment as the indictable-only offence;

(2) a summary offence, but only if it arises out of circumstances which are connected with those giving rise to the indictable-only offence.

In the case of (4) in the preceding paragraph the court has no discretion; any person charged jointly with the accused in a related either-way offence, who appears at the same time, must be sent for trial under s 51.

As to subsequent offences by a person sent for trial under s 51, see *below.* Where an indictable only offence is charged which arises out of the same facts as an earlier indictable only offence or either way offence, it must be sent to the Crown Court under s 51 (*R* (*on the application of Salubi*) *v Bow St MC* (2002) *The Times*, 4 June).

Procedure in the magistrates' court

CDA 1998, ss 50, 53

The preliminary hearing must take place before at least two magistrates; the Act excludes the proceedings from the necessity of an early administrative hearing (see JURISDICTION AND INITIAL PROCEDURE).

The CPS must be represented by a legally qualified advocate; unqualified persons are excluded from acting in indictable-only cases.

Legal representation

The court has power to grant a legal representation order in respect of an indictable offence and any related offences, to any accused jointly charged. If an application has not been submitted earlier, the matter is likely to be dealt with at the first hearing. Such an order is likely to be a 'through' order, covering proceedings both in the magistrates' court and at the Crown Court.

Adjournment and remand

CDA 1998, s 52(5)

Given the limited nature of the proceedings and the magistrates' court's functions, it should seldom be necessary to adjourn the proceedings, though there is power to do so where it is deemed necessary.

It may be appropriate on occasion to adjourn where the prosecutor seeks further time to investigate other offences which are related to the indictable-only offence.

Where:

(1) an adjournment is refused in such circumstances, and the accused is sent for trial; and

(2) the accused is subsequently charged with an either-way offence which is related,

the court may, in its discretion, send the accused to the Crown Court in respect of that subsequent offence.

As to adjournment in considering bail, see *below.*

Where proceedings are adjourned, the accused must be remanded on bail or in custody, and the provisions of BA 1976 apply.

Sending for trial; bail/custody

The court may send the accused to the Crown Court in custody or on bail. CDA 1998, s 52(1)(5)

As to venue see *Practice Direction* (*criminal: consolidated*) [2002] 3 All ER 904 para 21. As to the custody time limits, see CUSTODY TIME LIMITS.

The procedure on application for bail is the same as in any other first application in criminal proceedings (see BAIL) If, however:

(1) the court has insufficient information to make a decision, the proceedings may be adjourned for the necessary information to be put before the court; and

(2) on refusing an application for bail, it appears likely that before the case reaches the Crown Court, the accused will be likely to make a further, successful application (as where a hostel placement becomes available) the court may adjourn the hearing, before sending the accused for trial, for a further application to be made.

Once the accused has been sent to the Crown Court the magistrates' court has no further jurisdiction to entertain an application for bail.

Position of juveniles

A juvenile charged in his own right with an indictable-only offence is not eligible to be sent for trial under s 51, but where he is jointly charged with an adult with an indictable-only offence in respect of which the adult is sent to the Crown Court, the juvenile must also be sent to the Crown Court, where he appears or is brought before the court:

(1) on the same occasion as the adult; or

(2) on a subsequent occasion,

where the magistrates consider it to be in the interests of justice for the juvenile to be tried jointly with the adult.

In such circumstances, the juvenile may also be sent in respect of any related either-way or summary offences.

Subsequent offences; co-accused

Where: CDA 1998, s 51(12)

(1) an adult:
 (a) who has been sent to the Crown Court under s 51;
 (b) subsequently appears before the magistrates' court charged with an either-way or summary offence which fulfils the requisite conditions,

he may be sent to the Crown Court in respect of those offences;

(2) an adult has been sent to the Crown Court under s 51; and CDA 1998, s 51(5)(6)(12)

(a) a child or young person appears or is brought before the court on the same or on a subsequent occasion;
(b) charged jointly with the adult with an indictable offence,

the court *must* if it considers it in the interests of justice to do so, send that person to the Crown Court, both for that offence and for any either-way or summary offence which fulfils the statutory conditions.

Listing of first Crown Court appearance

CCR 1982, r 24ZA

Where notice of sending has been given, the accused's first appearance in the Crown Court must be no later than 28 days after receipt of the notice or, if he is in custody, no later than eight days after that date.

Procedure after sending for trial

SPER 1998

Where an accused is sent for trial under s 51, copies of the documents containing the evidence on which the charge or charges are based must, within 42 days of the first hearing in the Crown Court, be served on that person and given to the Crown Court. The prosecutor may apply orally or in writing to the Crown Court for this period to be extended or further extended. Where it is intended that an oral application be made, the prosecutor must give *written* notice to the accused and the court. Any written application must be sent to the accused and the court, specifying the grounds for the application.

The accused may make representations within three days of service.

If there is no oral hearing, the court must notify all parties of the outcome as soon as is reasonably practicable.

Application for dismissal

CDA 1998, s 52(6), 3, para 2(1)(2)(3)

A person sent for trial in such circumstances, on any charge or charges may apply to the Crown Court sitting at the place specified in the notice served upon him for any charge or charges to be dismissed.

No indictable only offences remaining

CDA 1998, s 52(6), Sched 3 paras 7, 8, 9

If, at the Crown Court, there comes a time when no indictable only offence remains in the indictment, the judge will conduct a form of mode of trial proceeding, and if the accused indicates that he will plead not guilty to any remaining either-way offences, or if he gives no indication of his plea, the judge will decide whether the case is more suitable for trial on indictment or summarily, and where the accused consents to summary trial, he will be remitted to the magistrates' court for trial.

Summary offences remaining

Where:

(1) the magistrates' court sent a person for trial under CDA 1998, s 42 for offences which include a summary offence,

CDA 1998, s 52(6), Sched 3, para 6

(2) and he pleads guilty to it in the Crown Court, the judge may deal within the limitation of his 'magistrates' powers';

(3) and he pleads not guilty to it,

the powers of the Crown Court cease.

SEX OFFENDERS REGISTER

Save for where an absolute or conditional discharge has been imposed for the offence, offenders who have committed specific sexual offences are required to notify their names and addresses to the police. SOA 1997, s 2

The magistrates' court by whom an offender is convicted:

(1) is required to serve on him, immediately after passing sentence, a notice informing him of his obligation to notifying details about himself to the police; but

(2) has no power to make any order as to notification.

The requirements of notification arise from the fact of conviction of one of the offences enumerated below.

Offences to which requirement applies

The requirement of notification applies to conviction of the following offences: SOA 1997, Sched 1

(1) Sexual Offences Act 1956:
  - (a) s 1 (rape);
  - (b) s 5 (unlawful sexual intercourse with a girl under 13);
  - (c) s 6 (unlawful sexual intercourse with a girl over 13 but under 16);
  - (d) s 10 (incest by a man);
  - (e) s 12 (buggery);
  - (f) s 14 (indecent assault on a woman);
  - (g) s 15 (indecent assault on a man);
  - (h) s 16 (assault to commit buggery);
  - (i) s 28 (causing etc prostitution of, intercourse with, or indecent assault on, a girl under 16);

(2) Indecency with Children Act 1960, s 1(1) (indecent conduct towards young child);

(3) Criminal Law Act 1977, s 54 (inciting girl under 16 to have sexual intercourse);

(4) Protection of Children Act 1978, s 1 (indecent photographs of children);

(5) Customs & Excise Management Act 1979 in relation to the importation of goods prohibited under the Customs Consolidation Act 1876, s 42 (goods including indecent photographs of children who were under the age of 16);

(6) Criminal Justice Act 1988, s 160 (possession of indecent photographs of children);

(7) Sexual Offences (Amendment) Act 2000 (breach of trust);

(8) Any attempt, incitement or conspiracy to commit the above offences; and

(9) Aiding and abetting the commission of any of the above offences.

SOA 1997, Sched 1, para 1(4)

(Note: a person is to be taken to have been under the age of 16 at any time if it appears from the evidence as a whole that he or she was under that age at that time.)

Requirements of the notice

The offender is required by law to notify the police:

CJCSA 2000, Sched 5

(1) within three days of the service of the notice, or, if he is in custody or otherwise detained, within three days of his release, of:
   (a) his name, and any other name he uses;
   (b) his date of birth; his home address, that is his sole or main residence in the United Kingdom, or if he has no such residence, any premises in the United Kingdom which he regularly visits;

(2) of any change of name, or of home address, within 14 days of the change;

(3) of any address where he resides or stays for 14 days or longer (ie either 14 days at a time, or a total of 14 days in any 12 month period.

The offender may give these notifications either by going to any police station in his local police area and giving them in person, or by sending notification in writing to any such police station.

This requirement applies even where the offender is already registered as a result of an earlier requirement.

Duration of requirement

SOA 1997, s 4

A requirement to register arises immediately on the passing of sentence, and maintains as follows in the case of:

(1) Imprisonment, or detention in a young offender institution for over 6 months – 10 years;
(2) Imprisonment, or detention in a young offender institution for six months or less – 7 years ;
(3) Admission to hospital under MHA 1983, s 37 (hospital order) – 7 years;
(4) Non-custodial sentences (including guardianship order under MHA 1983, s 37) – 5 years;
(5) Cautions – 5 years

Other periods apply to sentences imposed in the Crown Court.

Young offenders

For offenders under the age of 18 on the date of sentence, the notification periods shown above are halved, and the court may impose the notification requirement on the parent or guardian. SOA 1997, s 4(3)

SPECIAL MEASURES DIRECTIONS

An application may be made under under YJCEA 1999, s 19 for 'special measures' in the course of a trial. YJCEA 1999, ss 223–30

A witness who:

(1) is under 17; or
(2) suffers from a disability or disorder; or
(3) is suffering fear or distress about testifying, may be considered eligible for the following special measures (available to the magistrates' courts at the time of going to print):
  (a) screening witnesses from the accused;
  (b) evidence by live video link;
  (c) permitting evidence to be given in private;
  (d) video recorded evidence-in-chief, and
  (e) aids to communication in the case of a witness suffering from disability, disorder, or impairment.

Applying for a direction

Application is made:

(1) in the form prescribed in the schedule: SMDR 2002, r 2
  (a) which must be sent to the justices' chief executive and to each of the other parties,
  (b) to be received by the chief executive:
    (i) in the case of an application to the youth court within 28 days of the day on which the accused first appeared before the court in connection with the offence, and
    (ii) in any other case within 14 days of the accused indicating his intention to plead not guilty to the charges, though these times may be extended by a single magistrate without a hearing; SMDR 2002, r 3
(2) orally at the trial, SMDR 2002, r 4

or the court may of its own motion raise the issue of whether a direction should be given.

Where under (1) above no notice of opposition is served, the application may be determined without a hearing, but there must be a hearing where such notice is served.

Where an application under (2) above is made, the court must be satisfied that the applicant was unable to make the application under (1) in time.

(For guidance on the exercise of discretion in respect of evidence by live video link see *R (on the application of D) v Camberwell Green Youth Court (and others)* [2003] EWHC 227 Admin.)

Discharging or varying a direction

SMDR 2002, r 5 An application may be made to discharge or to vary a direction already given, by:

(1) serving a notice in writing,

(2) setting out any material change of circumstances alleged to have occurred since the direction was made,

(3) sent to the justices' chief executive and to each of the other parties,

(4) as soon as reasonably practicable after the change of circumstances occurs.

Any other party may oppose the application on the ground that it discloses no material change of circumstances.

Renewed applications

SMDR 2002, r 6 Where an application for a direction has been refused, it may be renewed if there is a material change of circumstances since the court refused the application. Such renewal must identify each alleged change of circumstances, and any other party may oppose it.

Live video link

SMDR 2002, r 7 Where an application is made for a witness to give evidence by means of a live link, then:

(1) unless the witness is a child in need of special protection (within the meaning of YJCEA 1999, s 21(1)(b);

(2) the party opposing the application must state why, in his view, the giving of a direction would not maximise the quality of the witness's evidence.

Where a direction is given, the witness must be accompanied at the live link only by persons acceptable to the court.

In regard to the Crown Court it has been said (*Practice Direction* (*criminal: consolidated*) [2002] 3 All ER 904, para 29.2) that an increased degree of flexibility is now appropriate as to who can act as supporter of a witness giving evidence by live video link. Where a special measures direction is made enabling a vulnerable, intimidated, or child witness to give evidence by means of a live video link, the court makes a direction as to the identity of the witness supporter, where practical, before the trial commences. In giving the direction, the trial judge will balance all relevant interests.

The witness supporter should:

(a) be completely independent of the witness and his or her family; and
(b) have no previous knowledge of or personal involvement in the case; and
(c) be suitably trained so as to understand the obligations of, and comply with, the national standards relating to witness supporters.

Providing these criteria are met, the witness supporter need not be an usher or court official. Thus, for example, the functions of the witness supporter may be performed by a representative of the Witness Service.

Where the witness supporter is someone other than a court usher, the usher should continue to be available both to assist the witness and the witness supporter, and to ensure that the court's requirements are properly complied with in the CCTV room.

Video recording of testimony

An application to enable the video recording of an interview with a witness to be admitted as the evidence-in-chief of that witness must be r 8 accompanied by: SMDR 2002, r 8

(1) the video recording which it is proposed to tender in evidence; and
(2) and must include certain formal details of the accused, the offence to be charged, the witness, and the date on which the recording was made; together with
(3) a statement of the circumstances in which the recording was made; and
(4) the date on which it was disclosed to the other party or parties;
(5) a statement as whether, and if so at what point in the recording an oath was administered to, or a solemn declaration made by, the witness; and
(6) a statement that, in the opinion of the applicant, either:
    (a) the witness is available for cross-examination; or
    (b) the witness is not so available, and the parties have agreed that there is no need for him to be.

Where the application is by the defence, the recording need not be sent to the prosecution until the close of the prosecution case, and may be determined even though the recording has not been served. SMDR 2002, r 8(6)(7)

Where the recording to be tendered is only part of a video recording of an interview with a witness, the application must specify that part and be accompanied by a recording of the entire interview, including those parts it is not intended to tender in evidence, and be accompanied by a statement as to the circumstances in which the recordng was made including certain information specified in the Rule.

A party receiving an application has 14 days in which to lodge notice of objection, giving his reasons why it would not be in the interests of justice for the recording, or part recording to be admitted.

Expert evidence

SMDR 2002, r 9 A party who proposes to adduce expert evidence (whether of fact or opinion) in connection with an application, or the renewal of an application for, or for varying or discharging any direction, must, not less than 14 days before the date set for the trial to begin, furnish the other party or parties to those proceedings, a statement in writing of any finding or opinion which he proposes to adduce by way of such evidence. If any of the other parties request it, he must provide them with a reasonable opportunity to examine the record of any observation, test, calculation, or other proceeding on which his finding or opinion is based.

SPENT CONVICTIONS

Where a person has been convicted of an offence and certain conditions are satisfied, he is, after the applicable rehabilitation period has expired, treated for the purposes of the Rehabilitation of Offenders Act 1974 as a 'rehabilitated person' in respect of that conviction, and the conviction is treated as 'spent'.

Effect of rehabilitation

The effect of ROA 1974 s 4(1) is that a person who has become a rehabilitated person for the purpose of the Act in respect of a conviction (known as a 'spent' conviction) shall be treated for all purposes in law as a person who has not committed, or been charged with, or prosecuted for, or convicted of, or sentenced for the offence or offences which were the subject of that conviction.

Section 4(1) does not apply, however, to evidence given in criminal proceedings (see s 7(2)(a)). Convictions are often disclosed in criminal proceedings. *Practice Direction* (*criminal: consolidated*) [2002] 3 All ER 904, para 6) provides that:

(1) During the trial of a criminal charge, reference to previous convictions (and therefore to spent convictions) can arise in a number of ways. The most common is when the character of the accused or a witness is sought to be attacked by reference to his criminal record, but there are, of course, cases where previous convictions are relevant and admissible as, for instance, to prove system.

(2) It is not possible to give general directions which will govern all these different situations, but it is recommended that both court and advocates should give effect to the general intention of Parliament by never referring to a spent conviction when such reference can reasonably be avoided.

(3) After a finding of guilty the court must be provided with a statement of the offender's record for the purposes of sentence. The record supplied should contain all previous convictions, but those which are spent should, so far as practicable, be marked as such.

(4) No one should refer in open court to a spent conviction without the authority of the court, which should not be given unless the interests of justice require.

(5) When announcing sentence the court should make no reference to a spent conviction unless it is necessary to do so for the purpose of explaining the sentence to be passed.

Excluded convictions which are 'spent'

Sentences of imprisonment for life, imprisonment, youth custody, or corrective training for a period exceeding 30 months, sentences of preventive detention, detention during HM pleasure or for life, or for a term exceeding 30 months passed under CYPA 1933, s 53, and custody for life are excluded from rehabilitation.

Where the sentence is imposed conviction is:	*The rehabilitation period begins on conviction and lasts for:*	*ROA 1974*
Imprisonment, detention in a young offender institution, youth custody, corrective training, 6–30 months	10 years*	
Imprisonment, detention in a young offender institution, youth custody, not exceeding 6 months	7 years*	s 5(2) Table A
Fine, or any other order not specified in Table B	5 years*	
Borstal training	7 years	
Detention CYPA 1933, s 53, PCC(S)A 2000, s 91, for a term exceeding 30 months	5 years	
Detention CYPA 1933, s 53, PCC(S)A 2000, s 91, for not more than 6 months	3 years	s 5(2) Table B
Detention in a detention centre	3 years	
Community punishment order, or community punishment & rehabilitation order	(a) 5 years for an adult (b) 2½ years for a juvenile	CJPOA 1994, Sched 9, para 11
(1) Probation order (2) Community rehabilitation order	(1) Date order ceases or 1 year, whichever is the longer (2)(a) 5 years for an adult (b) 2½ for a juvenile	
Detention and training order, PCC(S)A 2000, s 100	In the case of an offender: (a) 15 or over at date of conviction, 5 years if it was, 3½ years if it was not, for period exceeding 6 months; (b) under 15, a period beginning with date of conviction and ending 1 year after date on which order ceases to have effect	s 5(6A)
Secure training order, CJPOA 1994, s 1, conditional discharge, bind over, care order CYPA 1933, s 57, supervision order under PCC(S)A 2000, s 63(1), supervision order CYPA 1933 or CYPA 1963,	Duration of order plus 1 year	s 5(4)(5)
Committal to remand home CYPA 1933, s 54, committal to approved school CYPA 1933, s 57, attendance at an attendance centre	Duration of order plus 1 year	s 5(6)

Where the sentence is imposed conviction is:	*The rehabilitation period begins on conviction and lasts for:*	*ROA 1974*
Hospital order with or without restriction order	5 years or duration of the order plus 2 years (whichever is the longer)	s 5(7)
Disqualification, disability, prohibition, or other penalty	Duration of the order	s 5(8)
Absolute discharge	6 months	s 5(3)

* Subject to a reduction by half for an offender under 18 (for the full list of sentences and orders. See ROA 1974, s 5 + Table A + B)

SUMMARY TRIAL

There are a number of points relevant to summary trial which may be noted as follows:

General conduct of the proceedings

The general conduct of proceedings in the courtroom is a matter for agreement between the bench and the Clerk (*Hobby v Hobby* [1954] 2 All ER 365, *R v Consett JJ, ex p Postal Bingo* [1967] 1 All ER 605). It will vary from court to court according to the views of the presiding magistrate and the Clerk or legal adviser. The overall conduct of proceedings is the responsibility of the magistrates, but the efficiency of the court will generally depend on a delicate balance of functions between the two. The Clerk is under a duty to assist unrepresented parties to present their case, but must do so without appearing to become an advocate for the party concerned (*Practice Direction* (*criminal: consolidated*) [2002] 3 All ER 904, para 55.9).

In the case of an unrepresented accused, it is his duty to explain to him in simple language the substance of the charge. Where the accused, instead of putting questions to a witness, makes assertions, the clerk must assist him, by putting such questions to the witness as seem necessary. This will inevitably involve questioning the accused in order to elucidate the points he is seeking to make. This will usually be the Clerk's function (*R v Richmond & Gilling West MC, ex p Steel* [1993] Crim LR 711). As to apparent bias on the part of a legal adviser, and the risk of its 'infecting' the magistrates, see *R v Gough* [1993] 2 All ER 724.

Preliminary issues

The general rule is that in a summary trial before a magistrates' court, preliminary or incidental issues such as questions of admissibility or claims in bar of trial, should be decided as separate issues and not by means of a trial within a trial, nor is there any need for evidence to be repeated after a decision on admissibility (*F* (*An infant*) *v Chief Constable of Kent* [1982] Crim LR 682, *R v Epping & Ongar JJ ex p Manby* [1986] Crim LR 555). In general justices should be slow to treat matters as giving rise to preliminary rulings.

In relation to the admissibility of a confession in terms of PACE 1984, however, the court is bound to conduct a trial within a trial to determine the matter, where it is represented that the confession was obtained by oppression or improper means (*R v Liverpool JC ex p R* [1987] 2 All ER 668).

GIWA 1998, para 18.1

Where an accused has pleaded not guilty and wishes to raise a Welsh devolution issue under GWA 1998, he must do so in writing in accordance with DIW 1999, notice being given to the prosecutor, any other party and to the court, as soon as practicable after the plea is entered. Where proceedings, are to be committed or transferred to the Crown Court, the question whether such an issue arises is for the Crown Court to determine.

Disqualification of magistrates

Disqualification of magistrates from sitting on the summary trial of an offence is dealt with under JURISDICTION AND INITIAL PROCEDURE.

Publicity

Court proceedings should be open to the public provided there is room in court for the purpose, that the public do not interrupt the proceedings, and there is no specific reason why they should be excluded.

MCA 1980, s 121(4)

This general rule requires that the proceedings be held in open court, to which the press and public are admitted, and, in a criminal case, all evidence communicated to the court is communicated publicly. In respect of publication to a wider public, it permits of fair and accurate reporting of proceedings that have taken place in court, and the principle requires that nothing be done to discourage that (see CONTEMPT OF COURT) (*Daubney v Cooper* (1829) 10 B & C 237; *R v Denbigh JJ, ex p Williams* [1974] 2 All ER 1052; *Scott v Scott* [1913] AC 417).

Sitting *in camera*

It may be necessary to depart from the general rule stated above where the nature of the circumstances are such that its application would frustrate or render impossible the administration of justice, or would damage some other public interest for which protection is afforded by statute (*A-G v Leveller Magazine Ltd* [1979] 1 All ER 745).
There is authority for the court to sit *in camera:*

(1) under OSA 1920, s 8(4);

(2) under CYPA 1933, ss 37, 42 while a child is giving evidence in certain classes of case; and

(3) where the court, in the exercise of its inherent jurisdiction to regulate the conduct of its proceedings, decides to depart from the general rule.

In this last case, any departure from the general rule is justified only to the extent that it is necessary in the interests of justice (*R v Reigate JJ , ex p Argus Newspapers* [1983] Crim LR 564).

It is important to remember that it is not a question of convenience or expediency. Many issues such as whether the accused has given assistance to the police, or that he has a terminal disease of which he is unaware, can be dealt with by means of an agreed document handed to the court publicly.

An application for the court to sit *in camera* ought to be made *in camera* (*R v Tower Bridge MC, ex p Osborne* [1988] Crim LR 382).

Handcuffing of accused

It is exclusively a matter for the court to decide whether an accused is brought before the court in handcuffs, but it should not be permitted unless the prosecution can show that there are reasonable grounds for apprehending that he will be violent or will try to escape (*R v Cambridge JJ etc, ex p Peacock* [1993] Crim LR 219). Any application by the prosecutor to restrain an accused at trial by means of handcuffs should be heard *inter partes* (*R v Robinson* (1996) *The Times*, 29 October).

Anonymity of magistrates

The ends of justice cannot be served by members of the court withholding their names from the general public, the parties to the proceedings, their legal representatives, the press present in court to report those proceedings, or any *bona fide* enquirer (*R v Felixstowe JJ, ex p Leigh* [1987] 1 All ER 551).

Presence of accused

The presence of the accused is a necessary requirement throughout the trial save in exceptional circumstances, and, of course, any view of the locus is part of the trial (*R v Ely JJ, ex p Burgess* [1992] Crim LR 888, *R v Jones* [2002] 2 All ER 113).

Appearance of the parties

Unless there is statutory authority to the contrary, both parties to any proceedings ought to be present in court. Where, however, at the time and place appointed for the trial or adjourned hearing of an information the prosecutor appears but the accused does not, the court may proceed in his absence, but a warrant may be issued for his arrest where: MCA 1980, s 13(1)(5)

(1) the offence is punishable with imprisonment;

(2) the court thinks it undesirable to proceed in his absence; and

(3) the information is substantiated on oath.

A warrant may also be issued where the court proposes to disqualify the accused from driving; again, the information must be substantiated on oath.

Medical certificates and other excuses

Where an accused is unfit and has been attended by a medical practitioner, a certificate to this effect is often submitted, and in the majority of cases will suffice to secure an adjournment. However:

(1) It would be unrealistic to ignore the fact that accused persons may seek to defer the date of trial and may resort to a variety of expedients to that end, including the production of spurious or unconvincing medical excuses for non-attendance; and

(2) the court is not obliged to accept an excuse proffered, however convincing it may be; but

(3) if the magistrates suspect the grounds to be spurious or believe them to be inadequate, they should ordinarily express their doubts and give the accused an opportunity to resolve them. They may call for better evidence, require further enquiries to be made or adopt any other expedient that is fair to both parties.

The ultimate test must always be one of fairness and if the accused claims to be ill, and is supported by apparently professional support for his claim, the court should not reject that claim and proceed to hear the case in the absence of the accused without satisfying itself that the claim may properly be rejected and that no unfairness will be done (*R v Bolton JJ, ex p Merna* [1991] Crim LR 848, *R v Richmond JJ, ex p Haines* (1991) 155 JP 612).

Non-appearance of prosecutor

MCA 1980, s 15(1)

Where the prosecutor does not appear, the court may dismiss the information, or, if evidence was given on a previous occasion, may proceed in the absence of the prosecutor, or may adjourn the proceedings. If the proceedings are adjourned under these circumstances, the accused ought not to be remanded in custody unless he was brought from custody or is unable to find sureties.

If neither party appears, the court may dismiss the information, or, if evidence was given on a previous occasion, proceed in the absence of the parties.

The court has no power to dismiss an information without hearing any evidence:

(1) because it thinks it would be unfair or prejudicial to the accused to continue (*R v Birmingham JJ, ex p Lamb* [1983] 3 All ER 23); or

(2) in order to punish the prosecutor for some apparent inefficiency which is liable to be dispelled on investigation (*R v Hendon JJ, ex p DPP* [1993] 1 All ER 411); or

(3) where it is known that the case has been wrongly listed and that the prosecutor's arrival is imminent (*R v Dudley MC, ex p DPP* (1992) 157 JP 177, *R v Hendon JJ, ex p DPP* [1993] 1 All ER 411, *R v Sutton JJ, ex p DPP* [1992] 2 All ER 129),

nor should the power be exercised where the prosecutor is present but has not got the file (*DPP v Shuttleworth* (2002) 166 JP 417).

Where the court dismisses an information in these circumstances, without considering the case on the merits, there is nothing to prevent the court from hearing an identical information subsequently laid against the accused (*Holmes v Campbell* (1998) 162 JP 655).

Proceeding in absence

Where at the time and place appointed for the trial or adjourned trial of an information the prosecutor appears but the accused does not, the court may proceed in his absence, but where a summons has been issued, the court must not proceed unless satisfied either that: MCA 1980, s 11(1)(2)

(1) the summons was properly served within a time giving the accused a reasonable opportunity of appearing; or

(2) he appeared on a previous occasion when the hearing was adjourned.

The discretion to try an accused in his absence must be exercised judicially, with proper regard to the principle (enshrined in ECHR Art 6(1)) that an accused is entitled to a fair trial; and that must include a fair opportunity to be present to hear the evidence against him, and should he want to do so, to give evidence in his own defence and call witnesses (*R v Bolton JJ, ex p Merna* (*above*); *R v Richmond JJ, ex p Haines,* (*above*); *R v Dewsbury MC, ex p K* (1994) *The Times,* 16 March). The European authorities indicate that any waiver of the right to appear should be clear and unambiguous, but it does not mean that an accused has an unlimited opportunity to postpone appearance, or that he can hold up the proceedings indefinitely (*R v Ealing MC ex p Burgess* [2000] Crim LR 855 *R v Jones* (2002) *The Times,* 20 February).

The discretion to commence the trial in his absence:

(a) needs to be exercised with the utmost care and caution;

(b) if absence is attributable to involuntary illness or incapacity it will rarely, if ever, be right to proceed, unless he is represented and his representative asks for the trial to begin;

(c) it is generally desirable that he be represented, even if he has voluntarily absconded, since this provides a valuable safeguard against the possibility of error or oversight (*R v Jones, above*).

The seriousness of the offence, which affects the accused, the victim and the public, is not a matter relevant to the exercise of this discretion.

If the court proceeds in the absence of the accused and, on hearing evidence, learns that the accused put forward a defence when being interviewed by the police, it ought to adjourn the case and notify the accused to attend (*DPP v Gokceli* [1989] Crim LR 70).

(For the Court of Appeal's checklist of matters relevant to the exercise of discretion to proceed in the accused's absence see *R v Haywood* [2001] QB

862. The list is not comprehensive nor exhaustive but provides an invaluable guide (*R v Jones, above*).)

Statutory declaration: s 14

MCA 1980, s 14

Where the court has begun to try an information to which a summons relates, and at any time during or after the trial, the accused:

(1) makes a statutory declaration that he did not know of the summons or the proceedings until the date he specifies, being a date after the court has begun to try the information; and

(2) within 21 days of that date the declaration is served on the Clerk,

the summons and proceedings subsequent to it will be treated as invalid. A fresh summons may be issued on the original information, without regard to any time limits for summary proceedings. The information may not be tried by the same bench.

There is power to receive the declaration after the expiry of the 21 days if the court finds that it was not reasonable to expect him to serve the declaration within the 21 day period.

JCR 1999, Schedule

The Clerk may receive service of a statutory declaration.

Several accused: joint trials

Several accused may be joined in the same information. Where:

(1) an accused is charged on several informations, and the facts are connected; or

(2) two or more accused are charged on separate informations, and the facts are connected,

there is no reason, if the court thinks fit, why those informations should not be heard together. There must, however, be a common factual origin between the charges (*R v Barrel & Wilson* [1979] Crim LR 663; *Ludlow v MPC* [1970]1 All ER 567).

When such a situation arises:

(a) the court ought to enquire of both the prosecution and the defence, whether either party has any objection to the informations being heard together;

(b) if consent is forthcoming there is no problem;

(c) if consent is not forthcoming, the court should consider the rival arguments, and subject to any advice tendered by the Clerk, should rule as it thinks right in the overall interests of justice.

(*Norfolk Chief Constable v Clayton* [1983] 1 All ER 984, *R v Liverpool JC, ex p B* (1986) *The Times*, 13 May)

If the accused is absent, or not represented, the court must seek the views of the prosecution and, if necessary, the Clerk, ruling as it thinks fit in the overall interests of justice.

If the facts are sufficiently closely connected to justify such a course and there is no risk of injustice to the accused, absence of consent should not be considered as a bar. Where the court has determined to try a co-accused separately, it may reverse that decision at a later stage if fresh material arises justifying such a course (*R v Bingham JJ, ex p Baxter* [1987] Crim LR 771).

Where an accused is charged with a number of sets of offences, each relating to different days, it is a matter for the discretion of the court whether, in order to avoid any impression of bias, different offences should be tried before differently constituted courts (*R v Sandwich JJ, ex p Berry* [1982] Crim LR 121).

The issue of joint or separate trials should be decided before any question of the admissibility of evidence is considered (*R v Pervez & Khan* [1983] Crim LR 108).

The Clerk may, with the consent of both parties, give, vary, or revoke any order for separate or joint trials. JCR 1999, Schedule

Juvenile charged with an adult

Where an adult and a juvenile are charged jointly with the same offence, and:

(1) the adult pleads guilty and the juvenile not guilty, the latter may be remanded to the youth court for trial; MCA 1980, s 29(2)(a)

(2) the adult is committed for trial, or discharged, and the court finds summary trial more suitable in the case of the juvenile, who pleads not guilty, the latter may be remitted to the youth court for trial; MCA 1980, s 29(2)(b)

(3) the joint charges are indictable, the court must consider, in taking the mode of trial decision, whether it is necessary in the interests of justice to commit both for trial. MCA 1980, s 24

Where the charge is indictable only, the juveniles must be sent to the Crown Court under CDA 1998, s 51.

If the juvenile is tried in the adult court and found guilty, he may be remitted to the youth court for sentence, and indeed he must be remitted unless the adult court is prepared to deal with him by way of a fine, a conditional or absolute discharge, or binding his parent or guardian over. CYPA 1933, s 56 CYPA 1969, s 7(8)

No trial of cross-summonses

There is no power to try a summons and a cross-summons together, even if the parties consent to such a course (*R v Epsom JJ, ex p Gibbons* [1983] 3 All ER 523).

Discontinuance by DPP

POA 1985, s 23

Where the DPP has conduct of the proceedings he may, at any stage of summary proceedings, before the court has begun to hear the evidence, give notice to the Clerk that he does not want the proceedings to continue. In such a case, the proceedings are discontinued unless the accused gives notice that he wishes them to continue. Where that happens, the position is as if the DPP had never given notice.

Pre-trial disclosure

The subject of pre-trial disclosure is dealt with under a separate heading (see PRE-TRIAL DISCLOSURE). While AIR 1985 do not apply in the case of an accused charged with a summary offence, it is clear that the 'equality of arms' provisions in ECHR Art 6 require from investigating and prosecuting authorities disclosure of any material in their possession (see *Edwards v UK* (1992) 15 EHRR 417), and, in a contested case, particularly one which might lead to imprisonment on conviction, disclosure ought to be made. Where disclosure is not made the court will assess the impact of non-disclosure on the fairness of the trial (*R v Stratford JJ, ex p Imbert* (1999) 163 JP 693).

Defect in process

MCA 1980, s 123

No objection is allowed to any information, or summons or warrant to procure the presence of the accused before the court, for any defect in its substance or form, or for any variance between it and the evidence adduced on behalf of the prosecution at the hearing of the information, unless it appears to the court that any variance between the summons or warrant and that evidence is such that the accused has been misled, in which case, on the application of the accused, the court must adjourn the hearing.

Plea

MCA 1980, s 9(1); MCR 1981, r 13A

Once the accused appears, the court must state to him the substance of the information in simple language, and ask him whether he pleads guilty or not guilty. The question ought to be put to the accused himself albeit he is represented (*R v Wakefield JJ, ex p Butterworth* [1970] 1 All ER 1181; *R v Gowerton JJ, ex p Davies* [1974] Crim LR 253). Where he suffers from a physical or linguistic disability, he should have the assistance of an interpreter and, if necessary, legal representation (*R v Kingston-upon-Thames MC, ex p Davey* (1985) 149 JP 744).

MCA 1980, s 9(3)

Where a plea of guilty is entered, the court may convict without hearing any evidence, but before accepting it, the court should satisfy itself that the accused intends to admit the charge (*R v Blandford JJ, ex p G* [1966] 1 All ER 1021).

If:

(1) he adds any qualification to his plea, which, if accepted, would throw doubt on the validity of the plea; or

(2) anything is said by way of mitigation in court, or in, eg a pre-sentence report, which tends to show that the plea is inappropriate,

the court should enquire into the matter, and if in any doubt as to the accused's intentions, should enter a plea of not guilty and hear the evidence.

A corporation may plead guilty through its officers.

To enable the press and the public to know the circumstances of an offence of which an accused has been convicted and for which he is to be sentenced, in relation to each offence to which an accused has pleaded guilty the prosecution must state those facts in open court before sentence is imposed (*Practice Direction* (*criminal: consolidated*) [2002] 3 All ER 904, para 26).

Where there is a plea of not guilty, the court must permit the prosecutor to call such evidence as he wishes and is available. In the absence of any question of abuse of process they have no power (in view of MCA 1980, s 9(2)) to dismiss the information without hearing the available evidence (*R v Dorchester MC, ex p DPP* [1990] Crim LR 421; *R v Milton Keynes JJ, ex p DPP* [1991] Crim LR 712).

Unfitness to plead

Whereas no issue of unfitness to plead in its strict sense arises in summary proceedings, MHA 1983, s 37 and PCC(S)A 2000 (see MENTALLY DISORDERED OFFENDERS) provide a procedure by which a magistrates' court may deal with an accused person who is unfit to plead. The same procedure applies in the youth court (*R (P) v Barking YC* [2002] 2 Cr App R 294).

Where appropriate, a defence of insanity is available to an accused in the magistrates' court (*R v Horseferry Road MC, ex p K* [1996] 3 All 733). Where the offence is triable either way, it may be more convenient for the accused to elect trial at the Crown Court.

Change of plea

An accused may apply at any time up to sentence to change his plea from guilty to not guilty (*S (An Infant) v Manchester City Recorder* [1969] 3 All ER 1230).

It is a matter for the court, in its discretion, to permit a change (see *R v South Tameside MC ex p Rowland* [1983] 3 All ER 689, *R v Bow Street Stipendiary Magistrate, ex p Roche* (1987) *The Times*, 5 February).

Plea of guilty in writing: (1) s 12

MCA 1980, s 12(1)–(4)

Where a summons has been issued requiring a person (of 16 or over) to appear and answer to an information for a summary offence, not being an offence for which he is liable to be sentenced to imprisonment for a term exceeding three months, and the court has been notified that:

(1) the prescribed notice of the effect of the proceedings; and

(2) a concise statement in the prescribed form of such facts as will be placed before the court if the accused pleads guilty; and

(3) if any information relating to the accused will or may be placed before the court, a notice containing or describing that information,

has been served upon him, and has received notification in writing purporting to be signed by the accused, or a legal representative acting on his behalf, that the accused desires to plead guilty without appearing before the court, the Clerk will inform the prosecutor of the fact and the procedure below applies.

Plea of guilty in writing: (2) accused does not appear

MCA 1980, s 12(4)–(10)

If, at the time and place appointed:

(1) the accused does not appear; but

(2) it is proved that the documents referred to above have been served on the accused with the summons, and

(3) the court is informed that the plea of guilty tendered has not been withdrawn,

it may proceed to hear and dispose of the case in the absence of the accused, whether or not the prosecutor is also absent, as if both parties had appeared and the accused had pleaded guilty.

Before accepting the plea (for the court may decide to adjourn for proof in some other manner) and convicting the accused, the statement of facts, any information accompanying it, the notification under s 1(2), and any submissions tendered by the accused, must be read out by the Clerk, and no other material relating to the facts or to the accused may be placed before the court by the prosecutor, except after an adjournment under s 10(3). If at any time before the hearing the court receives any indication in writing that the accused wishes to withdraw his notification, the Clerk will inform the prosecutor and the case will be dealt with as if no notification had been given, and the court will adjourn or further adjourn the trial for it to be dealt with in the normal way, notice being given of the reasons.

MCA 1980, ss 12(4)(5)

Before the court can exercise this jurisdiction, the provisions of the Act must be closely adhered to (*R v Oldham JJ, ex p Morrissey* [1958] 3 All ER 559).

If the accused is convicted in his absence, the court is entitled to take account of:

(a) any previous convictions for summary offences contained in a notice to cite served on him; MCA 1980, s 104

(b) in relation to offences under road traffic legislation, any previous conviction or order arising from an offence involving obligatory endorsement which is specified in a statement produced under RTA 1988, s 13.

Where a claim for costs is notified to the accused under this procedure, the legal adviser is under a duty to bring that claim to the attention of the bench (*R v Coventry MC, ex p DPP* [1990] 3 All ER 277).

Plea of guilty in writing: (3) accused appears

Where the court has received a notification under s 12(4) but the accused does in fact appear, the court may still, if he consents, proceed as if he were absent, and may do the same if no notification has been received and the accused appears and informs the court that he desires to plead guilty. MCA 1980, s 12(4)

The procedure is modified to this extent, that the accused must be given an opportunity to make an oral submission in mitigation.

Change from summary trial

Where the court has begun to try an accused aged 18 or over, or more than one accused, summarily for an either-way offence, it may discontinue the trial and proceed with a view to committal for trial at any time before the conclusion of the prosecution evidence (see generally MODE OF TRIAL). Where this power is exercised, the court must adjourn the hearing. MCA 1980, s 25(1)(2)

Note that:

(1) Whilst the entering of a not guilty plea initiates the trial process, it is not sufficient of itself to begin a trial within the meaning of s 25(2) so as to permit the court to re-determine mode of trial;

(2) the trial process does not only begin with the giving of evidence: it may begin after a plea of not guilty where, eg the court hears submissions on a preliminary ruling of law (*R v Horseferry Road MC, ex p K* [1996] 3 All ER 719);

(3) the power is not available where the accused pleads guilty, and that plea is accepted by the court (*W Midlands Chief Constable v Gillard* [1985] 3 WLR 936; *R v Hammersmith JC, ex p 0* [1987] Crim LR 639);

(4) a court remanding an accused does not thereby 'begin to try' him (*R v St Helens JJ, ex p Critchley* (1988) 152 JP 102, *R v Southend MC, ex p Woods* (1988) 152 JP 970).

Evidence in the case: (1) general

The evidence presented to the court in any case may consist of the oral testimony of witnesses, the written statements of witnesses in the prescribed form and exhibits of a real or documentary nature. Certificates may be admissible by statute.

CJA 1967, s 10

Any facts of which oral evidence is admissible may be formally admitted, that admission being recorded in writing.

Evidence must be given in court, and it follows that the court is not entitled to interview police officers, officers of local probation boards etc, in relation to the case, in private. Again, in the absence of specialised knowledge, the members of the court ought not to practise as quasi-experts in their retiring room (see p 398 *below*).

Evidence in the case: (2) admissibility

When considering any question of admissibility, the magistrates are entitled to know the nature of the evidence it is proposed to tender. Thus:

(1) the normal procedure is for them to hear it, and if they decide that it is inadmissible, to ignore it in reaching their findings; the stage at which they consider such an issue is a matter for their discretion (*R v Epping & Ongar JJ ex p Manby* [1986] Crim LR 555);

(2) if it falls to them to decide whether, on account of the prejudicial effect outweighing its probative value, certain evidence should not be given, they will be informed of the nature of the evidence and if they rule that it should not be given, must ignore it in reaching their conclusions (see *R v Sang* [1979] 2 All ER 1222);

(3) while it is unusual, there is no reason to prevent them from holding a trial-within-a-trial (*R v Liverpool JC, ex p R* (*above*)); but,

(4) the magistrates dealing with the case cannot delegate the duty of deciding admissibility to another bench (*R v Ormskirk JJ, ex p Davis* [1994] Crim LR 850).

As to the admissibility of a confession under PACE 1984, however, see p 396 *below*.

Evidence in the case: (3) prosecutor's discretion

In summary cases the prosecution have an unfettered discretion as to which witnesses will be called until the case starts and an outline of the evidence is given as to which witnesses will be called. The court cannot compel the prosecution to call witnesses. If the prosecution refuses to call a witness and the court is satisfied that the interests of justice require that the witness should give evidence and that it would be unfair to the defence if he did not do so the court may call the witness itself (*R v Haringey JJ, ex p DPP* [1996] Crim LR 327); see also *R v Russell-Jones* [1995] 3 All ER 239.

The court also has power, in an appropriate case, to order disclosure of documents which are relevant and which the prosecution seek to withhold (*R v Bromley MC, ex p Smith and Wilkins; R v Wells St MC, ex p King* [1995] Crim LR 248). It does not follow that having examined a public interest immunity claim they are bound to disqualify themselves (but see *R v South Worcestershire MC, ex p Lilley* [1995] Crim LR 954).

Evidence of children and other witnesses

Any question whether a witness may be sworn for the purpose of giving evidence on oath must be determined by the court as follows: YJCEA 1999, s 55

(1) a witness under the age of 14 may not give sworn evidence; YJCEA 1999, s 55(1)

(2) a witness who has attained the age of 14 may give sworn evidence provided he has a sufficient appreciation of: YJCEA 1999, s 55(2)
   (a) the solemnity of the occasion; and
   (b) the particular responsibility to tell the truth which is involved in taking the oath.

If a witness is able to give intelligent evidence, ie he understands questions put to him as a witness and gives answers to them which can be understood, he is to be presumed to have a sufficient appreciation of the matters at (1) and (2) above unless evidence to the contrary is adduced.

If a witness of any age is competent to give evidence but by virtue of s 55(2) is not permitted to be sworn for the purpose of giving evidence, his evidence shall be given unsworn and if he has given a deposition as unsworn evidence the court shall receive that evidence as evidence in the proceedings. YJCEA 1999, s 56

Use of screens; anonymity of witness

An accused has the right to see and to know the identity of the prosecution witnesses. That right should only be denied in rare and unusual circumstances and, as such, it is a matter for the court's discretion. Where application is made for a witness to be allowed to give evidence behind a screen, the following should be noted:

(1) there must be real grounds for fear of the consequences if the evidence were given and the identity of the witness revealed;

(2) the evidence must be sufficiently relevant and important to make it unfair to make the prosecution proceed without it;

(3) the prosecution must satisfy the court that the creditworthiness of the witness has been fully investigated and disclosed;

(4) the court must be satisfied that, although some prejudice is inevitable, there will be no undue prejudice to the accused;

(5) the court should balance the need for protection of the witness, including the extent of that protection, against unfairness or the appearance of unfairness.

See also SPECIAL MEASURES DIRECTIONS.

The court may, in its discretion, make an order that a witness remain anonymous (*R v Watford MC, ex p Lenman,* [1993] Crim LR 388, *R v Taylor* [1995] Crim LR 253*; D v Foster* [1995] Crim LR 333).

Notes of evidence

While in summary proceedings there is no *statutory duty* imposed on the Clerk or legal adviser to take a note of the evidence, if he is to be able to fulfil his duties and obligations under the *Practice Direction,* a note of the evidence will almost certainly need to be taken.

On the other hand:

(1) the High Court has no power, where a note has been taken, to direct that a copy be provided for the use of the Crown Court on an appeal (*R v Clerk to the Lancaster JJ, ex p Hill* (1984) 148 JP 65);

(2) where a request for a copy of the notes is made by the solicitor representing an appellant on an appeal to the Crown Court, it has been said that the Clerk or legal adviser ought to 'look sympathetically' on such a request (*R v Clerk to Highbury Corner JJ, ex p Hussein* 1 WLR 1266);

(3) where an appellant is in receipt of a representation order, a copy of the notes must be supplied to his solicitor if he requests them; and

(4) the High Court has also suggested (*Hill v Wilson* (1984) 149 JP 252; *R v Clerk to Highbury Corner JJ,* (*above*)) that notes should be supplied to privately represented appellants.

The Clerk is required to provide notes of the evidence to:

MCR 1981, r 17(1)(b)

(a) the Crown Court when an offender is committed for senttence;

(b) the Crown Court when an offender is committed with a view to the making of a hospital order accompanied by an order under MHA 1983, s 41 restricting discharge; and

(c) the other magistrates' court when an offender is remitted there for sentence under MCA 1980, s 39.

Insofar as bail applications are concerned, the Clerk or legal adviser is required, where the court hears full argument, to make a note of that argument.

No case to answer

After hearing the evidence for the prosecution, the court may, of its own motion, or on a submission of no case to answer, dismiss the case. The High Court has said that the court is entitled to rule at the close of the prosecution case that the evidence does not disclose a case to answer where:

(1) there is no evidence to prove an essential element of the offence; or

(2) the evidence for the prosecution has been so discredited by cross-examination, or is so manifestly unreliable, that a reasonable bench, properly directing itself, could not safely convict on it.

(*R v Galbraith* [1981] 2 All ER 1060)

There is no obligation to give reasons for its decision (*Moran v DPP* (2002) 166 JP 467).

It is important to realise that:

(a) only a ruling on the submission is required at this stage, not a finding of guilty or not guilty;

(b) the court has a discretion to permit the prosecution to reopen its case, even on a point of substance, but this discretion must be exercised judicially (*R v Midhurst JJ, ex p Thompson* [1973] 3 All ER 1164), and only in exceptional circumstances (*James v S Glamorgan County Council* [1992] RTR 312).

Where the court is minded to dismiss an information prior to the start of the defence case, either of its own motion, or after hearing a submission, it ought not to rule without first calling on the prosecutor to address the bench *(R v Barking and Dagenham JJ, ex p DPP* [1995] Crim LR 953).

In a proper case, the court is entitled to allow the prosecutor an adjournment to supply a technical lacuna in his case (*Matthews v Morris* [1981] Crim LR 495).

If the court makes an error and returns a finding of guilt instead of ruling on the submission, the best course is for a rehearing to be arranged before a differently constituted bench (*R v Midhust JJ, ex p Thompson* (1974) 138 JP 359).

Apart from the two situations envisaged above, the court should not be asked to reach a decision until the whole of the case has been placed before it.

There is no obligation on the magistrates to give reasons for rejecting a submission of no case. Summary trial is a highly specific procedure and it is usually undesirable that magistrates be required to give detailed reasons for their assessment of the evidence and the witnesses at the end of the prosecution case (*Moan v DPP* (2002) *The Times*, 6 February).

Accused's right to present his case

At the conclusion of the evidence for the prosecution, the court must satisfy itself that the accused is aware that the stage has been reached at which evidence may be given for the defence, and that if he wishes, he may give

CJPOA 1994, s 35(2)

evidence. He must be warned that if he chooses not to give evidence or, having been sworn, refuses, without good cause, to answer any question, it will be open to the court to draw such inferences as appear proper from such failure or refusal.

CJPOA 1994, s 35(1)

Where the accused is represented, the court need not expressly enquire of the accused if his advocate states that the accused *will* give evidence. Otherwise, the court must enquire of that advocate in the following terms:

'Have you advised your client that the stage has now been reached at which he may give evidence and that, if he chooses not to do so, or having been sworn, refuses, without good cause, to answer any question, the court may draw such inferences as appear proper from his failure to do so?'

If the court is told that the accused has been so advised, the case will proceed. If told that he has not been so advised, the advocate should be directed to advise his client accordingly, and a brief adjournment ought to be permitted.

If the accused is not represented, he should be addressed as follows:

'You have heard the evidence against you. Now is the time for you to make your defence. You may give evidence on oath and be cross-examined like any other witness. If you do not give evidence or, having been sworn, refuse, without good cause, to answer any question, the court may draw such inference as may appear proper. That means that the court may hold it against you. You may also call such witnesses whom you have arranged to attend court. Afterwards, if you wish, you may address the court by arguing your case from the dock, but you cannot at that stage, give evidence. Do you now wish to give evidence?'

An accused has a right to give evidence; the justices have no discretion to direct from where that evidence should be given. He is entitled to give evidence from the witness box like any other witness, unless, in exceptional circumstances, as where he misconducts himself, or there are other considerations relating to the particular accused *(R v Farnham JJ ex p Gibson* (1991) 155 JP 792).

PACE 1984, s 79

The accused has the right to adduce evidence on his own behalf, but he must give evidence before his witnesses unless the court otherwise permits.

MCR 1981, r 13(2)(4)

The accused has a right to address the court, either at the conclusion of the prosecution evidence, whether or not a submission of no case is made, or at the conclusion of the defence *(R v Great Marlborough St Magistrate, ex p Fraser* [1974] Crim LR 47*; R v Middlesex CC, ex p Riddle* (1975) *The Times*, 8 October). The court is not entitled to reach a final decision before it without hearing such evidence and such submissions as the parties wish to place before them (*R v Dorking MC, ex p Harrington* [1983] 3 All ER 29, *R v Dorchester MC, ex p DPP* [1990] Crim LR 421).

Prosecution re-opening case

The court has discretion to allow the prosecution to re-open its case after the conclusion of the defence, where:

(1) there is some procedural gap in the evidence (*Price v Humphries* [1958] 2 All ER 725); or

(2) formal proof has been omitted, such as the production of a certificate (*Pigott v Sims* [1973] RTR 15) or the reading of a formal statement (*Matthews v Morris* [1981] Crim LR 495),

but after the court has retired further evidence may be called only in the most exceptional circumstances (*Webb v Leadbetter* [1966] 2 All ER 114, *French Dairies etc v Davis* [1973] Crim LR 630, but cf *Phelan v Back* [1972] 1 All ER 901).

Adjudication: (1) the finding

After hearing the evidence for both prosecution and defence, the court must either: MCA 1980, s 9(2)

(1) convict the accused; or

(2) dismiss the information.

The court is not obliged to give a reasoned judgment; it is enough for them to indicate the basis of their decision (*R (McGowan) v Brent JJ* (2001) 166 JP 29).

Where the accused is tried on alternative charges and the court convicts on the more serious:

(a) it is not entitled to dismiss the less serious; but

(b) must either convict on the lesser and impose a nominal penalty, or adjourn to see if an appeal is brought against the more serious (*DPP v Gane* [1991] Crim LR 711).

A court consisting of three magistrates must reach a decision on the finding; if it cannot reach a decision to convict, it must acquit. There is no power in such a case to order a rehearing before another bench (*R v Bromlev JJ, ex p Haymills (Contractors)* Ltd [1984] Crim LR 235). The position is otherwise where the court consisted of two justices only *(R v Redbridge JJ ex p Ram* [1992] 1 All ER 652).

The Clerk should, wherever possible, arrange for three magistrates to sit and adjudicate so that problems do not arise. The chairman of the bench does not have a casting vote.

Once the finding has been announced, the court is *functus officio* and may not alter its decision (*R v Essex JJ, ex p Final* [1962] 3 All ER 924).

As to the power under MCA 1980, s 142 to rectify mistakes, see pp 400, 401 *below*.

Adjudication: (2) Magistrates' special knowledge

One of the advantages of a court of lay magistrates is that the individual members bring a lot of varied experience into the courtroom and use it. Thus:

(1) it is not improper for a member of the court who has special knowledge (eg, a doctor) of the circumstances forming the background to the case, to draw on that special knowledge in interpreting the evidence he has heard; although

(2) it would be quite wrong if he were to go on, as it were, to give evidence himself, in contradiction of the evidence given in court; for

(3) a magistrate is not there to give evidence to himself, still less is he there to give evidence to his colleagues; but

(4) he is entitled to employ his special knowledge in considering, weighing up, and assessing the evidence given before the court.

There is no reason why such a magistrate should not (and if requested by his fellows he certainly should) tell them the way in which his specialised knowledge has caused him to look at the evidence (*Wetherall v Harrison* [1976] 1 All ER 241). He ought, however, to wait until he is asked to make a contribution, and should not press his views on the rest, or give evidence contradicting that given in court. He may explain the evidence, give his own view as to how it should be decided and leave it to them to form their own conclusions.

In the absence of any specialised knowledge, it is quite wrong for the magistrates to practise as quasi-experts in their retiring room *(R v Tiverton JJ, ex p Smith* (1981) 145 JP 177).

Adjudication: (3) reasons

ECHR Art 6(1) requires that the accused receive a fair trial and that the court give reasons for its decisions. This latter requirement will vary according to the nature of the proceedings, and the decision made (*Stephen v GMC* [1999] 1 WLR 1293).

Giving reasons is essentially to inform the accused why he has been found guilty – this can be done in a few sentences (*R (McGowan) v Brent JJ* [2001] EHWC Admin 814).

Magistrates:

(1) need not give reasons for their finding elaborately or in the form of a judgment (*McKerry v Teesdale & Wear Valley JJ* [2000] Crim LR 594); but

(2) in giving their reasons must show that:
   (a) they have applied their minds to the ingredients of the offence(s);

and

(b) they have appreciated the state of mind of the accused. If the accused or any person aggrieved wishes to have more detailed reasons for the decision, he may apply to the magistrates to state a case for the opinion of the High Court (*McKerry v Teesdale & Wear Valley JJ,* (*above*)).

The explanation should be in terms of the magistrate(s) own choosing, taking care to ensure that the explanation is clear and accurate; it is a duty which cannot be delegated.

Magistrates are entitled to the asistance of their legal adviser in drafting their reasons (*Practice Direction (criminal: consolidated)* [2002] 3 All ER 904).

Juveniles : (1) duty of adult court to remit to youth court

A child or young person should normally be dealt with by a youth court acting for the place where he normally resides. The adult court *must,* after convicting a juvenile, remit him to a youth court for sentence *unless* satisfied that it can deal with him by way of: PCC(S)A 2000, s 8

(1) an absolute or conditional discharge;

(2) a fine;

(3) an order that a parent or guardian enter into a recognisance to take proper care of him and exercise proper control over him; or

(4) a referral order,

with or without any ancillary order(s) that the court has power to make.

The Clerk may remit the offender to another court for sentence. Note that: JCR 1999, Schedule

(a) remittal must be to a youth court acting either for same place as the remitting court, or to a court for the place where the offender habitually resides;

(b) the remitting court will give directions as to the offender's release on bail or remand in custody, and the Clerk will forward a certificate to the relevant youth court;

(c) there is no appeal against the remittal although appeal will lie against any order made by the court to which the offender is remitted.

Juveniles: (2) referral to youth offender panel

The adult court has powers similar to those of the youth court, to refer a juvenile offender to a youth offender panel (see YOUTH COURT).

Adult: remittal to another magistrates' court

Where the court has convicted an offender who has attained the age of 18 of an offence punishable with imprisonment, or one in respect of which it has a power or a duty to disqualify him from driving under RTOA 1988, PCC(S)A 2000, s 10(1)(2) ss 34, 35 or 36, it may remit him to another magistrates' court to be dealt with, provided that:

(1) that other court has convicted him of another such offence in respect of which it has not yet passed sentence on him, committed him to the Crown Court for sentence or dealt with him in any other way; and

(2) that other court consents to him being remitted.

JCR 1999, Schedule

The Clerk may remit the offender to another court for sentence.

PCC(S)A 2000, s 10(3)

Where this procedure is adopted, the convicting court adjourns the trial and the usual provisions relating to bail on remand apply, as if the reference to the court before which the offender is to be brought or to appear were references to the court to which he is remitted.

PCC(S)A 2000, s 10(7)

The only order in relation to sentence which may be made by the remitting court is a restitution order; the court to which he is remitted has power to deal with the offender in any way in which it could have done if all the proceedings had taken place before it.

It may even remit him back to the convicting court.

It should be noted that:

PCC(S)A 2000, s 10(8)

(a) 'conviction' includes a finding under MCA 1980, that the accused did the act or made the omission, followed by a remand for a medical examination and report; and

(b) the offender has no right of appeal against remittal.

Dealing with sentence

If the accused is convicted, and the court does not propose to remit the offender to another magistrates' court or to the youth court, it has the choice of proceeding to sentence, whether on the same, or an adjourned, occasion, of deferring sentence, or, in a proper case, of committing the accused to the Crown Court for sentence. See generally, as to the situation leading up to sentence, DEALING WITH AN OFFENDER.

Power to reopen cases to rectify mistakes

MCA 1980, s 142

A magistrates' court may vary or rescind a sentence or other order imposed or made by it when dealing with an offender if it appears to the court to be in the interests of justice so to do, unless

(1) the Crown Court has determined an appeal against:
   (a) that sentence or order;
   (b) the conviction in respect of which that sentence or order was imposed or made; or
   (c) any other sentence or order imposed or made by the magistrates'

court when dealing with the offender in respect of that conviction (including a sentence or order replaced by that sentence or order); or

(2) the High Court has determined a case stated for its opinion on any question arising in any proceeding leading to or resulting from the imposition or making of the sentence or order.

Where a person is convicted and it subsequently appears to the court that it would be in the interests of justice (ie on proper judicial grounds: *R v Camberwell Green MC, ex p Ibrahim* (1984) 148 JP 400) that the case should be heard again by a different bench, the court may so direct regardless of that person's plea unless:

(1) the Crown Court has determined an appeal against:
  (a) the conviction; or
  (b) any sentence or order imposed or made by the magistrates' court when dealing with the offender in respect of the order; or
(2) the High Court has determined a case stated for its opinion on any question arising in any proceeding leading to or resulting from the conviction.

There is no time limit on the exercise of this power to re-open, nor is there any requirement that the power is exercised by the magistrates who originally convicted the person or who passed sentence etc. CAA 1995, s 26

Where a direction of this nature is made, any finding of guilt, and any sentence or other order made in consequence of it, ceases to have effect. If the sentence or other order is varied as a result of the rehearing, it takes effect from the beginning of the day on which it was originally imposed, unless the court otherwise directs. MCA 1980, s 142(3)(5)

TICs

When passing sentence upon an offender, the court may, if:

(1) informed that there are outstanding charges against him, and that

(2) he admits each of them and asks for them to be taken into consideration on sentence,

take into consideration those offences still outstanding which he admits. The object of this practice is to give a convicted offender the opportunity, when he has served his sentence, of starting with a clean sheet and to prevent, if possible, his being immediately arrested for some other offence committed before the offence(s) for which he was convicted.

Once the admitted offence has been established, the court may pass sentence for the matters charged, and in so doing may pass a sentence longer than it might otherwise have passed, provided it does not exceed the maximum for the offence, or the court's powers.

Pre-conditions

An offence to be taken into consideration must be *similar* to that or those in respect of which the offender has been convicted. An offence should not be taken into consideration where:

(1) it is wholly dissimilar, even where the prosecutor consents, unless the court considers it proper to do so in the circumstances of the case *(R v McLean* (1911) 6 Cr App R 26);

(2) the court would have no jurisdiction to try it (*R v Simons* [1953] 2 All ER 599) particularly where it is an offence of a purely military character (*R v Anderson* (1958) 122 JP 282) or where it was committed in Scotland, where there is no similar procedure (*Hilson v Eassom* (1914) 7 Adam 390);

(3) it relates to road traffic matters, involving potential disqualification and endorsement, unless the offences before the court are of a similar nature (*R v Collins* [1947] 1 All ER 147; *R v Simons,* (*above*); *R v Jones* [1970] 3 All ER 815).

Procedure

Since the procedure involves an offender convicted of one or more offences being punished for other offences with which he has not been charged, tried or convicted, and to which he has never pleaded guilty, it is *essential,* if justice is to be done, that the court satisfies itself that he admits his guilt in relation to each of the outstanding matters, and *wishes* to have it taken into consideration. To this end:

(1) it is usual for the police to prepare and serve upon the offender a list of such offences, obtaining his signature to it;

(2) the offender, not his counsel, should be asked in open court whether he has received and signed that list, and whether:
  (a) he has gone through it with his legal representative
  (b) he admits each of the offences contained in it; and
  (c) whether he wishes them to be taken into consideration;

(3) in the case of a lengthy list, it may be necessary to take the offender through the offences, page by page;

(4) any offence not admitted will be struck out of the list.

The Clerk should ensure that the form has been signed (*DPP v Anderson* [1978] 2 All ER 512, *R v Marquis* (1915) 115 JP 329; *R v Nelson* [1967] 1 WLR 449).

The number of such offences should be entered in the court register.

Ancillary orders

When taking an offence into consideration, the court may make:

(1) a compensation order (see COMPENSATION); and

(2) a restitution order (see FORFEITURE etc).

TRANSFER FOR TRIAL

Transfer for trial under CJA 1987 and CJA 1991 is an administrative act by the prosecutor which dispenses, in the class of case to which it applies, with the need for committal proceedings. A notice may be served as soon as the magistrates' court is seised of the case, and there is no need, in the case of an offence triable either way, to wait for determination of the mode of trial (*R v DPP, ex p Brewer* [1995] Crim LR 168).

Its purported advantages are that it avoids delay and brings the case before the court of trial at an early stage in its development.

At present the procedure applies to two classes of case, namely serious fraud cases, in accordance with CJA 1987, s 4, and certain sexual offences and offences of violence or cruelty in which children are involved, under CJA 1991, s 53 and Sched 6.

Serious fraud cases

When conducting proceedings for a serious or complex fraud, certain 'designated' authoities may take advantage of the procedure and avoids formal committal proceedings by giving to the magistrates' court notice of transfer. CJA 1987, s 4(2)

The authorities designated are:

(1) The Director of Public Prosecutions;
(2) The Director of the Serious Fraud Office;
(3) The Commissioner of Inland Revenue;
(4) The Commissioner of Customs & Excise; and
(5) The Secretary of State.

Conditions for giving of notice

Notice of transfer may be given where: CJA 1987, s 4(1)

(1) a person has been charged with an indictable offence; and
(2) in the opinion of the designated authority, or one of its officers the evidence of the offence charged:
    (a) is sufficient for the person charged to be committed for trial; and
    (b) evidence reveals a case of fraud of such seriousness or complexity that it is appropriate that the management of the case be taken over by the Crown Court without delay; and

(c) notice of transfer certifying that opinion is given to the magistrates' court before that court begins to enquire into the case as examining justices.

Sexual offences and offences involving cruelty

CJA 1987, s 53

Where there is a child witness, the notice of transfer procedure applies where a person has been charged with:

(1) an offence involving an assault on, injury to, or a threat of injury to, a person; or

(2) an offence of cruelty to a person under 16, under CYPA 1933, s 1; or

(3) an offence under SOA 1956, IWCA 1960, SOA 1967, CLA 1977, s 54 or POCA 1978; or

(4) an offence of attempting or conspiring to commit, or aiding or abetting, counselling or procuring the commission of any of the above offences.

A 'child' for the purposes of:

(a) offences under (1) or (2) above is a person under 14; and

(b) offences under (3) is a person under 17,

but where a video recording has been made by the child witness when he was below the relevant age, the age limits are raised to 15 and 18 respectively.

For the purposes of offences under (4) above, the age is that which is appropriate to the substantive offence.

A notice may include offences not involving a child witness, where these may be properly joined in the same indictment (*R v Wrench* [1996] Crim LR 265).

Conditions for giving of notice

CJA 1987, s 4(1)

Notice of transfer may be given, where the proceedings are being conducted by the DPP, who is of opinion that:

(1) the evidence of the offence would be sufficient for the person charged to be committed for trial; and

(2) a child who is alleged to be the person against whom the offence was committed, or to be a witness to its commission, will be called as a witness at the trial; and

(3) for the purpose of avoiding any prejudice to the welfare of the child the case should be taken over and proceeded with at the Crown Court without delay.

The powers of the DPP may be exercised by Crown Prosecutors to whom authority has been generally delegated (*R v Liverpool CC ex p Bray* [1987] Crim LR 51).

PROVISIONS COMMON TO BOTH SETS OF PROCEDURE

Residual functions of magistrates

On the giving of notice of transfer, all functions of the magistrates' court cease, save for the powers: CJA 1987, s 5

(1) to remand the person charged, in custody or on bail, until such time as he appears before the Crown Court, the date, time, and place of that appearance being stated in the notice of transfer;

(2) to treat a person whose written statement is tendered in evidence for the purpose of the transfer as a person who has been 'examined' (in committal proceedings) by the magistrates' court; and

(3) to make representation orders both for the proceedings in the magistrates' court and those in the Crown Court.

Form of notice

The notice must specify: CJA 1987, s 5(1)(2), NTR 1992, regs 2–4

(1) *the proposed place of trial,* and in selecting the place, the designated authority must have regard to the considerations which MCA 1980, s 7 requires committing magistrates to have regard when selecting the place at which an accused is to be tried;

(2) *the charge or charges* to which it relates, and must include, or be accompanied by, such additional matter as may be prescribed by regulations;

(3) if the accused is on bail at the time the notice is given, whether he is required to attend at the magistrates' court on the date fixed, or whether that requirement is transformed into a requirement that he attend at the Crown Court in due course; if he is remanded in custody at the time when the notice is given, he will be produced at the magistrates' court on the remand date unless he has given his consent to being dealt with in his absence (see ADJOURNMENT AND REMAND);

(4) if notice is given after the person to whom it relates has been remanded on bail to appear before a magistrates' court on an appointed day, the requirement that he appear ceases on the giving of the notice, unless the notice states that it is to continue, and it amounts to a requirement to appear before the Crown Court at the place of trial specified in the notice, or at any place substituted for it by a direction under SCA 1981, s 76; CJA 1987, s 5(6)(7)

CJA 1987, s 5(7A) (5) if the notice states that the requirement is to continue, and the person appears before the magistrates' court, it has in addition to its powers outlined above, the power to enlarge, in the surety's absence, any recognisance taken from him, so that he is bound to secure that the person charged appears before the Crown Court.

Juveniles

As far as an accused juvenile is concerned, a notice of transfer in respect of him:

(1) may not be given once the youth court has determined to try him summarily under MCA 1980, s 24 (*R v Fareham, YC & Anor, ex p M* [1999] Crim LR 325); and

(2) should not be given unless the DPP is satisfied that the requirements of MCA 1980, s 24 are met *and* that it should be possible for the Crown Court to sentence the offender to be detained under PCC(S)A 2000, s 91.

Venue: (1) fraud etc

Where a notice of transfer is served under CJA 1987, s 4 (cases of serious or complex fraud) the proposed place of trial to be specified in the notice shall be one of the following Crown Court centres:

(1) Midland Circuit: Birmingham (also sitting at West Midlands trial centre), Leicester, Northampton, Nottingham, Wolverhampton (also sitting at West Midlands trial centre);

(2) North Eastern: Bradford, Leeds, Newcastle, Sheffield, Teesside;

(3) Northern: Liverpool, Manchester;

(4) South Eastern: Central Criminal Court, Chelmsford, Harrow, Kingston, Knightsbridge, Luton, Maidstone, Middlesex Guildhall, Norwich, Oxford, Reading, Snaresbrook, Southwark, Wood Green;

(5) Wales and Chester: Cardiff, Chester, Mold, Swansea, Warrington;

(6) Western: Bristol, Plymouth, Portsmouth, Truro, Winchester.

(*Practice Direction* (*criminal: consolidated*) [2002] 3 All ER 904, para 21.11)

Venue: (2) child witness cases

Where a notice of transfer is served under CJA 1991, s 53 (child witness cases) the proposed place of trial to be specified in accordance with para 1(1) of Sched 6 to the 1991 Act shall be a Crown Court centre which is equipped with live video link facilities. The following Crown Court centres are so equipped: Birmingham, Bradford, Bristol, Caernarfon, Cardiff, Carlisle, Central Criminal Court, Chelmsford, Croydon, Exeter, Gloucester,

Grimsby, Guildford, Harrow, Hull, Leeds, Leicester, Lewes, Lincoln, Liverpool, Maidstone, Manchester, Mold, Newcastle, Northampton, Norwich, Nottingham, Plymouth, Portsmouth, Preston, Reading, Sheffield, Southwark, St Albans, Stafford, Swansea, Teesside, Truro, Winchester, Wolverhampton.

(*Practice Direction* (*criminal: consolidated*) [2002] 3 All ER 904, para 21.12)

Bail

Where the magistrates' court has remanded a person in custody to whom a notice of transfer relates, it has power (subject to BA 1976, s 4 and POA 1985, s 22): CJA 1987, s 5(3)

(1) to order that he be kept in custody until delivered in due course of law; or

(2) to release him on bail in accordance with the Bail Act 1976, by directing him to appear at the Crown Court for trial,

and, where release is conditional on his providing one or more sureties, and in accordance with BA 1976, s 8(3) the court fixes the amount in which the surety is bound with a view to the recognisances being entered into subsequently, the court *must* make an order under (1) *above.*

Where:

(a) the person to whom the notice relates has given his *written* consent; and CJA 1987, s 5(4)(5)

(b) the court is satisfied that when he gave his consent he knew that a notice of transfer had been issued,

the court may exercise its powers without his being brought before it, in any case in which (by virtue of MCA 1980, s 128(3A)) it would have power to remand him further on an adjournment such as is mentioned in that section.

Where notice of transfer is given *after* the person to whom it relates has been remanded on bail to appear before a magistrates' court on an appointed day, the requirement that he so appear ceases on the giving of notice, unless the notice states that it is to continue.

A requirement to appear before a magistrates' court then amounts to a requirement to appear before the Crown Court at the place specified in the notice of transfer as the place of trial, or at any place substituted for it by a direction under SCA 1981, s 75.

Documents etc to be sent to the Crown Court in fraud cases

NTR 1988 r 7, NTRC, 1992, r 6

As soon as practicable after the magistrates' court has discharged the functions reserved to it by the Act, the clerk sends to the appropriate officer of the Crown Court:

(1) a list of the names, addresses and occupations of the witnesses in respect of whom witness orders have been made;

(2) a copy of the record made in pursuance of BA 1976, s5;

(3) any recognisance entered into by a surety, and a statement of any enlargement of it;

(4) a copy of any representation order made;

(5) a copy of any application for public funding which has been refused; and

(6) a statement of means in Form B if appropriate.

Reporting restrictions

Restrictions similar to those applying to committal proceedings (see COMMITTAL PROCEEDINGS) apply to the reporting of cases in which a notice of transfer is given.

YOUTH COURT

Both children and young persons are presumed to have full criminal responsibility. The rebuttable presumption that a child is incapable of committing a crime (ie until the presumption is rebutted by proof on the part of the prosecutor that the child in fact knew that what he did was seriously wrong) no longer exists (*C v DPP* [1994] Crim LR 523).

A 'child' is a person under the age of 14; a 'young person' is a person who has attained the age of 14 but is under 18. CYPA 1969, s 107(1)

It is the duty of the court before whom a juvenile is brought to enquire of his age if it is not correctly stated; however, the proceedings will not be invalidated by subsequent proof of a different age. The age declared by the court is deemed to be the correct one. CYPA 1969, s 99(1)

The absence of any power in the adult court to impose a detention and training order indicates that, in general, Parliament considers that a non-custodial sentence should be passed in respect of juveniles, rather than a term of detention under PCC(S)A 2000, s 91, and that wherever possible, children and young persons, should be dealt with in the youth court (see further *R (on the application of W) v Southampton Youth Court, R (on the application of K) v Wirral Borough MC* (2002) 166 JPN 709).

Jurisdiction

In criminal cases, a youth court has jurisdiction to deal with all offences committed by a juvenile, except homicide which must be dealt with at the Crown Court. A juvenile charged with an offence other than homicide must be dealt with in the youth court unless:

(1) the offence is such as is mentioned in PCC(S)A 2000, s 91(1) (under which young persons convicted of grave crimes may be sentenced to be detained for long periods), and the court considers that, if found guilty, it ought to be possible to sentence him in pursuance of that section; or MCA 1980, s 24(1)

(2) he is charged jointly with an adult and the adult court considers it necessary in the interests of justice to commit the cases of both for trial, or to send the case or transfer the case to the Crown Court for trial; or

(3) he is charged jointly with an adult; or

(4)(a) the charge arises out of circumstances connected with an offence with which an adult is charged; or

(b) an adult is charged with aiding and abetting or procuring an offence by a juvenile; or

(c) a juvenile is charged with aiding and abetting or procuring an offence by an adult.

In (3) and (4) (a)–(c) there is a discretion and it is for the court to determine whether the trial should be in the adult court or the youth court.

Juveniles may be remitted to the youth court from both the Crown Court and the adult magistrates' court.

CYPA 1933, s 44 In dealing with a juvenile who is brought before it, a youth court must, like any other court, have regard to his welfare and, in a proper case, must take steps to remove him from undesirable surroundings and to secure that proper provision is made for his education and training.

CYPA 1933, s 59 The terms 'conviction' and 'sentence' are not used in relation to a juvenile dealt with summarily; reference is made to a 'finding of guilt' or an 'order made on a finding of guilt'.

ECHR Art 6 requires a juvenile charged with a criminal offence to be treated in a manner which takes full account of his age, level of maturity, and intellectual and emotional capacities. It requires that steps be taken to promote his ability to understand and participate in the proceedings (see the 'Bulger' cases of *T v UK, V v UK* [2000] Crim LR 187).

Composition of the court: (1) outside the Metropolitan Area of London

Outside the Metropolitan Area of London a youth court is composed of either:

(1) a District Judge (magistrates' courts) sitting alone; or

(2) not more than three magistrates; and

(3) except where a District Judge is sitting alone, the court must include a man and a woman except where, by law, a single magistrate is authorised to act.

Where a court is not properly constituted, and it is inexpedient in the interests of justice for there to be an adjournment, the court may sit without there being a man and a woman, owing to circumstances unforeseen:

(a) when the court was arranged; or

(b) where a magistrate cannot properly sit as a member of the court.

A youth court must be chaired by the chairman or a deputy chairman of the Youth Court Panel except where, owing to circumstances unforeseen when the members of the court were chosen, a chairman:

(i) was not present; or

(ii) could not properly sit as a member of the court.

Composition of the court: (2) the Metropolitan Area of London: Inner London and the City of London

Similar provision to that above is made for youth courts in the Metropolitan Area of London, for magistrates who are nominated as chairmen and panel members by the Lord Chancellor.

Where a court cannot be fully constituted, and it appears to the chairman that an adjournment is not in the interests of justice, he may proceed with one magistrate, whether a man or a woman.

If, owing to illness or to an emergency, a chairman is not available, any District Judge (magistrates' courts), or any of the magistrates, may, with the consent of the Lord Chancellor, sit temporarily as chairman

Grave crimes; committal for trial

Where:

(1) a child or young person is charged with homicide; or MCA 1980, s 24(1)(b)

(2) a child or young person is charged with:
  (a) an offence punishable in the case of an adult with a term of imprisonment for 14 years or more; or
  (b) an offence under SOA 1956, s 14 (indecent assault on a woman); or
  (c) an offence under SOA 1956, s 15 (indecent assault on a man); or

(3) a young person is charged with:
  (a) an offence under RTA 1988 (causing death by dangerous driving); or
  (b) an offence under RTA 1988, s 3A (causing death by careless driving while under the influence of drink or drugs),

if the conditions of MCA 1980, s 24(1) are satisfied the youth court must commit the juvenile to the Crown Court for trial: the Act unambiguously requires that (*R(C and Another) v Sheffield Youth Court* (2003) *The Times*, 23 January) (see COMMITTAL PROCEEDINGS).

Declining jurisdiction

A decision under (2) and (3) of the preceding paragraph is a most important one. The power of the Crown Court to impose a term of detention under PCC(S)A 2000, 91, is available only on trial on indictment. Whilst a youth court must be vigilant in not dealing with a serious offence summarily (*R v Learmouth* (1988) 153 JP 18) the general policy of the present legislation is that wherever possible juveniles should be tried by a youth court (see MCA 1980, s 24).

The youth court should start its consideration of jurisdiction on the basis that:

(1) there is a *strong presumption* against sending a juvenile offender for trial in the Crown Court, unless

(2) the court is satisfied that such a committal is *clearly required.*

(*R (on the application of M) v Waltham Forest YC & DPP, R (on the application of W) v Thetford YC & DPP* (2002) 166 JP 453)

A number of factors fall to be considered:

(1) the power to commit a juvenile for sentence to the Crown Court no longer exists;

(2) the court's sole custodial option is a detention and training order (see CUSTODIAL SENTENCES);

(3) a detention and training order may only be imposed on an offender aged 12, 13, or 14 if the court finds as a fact that he is a 'persistent offender' (see pp 183, 184);

(4) there is no lower age limit for detention under s 91 other than the age of criminal responsibility (10); the facility is designed specially for children and young persons;

(5) a juvenile should not be committed for trial in the Crown Court unless the offemce is so serious that detention under s 91 is a realistic option on conviction; and

(6) the detention and training order option leads to the inference that a term of two years' detention (which is the maximum) is considered appropriate for offences which would carry longer terms in the case of an adult.

For age as a consideration, see *below*.

No decision on jurisdiction should be taken before the court has considered representations on the subject from the prosecutor and the accused's representative.

Age of juvenile as a consideration

The age of the juvenile is a major consideration, alongside the court's powers of sentence, in the decision whether or not to accept jurisdiction.

Age: (1) 10–14 years old

In the case of a juvenile:

(1) aged 10 or 11, there is no custodial sentence that may be imposed in the youth court on a child of this age (he does not qualify for a detention and training order); the punishment will need to be a non-custodial one; it is unlikely that Parliament intended an offender of such an age to be sentenced at the Crown Court under s 91;

(2) aged 12, 13, 14, a detention and training order up to a maximum term of two years may only be imposed on an offender of this age where the court finds as a fact that he is a 'persistent offender' (see pp 183, 184), thus where:
   (a) in the case of a 'persistent offender', the court considers that realistically it ought to be possible in the event of conviction for him to be sentenced to a term in excess of two years, it *must* decline jurisdiction;
   (b) in the case of an offender who is not found to be a 'persistent offender', where on conviction the appropriate sentence would be a custodial term in the region of two years, it *may* decline jurisdiction.

The court should still remind itself that the seriousness of the offence and the Crown Court's sentencing powers are the principal considerations; the court should not decline jurisdiction where it considers a custodial term of *less than two years* appropriate.

Age: (2) young persons

Offenders ages 15, 16, and 17 are eligible for a detention and training order up to a maximum of two years. The question for the youth court in deciding whether or not to accept jurisdiction, is whether, on conviction, it would be appropriate for the Crown Court to exercise its powers of detention under s 91 for a period longer than two years. If the court is of that opinion it ought to decline jurisdiction.

Position of 17-year-olds

CJA 1991 provides for 17-year-olds to be dealt with as young persons for all criminal justice purposes save for the following pre-trial matters:

(1) all purposes of PACE 1984;
(2) the notification of persons responsible for the welfare of juveniles detained by the police (CYPA 1963, s 34);
(3) recognisances for the release of juveniles arrested on warrant (CYPA 1969, s 29);
(4) all purposes of BA 1976; and
(5) all remand purposes (in particular CYPA 1969, s 23; CJA 1991, s 60(1)).

Youth Court

Juvenile attaining 18 during proceedings

Where:

(1) a young person brought before the youth court, charged with an offence, attains the age of 18 before his trial has started, that court may remit him to the adult court for trial; CDA 1998, s 47

CYPA 1933, s 48

(2) in the course of proceedings it is discovered that the accused, who was believed to be a young person, has in fact attained the age of 18, the court may, if it thinks fit to do so, proceed with the hearing, and determine the proceedings;

PCC(S)A 2000, s 9(1)(2)(b)(4)

(3) proceedings have begun and a young person attains the age of 18 before their conclusion, the youth court may either:
   (a) continue with the case and make any order which it could have made had the offender not attained 18 (*Re Daley* [1963] 3 All ER 657); or
   (b) at any time after conviction and before sentence, may remit him to the adult court for sentence, and that court may deal with him in any manner in which it could have dealt with him had the proceedings taken place in the adult court, (but see AGE OF OFFENDER and *R v Ghafoor* [2002] 116 JPR 601).

The youth court cannot, however, deal with any further charges preferred after it is known that he has attained 18 (*R v Chelsea JJ, ex p DPP* [1963] 3 All ER 657).

There is no appeal against a remittal although an appeal will lie against any order made by the court to which the offender is remitted.

JCR 1999, Schedule

The Clerk may remit the offender to another court for sentence.

Age in relation to mode of trial

In relation to the court's powers to determine mode of trial, it is the age of the accused when he first appears before the court in answer to the charge that is in point *(R v Nottingham JJ, ex p Taylor* [1991] 4 All ER 860). Thus if, before he reaches the age of 18, an accused appears before the court, whether for the first time or on remand, charged with an indictable or either way offence, and:

(1) he pleads guilty when the charge is first put to him; or
(2) the mode of trial was discussed with him, or his legal representative, and decided, the decision being recorded in clear terms,

then whether or not the evidence was called on that occasion, his attaining 18 before the trial has no effect upon the mode of trial which has already been determined; he must be treated as though he were 17. It is only if the mode of trial was not determined that his attaining 18 has any effect (*R v Nottingham JJ, ex p Taylor* (*above*)) and he will have the right to trial by jury.

Age in relation to sentence

In relation to any order made on a finding of guilt, the determining factor is usually the day on which the accused pleads guilty or is found guilty (*R v Danga* [1992] Crim LR 219). It is an abuse of the court's power to adjourn a case so that an offender can attain a particular age during the period of adjournment (*Arthur v Stringer* (1986) 151 JP 97). As to a similar delay on the part of the prosecutor, see *R v Rotherham JJ ex p Brough* [1991] Crim LR 522 (but see AGE OF OFFENDER and *R v Ghaboor* [2002] 116 JPR 601).

Provisions special to youth courts

Youth courts will sit as often as is necessary for the purpose of exercising any jurisdiction conferred upon them.

Custody time limits

In general, the custody time limits that apply in the youth court are the same as those applying in the adult court (see CUSTODY TIME LIMITS), but special limits apply under YC(TL)R 1999 in relation to proceedings instituted in a 'relevant court' in a 'relevant area', such courts and areas being specified in the Schedule to the Regulations. Under these Regulations, the maximum period:

(1) where a juvenile is arrested in connection with an offence
  (a) whilst under the age of 18, and
  (b) in a relevant area,

  to be allowed for the stage beginning with his arrest and ending with the date fixed for his first appearance in a relevant court – **the initial stage** – is 36 days;

(2) to be allowed to the prosecution for the completion of the stage beginning with the date of the first appearance and ending with the start of the trial in the relevant court – **the overall limit** – is 99 days;

(3) where a juvenile;
  (a) was under the age of 18:
    (i) at the time of his arrest for an offence; or
    (ii) where he was not arrested, at the time of the laying of an information charging him with an offence; and
  (b) is convicted of the offence in a relevant court, between his conviction and his being sentenced in a relevant court is 29 days.

Applications by the prosecution for a extension of the initial or overall periods are governed, as in the adult court, by the provisions of reg 7.

Process

The appearance of a child or young person before the court is secured in the same manner as in the case of an adult, by being charged and bailed, or being brought before the court in custody, or as the result of an information laid before a magistrate or the Clerk, followed by a summons (see INFORMATION, SUMMONS, etc).

Publicity; open court

Special rules apply to the persons who are entitled to be present at the sitting of a youth court. The only persons entitled to be present are:

(1) members and officers of the court;

(2) parties to the case before the court, and their legal representatives;

(3) witnesses, and others directly concerned with the case in progress;

CYPA 1933, s 47(2)

(4) *bona fide* representatives of newspapers or news agencies; and

(5) such other persons as the court specifically authorises to be present.

Attendance of parent/guardian

CYPA 1933, s 34A

Where a juvenile is charged with an offence, or is brought before the court for any other reason, the court:

(1) *may* in any case; and

(2) *must* in the case of a juvenile under 16,

require a parent or guardian of that juvenile to attend at the court during all stages of the proceedings unless, and to the extent that, the court is satisfied that it would be unreasonable to require it, having regard to the circumstances of the case.

Where a local authority has parental responsibility for a juvenile who is in its care or who is provided with accommodation by it, that authority is treated as parent or guardian for this purpose.

Right to representation

Legal representation under public funding is available to a juvenile as it is to an adult, (see DEFENCE PUBLIC FUNDING) although in relation to persons under 17 the application needs to be made by a parent or guardian.

Presence of juveniles; clearing the court

CYPA 1933, s 36

A child other than an infant in arms is not permitted to be present in court during any criminal proceedings in respect of another person, except when required as a witness, or authorised for the purposes of justice. In any other case the court must order a child to be removed.

CYPA 1933, s 37(1)(2)

Where a child or young person is called as a witness in any proceedings relating to an offence against, or any conduct contrary to, decency or morality, the court may direct that any persons other than members or officers of the court, and persons directly concerned with the case, be excluded during the taking of that witness's evidence. The power does not permit the exclusion of *bona fide* representatives of the press. It is without prejudice to any other power to sit *in camera* (see SUMMARY TRIAL).

Restrictions on reporting

No report of any youth court proceedings shall be published which reveals, the name, address or school, or include any particulars calculated to lead to the identification of any juvenile concerned in the proceedings (including any juvenile who is a witness), nor may any picture be published of such a juvenile.

CYPA 1933, s 49(1)

The court may dispense to any extent with this prohibition where satisfied that:

(1) it is appropriate to do so for the avoidance of injustice to the child or young person, or

(2) it is necessary for the purpose of apprehending him or bringing him before the court or returning him to custody, although in this case:
   (a) only where the juvenile is charged or has been convicted of a violent or sexual offence, and
   (b) where application is made on notice by or on behalf of the DPP.

A 'report' is a report in a newspaper and a report included in a service programme and similarly as respects pictures.

The power to waive anonymity in such circumstances needs to be approached with 'great care, caution and circumspection' and should not be used for the purpose of 'naming and shaming'. It is quite proper to hear representations from members of the press present (*McKerry v Teesdale & Wear Valley JJ* [2000] Crim LR 294).

(Note: where a juvenile appears before the adult court there is a similar power to restrain publication of certain matters, both in relation to the juvenile and to any juvenile who is a witness in the proceedings: CYPA 1933, s 39.)

Order of proceedings

In general, the order of proceedings in a criminal trial in a youth court takes the form of a summary trial in the adult court. The proceedings are governed by the Magistrates' Courts (Children and Young Persons) Rules 1992.

Pleading guilty by post

MCA 1980, s 12 permits persons who have been summoned to appear before a magistrates' court to answer an information for a summary offence, provided the offence does not carry a penalty in excess of three months' imprisonment, to plead guilty in writing without appearing in court (see SUMMARY TRIAL). CJA 1991, s 69 applies the provisions of s 12 to accused persons aged 16 and 17 whose cases are to be dealt with in a youth court.

Explanation of charge

CYPR 1992, rr 6, 7

In criminal proceedings, when the accused appears, the court must explain to him the nature of the proceedings, and, where he is charged with an offence, the substance of the charge, in simple language suitable to his age and understanding (without elaborate or detailed explanations – *R v Blandford JJ, ex p G (An Infant)* [1966] 1 All ER 1021), and must ask him whether he pleads guilty to it or not.

Assistance by parents etc

CYPR 1992, rr 5, 8(2)

Except where he is legally represented, the court must allow the juvenile's parent or guardian to assist him in conducting his case, including the cross-examination of witnesses for the prosecution.

If the parent or guardian cannot, in the opinion of the court, reasonably be required to attend, any relative or other responsible person may be allowed to take their respective places for this purpose.

Procedure on not guilty plea

CYPR 1992, r 8

Where the juvenile does not plead guilty, the court will hear the evidence of prosecution witnesses in support of the charge, who may at the close of their evidence-in-chief be cross-examined by, or on behalf of, the juvenile. In a case where he is not legally represented or assisted in his defence, if he makes assertions by way of cross-examination instead of framing questions, it is for the court to put to the witness such questions as it thinks necessary on his behalf, and for this purpose may question the accused in order to bring out or clear up any point arising out of those assertions.

CYPR 1992, r 9

Where a *prima facie* case is made out, the accused must be told, if he is not legally represented, that he may give evidence or address the court, and that the court will hear the evidence of his witnesses, if any.

Adjournment and remand

CYPA 1969, s 23

The proceedings of a youth court may be adjourned, and the accused or offender remanded in the same manner as in the adult court (see ADJOURNMENT AND REMAND). A juvenile may be remanded during proceedings on bail, or if bail is refused, in the case of:

(1) children aged 10 or 11, into local authority accommodation, either
  (a) without conditions, or
  (b) with bail-like conditions imposed on the child and/or requirements imposed on the local authority.

The local authority may apply for a secure accommodation order;

(2) children aged 12, 13, and 14, remand is on the same basis as in (1) above, but in addition, the court may:

(a) order curfew tagging;
(b) impose a security requirement;

(3) young persons aged 15 and 16, remand is on the same basis as for (1) and (2) above;

(4) a young person aged 17, remand is on the same basis as an adult for purposes of bail and custody. If bail is refused the juvenile will be remanded to prison accommodation.

In certain circumstances a juvenile may be remanded to the custody of a constable for a period of up to 24 hours. MCA 1980, s 128(7)

The only provisions that are special to the juvenile court are:

(i) an accused juvenile may be refused bail 'for his own welfare'; and

(ii) the juvenile's parent or guardian may be asked to stand surety for his compliance with any conditions of bail imposed, in addition to standing surety for his appearance.

A youth court need not adjourn proceedings for an offence at any stage, by reason only that it commits the accused for trial for another offence, or he is charged with another offence; MCA 1980, s 10(3A)

Procedure after finding of guilt

Where a juvenile is found guilty, whether on a plea of guilty or otherwise: CYPR 1992, r 10(1)

(1) he and his parent or guardian, if present, must be given the opportunity of making a statement;

(2) the court must take into consideration such information as to his general conduct, home surroundings, school record, and medical history as may be necessary to enable it to deal with the case in his best interests, and in particular, must take into consideration such of that information as is provided by a local authority;

(3) if such information is not fully available, the court must consider the desirability of adjourning the proceedings for such enquiry as is necessary (see ADJOURNMENT AND REMAND); CYPA 1969, s 9

(4) a written report by a probation officer, local authority, local education authority, educational establishment, or registered medical practitioner may be received without being read aloud;

(5) if the court considers it necessary in the interests of the juvenile, it may require him, or his parent or guardian if present, to withdraw from the court.

Written reports

It is the duty of the local authority, unless they are of opinion that it is unnecessary to do so, to provide the court with information as to the home CYPA 1969, s 9(1) surroundings, school record, health, and character of a juvenile, and the court must arrange for any written reports which it has to be made available to:

CYPR 1992, r 10(3)

(1) the juvenile's legal representatives;

(2) the juvenile's parent or guardian, if present at the hearing; and

(3) the juvenile himself, except where the court otherwise directs on the ground that it appears either impracticable to disclose the report to him, having regard to his age and understanding, or undesirable to do so, having regard to any serious harm which he might suffer thereby.

CYPR 1992, r 10(4)

In a case where the juvenile is not represented, and where a report has not been made available to him in pursuance of (3) *above,* but has been considered without being read aloud, or where the juvenile, his parent or guardian have been required to withdraw:

(1) the juvenile must be told the substance of any part of the information bearing on his character or conduct which the court considers material to the manner in which the case should be dealt with, unless it appears impracticable to do so having regard to his age and understanding;

(2) the parent or guardian, if present, should be told of any information which has reference to his, ie the parent or guardian's character or conduct, or to the juvenile's character, conduct, home surroundings or health.

Where a juvenile, or his parent or guardian, has been told the substance of such information and wishes to adduce further evidence in respect of those matters, the court must adjourn the proceedings for such evidence to be adduced, provided that it would be material. If necessary, the court will require the maker of any report tendered to attend the adjourned hearing.

Duty to explain disposal

CYPR 1992, r 11(1)

Before finally disposing of a case, or before remitting it to another court, the court must:

(1) inform the juvenile, and his parent or guardian if present, or any person assisting him in his defence, of the manner in which it is proposed to deal with the case; and

(2) allow any of those persons to make representations;

though the juvenile need not be informed if the court thinks it undesirable to do so.

Duty to explain effect of order

On making any order, the court must explain to the juvenile its general nature and effect unless, in the case of an order requiring his parent or guardian to enter into a recognisance, it appears undesirable to do so. CYPR 1992, r 11(2)

Juvenile failing to attend trial: considerations before deciding whether to proceed in absence

Whilst a court has discretion to proceed with a trial in the absence of the accused, that discretion ought rarely to be exercised against an accused who had not voluntarily absented himself because of the emphasis in the United Nations Standard Minimum Rules for the Administration of Juvenile Justice of proceedings being conducted in an atmousphere of understanding which allows a juvenile to participate and express himself freely. The exercise of the court's discretion must reflect the importance of the consideration that a juvenile may not have the same development and understanding as an adult and will not have the opportunity to respond to prosecution evidence as it is given (*R (on the application of R) v Thames Youth Court* [2002] 166 JPR 613).

SENTENCE, PENALTY, OR OTHER ORDER

Youth offending teams

The principal aim of the youth justice system is to prevent offending by juveniles, and under the Act, each local authority, or two or more local authorities acting together, has established one or more youth offending teams (YOTs), composed of the persons listed in CDA 1998, s 39, acting in co-operation with: CDA 1998, s 37

(1) every chief officer of police whose police area lies wholly or in part within the local authority area; and
(2) every probation committee, health authority or Primary Care Trust, whose area lies wholly or in part within the local authority area,

whose duty is to:

(a) co-ordinate the provision of youth justice services for all those in the authority's area who need them; and CDA 1998, s 39(7)
(b) to carry out such functions as are assigned to them by the Youth justice plan (see *below*) formulated by the local authority.

Youth justice plans

Each local authority, after consultation with relevant persons and bodies, is obliged to formulate and implement for each year, a 'youth justice plan', setting out: CDA 1998, s 40

(1) how youth justice services in their area are to be provided and funded; and

(2) how YOTs are to be composed and funded, how they are to operate and what functions they are to carry out.

CDA 1998, s 41

The plan must be submitted, by direction of the Secretary of State, to the Youth Justice Board, whose functions include the monitoring of the youth justice system and services, and to identify, make known and promote good practice.

REFERRAL ORDER

General

Where:

(1) neither the offence of which the juvenile has been convicted nor any 'connected offence' is one for which the sentence is fixed by law; and

(2) the court is not proposing to impose a custodial sentence or to make a hospital order in respect of those offences; and

(3) the court is not proposing an absolute discharge,

the court:

(a) *must* where the offender:

PCC(S)A 2000, 16(1), 17(1)(5)

(i) pleaded guilty to the offence and to any connected offence;

(ii) has never been convicted (and that includes an offence for which he was conditionally discharged) by or before a court in the United Kingdom of any other offence; and

(iii) has never been bound over in criminal proceedings to keep the peace or to be of good behaviour; and

PCC(S)A 2000, ss 16(1), 17(2)(5)

(b) *may*, where the offender;

(i) is being dealt with for the offence and one or more connected offences;

(ii) although he pleaded guilty to at least one of those offences, he also pleaded not guilty to at least one other;

(iii) he has never been convicted (and that includes an offence for which he was conditionally discharged) in the United Kingdom of any other offence; and

(iv) he has never been bound over to keep the peace or to be of good behaviour,

deal with the offender for the offence by referring him to a youth offender panel, which will agree (in the form of a 'youth offender contract') a programme of behaviour with him, designed to prevent him re-offending.

When a referral order is made it is the duty of the YOT to establish a youth offender panel for that offender.

An offence is 'connected' with another if the offender falls to be dealt with for it at the same time as he is dealt with for the other offence whether or not he was convicted of those offences at the same time or by, or before, the same court. PCC(S)A 2000, s 16(4)

Administrative matters

The order will:

(1) specify the youth offending team responsible for its implementation;

(2) require the offender to attend each of the meetings of the panel which will be established in his case; and

(3) specify the period, not being less than three nor more than 12 months, for which any contract entered into by him with the panel is to have effect.

On making a referral the court must explain to the offender, in ordinary language, the effect of the order, and the consequences which may follow if no youth offender contract takes effect, or if the offender breaches any of the terms of such a contract.

The court may, if it thinks fit, order that an 'appropriate person', that is a parent or guardian with whom the offender is allowed to live, or a representative of the local authority where he is looked after by them, to attend meetings of the panel, but:

(a) not if it would unreasonable to do so; or

(b) to the extent that it would be unreasonable.

The court will send a copy of the order to such person, if he was not present in court at the time it was made.

The programme

The programme may include any of the following:

(1) making financial or other reparation to any person who appears to the panel to be a victim, or to be otherwise affected by the offence;

(2) attendance at mediation sessions with any victim or other person;

(3) carrying out unpaid services in or for the community;

(4) being at home during specified times;

(5) attendance at school or other educational establishment, or being at work;

(6) participation in specified activities;

(7) attending a specified person at specified times and places;

(8) staying away from specified persons or places; and

(9) conditions enabling compliance with the programme to be supervised and recorded.

Improper combinations

PCC(S)A 2000, s 19

Where the court makes a referral order in respect of an offence, it may not deal with the offender by;

(1) imposing a community sentence;
(2) imposing a fine;
(3) making a reparation order;
(4) making a conditional discharge;
(5) binding him over;
(6) binding over his parent or guardian, or
(7) making a parenting order.

Where the compulsory referral conditions are satisfied the court cannot defer sentence, but may still exercise its powers of adjournment and remittal to another court. Its powers under the mental health legislation are unaffected.

Breach

PCC(S)A 2000, Sch 1, para 5

If no youth offender contract takes effect between the offender and the panel, or the offender breaches any of the terms of the contract, the youth offender panel may refer the offender back to court, sending a report to the youth court for the petty sessions area in which the offender resides or will reside, or a magistrates' court for that area where he will have attained 18 on first appearing at the court on the referral back, which will issue a summons, or if appropriate, a warrant to bring him before the court.

If the court is satisfied that any decision of the panel which resulted in the offender being referred back to the court was a finding of fact that the panel was entitled to make or was an exercise of discretion which the panel exercised reasonably, the court has power to revoke the order.

Where the order is revoked, the court:

(1) may deal with the offender in any way he could have been dealt with for the offence which made the order; and
(2) shall have regard to:
    (a) the circumstances of his referral back to court; and
    (b) where the contract has taken effect, the extent of the offender's compliance with it.

Application to adult court

The referral provisions apply also to a relevant juvenile who is dealt with in the adult court, where that court decides not to remit him to the youth court for sentence.

Other Orders

If, on trying a juvenile summarily, the youth court finds him guilty, it may, subject to the relevant level on the standard scale of fines for the particular offence: MCA 1980, s 24(1)(3)(4)

(1) impose a fine of an amount not exceeding £1,000 (£250 in the case of an offender under the age of 14); or

(2) exercise the same powers as it could have exercised if he had been found guilty of an offence which, but for PCC(S)A 2000, s 89(1), it could have sentenced him to imprisonment for a term not exceeding the maximum term of imprisonment for the offence on conviction on indictment, or six months, whichever is the less.

A youth court's powers in respect of a child or young person convicted of an offence are, in some cases, similar to those of the adult court.

The youth court may:

(1) make the following orders which the adult court can make:
   - (i) absolute and conditional discharge (see *below*);
   - (ii) referral order;
   - (iii) a fine;
   - (iv) binding over of parent etc (see *below*);

(2) make the following orders (which the adult court may not make in respect of a juvenile:
   - (i) attendance centre order (see COMMUNITY SENTENCES);
   - (ii) supervision order (see COMMUNITY SENTENCES);
   - (iii) community rehabilitation order (see COMMUNITY SENTENCES);
   - (iv) community punishment order (see COMMUNITY SENTENCES);
   - (v) community punishment and rehabilitation order (see COMMUNITY SENTENCES);
   - (vi) curfew order (see COMMUNITY SENTENCES);
   - (vii) drug treatment and testing order (see COMMUNITY SENTENCES);
   - (viii) a parenting order (see below);
   - (ix) a compensation order;
   - (x) an action plan order (see COMMUNITY SENTENCES);
   - (xi) a reparation order (see COMMUNITY SENTENCES); and
   - (xii) a detention and training order (see CUSTODIAL SENTENCES).

(Where a juvenile has already been the subject of a final warning from a constable under CDA 1968, s 65 and is convicted of an offence within two years of that warning, the court may not impose a conditional discharge unless there are exceptional circumstances which must be stated in open court.) CDA 1998, ss 55(4), 65

Binding over parent or guardian

PCC(S)A 2000, s 150

Where a juvenile is found guilty of an offence, the court by which he is sentenced has power:

(1) with the consent of his parent or guardian, to order that person to enter into a recognisance to take proper care of him and exercise proper control over him; and

(2) if the parent or guardian refuses consent and the court considers the refusal unreasonable, to order that person to pay a fine not exceeding £1,000.

Where the court has passed a community sentence on the offender, it may include in the recognisance a provision that his parent or guardian ensure that he complies with the sentence.

Where the relevant juvenile has not attained the age of 16, the court:

(a) *must* exercise the power to bind over the parent or guardian if it is satisfied that, having regard to the circumstances, its exercise would be desirable in the interests of preventing him committing further offences; and

(b) if it does not exercise that power, must state in open court that it is not so satisfied, and why not.

Amount; duration of recognisance

PCC(S)A 2000, s 150(3)

The maximum:

(1) amount of such a recognizance is £1,000;

(2) period of the bind over is three years, or, where the relevant juvenile will attain the age of 18 within a shorter period, that shorter period.

PCC(S)A 2000, s 150(4)

As in the case of any other recognisance, the means of the parent or guardian concerned, so far as they appear to the court, must be taken into account, in fixing the amount of the recognisance.

Appeal; variation; revocation

PCC(S)A 2000, s 150(8)(9)(10)

A parent or guardian may appeal to the Crown Court against the making of the order.

The court which made the order may, on the application of the parent or guardian, vary or revoke the order if it appears in the interests of justice to do so, having regard to any change of circumstances since it was made.

Forfeiture

In the event of forfeiture of a recognisance, MCA 1980, s 120 applies as it does to recognisances for keeping the peace.

PARENTING ORDER

In respect of a child or young person convicted of an offence, the youth court: CDA 1998, ss 8, 9(3)

(1) *may* make a parenting order; and

(2) *must* make such an order, where the offender is under the age of 16,

where it is satisfied that the order would be desirable in the interests of preventing the commission of any further offence by him.

If the court is not so satisfied, it must so state in open court, and state why it is not.

Before making a parenting order in the case of (2) *above*, the court must obtain and consider information about the juvenile's family circumstances and the likely effect of the order on those circumstances

A parenting order requires the parent or guardian of the child or young person:

(a) to comply, for a specified period not exceeding 12 months, with such requirements as are specified in the order; and

(b) to attend, for a concurrent period not exceeding three months, and not more than once a week, counselling or guidance sessions as directed by the responsible officer.

Before making the order the court must explain to the parent in ordinary language:

(i) the effect of the order and of any requirements proposed to be included in it;

(ii) the consequences if he fails to comply with the requirements; and

(iii) that the court has power to review the order on the application of the parent or of the responsible officer.

Failure to comply

Failure, without reasonable excuse to comply with any requirement of the order, or any specified directions given by the responsible officer, is an offence punishable with a fine on level 3. CDA 1998, s 9(7)

Discharge, variation etc

If, on the application of the responsible officer or the parent, the court considers it appropriate to do so, it may: CDA 1998, s 9(5)

(1) discharge the order; or

(2) vary the order by inserting in it any provision that could have been included in it when it was made.

If an application to discharge the order is dismissed, no further application may be made without the consent of the court which made the order.

Reparation Orders

'Reparation' here means an order to make reparation otherwise than by the payment of compensation.

PCC(S)A 2000, s 73(1)(2)(3)(4)(6)

Where a child or young person is convicted of an offence other than one for which the sentence is fixed by law, the youth court may make a reparation order requiring the offender to make reparation as specified in the order, to a specified person or persons identified as a victim of the offence, or a person otherwise affected by it, provided that:

(1) it does not pass on him a custodial sentence, or make a community punishment order, a community punishment and rehabilitation order, or a supervision order including requirements authorised by Sched 6, an action plan order, or a compensation order;

(2) the person to whom reparation is to be made consents; and

(3) the court has been notified by the Home Secretary that arrangements for implementing such orders are available in the area proposed to be named in the order.

PCC(S)A 2000, s 73(8)

The court must, as in the case of a compensation order (see COMPENSATION ORDERS) give its reasons if it does *not* make an order in a case where it has power to do so.

Before making an order

PCC(S)A 2000, s 73(5)(7)

Before making an order the court must:

(1) obtain and consider a written report by an officer of a local probation board, local authority social worker or a member of a youth offending team indicating the type of work suitable to the offender, and the attitude of the victim or victims to the requirements proposed to be included in the order; and

(2) explain to the offender in ordinary language:
   (a) the effect of the order, and of the requirements proposed to be included in it;
   (b) the consequences if he fails to comply with any of these requirements; and
   (c) the court's power to review the order on the application either of the offender or the responsible officer.

Requirements of the order

PCC(S)A 2000, s 74(1)(2)(8)

The requirements specified in the order must be such that, in the court's opinion, are commensurate with the seriousness of the offence, or the combination of that offence and one or more offences associated with it, and must, so far as is practicable, be such as to avoid any conflict with:

(1) the offender's religious beliefs, or

(2) the requirements of any (other) community order to which he is subject; and

any interference with the times, if any, at which the offender normally works or attends school or any other educational establishment; and the order must not require the offender:

(a) to work for more than 24 hours in aggregate; or

(b) to make reparation to any person without the consent of that person.

The order will name the petty sessions area in which it appears that the offender resides, or will reside, and any reparation required by the order will be made under the supervision of the responsible officer, and within a period of three months from the date the order is made.

Failure to comply with the order

Schedule 8 has effect for dealing with the discharge, revocation, and amendment of reparation orders. The appropriate court for dealing with these matters is the youth court acting for the petty sessions area for the time being named in the order.

PCC(S)A 2000, s 75, Sched 8, paras 2, 4, 5

Where an action plan or a reparation order is in force, and it is proved to the satisfaction of that court:

(1) that an offender has failed to comply with any requirement included in an order; and

(2) that the order was made by the Crown Court, it may commit him in custody or release him on bail until he can be brought or appear before the Crown Court.

INDEX